# Protecting All

HUMAN DEVELOPMENT PERSPECTIVES

# Protecting All
## Risk Sharing for a Diverse and Diversifying World of Work

Truman Packard, Ugo Gentilini, Margaret Grosh, Philip O'Keefe, Robert Palacios, David Robalino, and Indhira Santos

**WORLD BANK GROUP**

ISBN (paper): 978-1-4648-1427-3
ISBN (electronic): 978-1-4648-1428-0
DOI: 10.1596/978-1-4648-1427-3

*Cover design and image:* Debra Naylor, Naylor Design Inc.

**Library of Congress Cataloging-in-Publication Data has been requested.**

# Human Development Perspectives

The books in this series address main and emerging development issues of a global/regional nature through original research and findings in the areas of education, gender, health, nutrition, population, and social protection and jobs. The series is aimed at policy makers and area experts and is overseen by the Human Development Practice Group Chief Economist.

## Previous titles in this series

Damien de Walque, *Risking Your Health: Causes, Consequences, and Interventions to Prevent Risky Behaviors* (2014).

Rita Almeida, Jere Behrman, and Davide Robalino, *The Right Skills for the Job? Rethinking Training Policies for Workers* (2012).

Barbara Bruns, Deon Filmer, and Harry Anthony Patrinos, *Making Schools Work: New Evidence on Accountability Reforms* (2011).

Harold Alderman, *No Small Matter: The Impact of Poverty, Shocks, and Human Capital Investments in Early Childhood Development* (2011).

# A White Paper
## of the World Bank's Social Protection and Jobs Global Practice

"A white paper is an authoritative report or guide that informs readers concisely about a complex issue and presents the issuing body's philosophy on the matter. It is meant to help readers understand an issue, solve a problem, or make a decision. White papers are a *"tool of participatory democracy . . . not* [an] *unalterable policy commitment." "White papers have tried to perform the dual role of presenting firm government policies while at the same time inviting opinions upon them."*

—Wikipedia, drawing on Gordon Graham, "What Exactly Is a White Paper?" (The White Paper FAQ, thatwhitepaperguy.com, retrieved March 16, 2015); Audrey D. Doerr, "The Role of White Papers," in G. B. Doern and Peter Aucoin, eds, *The Structures of Policy-Making in Canada* (Toronto: MacMillan, 1971), 179–203; and John E. Pemberton, "Government Green Papers," *Library World* 71 (August 1969), 49.

# Contents

## Boxes

## Figures

## Photo

## Tables

# Foreword

Well-functioning labor markets and well-designed social policy are mutually dependent and mutually reinforcing. Social policy not only is about making society more equitable but also is an essential ingredient in making a country's economy more efficient. A central purpose of social policy is to foster growth by sharing risk—too much risk is bad: a reliable safety net supports individuals' enterprise, business startups, and innovation; but too little risk is also bad, as shown by the performance of the communist economic system.

Since the time after the Second World War, when social policy became deeply integrated in advanced economies, the world has changed. But the policy objectives—alleviating poverty, protecting against risk and uncertainty, assisting planning over the life course, and investing in health and skills—have not, and should not.

The traditional model of social protection in rich countries was based on the assumption that the majority of working people would be in full-time employment for most of their working lives, and that they would pay mandatory contributions and payroll (labor) taxes in exchange for coverage. Increasingly, the viability of this traditional, employment- and payroll-based insurance model is being challenged by the decline of standard employment contracts. In advanced economies, the changing nature of work is making long-term employment less frequent, with more people in part-time work, self-employment (often holding multiple jobs), the gig economy, and zero-hour contracts, and as a result, coverage is declining. In this changing world, what happens and what should happen to the traditional model of social protection tied to formal wage employment?

In developing economies, where there has been little progress in expanding formal employment, traditional social protection systems generally never achieved a significant scale. In Bangladesh, India, Indonesia, Nigeria, and Pakistan—which together make up about one-third of the world's population—coverage of social insurance languishes in the single digits, with virtually no change over recent decades. Most workers—especially the poor—are engaged in informal livelihood activities with little or no access to social protection. In low-income countries, social assistance (i.e., noncontributory transfers) cover less than 20 percent of the poor. What happens, and what should happen, to workers in informal subsistence agricultural and service jobs? How can workers be guaranteed at least a minimum level of consumption and manage risks in a diverse and diversifying world of work? The issue is relevant not only in developing economies: the absence of universal health coverage persists also in many high-income economies.

In addressing these key questions, this white paper is very explicit that the original objectives of social policy remain; the ways in which societies seek to achieve those objectives, however, need to fit the world as it is now and as it will likely be. Bluntly, the welfare state (like Shakespeare plays) should not be set in aspic.

The white paper therefore explores how the traditional model should adapt in order to serve the needs of everyone, regardless of their employment status, and to be responsive and resilient in the face of economic, social, and demographic change. What is needed, in other words, is a new social contract, a central point in the *World Development Report 2019: The Changing Nature of Work*. Given the endemic nature of the challenge, the authors argue that social protection should be organized in ways that are less dependent on a person's work situation. Poverty relief through social assistance can and should be enhanced to include larger swaths of informal sector workers, and benefits offering insurance (e.g., against medical risks, disability, or old-age poverty) could be financed through broadly based taxation unrelated to the nature of a person's job status. Recent experience with flagship safety net programs, for example, in the Arab Republic of Egypt, Ethiopia, Indonesia, Pakistan, and the Philippines demonstrate that it is possible to extend protection to more people living in or vulnerable to poverty, regardless of employment status. New technologies, including digital identification and payment systems, are making this outcome even more possible.

Once robust basic protections are in place, people could keep upgrading their security with various progressively subsidized contributory plans—with contributory social insurance, public or private, pay-as-you-go or funded, or anything in between—in which conducive conditions exist, but also through a range of voluntary options, where the state and markets are able to offer them. The white paper wholly endorses the objective of universal social protection espoused by the international development community. Its purpose is to show new pathways for achieving that objective.

We recognize that the rapidly changing nature of work across countries at all levels of development requires new thinking to ensure continuing robust and effective social protection. The imperative for clarity is reinforced by the persistence of the view that in the end we will all converge on the model of a standard employment contract and the design of social protection that is dependent on it. Aimed at readers interested in social protection, the white paper examines options that reflect current reality: new, changing, and more diverse forms of work in developing economies, emerging market economies, and high-income countries.

The white paper has five key messages for policy makers:

- The foundation of effective risk sharing is poverty prevention and subsidized protection against catastrophic losses, financed from broad-based taxes.
- With robust protections from impoverishment in place, available to all people wherever and however they work, government mandates can be less distortive.
- Rather than protect workers *from* change, governments can shift efforts to protecting them *for* change: supporting job transitions and reemployment.
- Given daunting resource and capacity limitations in most countries, the white paper proposes arrangements that cover the needs of the least well off first, before expanding coverage to other households (the authors refer to this strategy as "progressive universalism").
- Digital technology can be harnessed to mobilize tax resources and to deliver protection more effectively, efficiently, and equitably.

Nicholas Barr
Professor of Public Economics
London School of Economics

Michal Rutkowski
Global Director
Social Protection and Jobs
World Bank Group

# Acknowledgments

This volume was prepared by a core team of staff from the World Bank Group's Social Protection and Jobs Global Practice: Truman Packard (team leader), Ugo Gentilini, Margaret Grosh, Philip O'Keefe, Robert Palacios, David Robalino, and Indhira Santos. Substantial analytical input was provided by Arvo Kuddo, Zaineb Majoka, Veronica Michel Gutierrez, Claudio Montenegro, and Jose Romero. Vanessa Moreira da Silva provided invaluable data-management, data visualization, and analytical assistance. The team was supported by Angela Maria Rubio, Federico Antonio Beckley, and Helena Makarenko. Jewel McFadden of the Development Economics unit was the acquisitions editor who advised on publication standards, and Michael Harrup from the Global Corporate Solutions Editorial Production team was the book's proactive, helpful, and patient production manager.

The team worked under the supervision of Michal Rutkowski, Global Director of the Social Protection and Jobs Global Practice. Nicholas Barr, Professor of Public Economics at the London School of Economics and Political Science, provided mentoring and expert advice to the team.

The *white paper*, as it has come to be known, is the product of what has been a collective effort from the start in January 2017. The team's thinking and the volume have benefited from excellent and timely input from colleagues in the Social Protection and Jobs Global Practice: Ignacio Apella, Ali Bargu, Alvaro Gonzalez, Matteo Morgandi, Maria Laura Oliveri, Karen Peffley, Juul Pinxten, Abla Safir, Maria Laura Sanchez-Puerta, and

Michael Weber. These colleagues gave generously of their time and consistently responded to requests for supporting evidence and analysis with patience and good cheer. Thank you.

The team is additionally grateful for the valuable written submissions received over the course of its deliberations from members of the practice: Syud Amer Ahmed, Colin Andrews, Elizabeth Ruppert Bulmer, Mark Dorfman, Melis Guven, Qaiser Khan, Johannes Koettl, Hilma Mote, Ahmet Fatih Ortakaya, Montserrat Pallares Miralles, Stefano Paternostro, Iffath Sharif, Paul Siegel, Sandor Sipos, Ramya Sundaram, Mauro Testaverde, Nithin Umapathi, Ian Walker, Thomas Walker, Mitchell Wiener, Hernan Winkler, and Ruslan Yemtsov.

The team owes a debt of gratitude to formal peer reviewers and other World Bank colleagues—Omar Arias, Daniel Cotlear, Aline Coudouel, Francisco Ferreira, Emanuela Galasso, Tina George, John Giles, Gabriela Inchauste, Himanshi Jain, Steen Jørgensen, Kathy Lindert, Dhushyanth Raju, and Mitchell Wiener—being patient and generous with their time and for detailed comments on earlier drafts and suggestions that substantially strengthened the volume.

Finally, the authors and the Social Protection and Jobs Global Practice would like to acknowledge the valuable contribution of individuals and agencies in the social protection and jobs policy community that challenged us and sharpened our thinking. Vital feedback was received from Gordon Betcherman, Professor of International Development and Global Studies at the University of Ottawa; Agnieszka Chlon-Dominczak, Associate Professor in the Institute of Statistics and Demography at the Warsaw School of Economics; Gary Fields, Professor of International and Comparative Labor and Economics at Cornell University; Indermit Singh Gill, Professor of Practice of Public Policy in the Sanford School of Public Policy, Duke University; Florian Höllen of Germany's Federal Ministry for Economic Cooperation and Development; Deborah Greenfield, Deputy Director-General for Policy at the International Labour Organization and her team; Sharan Burrow, General Secretary at the International Trade Union Confederation and her team; and Marjeta Jager, Deputy Director-General for International Cooperation and Development, and Andriana Sukova, Deputy Director General, Employment, Social Affairs and Inclusion of the European Commission.

The observations, interpretations, arguments, conclusions, and remaining errors made in this volume are attributable only to the authors.

# About the Authors

**Truman G. Packard** joined the World Bank staff in 1997 and is currently a Lead Economist in its Social Protection and Jobs Global Practice, working on labor market policy in Argentina, Brazil, and Chile. His prior assignment was providing social protection and jobs policy assistance to Indonesia, Malaysia, and Vietnam, and leading the World Bank team that delivered the regional report *East Asia Pacific at Work: Employment, Enterprise and Well-Being* in 2014. He also served on the teams that produced *Golden Growth: Restoring the Lustre of the European Economic Model*, published in 2012, and the *World Development Report 2009: Reshaping Economic Geography*. Truman led the World Bank's Human Development program in the Pacific Islands, Papua New Guinea, and Timor-Leste and has been part of teams delivering financial and knowledge-transfer services to various governments in Europe and Central Asia, East Asia and Pacific, and Latin America and the Caribbean. Trained as a labor economist, Truman's work has focused primarily on the impact of social insurance—including pensions, unemployment insurance, and health coverage—on household labor supply decisions, employment outcomes, saving behavior, and risk management. Truman holds a Ph.D. in economics from the University of Oxford.

**Ugo Gentilini** serves as the Global Lead for Social Assistance in the World Bank's Social Protection and Jobs Global Practice. He has conducted analytical and operational work on social assistance in the context of jobs and labor market activation, fragility and displacement, resilience and crises, and food security and nutrition, as well as urbanization and mobility.

He has authored or coauthored dozens of publications, including flagship reports, operational tools, and articles in peer-reviewed journals as well as the blogosphere. His latest coedited book, forthcoming in 2019, will examine universal basic income. Before joining the World Bank staff in 2013, he was with the United Nations World Food Programme, where he worked on safety nets. A Swedish-Italian national with a Ph.D. in development economics, he hosts a weekly newsletter on social protection.

**Margaret Grosh** is the Senior Advisor for the World Bank's Social Protection and Jobs Global Practice. She has written, lectured, and advised extensively on social protection programs, especially on targeting and cash transfer programs, globally and for Latin America. She has extensive experience with social protection both for responding to a crisis and for improving equality of opportunity. Earlier in her career, she served as Lead Economist in the World Bank's Latin American and Caribbean Region Human Development Department and led the Social Assistance team in the World Bank's Global Social Protection Department, and before that, the Living Standard Measurement Study in its Research Department. She holds a Ph.D. in economics from Cornell University.

**Philip O'Keefe** is the Practice Manager in the World Bank's Social Protection and Jobs Global Practice for East Asia and Pacific, based in Sydney. Previously, he was Lead Economist for Social Protection and Labor in East Asia and Pacific, and Lead Economist for the Human Development Sector for the East Asia and Pacific region. He has worked in the World Bank's East Asia and Pacific, South Asia, and Europe and Central Asia regions on social protection and labor issues, including field positions in China, Hungary, and India. He is the lead author of the Bank's East Asia and Pacific flagship report on aging and has published regularly on social security and labor market issues in East and South Asia and transition economies. Prior to joining the World Bank staff, he was a lecturer at the University of Warwick. He holds undergraduate degrees in history and literature and in international law from the University of Sydney and postgraduate degrees in development economics and law from the London School of Economics and Political Science and the University of Oxford.

**Robert Palacios** is a Lead Specialist in the World Bank's Social Protection and Jobs Global Practice. His most recent previous assignment was as the Global Lead for the Pensions and Social Insurance Global Solutions Group. Between 1992 and 1994, he was a member of the Research Department team that produced the World Bank's influential volume on international pension systems, *Averting the Old Age Crisis: Policies to Protect the Old and Promote Growth*. Since 1995, he has worked in more than 30 countries in eastern Europe, East and South Asia, Latin America, and Africa. His publications include articles and books on old-age poverty, health insurance, and a wide range of pension policy issues. Between 2007 and 2010, he was based in India, where he provided support to the effort to roll out the biometric identification system known as Aadhaar. Upon his return to Washington, DC, he played a key role in establishing the World Bank's Identification for Development (ID4D) initiative, developing the ID4D diagnostic tool, which has been applied in 25 countries. He continues to advise multiple country teams across the world.

**David Robalino** is a Senior Advisor for McKinsey and Professor of Public Finance at the American University of Beirut. Until recently he was the Manager and Lead Economist of the World Bank's Jobs Group and Codirector of the Labor and Development Program at the Institute of Labor Economics (IZA). David's policy work and research focuses on issues related to jobs, social insurance, and fiscal policies. He has worked in more than 60 countries around the world providing advice to governments and international organizations. David completed his graduate studies at the University of the Sorbonne and the RAND Graduate School.

**Indhira Santos** is the the Global Lead for Labor and Skills in the World Bank's Social Protection and Jobs Global Practice. She was a primary author of the *World Development Report 2019: The Changing Nature of Work* and the *World Development Report 2016: Digital Dividends*. She has worked on the Africa, Europe and Central Asia, and South Asia regions at the World Bank since joining as a Young Professional in 2009. Prior to joining the World Bank staff, she was a research fellow at Bruegel, a European policy think tank in Brussels, between 2007 and 2009. She has also worked for the Economic Research Center of the Pontificia Universidad Católica Madre y Maestra in the Dominican Republic and the Dominican Republic Ministry of Finance. She was a Fulbright Scholar at Harvard University, where she obtained her Ph.D. in public policy and a Master of Public Administration in international development.

# Abbreviations

| | |
|---|---|
| ALM | active labor measure |
| BDS | business development services |
| BISP | Benazir Income Support Program (Pakistan) |
| BPC | business plan competition |
| BPC | Benefício de Prestação Continuada (Continuous Cash Benefit; targeted social pensions for elderly and disabled; Brazil) |
| CCT | conditional cash transfer |
| DB | defined benefit |
| DC | defined contribution |
| EAT | Entrepreneurship Aptitude Test |
| EC | European Commission |
| EITC | earned income tax credit |
| EU | European Union |
| FGTS | Fundo de Guarantia do Tempo de Serviço (Mandatory individual savings for unemployment; Brazil) |
| GDP | gross domestic product |
| GMI | guaranteed minimum income |
| GP | general practitioner |
| HIC | high-income country |
| IDA | International Development Association |
| ILO | International Labour Organization |
| IMF | International Monetary Fund |
| IRR | internal rate of return |
| IT | information technology |
| JLE | job-linked externalities |
| KYC | know your customer |

| | |
|---|---|
| KYEOP | Kenya Youth Employment and Opportunities Project |
| LIC | low-income country |
| LMIC | lower-middle-income country |
| LTC | long-term care |
| MDC | matching defined contribution |
| MIS | management information system |
| M/SME | micro/small or medium enterprise |
| MTR | marginal tax rate |
| NDC | notional defined contribution |
| NIT | negative income tax |
| NSE | nonstandard employment |
| OECD | Organisation for Economic Co-operation and Development |
| OPL | Old Poor Law (England) |
| PBI-JKN | subsidized health coverage program (Indonesia) |
| PBS | Pensión Básica Solidaria (social old-age pension; Chile) |
| PSU | public service unit (China) |
| RGPS | Regime Geral de Previdência Social (General Social Security Regime; for private sector workers; Brazil) |
| RR | replacement rate |
| SAR | special administrative region |
| SHI | social health insurance |
| SME | small and medium enterprise |
| SNAP | Supplemental Nutrition Assistance Program |
| SP | social protection |
| STI | sexually transmitted infection |
| TUBI | tapered universal basic income |
| TUSI | tapered universal social insurance |
| UBI | universal basic income |
| UHC | universal health coverage |
| UK NEST | National Employment Savings Trust (United Kingdom) |
| UMIC | upper-middle-income country |
| USI | universal social insurance |
| VAT | value added tax |
| WDR | *World Development Report* |
| WLD | world |

# Overview

Forces disrupting markets and changing the nature of work present a fundamental challenge to prevailing employment-based risk-sharing policies in countries at all levels of development. These forces are diversifying the ways people earn their livelihoods. Work in low- and middle-income countries has always been diverse, fluid, and overwhelmingly informal: unobservable and beyond the reach of the state's ability to enforce the obligations and benefits of a country's social contract. In contrast to this diversity and fluidity, prevailing employment-based risk-sharing policies assume a level of homogeneity and stability in the ways people work that reflects the reality of only a minority of workers in these countries. More recently, the assumed homogeneity and stability of work has changed even in the high-income countries where these policies were conceived of and developed. Both these situations raise concerns that current risk-sharing policies are losing relevance for working people. The changing nature of work challenges the assumptions underpinning the policy tools for managing risk and uncertainty, which have for the most part remained built around the assumption that most people are in a stable, "standard" employment relationship.

This volume proposes a package of protections, labor benefits, and services that are more relevant to the diverse and diversifying world of work. Here are five key messages for policy makers. The foundation of risk-sharing policy is poverty prevention and subsidized protection from catastrophic losses, financed from broad-based taxes. With robust protections in place, available to all people wherever and however they work, governments' mandates can be less distortive. Rather than protect workers *from* change, governments can shift their efforts to protecting them *for* change by supporting transitions and reemployment. Given daunting resource and capacity limitations in most countries, a *progressive* universalization of risk-sharing coverage will be more fiscally viable and sustainable. Digital technology can be harnessed to mobilize tax resources for this extended coverage and to deliver protection more effectively, efficiently, and equitably.

This overview summary is a stand-alone synthesis that follows the structure and sequence of the volume. We begin with a statement explaining our objectives and establishing the scope of the volume. Following that, we motivate the need for change in the prevailing approach to risk-sharing policy, then we propose packages of consumption support and labor-market protections that are more suitable for the diverse and diversifying world of work. We close with a discussion of the financing and administration issues that will arise in any country that decides to undertake the outlined approach to risk-sharing policy.

## Statement of Objectives and Scope

This volume—a white paper by the World Bank's Social Protection and Jobs Global Practice—focuses on the policy interventions made to help people manage risk, uncertainty, and losses from events whose impacts are channeled primarily through the labor market. Its objectives are to scrutinize the relevance and effects of prevailing risk-sharing policies in low- and middle-income countries; to take account of how global drivers of disruption shape and diversify the ways in which people work; in light of this diversity, to propose alternative and more relevant risk-sharing policies and ways to augment and improve current policies to make them more relevant and responsive to peoples' needs; and to map a reasonable transition path from the current policy approach to an alternative approach that substantially extends protection to a greater portion of working people and their families. This volume is a contribution to the broader global discussion of the changing nature of work and how policy can shape its implications for the well-being of people (ILO 2019; World Bank 2019b).

We use the term *risk-sharing policies* broadly in reference to the set of institutions, regulations, and interventions that societies put in place to help households manage shocks to their livelihoods. These policies include formal rules and structures that regulate market interactions (worker protections and other labor market institutions) and instruments that help people pool risks (social assistance and social insurance), save and insure affordably and effectively (mandatory and incentivized individual savings and other financial instruments), and recover from losses in the wake of shocks to their livelihoods (active reemployment measures). This volume is focused particularly on risk-sharing policies that assume a stable, subordinate wage or salaried employment: the so-called *standard employment relationship*. Principal among these policies is the model of social insurance that is by design financed primarily with statutory employer and employee contributions structured as earmarked levies on firms' wage bills and that conditions eligibility to coverage on a person's history of contributions.

Effective risk-sharing policies are foundational to building equity, resilience, and opportunity, the strategic objectives of the World Bank's Social Protection and Jobs Global Practice (World Bank 2012). Given the failures of factor markets and the market for risk, the rationale for policy intervention to augment people's options for managing shocks to their livelihoods is well-understood and -accepted (Barr 2001, 2012; Ravallion 2016). By helping to prevent vulnerable people from falling into poverty—and people in the poorest households from falling deeper into poverty—effective risk-sharing interventions dramatically reduce poverty. In contexts where they reach most people, risk-sharing policies can make economic growth more equitable by safeguarding households' vital assets. Households and communities with access to effective risk-sharing instruments can better maintain and continue to invest in these vital assets, first and foremost, their human capital. In doing so, they can reduce the likelihood that poverty and vulnerability will be transmitted from one generation to the next. Risk-sharing policies foster enterprise and development by ensuring that people can take appropriate risks that are required to grasp opportunities and secure their stake in a growing economy.

However, in many low- and middle-income countries, most people are underinsured; living and working without access to modern credit, saving, or risk-pooling instruments; and overly reliant on risk-sharing mechanisms that depend on strong family and community ties. These traditional risk-sharing structures are important but are growing more precarious; they can be overwhelmed by large, systemic shocks; and they can place limits on individuals' and households' pursuit of prosperity. Furthermore, even in contexts where many people have access to financial risk-sharing instruments, uncertainty looms large, confounding even the most sophisticated credit and insurance markets. The state has stepped in to help people manage risk and uncertainty in the labor market.

But in many countries, the prevailing set of industrial-era, employment-based risk-sharing policies often does more harm than good, becoming an obstacle to jobs rather than providing effective protection. Transfers from government budgets to cover deficits between statutory contributions and benefit payments to the eligible minority constrain governments' ability to pursue more equitably spread human-capital investments with potentially higher yields in economic development and well-being. Global drivers of disruption to factor markets—the labor market in particular—are aggravating this problem in low- and middle-income countries, where it has long existed, and are creating similar issues in high-income countries, where an increasing diversity of forms of work is challenging the effectiveness and relevance of industrial-era, employment-based risk-sharing models.

The ideas presented in this volume challenge the status quo. To avoid unnecessary misunderstandings rooted in semantics, we would like to clarify from the outset how we use key concepts and terms. The first concept is *economic informality* (variously referred to as the *informal sector*, the *informal economy*, or the "*gray*" or "*shadow economy*"). To distinguish "informal" from "criminal" per the International Labour Organization (ILO) (2015), the World Bank (2019a), and Perry et al. (2007), the salient characteristic of *informal* economic activity is its lack of observability by the government for the purposes of policy making and implementation. The salient characteristic of *informal employment* or *informal work* is the lack of access to, or purposeful avoidance of, state-financed or -mandated risk-sharing instruments (whether those instruments purely or partially pool the risk of losses, redistribute income, or simply help people to save) and the accompanying lack of access or recourse to legislated worker protections.

The second concept is *social insurance* (sometimes referred to as social security). In this volume, we set out arguments for departing from what has become an unhelpfully narrow use of the term, limited to programs structured to mimic market insurance (most visibly by limiting eligibility to and structuring financing through statutory contributions, which are typically levied as a percentage of firms' wage bills). We argue that this narrow definition of social insurance is outdated and a source of exclusion. The vital, inalienable feature of social insurance is that it provides coverage against losses that markets cannot cover, or, without state intervention, can cover only with difficulty and at a prohibitive price. Because noncontributory social assistance programs (referred to variously in the literature as social welfare, social transfers, or safety nets) are financed from the pool of taxes and other state revenues, in this volume they are considered conceptually equivalent to any other publicly financed intervention to support households' consumption. More plainly put, when the policy objective is to help people manage risk and uncertainty, as a state-financed risk-pooling instrument, social assistance is *the* essential foundation of social insurance.

## The Need for a More Effective and Relevant Risk-Sharing Model

Despite the disruptive changes shaping markets in countries around the world, a key feature of the labor markets in developing countries has remained stubbornly unchanged: the dominance of the informal economy and ubiquity of informal work. This informality is particularly threatening to the effectiveness of the prevailing employment-based approach to risk-sharing policy. On average, approximately two-thirds of working people in developing countries earn their living in the informal economy. From the standpoint of risk-sharing policy, the most salient feature of work in the informal economy is that, for the most part, it is undertaken without work contracts and thus without the benefits of contributory social insurance schemes or mandatory worker protections. Work arrangements in the informal economy are also diverse and very fluid—people move in and out of jobs regularly, can hold several market engagements at the same time, and may hold jobs with characteristics of both economic formality and economic informality. As a result, the share of workers participating in contributory social insurance plans—historically, a hallmark of formal work—has remained low or stagnant in most developing countries. Figure O.1 compares administrative data on participation in contributory social insurance plans collected from a range of low- and middle-income countries during the 1990s and again in the 2010s. There is disappointingly little change in the share of working people that participate in and can count on contributory social insurance coverage (Rutkowski 2018). Longstanding and more recently emerging trends, such as premature deindustrialization and new labor market disruptors—also seen in developed countries—suggest that the situation is unlikely to change fundamentally in the coming decades.

Even in developed economies, global drivers of labor market disruption—such as technological advances; economic integration; and social, demographic, and climate change—have resulted in greater diversity and fluidity of work than has previously characterized most people's experiences. This diversity includes numerous forms of self-employment, fixed-term and part-time work, "gig economy" jobs, other flexible work arrangements, and, for many with higher skills, so-called portfolio careers: multiple concurrent, part-time engagements. Legal systems often struggle to characterize such jobs within traditional categories of employment relationships. Although such workers remain a minority in the workforces of most countries, the rate of growth of such jobs could outstrip the growth in more traditional wage and salaried employment. Digital "platform" firms, which employ a greater share of such workers than their traditional "brick-and-mortar" rivals, have expanded exponentially compared to their rivals (World Bank 2016, 2019b).

These patterns in the evolution of labor markets and the nature of work suggest that convergence across lower- and higher-income countries is indeed happening—just not in the expected direction. The world of work in upper-middle- and high-income countries is becoming more fluid and diversified, to a greater or lesser extent, than that of the second half of the twentieth century, when most people worked in standard employment relationships. And in most developing countries, jobs are not formalizing at the rate that was expected. In the social protection policy domain, perennial issues of undercoverage of contributory social insurance and worker protections persist in lower-income countries, while incomplete (and sometimes regressive) coverage is a growing concern in higher-income countries. This concern is

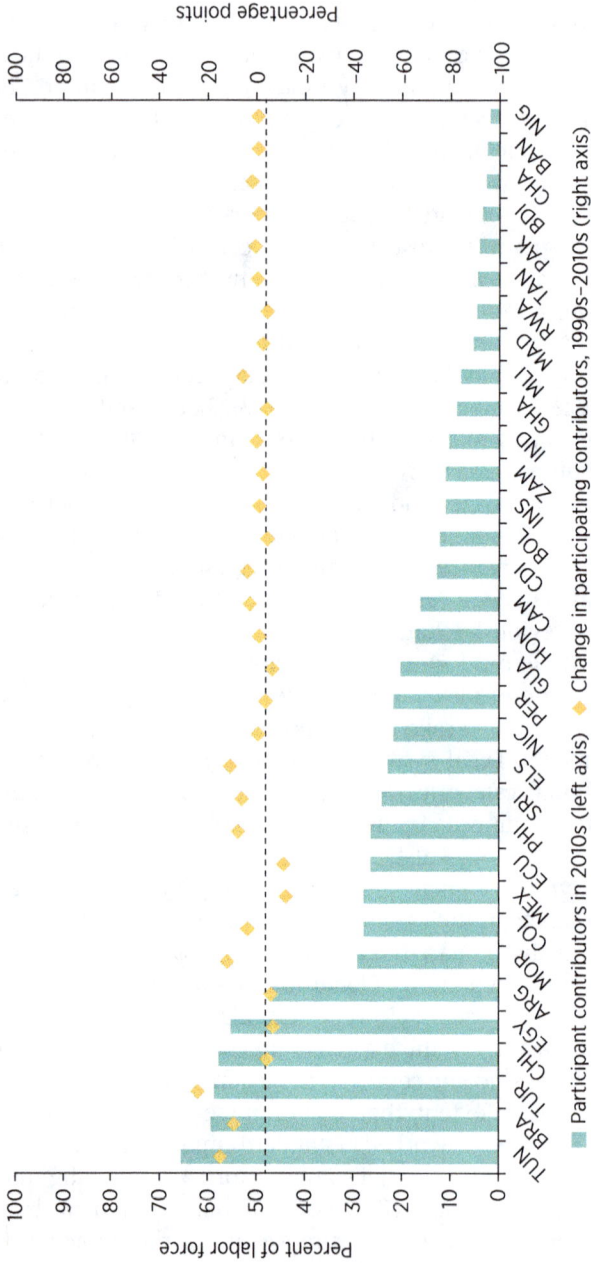

Figure O.1 Changes in Coverage of Employment-Based Social Insurance Have Been Disappointing

■ Participant contributors in 2010s (left axis) ◆ Change in participating contributors, 1990s–2010s (right axis)

**Source:** Rutkowski 2018; World Bank Pensions Database.

**Note:** The figure shows participation rates in contributory pension schemes from the 1990s to the 2010s. The dashed horizontal line represents no change in rates of contribution over time.

**Figure O.2 Convergence of Work Arrangements and Social Protection Coverage Is Happening—but Not as Expected**

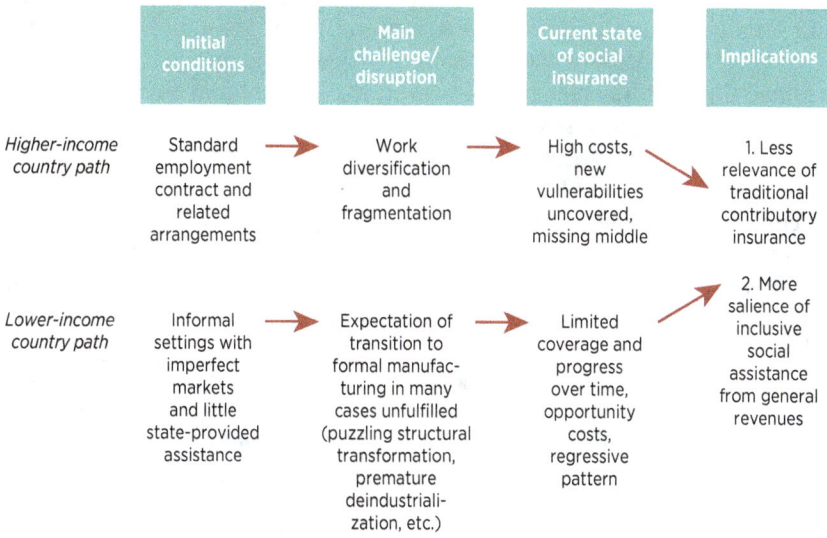

| | Initial conditions | Main challenge/ disruption | Current state of social insurance | Implications |
|---|---|---|---|---|
| *Higher-income country path* | Standard employment contract and related arrangements | Work diversification and fragmentation | High costs, new vulnerabilities uncovered, missing middle | 1. Less relevance of traditional contributory insurance |
| *Lower-income country path* | Informal settings with imperfect markets and little state-provided assistance | Expectation of transition to formal manufacturing in many cases unfulfilled (puzzling structural transformation, premature deindustriali-zation, etc.) | Limited coverage and progress over time, opportunity costs, regressive pattern | 2. More salience of inclusive social assistance from general revenues |

most acute in countries where populations are aging rapidly. In both cases, these trends weaken the salience of contributory social insurance systems (figure O.2).

This is not to say that greater formalization of work is no longer a desirable objective. When people engage in market activities formally, their work can be legally recognized and protected from market failures and abuses. When people work informally, they are at much greater risk of exploitation. But formalization does not have to be synonymous with homogeneity, and certainly not with dependent wage or salaried employment in factories or firms. However, because prevailing risk-sharing policy models are designed around and operate on the assumption of predominant and steadily increasing standard employment, a diverse and diversifying world of work puts the relevance and effectiveness of these models in jeopardy.

Although the relevance of these approaches is increasingly in question, their *objectives* are more vital than ever. The objectives of risk-sharing policy remain as they always have been—to prevent poverty, cover catastrophic losses, smooth consumption, help households and markets manage uncertainty, and, by achieving all this, to provide the foundation for more efficient and equitable economic and social outcomes. These objectives should continue to guide efforts to improve risk-sharing policies so that they serve the needs of all people and become more adaptable and resilient to dynamic economic, social, and demographic forces.

A more relevant risk-sharing policy model requires institutions and instruments that are accessible no matter how people engage in markets for their livelihoods. Developing such instruments, in turn, will require revisiting some of the rigid distinctions between "social assistance" and "social insurance" that are prevalent among policy experts and practitioners. To achieve the specific objectives of preventing poverty and covering potentially impoverishing losses, the de jure distinction between contributory social insurance and noncontributory social assistance will have to be blurred and potentially, in time, abandoned entirely. Seeing as the liabilities of contributory social insurance are increasingly financed in many countries through general revenues—a current, regrettably regressive outcome of the design of these countries' benefit and tax systems—this proposition is less revolutionary than it sounds. The approach to risk-sharing policy we advocate in this volume will require revisiting the current mingling of social objectives—enabling actuarial risk pooling, eliminating poverty, and pursuing equity through redistribution—to achieve a more explicit alignment of risk-sharing instruments and objectives and a more holistic approach to financing on both the revenue and expenditure sides.

## The Policy Package for Poverty Prevention and Livelihood Shocks

We propose a comprehensive policy package of protection with a publicly financed, guaranteed-minimum risk-pooling mechanism at its core and additional layers of mandated, nudged, and wholly voluntary insurance (figure O.3). Drawing on principles of actuarial and public economics, each segment of the proposed package is composed according to the *nature* of shocks (the size of losses, the probability of occurrence, and the extent of market failures to provide coverage for them). The innermost core represents the guaranteed minimum support to prevent impoverishment and mitigate the most catastrophic losses for which there are no effective market-insurance instruments. Interventions to cover the risks of more frequently occurring, lower-loss events for which protection would have substantial external social benefits—preventive actions, for example—could be included in the guaranteed minimum support.

The most important feature of this innermost core of the package is that it covers losses that, if left uncovered, impose an unacceptable social cost. This point is important to underscore, because this coverage is too important to be left to people's will or to the presumed steadfast compliance of employers. In the three remaining segments of the stylized package of protection, responsibility for financing and provision shifts gradually away from purely public resources and direct government provision to household or individual

Policy package of protection

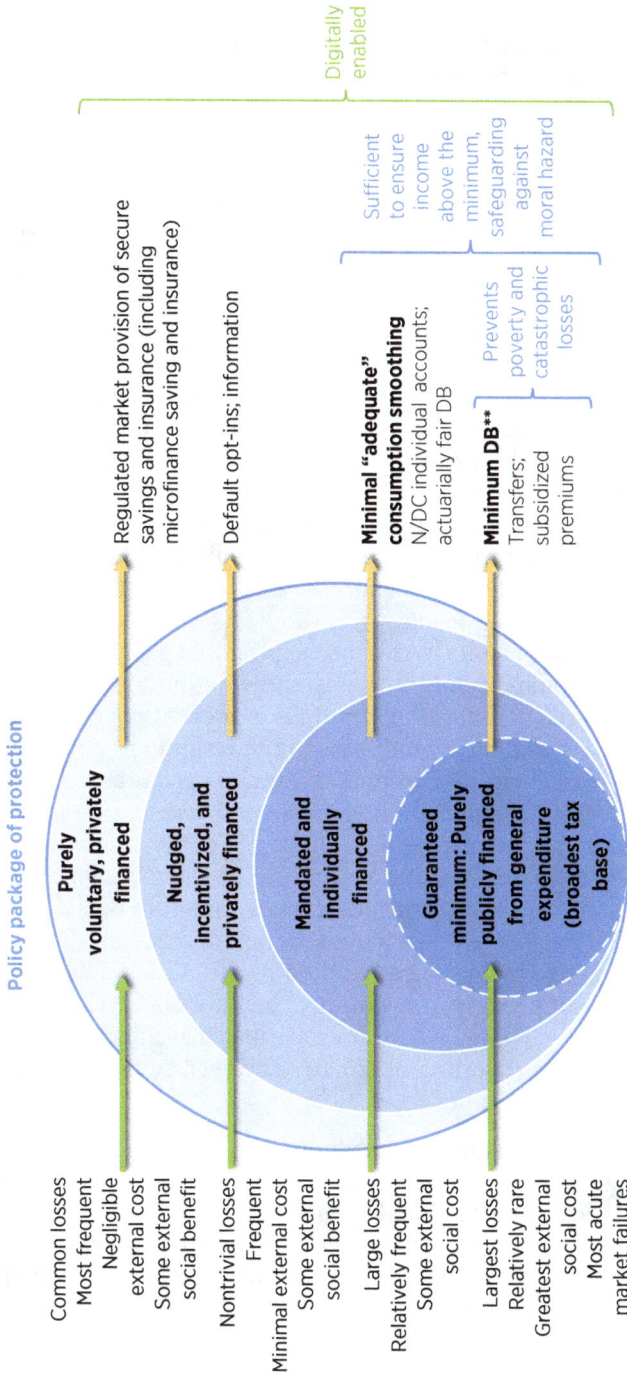

Common losses
Most frequent
Negligible
external cost
Some external
social benefit

Nontrivial losses
Frequent
Minimal external cost
Some external
social benefit

Large losses
Relatively frequent
Some external
social cost

Largest losses
Relatively rare
Greatest external
social cost
Most acute
market failures

**Purely voluntary, privately financed**

**Nudged, incentivized, and privately financed**

**Mandated and individually financed**

**Guaranteed minimum: Purely publicly financed from general expenditure (broadest tax base)**

Regulated market provision of secure savings and insurance (including microfinance saving and insurance)

Default opt-ins; information

**Minimal "adequate" consumption smoothing** N/DC individual accounts; actuarially fair DB

**Minimum DB**** Transfers; subsidized premiums

Digitally enabled

Sufficient to ensure income above the minimum, safeguarding against moral hazard

Prevents poverty and catastrophic losses

*Note:* DB = defined benefit; N/DC = notional/defined contribution. **Replaces contributory minimum guarantees and tax incentives.

9

financing and market provision. As a whole, the package represents a coherent set of interventions that extend protection and augment people's ability to manage risk and uncertainty. We characterize this comprehensive, coherent, and concerted approach to risk sharing as "insurance assistance."[1]

How each segment of the proposed package is financed matters for the efficiency and effectiveness of risk sharing. A key principle shaping the package is that poverty-prevention and redistribution objectives (that is, vertical redistribution) should be pursued transparently with instruments financed from broad-based taxes, whereas statutory contributions should be reserved to finance consumption-smoothing instruments with actuarially fair parameters (that is, horizontal redistribution). Traditionally, industrial-era contributory social insurance systems have mingled different forms of redistribution, either directly, through budget financing of deficits (or the buildup of contingent liabilities implying future budget subsidies) or through redistributing between different groups of contributors. By consolidating poverty-prevention and redistribution objectives in the core of the package and financing it entirely from general revenues, governments can increase coherence across the publicly and individually financed layers of the package and reduce perverse incentives.

Because most working people go without insurance coverage or are underinsured, the most vital element of the proposed package is a publicly financed risk-pooling mechanism (that is, the innermost core). The policy objective of the core guaranteed minimum is to prevent poverty and manage catastrophic losses that, even if they do not result in impoverishment, can jeopardize household investments in human capital because of their rapid onset and size. Though definitions of a *catastrophic* loss vary, a broadly applied definition is a loss that wipes out 30 percent or more of a household's disposable income. To serve as the core of a comprehensive policy package of insurance assistance, the guaranteed minimum would ideally be available to all in need, be set at adequate benefit levels, incentivize work, respond to changing circumstances, and be fiscally sustainable. Although these features are long-accepted attributes of an ideal safety net, experience across countries shows how difficult they are to achieve and that there are tensions among them (Grosh et al. 2008). However, some important lessons emerge from global experience:

- To meet the goals of the guaranteed minimum and avoid excluding households through rigid rationing, programs need to operate as *entitlements* with accommodative budgets and open, on-demand eligibility processes.
- All residents who are in need should be eligible to receive the guaranteed minimum, and specific social groups, such as the working poor, should not be excluded by design.
- To increase fiscal sustainability, the guaranteed minimum should have a benefit structure that gradually tapers as income or wealth rises in order to avoid sharp discontinuities or "eligibility cliffs" that discourage work.

- Eligibility thresholds should be set high enough to avoid treating households with similar (low) levels of welfare substantially differently. This feature also would help sustain protection for families who move frequently in and out of poverty and would reduce the risk of exclusion errors and a hollow guarantee.

Various instruments are available to achieve the guaranteed minimum, with different strengths and weaknesses and varying suitability to a particular country's wealth and administrative capacity. At one end of the spectrum, a guaranteed minimum income (GMI) program can be characterized as a "minimal-minimum" model: such programs involve strict, means-based targeting intended to achieve poverty prevention at the lowest possible fiscal cost but with a higher risk of undercoverage of poor people, sharp discontinuities in benefits, and disincentives to work. At the other extreme, a universal basic income (UBI) could be considered a "maximal-minimum" option when set generously. A UBI would have no errors of exclusion and would create fewer disincentives to work but would require a substantially larger volume of public resources to finance at an adequate level. An intermediate option is a negative income tax—or an equivalently tapered benefit in countries where coverage of the income tax system is limited—that has a higher eligibility threshold than a GMI and a gradual withdrawal of benefits. The taper could extend all the way up the welfare distribution, or, more likely, taper to zero at some point of the distribution at which the likelihood of exclusion errors is very low. All else equal, tapering the guaranteed minimum benefit would lower fiscal costs and increase the program's impact on poverty, hence presenting a more cost-effective approach if poverty reduction is the core objective. Another intermediate option is a smaller GMI supplemented with age-categorical transfers, such as a child allowance or a cash transfer to the elderly, or combined with an earned income tax credit for low-income workers above the eligibility threshold. The common, essential feature of all these alternatives is that the minimum guarantee is financed from *the largest available risk pool*, the national budget (often supplemented with international sources of aid and development financing), and is available when and where required.

A growing number of developing countries, including those at the lowest levels of income and institutional development, are already moving toward providing some form of guaranteed minimum protection. There are three trends in how these countries are offering minimum protection, all of which are consistent with the progressive realization of the guaranteed minimum protection shown in figure O.3: (i) new and growing national "flagship" social protection programs, some of which have near or full coverage of the intended beneficiary population; (ii) an aggregation of separate poverty-focused interventions that when combined give the system of benefits the characteristics of a substantial minimum guarantee and that taper away at differing points in the wealth distribution; and (iii) an increasingly blurred distinction between social insurance and social assistance, whether by default or by design, that results in a core guaranteed minimum for poor and sometimes also near-poor households. But although many countries are far along a path to realizing the vision of protection for all presented in this volume, formidable challenges remain to extending coverage, ensuring adequacy, reducing fragmentation, and supporting market engagement.

A second element of the proposed guaranteed minimum protections is universal access to contingent coverage of catastrophic losses through public subsidies. Many social protection systems currently lack protection against catastrophic losses for those without a history of contributing to traditional social insurance plans. A guaranteed minimum package, as conceptualized in figure O.3, should help address this lack of coverage or undercoverage, but it will require public subsidies. Many shocks impose losses that would over-whelm even the most generous flat benefit. The combination of a poverty-prevention benefit and publicly financed coverage of contingent risks can achieve progressive protection for all. This approach is already observed in how a growing number of countries structure health insurance, approaching the goal of universal health coverage (UHC) through the government subsidizing actuarially set premiums for people who are not able to afford them. As with the poverty-prevention transfer, the subsidy for contingent coverage can be reduced as people's income or consumption rises. This tapered subsidy for a risk-pooling premium would complement the poverty-prevention transfer as a second essential element of the guaranteed minimum (the innermost core of figure O.3). Tapering is possible in contexts where governments' administrative and implementation capacities allow them to observe people's means. The tapered subsidy for risk-pooling premiums could purchase contingent coverage for longevity, health and disability, the costs of long-term care for functional dependency, and exceptionally long unemployment spells. By designing the poverty prevention and shock-responsive elements of the guaranteed minimum together, governments can reduce perverse incentives.

The guaranteed minimum can also help lower distortions on firms' and individuals' choices caused by statutory contributions that finance additional mandatory insurance coverage (the second ring of figure O.3). The statutory contributions set to finance traditional contributory social insurance can have a substantial tax element because, for most people, the mandate forces a choice to save or insure that they would otherwise not make, even if the terms of the plan were set purely actuarially. Because the terms of traditional social insurance plans are devised to achieve income as well as risk redistribution, the tax element is substantial. The package proposed in this volume allows a reduction of this tax element through two channels. First, to the extent that the minimum income guarantee keeps people out of poverty (and keeps lower-earning households protected from catastrophic losses), a large component of redistribution could be stripped out of plans financed with statutory contributions, leaving contributory plans as instruments purely for consumption smoothing or additional, actuarially fair insurance coverage. Unlike in traditional models, the afore-mentioned subsidies would be *explicit, transparent,* and financed from a broader revenue base than statutory, earmarked levies on firms' observable wage bills. Second, by eliminating implicit redistribution, remaining man-datory contributions would be linked entirely to the benefits a participant receives, reducing—though not eliminating—the distortion created by the mandate to contribute. This change might even allow the government to reduce the level of statutory contributions required.

Furthermore, the mandated segment of the package safeguards the fiscal sustainability of the guaranteed core from moral hazard and protects people from their own improvidence or myopia and from the failures of markets to provide affordable, reliable insurance. Human limitations combine with mar-ket failures to create a strong rationale for the state to compel additional sav-ing and insurance efforts. But many governments are mandating more such efforts than they need to. Mandatory contributions from working individuals (and their employers) serve two primary purposes. First, mandatory, actuari-ally fair arrangements reduce the risk of moral hazard that naturally arises from the government providing the minimum guaranteed core of protection. Second, a remaining mandate provides a vehicle for consumption smoothing that may not be available in the market. Because of adverse selection, annu-ity markets, for example, have not developed organically in most countries. This market failure provides a rationale for government intervention.

Beyond the guaranteed minimum and mandated segments of the policy package, there is potential to strengthen *nudged* and purely voluntary sav-ings and insurance for additional consumption smoothing. These layers of the protection package are important, though experience with them to date has been disappointing, reflecting cognitive and behavioral limitations on the demand side and informational and capacity constraints on the supply side (World Bank 2006; Barr and Diamond 2010; Kahneman 2011; Thaler and Sunstein 2008). Successful examples of nudged or purely voluntary savings and insurance programs draw on insights from behavioral econom-ics, using simple commitment devices or behavioral nudges such as opt-in defaults within business registration and taxation systems. Such approaches have shown promise in developed and developing countries (for example, New Zealand's Kiwi Saver retirement-savings scheme and commitment devices in telephone payment platforms in Kenya that have increased savings).

The path toward achieving the full package of protection, particularly the guaranteed minimum, will need to be progressive, ensuring that people already in poverty and the most vulnerable to impoverishment benefit first,

**Figure O.4 Countries Can Take Specific Steps to Move from Current Risk Sharing to Comprehensive Coverage**

a. Stylized state of social protection in a typical low- or middle-income country

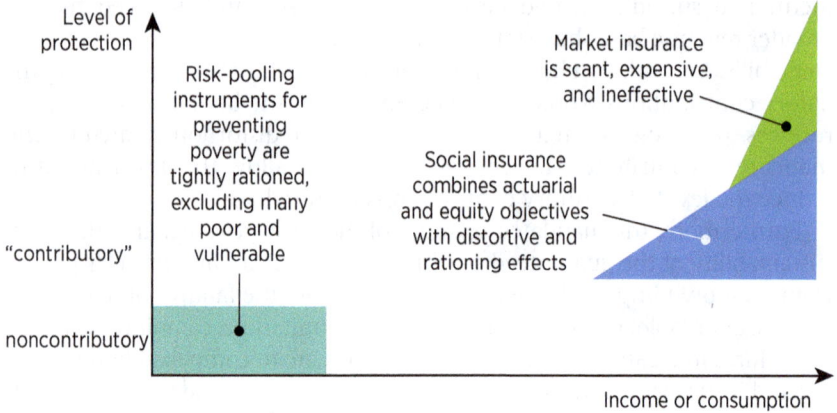

Level of protection

Risk-pooling instruments for preventing poverty are tightly rationed, excluding many poor and vulnerable

Market insurance is scant, expensive, and ineffective

Social insurance combines actuarial and equity objectives with distortive and rationing effects

"contributory"

noncontributory

Income or consumption

b. Policy actions to fill the current gaps in protection

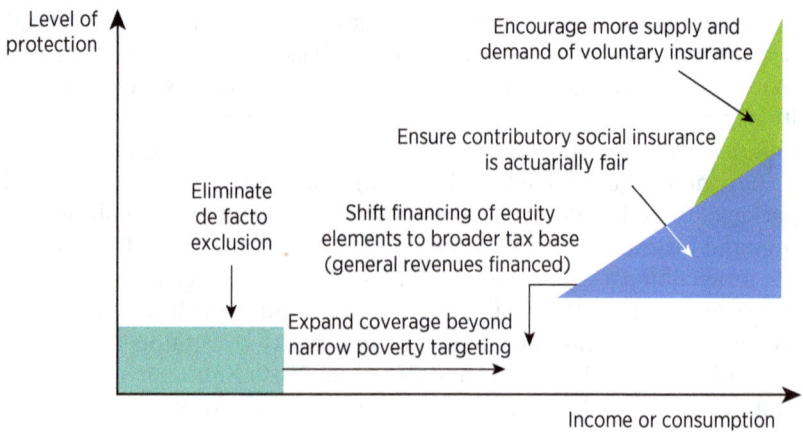

Level of protection

Encourage more supply and demand of voluntary insurance

Ensure contributory social insurance is actuarially fair

Eliminate de facto exclusion

Shift financing of equity elements to broader tax base (general revenues financed)

Expand coverage beyond narrow poverty targeting

Income or consumption

■ Social assistance          ■ Market insurance (voluntary)
■ Social insurance (mandatory)  ■ Subsidized premiums for insurance coverage

*continued next page*

**Figure 0.4** (*continued*)

c. Comprehensive insurance assistance

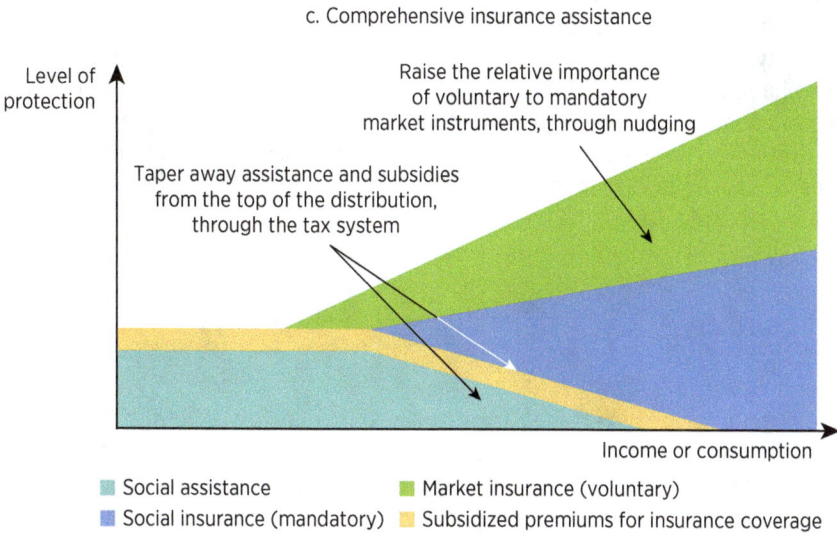

Level of protection

Raise the relative importance of voluntary to mandatory market instruments, through nudging

Taper away assistance and subsidies from the top of the distribution, through the tax system

Income or consumption

- Social assistance
- Social insurance (mandatory)
- Market insurance (voluntary)
- Subsidized premiums for insurance coverage

or at least in tandem with the rest of society. Figure O.4 presents a simple step-by-step illustration of how current social protection arrangements in an archetypal low- or middle-income country would need to be reformed to achieve the objective of comprehensive insurance assistance presented in this volume. Panel a shows de jure gaps in coverage. Importantly, even when social assistance programs are designed to cover the poorest, many families living in poverty are excluded de facto, because of either budget or delivery limitations. Furthermore, exacerbating de jure and de facto exclusion from social assistance and social insurance, market insurance is scant and available at prices only the wealthiest people can afford. Panels b and c indicate the structural reforms a government would undertake to close coverage gaps, starting with measures to eliminate de facto exclusion of the poorest people, and expand entitlement beyond narrow poverty targeting. Inclusion, equity, and redistribution—including subsidies for the premiums of contingent coverage—would be shifted to broader-based (general-revenue) financing. Statutory contributions would be limited to actuarially fair consumption-smoothing plans, and measures would be taken to expand financial inclusion and access to market-provided credit, saving, and insurance instruments.

A guaranteed minimum will not be put in place overnight. In the absence of existing broad-based programs to replace or extend protection from poverty, choices will need to be made on where to start, in terms of both categories of the population and communities across geography. Applying the concept of "progressive universalism," borrowed from the UHC movement, will ensure that the poorest people have the highest priority in the expansion of protection. The pace of implementation will also have to match countries' progress in building administrative and taxation capacity, such that governments have both the ability to assess the welfare needs of their populations and the fiscal space to meet those needs. This overview summary closes with a more detailed discussion of financial and administrative issues.

## Helping People Manage Labor Market Risks and Uncertainty

Labor policies are also risk-sharing policies. In addition to being the primary channel through which people obtain their livelihoods and prosperity, working is the most widespread and effective measure people take to manage risk. Ensuring ample opportunities for safe, fairly remunerated work remains a powerfully effective policy response to risk and uncertainty. However, the labor market is itself a source of risk and uncertainty. The power and information to set the terms of work relationships are spread unevenly, which can leave people disadvantaged and vulnerable to exploitation. Redundancy in the wake of a technology or trade shock and subsequent long-term unemployment can be a catastrophic loss for individuals and their families. In this sense, labor market policies—just like social assistance and insurance—provide tools and protections that help workers and their families prevent, save, and pool to mitigate the risks of losses and to cope better in the wake of a shock. For this reason, there is an equally important role within an overall risk-sharing framework for labor market policies, especially for policies that regulate the interactions between parties transacting in the labor market.

The vital principle for policy makers to follow when crafting labor regulations is to avoid extremes. The *World Development Report 2013: Jobs* (World Bank 2012) presented the concept of a broad "plateau" between extreme "cliffs" of too little and too much regulatory intervention (see figure O.5). A *plateau* is a compelling and powerful metaphor, and one that this volume espouses fully as a policy principle to guide the design of labor market regulation. However, the plateau has not yet been sufficiently developed to provide actionable policy guidance. More analytical effort is required to empirically and convincingly identify its features, most importantly its inflection points—that is, where "too little" stops and "too much" starts—and the levels at which regulation is relatively beneficial and benign that lie in between the two extremes.

**Figure O.5  To Minimize Adverse Labor Market Outcomes, Countries Should Avoid Regulatory Extremes**

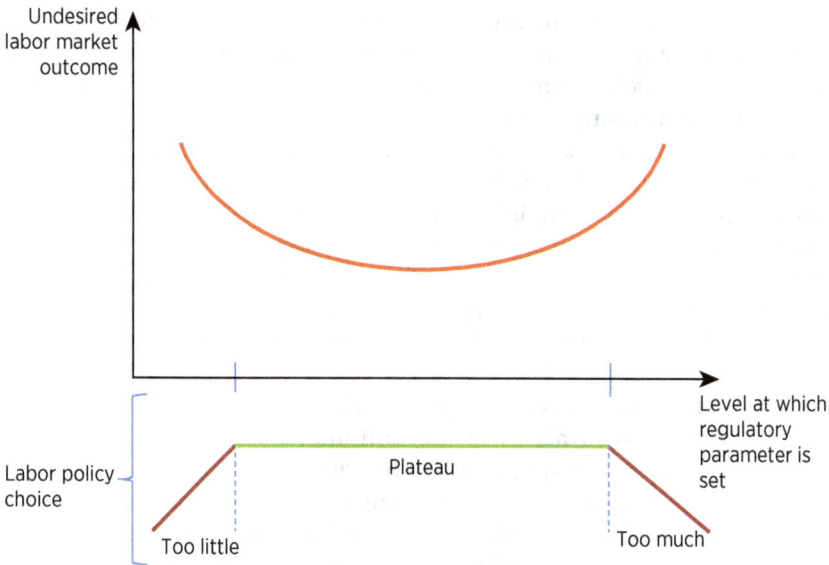

The ILO's core labor standards represent vital bulwarks that safeguard hard-won advances in human well-being and remain a key development benchmark used in the World Bank's annual *Country Policy and Institutional Assessment*. Beyond these core standards, regulations to keep markets competitive and contestable, and a framework for accessible social dialogue, regulatory mandates on their own can become less effective and costlier instruments for risk sharing. In countries where governments are resource- and capacity-constrained, labor regulation is still being deployed as the principal instrument of risk-sharing and redistribution policy. This use can result in labor regulations that are de jure too restrictive, making de facto compliance too difficult for many firms. In the mid- and late industrial era, when most governments lacked the fiscal and administrative capacity to provide labor-market protections, this approach probably made sense. However, this is no longer the case now that the capacity to deliver timely transfers of cash and other resources has grown exponentially even in low- and middle-income countries.

A diverse and diversifying world of work demands fresh thinking about the role of labor policy and the regulatory instruments that governments should prioritize. To guide thinking on the evolution of labor policies, this volume mentions several features of global labor markets that overlay the megatrends discussed earlier. There is a growing premium for firms and workers that adapt quickly to the changing nature of production and work. However, much of labor market regulation is designed to protect firms and people from change, that is, to preserve jobs, firms, and even entire sectors. Labor market policies in most countries do not yet accommodate diversity and fluidity of working forms well. Worker protection policies, and labor regulation specifically, assume a level of homogeneity and stability that does not characterize most work arrangements. Reflecting this orientation toward preserving specific jobs, the volume, coverage, and efficiency of active reemployment assistance and income-protection arrangements remain low in many countries and are insufficient to facilitate more frequent livelihood disruptions and labor market transitions, including those of people who have been dislocated by structural changes from automation and trade.

Greater effort is also needed to prevent abuses of uneven market power and to ensure broader access to the institutions of collective action and industrial relations. The market power of firms is growing in many parts of the world. Ensuring competitive and contestable markets has long been a challenge in low- and middle-income countries, where governance institutions are weak and can be vulnerable to oligopolistic pressures. However, the dangers of market concentration are increasing in high-income countries as well. Concentration is often accompanied by restrictive and even exploitative business practices. Alongside market concentration, the declining influence of labor unions has reduced the power of an important accountability instrument. Yet for many working people, these institutions have never been strongly relevant or even accessible. The same is true of employer and professional associations. This observation suggests a need for revitalized efforts to counter the concentration of market power and new institutions to give working people greater voice. This volume argues for changes to the institutions of social dialogue that would make them more representative of a diverse and diversifying world of work.

Societies need no longer rely as much on the place and stability of employment to extend reliable and resilient protection from shocks and losses, or even to pursue greater equity. When the prevailing risk-sharing models—including labor market policies—were put in place, the employer and the firm were the assumed superior provider of protection and continuity, primarily through seniority-based advancement or internal labor markets. Partly because of the inadequacy of government-provided risk-sharing arrangements, such as formal social protection systems, firms were expected to be the platform for risk pooling, mandatory precautionary saving, and skill renewal. Labor regulations and mandates on firms were used to provide more than just basic protections. They were the tools at hand in the developing countries at the time to prevent in-work poverty, smooth consumption in the wake of shocks, and help people make market transitions. These same tools were later adopted by many newly independent or transitioning countries with little or no adaptation and with the expectation that economic development would shift most working people off of farms and into factories and firms. However, the path of structural transformation is less clear today. And advances in government capacity, even in many low-income countries, have made alternative and more reliable risk-sharing instruments available.

In a diverse and diversifying world of work, the gains from protecting working people are far more attractive than the costs of protecting certain jobs. With more effective guaranteed poverty-prevention and consumption-smoothing instruments in place, underpinned with more public resources allocated to reemployment support, there is room to loosen restrictions on firms' contracting and dismissal decisions. Governments' efforts and resources can be shifted to protecting people *for* change. This "flexicurity" approach to helping people manage market shocks and transitions is a robust and resilient policy response to a diverse and fluid world of work. Once a buzzword of labor policy in Europe in the 1990s, the flexicurity approach has lost its luster because many reforming governments have quickly pursued flexibility but have been slow to deliver the promised security (Gill and Raiser, 2012; Bussolo et al. 2018). Flexible hiring and dismissal procedures need to be balanced with increased and more effective protections outside of the employment contract. Without reemployment support to meet the income and other needs of people who lose jobs, lifting restrictions on hiring and dismissal decisions would shift an unreasonable risk burden onto working people.

Even with the best labor policies in place, targeted interventions will be required to stimulate demand and productivity. The global drivers of disruption could limit the structural shift of labor out of low-productivity agriculture into more productive sectors. In some regions, and for some population groups, job opportunities can be very limited, requiring more proactive policies to create jobs or improve the quality of existing jobs. The social externalities of work are sometimes sufficiently substantial to justify policies that stimulate private investments on the condition that they improve job outcomes for certain population groups. The idea of subsidizing demand for job creation is not new and has motivated many costly mistakes. However, the approach proposed in this volume is fundamentally different. Traditional job-creation programs focus on the private or "internal" rate of return (IRR) on their investments. However, in the presence of jobs externalities, the IRR is a poor indicator of success for such projects (Robalino, Romero, and Walker 2019). Instead, from a normative point of view, projects could be ranked based on the level of their job-linked externalities. Targeted subsidies can equate the private and social benefits of the investment and are more likely to maximize the number of jobs created. Of course, when it comes to targeting public subsidies to stimulate job creation, the proverbial devil is in the details. Criteria for project identification and expectations for market performance must be set very high to avoid rent seeking and capture by elites.

In this context, this volume proposes a package of labor policies aimed at protecting working people from labor-market- and work-related risks and uncertainty that depends less than the prevailing approach on where or how people work (figure O.6). Just as the proposed package of poverty prevention and consumption support, this package has a publicly financed guaranteed minimum of protection at its core and supplementary layers of mandated, nudged, and fully voluntary policies. It should be considered together with the insurance assistance package presented earlier (figure O.3).

The core of the proposed labor package is aimed at preventing abusive exploitation and catastrophic losses and addressing areas where market failures can be the most harmful to households, communities, and society. The potential harm justifies financing these protections from general

**Figure O.6  Labor Policies Are Also Tools for Effective Risk Sharing**

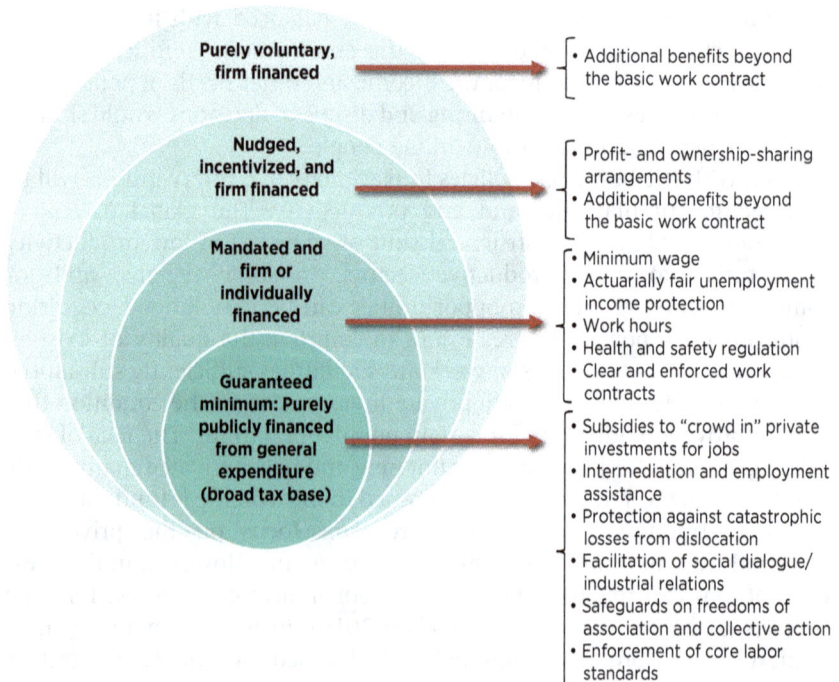

**Purely voluntary, firm financed**
- Additional benefits beyond the basic work contract

**Nudged, incentivized, and firm financed**
- Profit- and ownership-sharing arrangements
- Additional benefits beyond the basic work contract

**Mandated and firm or individually financed**
- Minimum wage
- Actuarially fair unemployment income protection
- Work hours
- Health and safety regulation
- Clear and enforced work contracts

**Guaranteed minimum: Purely publicly financed from general expenditure (broad tax base)**
- Subsidies to "crowd in" private investments for jobs
- Intermediation and employment assistance
- Protection against catastrophic losses from dislocation
- Facilitation of social dialogue/industrial relations
- Safeguards on freedoms of association and collective action
- Enforcement of core labor standards

revenues so that provision and access is assured. Put another way, provision and access to the protections in this core is not denied on the basis of how or where people work. These protections are given to everyone who needs them, regardless of their work arrangements. The goal is to prevent losses with high social costs, such as exploitative abuses, discrimination, trafficking, the worst forms of child labor, and hazardous working conditions.

A minimum guaranteed package of labor protection should also include effective mechanisms to increase workers' voice: their influence in setting labor policies. Weak enforcement of labor laws and protections often leaves workers (even those with formal contracts) de facto unprotected. Informality makes enforcement even more challenging. Thus, the government has a role in ensuring that all workers, including people in the informal economy, who are often not organized or heard in policy debates, are represented at the tables of social dialogue.

Additionally, the guaranteed minimum should mitigate the rarest events and largest losses and those with clear social externalities. Of greatest priority among these events are relatively permanent shocks that affect individuals or sectors, such as structural displacement. Employment assistance programs such as skill programs, entrepreneurial support, and intermediation, when well-designed, can help workers both mitigate and manage work-related risks by improving the speed and quality of labor market transitions. These policies are today mostly financed from general revenues. Because these services are still needed, especially by vulnerable populations, employment assistance services are considered part of the core guaranteed minimum. That said, under some conditions these policies may be cofinanced by firms, industries, or individuals.

Beyond the core minimum, additional layers of mandated, nudged, or fully voluntary labor policies are needed. These additional policies recognize the importance of firms and individuals bearing responsibility and taking actions above and beyond the protections provided directly by governments. Just as important, these additional layers aim to decrease adverse selection and moral hazard. Some of the risks discussed here are also insurable by individuals either alone or in combination with employers.

Although some protections would remain tied to jobs, the proposed package would contain fewer such protections than prevailing models. A case in point is severance pay. Originally intended as a device to deter firms from overly hasty dismissals and to compensate workers for breach of assumed or explicitly-defined indefinite employment contracts, in the absence of national unemployment income protection plans, employer-financed severance pay has grown far beyond its original purpose and in some countries has become a deterrent to formal hiring. As more governments have gained the capacity to administer social protection systems, the relative unreliability and distortive costs of firm-provided severance pay have grown ever more apparent. We argue for greater reliance on nationally administered plans of unemployment income support. Following actuarial principles, the most effective income support in the wake of job loss from normal churn in the labor market involves individual savings underpinned with publicly financed risk pooling for longer-than-expected unemployment spells and to support people with low capacity to save. Severance pay provides only ineffective and unreliable risk pooling when compared to national unemployment income-support plans. Individuals' mandatory savings for unemployment can be complemented by additional nudged or voluntary savings. Evolving beyond employer-provided arrangements would also rebalance risks between firms, workers, and government. National unemployment income support plans can be a far less distortionary protection instrument and lower the prospect of job lock and the extent of the losses that accompany unemployment.

## Financing and Implementation Challenges: An Aspiration within Reach

To adequately fund the proposed guaranteed minimum package against poverty and catastrophic losses and to provide labor market support, most developing countries will have to spend more on risk-sharing policies than they do today. To increase this spending in a fiscally sustainable manner, governments will need to reallocate current inefficient and regressive public spending *and*, in most cases, raise more revenue than they have managed to raise historically. At present, low-income countries on average raise just under 15 percent of their gross domestic product (GDP) in revenue, and middle-income countries raise only about 18 percent of GDP (World Bank 2019b). Without better revenue performance, funding an adequate minimum package of consumption support and labor market services will remain challenging. In some countries, governments may in the short run continue to provide insufficient resources to fully realize the vision of risk sharing proposed in this volume. However, even in such cases, a revised vision for achieving universal protection still provides a more feasible framework with which to move progressively toward complete coverage of risk-sharing arrangements than existing policies.

Financing the expansion of protection requires a comprehensive look at fiscal incidence across the entire tax and transfer system. Assuming additional revenues will be needed to finance a guaranteed minimum package in most developing countries, the effects of taxes and of transfers need to be examined jointly in order to understand their net impact.

The most obvious and administratively easiest measure to fund these new protections is to reallocate financing from generalized consumer food and fuel price subsidies. On average, across low- and middle-income countries, these price subsidies continue to absorb about double the amount allocated to social safety-net spending, and spending on price subsidies is nearly always regressive (World Bank 2018). Resources that countries are already spending on social safety-net programs could also be consolidated and made more effective. However, even with such measures, most countries will need significant additional revenues to offer comprehensive insurance assistance and effective labor market intermediation services. There are likely to be trade-offs between revenue instruments, including their potential for revenue mobilization, their redistributive potential, and their tax administration demands.

The ultimate administrative asset governments can build to finance and sustain effective risk-sharing policies is a progressive tax system. Although the challenges to building such systems are formidable and daunting for governments in most low- and middle-income countries, the countries with the most effective progressive tax systems today overcame similarly formidable challenges. In assessing the potential sources of incremental revenue beyond reallocation of subsidies, it appears that more intensive use of value added taxes (VATs) will be the most realistic measure for governments to take. Wherever possible, more effective use of VATs should be complemented by improved collection of more progressive and currently underexploited revenue sources (such as property and inheritance taxes) and novel revenue instruments (such as carbon taxes). Although recent global experience demonstrates the revenue-raising potential of VATs and other levies on consumption, these taxes can have regressive impacts in the absence or insufficiency of compensating transfers for poorer households. The impacts of various revenue instruments should be considered as part of a comprehensive assessment of the net effect on households of the public transfer and tax system (Lustig 2018).

The expansion of mobile payments and digital commerce has the potential to transform how and how much revenue is raised and, over time, to narrow the historical divide between the formal and informal economies. Thanks to technological change, more economic activity—production and consumption—is becoming observable for the purposes of policy making and implementation. As economic activity becomes observable, the relative size of the informal economy and the scope for informal employment should decline. This transformation is especially dramatic, and potentially consequential for risk-sharing policy, in low- and lower-middle-income countries. According to the latest *State of the Industry Report on Mobile Money* published by the GSM Association, by 2018 there were 690 million registered mobile money accounts worldwide, an increase of 25 percent since 2016.

Importantly, the most rapid growth in mobile money and digital commerce is taking place in Africa and Asia. Two-thirds of adults in Kenya, Rwanda, Tanzania, and Uganda actively used mobile payment accounts in 2017. Today in Kenya, the value of annual mobile transactions is four times the size of the formal sector wage bill. In Asia, China leads the way in moving away from cash, and this shift appears imminent in South Asia's larger economies as well. This shift has major implications for the nature of the informal economy and for which risk-sharing policies are viable in any given country. Financing traditional social insurance with an earmarked statutory levy on formal payrolls was a pragmatic solution when governments were not able to observe most economic activity. However, the consumption that is taking place digitally is effectively formalizing—that is, making observable—large swathes of the economy. While incomes should also be increasingly observable, the damaging distortions from a mandatory contribution levied on consumption are likely to be far lower than those from one levied on income. Along with lower transaction costs, this change opens new opportunities to effectively mandate or encourage people to save.

A critical element of putting into practice the proposed guaranteed-minimum protection package is technology-augmented administration, specifically the capacity to monitor the welfare of working people no matter where or how they work. Many middle-income countries already harness the power of digital administrative data. By linking multiple registries, including those for identity, property, vehicles, financial assets, energy consumption, and taxation, a growing number of countries are increasingly able to use the information contained in them to assess the welfare of individuals and households. Improved technology-augmented administrative capacity is within the reach of lower-income countries too. Lower-income countries tend to have less data because they are not yet as digitized and because there are fewer points of contact between their governments and their populations. But this is changing rapidly. In the meantime, these countries are collecting data that can achieve similar results to connecting administrative databases. The costs associated with this exercise are surprisingly low, partly because of improvements in technology that allow for mobile electronic data collection. A strong grievance-redress system could also be set up to effectively deal with errors in assessing need and other issues that arise with benefit delivery. The combination of guaranteed minimum protections proposed in this volume would extend coverage further up the income distribution than is currently achieved in most low- and middle-income countries (as depicted in figure O.4). In policy terms, this expansion reduces the risk of exclusion errors. Added administrative capacity to assess and rank the welfare of households in real time should help to address the well-founded concerns about overly restrictive, insufficiently dynamic, and inadequately contestable targeting.

The broad spread of digital payments will also help extend coverage of more effective risk-sharing arrangements well beyond the structural confines of traditional, employment-based social insurance models. Motivated partly by fiscal savings, *government-to-person*, or G2P, payments ranging from salaries to cash transfers to the poor are increasingly made digitally. This change is helping to extend financial inclusion to people living in or close to poverty, who historically have operated outside the formal financial system. Facilitated by digital identification, new technologies are increasing access to digital payment systems and lowering the transaction costs of G2P payments. A parallel reduction in the costs of *know-your-customer* (KYC) measures—the efforts made by financial service providers to obtain information about the identities of their customers—brought about by electronic authentication, has also helped spread financial inclusion. For example, the newly launched Aadhaar identification system in India has contributed to a huge increase in the proportion of Indians who hold a bank account. The savings generated by digital G2P payments can also in themselves be part of the incremental revenue mobilization that will be needed to fund more inclusive and adequate risk-sharing policies.

## Note

1. Though long-time social protection specialists and practitioners might find this term ungainly, it emphasizes the insurance *function* rather than the insurance or actuarial mechanism. As Barr (2001) notes, "Even where institutions are not insurance in the second sense, they might still be regarded as insurance in that they offer protection against risk." The term also considers individual saving effort (including credit) and prevention measures as integral instruments to augment households' abilities to manage risk, following Ehrlich and Becker (1972) and Gill and Ilahi (2000). The full economic and policy rationale for the package is discussed in chapters 2 and 3, and appendix C presents simulations of an example of the approach.

## References

Barr, N. 2001. *The Welfare State as Piggy Bank*. New York: Oxford University Press.

———. 2012. *The Economics of the Welfare State*. 5th ed. New York: Oxford University Press.

Barr, N., and P. Diamond. 2010. *Pension Reform: A Short Guide*. New York: Oxford University Press.

Bussolo, M., M. E. Davalos, V. Peragine, and R. Sundaram. 2018. *Toward a New Social Contract: Taking on Distributional Tensions in Europe and Central Asia*. Europe and Central Asia Studies. Washington, DC: World Bank.

Ehrlich, I., and G. Becker. 1972. "Market Insurance, Self-Insurance, and Self-Protection." *Journal of Political Economy* 80: 623–48.

Gill, I., and N. Ilahi. 2000. "Economic Insecurity, Individual Behavior, and Social Policy." Office of the Chief Economist, Latin America and Caribbean Region, World Bank, Washington, DC.

Gill, I., and M. Raiser. 2012. *Golden Growth: Restoring the Lustre of the European Economic Model.* Washington, DC: World Bank.

Grosh, M., E. Tesliuc, A. Ouerghi, and C. Del Ninno. 2008. *For Protection and Promotion: The Design and Implementation of Effective Safety Nets.* Washington, DC: World Bank.

GSM Association. 2019. *The 2018 State of the Industry Report on Mobile Money.* London: GSM Association.

ILO (International Labour Organization). 2015. "Transition from the Informal to the Formal Economy Recommendation, 2015 (No. 204)." ILO, Geneva.

———. 2019. *Work for a Brighter Future: Global Commission on the Future of Work.* Geneva: International Labor Office.

Kahneman, D. 2011. *Thinking, Fast and Slow.* New York: Farrar, Strauss and Giroux.

Lustig, N. 2018. *Commitment to Equity Handbook: Estimating the Impact of Fiscal Policy on Inequality and Poverty.* Washington, DC: Brookings Institution Press.

Perry, G., W. Maloney, O. Arias, P. Fajnzylber, A. Mason, and J. Saavedraq-Chanduvi. 2007. *Informality: Exit and Exclusion.* Washington, DC: World Bank.

Ravallion, M., 2016. *The Economics of Poverty.* Oxford, UK: Oxford University Press.

Robalino, D., J. Romero, and I. Walker. 2019. "Allocating Matching Grants for Private Investments to Maximize Jobs Impacts." Unpublished manuscript, Jobs Group, Social Protection and Jobs Global Practice, World Bank, Washington, DC.

Rutkowski, M. 2018. "Reimagining Social Protection." *Finance & Development* 55 (4).

Thaler, R. H., and C. R. Sunstein. 2008. *Nudge: Improving Decisions about Health, Wealth, and Happiness.* New Haven, CT: Yale University Press.

World Bank. 2006. "Pension Reform and the Development of Pension Systems: An Evaluation of World Bank Assistance." Independent Evaluation Group, World Bank, Washington, DC.

———. 2012. *World Development Report 2013: Jobs.* Washington, DC: World Bank.

———. 2016. *World Development Report 2016: Digital Dividends.* Washington, DC: World Bank. https://openknowledge.worldbank.org/handle/10986/23347.

———. 2018. *The State of Social Safety Nets 2018.* Washington, DC: World Bank.

———. 2019a. *Global Economic Prospects: Darkening Prospects.* January. Washington, DC: World Bank.

———. 2019b. *World Development Report 2019: The Changing Nature of Work.* Washington, DC: World Bank. https://openknowledge.worldbank.org/handle/10986/30435.

———. 2019c. *Women, Business, and the Law 2019: A Decade of Reform.* Washington, DC: World Bank.

# 1

# Prevailing Risk-Sharing Policies and Drivers of Disruption in the World of Work

## The Enduring Legacy of Employment-Based Risk-Sharing Institutions

Late-industrial-era risk-sharing policies that were conceived in today's high-income countries continue to be adopted in many low-income countries (see figure 1.1).[1] This pattern has persisted since the early- and mid-twentieth century, even in mainly agrarian economies where manufacturing has never taken a firm hold. At independence, the newly sovereign states of Africa, the Middle East, and Asia inherited many of the retreating colonial powers' norms and institutions, and the new governments expected to travel a similar path of economic development to high incomes as the Europeans had done. In Latin America, where independence from Spain and Portugal came much earlier, norms and institutions from industrializing Europe were adopted almost in parallel and were further augmented by close trade relationships and large waves of migration. At the time, and from the perspectives of these countries, it was logical for policy makers to envision and plan risk-sharing policies—such as worker protections and social insurance—for a labor force that would be mainly employed in factories and firms, as was the case in European and other high-income countries in the early twentieth century and post–World War II period. Indeed, many of the newly independent countries sought to accelerate their progress down this path of structural

**Figure 1.1 Since the Early- and Mid-Twentieth Century, Europe's Industrial-Era Risk-Sharing Model Has Been Adopted Widely, Even in Preindustrial Economies**

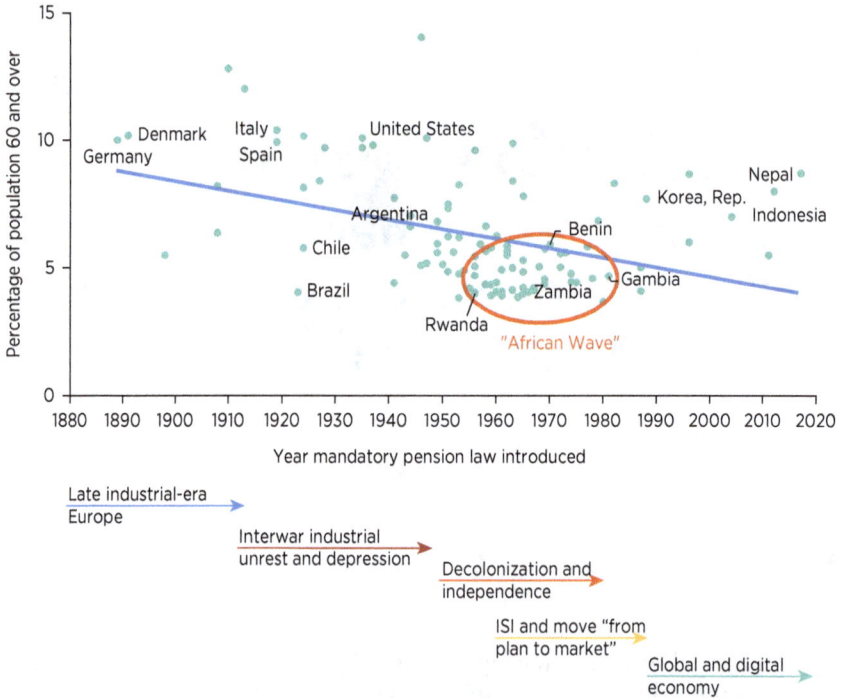

*Source:* World Bank Pensions Database.

*Note:* This figure shows the year in which mandatory social insurance (pensions) were introduced and the share of the population 60 years of age and older for various countries. ISI = import-substituting industrialization.

transformation and development by nurturing infant industries with import-substitution industrial policies.

The leaders of newly independent countries expected that structural transformation and economic development would propel people out of farming in rural areas and raise the share of people living in cities and working full-time in large manufacturing enterprises. The example set by the high-income countries was clear and became the expected path of economic development: people would migrate away from the traditional family- and community-based risk-sharing structures that had supported them for centuries, but which relied on the strong kinship ties that only a mainly rural, agricultural economy could sustain. As part of the fast-spreading expectations of economic development, across continents and in diverse settings, a surprisingly uniform aspirational norm of the so-called good job took hold, was held up as a standard, and, in many places, was codified into law. That norm was full-time, stable, and subordinate wage or salaried employment for a single employer on a factory assembly line or behind a desk in a firm or government office. Even if such a job would only ever be a distant aspiration for most people in low- and middle-income countries, this *standard employment relationship* was the legal bedrock on which the risk-sharing policy apparatus adopted from European and other industrialized economies was enthusiastically constructed.

The standard employment relationship, although never widespread, became the aspirational gold standard. In most low- and middle-income countries in the second decade of the twenty-first century, the segment of people whose work resembles that standard and who are thus covered by statutory worker protection and social insurance is very small and relatively well-off. In many countries of Sub-Saharan Africa, the covered segment consists of barely 10 percent of the working population, usually at the highest end of the income distribution. Given the unexpectedly slow pace and uncertain direction of structural transformation, this situation is likely to be the case for many years to come. Even in fast-growing East Asia, where the process of structural transformation closely followed the expected path, at currently observed rates of development, it would take Malaysia until 2030 to reach levels of income per capita associated with full coverage of employment-based, contributory social insurance. Thailand, the Philippines, and Vietnam would have to wait until after 2050 to achieve full coverage.

Policy, institutional, and administrative coordination has been poor or absent between employment-based, contributory social insurance (that is, insurance plans to which workers and employers make statutorily defined contributions) and newer social-protection transfer models. In the lowest-income countries, despite recent advances in the design and deployment of formal in-kind and cash transfer programs, the lack of coordination has left a large and vulnerable gap of underinsured people: most households in that gap are ineligible to receive formal assistance transfers and are unable to receive employment-based worker protection and insurance arrangements. In these settings, maintaining an industrial-era, employment-based, contributory social insurance model augments this problem by causing distortions that constrain the economy's growth potential, create obstacles to the movement of labor and talent that institutionalize inequality, and fuel the growth of contingent liabilities that absorb public resources away from more broadly beneficial spending on infrastructure and services, particularly the health and education services that are vital to building human capital (World Bank, 2012).

Although the definition of a job has expanded to capture more forms of work, the policy instruments deployed to help people manage risks in the labor and capital markets have not. Why does this persistent pattern of policy making matter to eliminating poverty and promoting shared prosperity? Three reasons stand out. First and foremost, the clear majority of poor people, and those who are vulnerable to poverty, depend on work for their livelihoods (see figure 1.2). Given the various failures of product and factor markets—and the markets for risk in particular—it is no longer controversial for the state to intervene to augment people's options for managing shocks to their livelihoods. Indeed, it has become widely accepted in policy circles that risk-sharing interventions contribute to the fight against poverty and to greater equity. Second, by helping to prevent vulnerable people from falling into poverty and prevent people in the poorest households from falling *deeper* into poverty, risk-sharing interventions can dramatically reduce the number of poor and the likelihood that poverty will carry forward from one generation to the next. Third, risk-sharing policies can make economic growth more equitable by safeguarding the population's

Figure 1.2   **Most Poor People Depend on Work for Their Livelihoods, and Work Is Very Diverse**

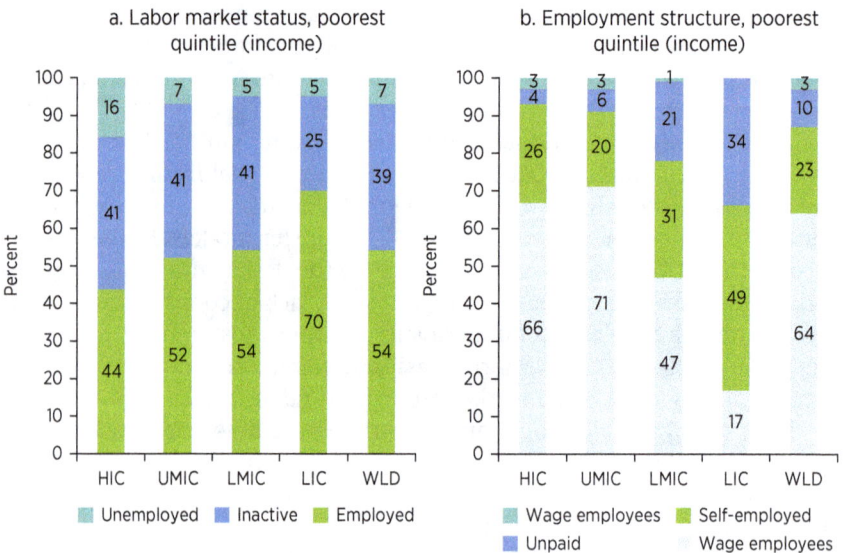

a. Labor market status, poorest quintile (income)

b. Employment structure, poorest quintile (income)

*Source:* I2D2 database, surveys circa 2017.

*Note:* This figure shows the labor market status and employment structure of the poorest quintile of inhabitants, by country income group. HIC = high-income countries; LIC = low-income countries; LMIC = lower-middle-income countries; UMIC = upper-middle-income countries; WLD = world.

human and physical capital and ensuring that all enterprising people are able to grasp economic opportunities for advancement.

But if the state intervenes with policy instruments designed for a different context and to cover forms of employment held by only a few people, its interventions will lack relevance (at best) and become distortive and regressive (at worst). When risk-sharing policies are inappropriate and of limited relevance and coverage, not only are most working people left to cope with shocks as best they can on their own, but also a country's equity outcomes and growth potential are compromised. The mismatch between the way most people work and how the prevailing risk-sharing policies assume they work has been the fundamental problem in low- and middle-income countries for decades.

The same mismatch is quickly becoming a fundamental problem of risk-sharing policies in countries with postindustrial economies. Technological advancement, economic integration, demographic change, and social transformations are disrupting economies, diversifying the world of work, and challenging norms, such as the standard employment relationship around which risk-sharing policies in high-income countries have developed for more than a century. The drivers of disruptive change—sometimes called megatrends—have firmly pushed the high-income economies out of their postindustrial equilibrium, in which it was taken for granted that most people worked in standard employment, and are forcing many governments to make their best guess as to what the future of work will look like (ILO 2015a; OECD 2018). The continuing disruptions wrought by digital technologies, automation, and artificial intelligence will challenge even the best predictions of how people will work and how much work there will be when countries and the global economic system reach their next equilibrium (ILO 2015a, 2015b; Avent 2016). But people's need for effective risk-sharing policies won't wait until then, and, indeed, it may grow in the interim.

Faced with the need to establish new risk-sharing models, policy makers in low- and middle-income countries may hold an advantage. The receding relevance of prevailing risk-sharing institutions and the consequent disruption in high-income countries can be disheartening to policy makers in low- and middle-income countries. But rather than being discouraged by the scope and pace of disruptive change or paralyzed by uncertain predictions of what lies ahead, policy makers in low- and middle-income countries can take some comfort in knowing that they are in an ironically advantageous position. In these countries the industrial-era risk-sharing models and the standard employment relationship are of limited relevance today. Rather than an indication of poor development progress, their lack of attainment of those aspirations and uptake of those models means that the political, fiscal, and other adjustment costs of pursuing risk-sharing policies which are more appropriate to a diversely employed labor force will be much lower for them than for the high-income countries.

## Historical and Institutional Foundations of Prevailing Risk-Sharing Policies

The risk-sharing policies enacted in almost all low- and middle-income countries reflect the norms of an industrial-era, high-income-country world of work. Even some of the poorest countries have adopted many elements of the classical welfare state wholesale. This policy apparatus can include employment-based, contributory social insurance, statutory minimum wages, limits on hiring and dismissals, provisions for severance pay, and relatively comprehensive worker health and safety structures, at least in the statute books. In their countries of origin, these models were developed in the late stages of the industrialization process to counter worker exploitation and other abuses, augmented in response to labor unrest and the Great Depression during the interwar period, and further fortified in the decades of high growth after World War II. Many of the social aspirations, norms, and institutions that took hold during that period remain a powerful point of reference today in countries at every level of development.

In the countries of origin and at the time the employment-based risk-sharing models were conceived, the world of work was relatively homogenous and growing more so, the path from school to work was well defined, and people's employment was relatively stable. Intended to achieve a greater balance of power between workers and firms, and to correct many other market failures, this policy apparatus was designed to support the way that most people worked at that time. The path most people followed went directly from school—sometimes through vocational training or university—into full-time work, usually for someone else. By their late teens and early twenties, most people were looking for full-time work in factories or firms that would provide a long employment ladder that they could steadily climb, rung by rung. The expectation most people held was that if they worked diligently, they would remain inside the firm and rely on *internal labor markets* for career advancement. Unionization and collective bargaining were based on well-defined and enduring occupational categories. Losing a job was a relatively rare experience, which workers and firms, sometimes with governments' help, could insure against. Pension plans that were based on final salaries rewarded long tenure. And the firm was assigned enormous responsibility for implementing social policy. In the United States, for example, firms took up many administrative and financial functions to cover the costs of health care. In other countries, governments delegated agency to employers (or to trade associations) to manage the financing channels for benefits, monitor and report on eligibility conditions, and fulfill many other functions to administer social insurance plans designed and mandated to protect people from losses such as the death or disability of an income-earner or the inability to work in old age.

Assistance transfers for the poorest and other vulnerable members of society have also played a historically important role in risk-sharing, even if they were not always explicitly conceived of as insurance. Most accounts of the modern welfare state begin with the 1601 Old Poor Law (OPL) in England. Although the OPL didn't (and wasn't supposed to) have significant poverty-eliminating and redistributive effects, it provided a degree of protection for poor and vulnerable people, and it helped break the historical link between harvest failures and mortality. In 1834, reforms to the OPL reduced spending on the law from about 2.5 percent of national income in 1830 to 1 percent in 1840 (Lindert 2013). Wider use was made of workhouses: they had long existed, and by the late eighteenth century, 1–2 percent of the population of London sought relief in some 80 workhouses (Ravallion 2016). This policy was relevant because its basic principles were subsequently enshrined in the welfare regimes of colonies like the United States and India. In the latter, for example, limited protection from shocks became the main focus of interventions such as India's famine relief policies (Ravallion 1987, 2016). In the United States, the OPL influenced broad thinking and approaches to antipoverty policy until the New Deal, when some of the country's federal-level social-protection interventions were established. The industrialized world saw a boom in social spending in the second half of the twentieth century (Lindert 2004).

The features that distinguish policy-provided assistance and redistribution from *social insurance* programs have always been chosen ad hoc to reflect administrative constraints or strategic and political concerns. By the middle of the twentieth century, social assistance programs were common throughout Europe and North America. Some countries relied heavily on these programs. New Zealand, for example, chose to rely exclusively on a universal pension to address the decline of income in old age. In contrast, Germany, and eventually many other countries, introduced an alternative plan based on the concept of market insurance (see box 1.1). The invention of social insurance marked a major new role for government. At the same time, the concept of statutory and specific contributions to finance this insurance meant that employers played an important part in the day-to-day functioning of the system. It was both intuitively appealing and politically expedient to structure the financing of social insurance arrangements as statutory worker and employer contributions that mimicked the premiums people paid for market insurance. The choice of this method of financing over alternatives was largely pragmatic. Governments had more limited administrative abilities and presence in people's day-to-day lives. Employers could monitor and report when employment began and ended and under what circumstances, and wages were more observable than other resource flows in the economy (Palier 2010).

## Caesar, Bismarck, and Seddon

At the end of the nineteenth century, industrialization and urbanization led many working people into wage employment and sparked the demand for insurance against work injury, old age, death of the bread-winner, and so on. This insurance model could have been organized and financed in different ways, but mandating that workers and employers deduct a portion of their easily observable wages, and then basing the benefits paid out on the same, was an administratively con-venient and seemingly reasonable approach.

Today, the global dominance of so-called contributory pension schemes is taken for granted. What were originally convenient, prag-matic solutions to late-nineteenth-century limitations on governments' information and administrative capacities have, in the decades since, been elevated to principles (ILO and ISSA 1998; ILO 2018). But there have always been other options for how to finance and structure social insurance. As the Tax History Project explains, "Caesar Augustus insti-tuted an inheritance tax to provide retirement funds for the military. The tax was 5 percent on all inheritances except gifts to children and spouses. The English and Dutch referred to the inheritance tax of Augustus in developing their own inheritance taxes."[a]

Most people trace modern contributory pensions to those that started in Germany in 1889. The so-called Bismarckian model is distin-guished by a financing structure based primarily on explicit de jure employer and employee (and sometimes even government) contribu-tions and benefits proportional to the covered workers' salary. The first chancellor of the German Empire and the historical figure most closely associated with modern social insurance, Otto Von Bismarck, in fact proposed that a tax on the tobacco monopoly should finance a flat pension. But this idea was rejected by the Reichstag, who argued that workers should finance their own retirement. As Fenge, de Menil, and Pestieau (2008) write, "that the old age pensions he called for came to be financed with wage-based taxes was an accident." Nevertheless, Bismarckian social insurance bases a person's eligibility for coverage on a specific history of contributions and pays benefits in proportion to the covered person's lost salary in the wake of an earnings shock.

Participation in these social insurance arrangements in the industri-alizing countries was initially low but gradually increased as a greater share of the workforce moved into factories and firms and labor markets were formalized, that is, workers and their employers were registered and monitored by government authorities to comply with various regulations including social insurance contributions from

*continued next page*

**Box 1.1** (*continued*)

payroll, income, and corporate taxes. By the middle of the twentieth century, the coverage of social insurance financed at least in part by dedicated contributions from payrolls had become almost universal in the parts of Europe that had chosen the Bismarckian approach and would soon catch up in North America and Japan. The Republic of Korea reached these high rates of participation in the 1990s after its spectacular period of economic growth.

Meanwhile, New Zealand—the first country to legislate a minimum wage and the first to extend suffrage to women—took a different path to financing social insurance and remains exceptional among rich countries. Richard J. Seddon, the 15th prime minister of New Zealand, introduced a flat pension for all (white) citizens in 1891 that was financed from the budget without a statutory employer or employee contribution or another earmarked tax. More than 125 years later, these arrangements survive with some modifications (nonwhites now receive the pension in New Zealand), a true testament to the inertia of pension policy.

*Sources:* Palier 2010; Willmore 2007.

a. For further information, see http://www.taxworld.org/History/TaxHistory.htm.

In addition to sharing risk in a purely actuarial sense, governments found it politically palatable to pursue additional social objectives through the new social insurance plans. Governments chose to pursue the elimination of poverty, redistribution, and workforce management through changes in the eligibility requirements and benefit parameters of programs that were initially presented as contribution-financed. People whose eligibility to draw from the new risk pool was visibly related to their history of contributions would feel more ownership and maintain a stronger interest in ensuring the stability of the model. Later generations of policy makers who tried to alter the terms of the risk-sharing arrangements would have a politically powerful constituency to contend with.

The employment-based contributory model of risk sharing was adopted widely and would soon dominate social protection spending, despite limited coverage. Along with social health insurance (SHI), the contributory model for covering disability, survivor, and old age pensions spread across the world and became the most important element of the social protection system in terms of the allocation of public resources. Globally, average social insurance expenditures are roughly three times social assistance spending, and this ratio continues to rise along with income levels. In Europe and North America, the coverage of contributory schemes became practically universal, a reflection of a labor market dominated by standard wage or salaried employment. In low- and middle-income countries, however, participation and coverage rates reflected the diversity and fluidity of employment in the informal economy as well as the large proportion of the population that was engaged in agriculture. In the poorest countries, much of the population continued to toil in a subsistence economy. Incomes were not observable. The main exception was Eastern Europe and the former Soviet Union, where the state's role as employer made it possible to implement social insurance even for farmers. In the postsocialist period, however, as countries transitioned from planned to market economies, participation rates have fallen back to those observed in other countries with similar income levels. In developing countries, stagnant coverage rates had raised questions as to the viability of the employment-based approach to risk-sharing long before current concerns with the changing nature of work were being discussed in richer countries.

There is little reason to think that participation and coverage rates will rise significantly in the foreseeable future. Comparing the most recent coverage data from low- and middle-income countries with data from the early and mid-1990s (figure 1.3) shows little if any improvement. In India, for example, the percentage of workers who contribute to pensions has increased at the dismal rate of 1 percentage point per decade since the 1950s, barely reaching 10 percent today. At that rate, universal coverage would not be achieved until the end of the twenty-first century. With the partial exception of China, the employment-based social insurance model and accompanying statutory worker protections have effectively excluded as much as two-thirds of the developing world's population.

For newly independent countries in the earliest stages of the industrialization process, these risk-sharing models were a particularly poor fit. The models rested on three foundational assumptions about the way people earned their livelihood: first, that most people have a single economic activity; second, that most people work full-time in a subordinate salaried or wage relationship for a firm; and third, that their occupation and employment will be stable over a long term and require only infrequent, short periods of skill updating. For many low- and middle-income countries, these foundational assumptions stand in stark contrast to how the majority of people earn their livelihoods. Most households rely on a wide range of subsistence and market activities for their livelihoods, work for themselves, and live far from the sort of firms that can offer internal labor markets and career ladders or that have the capacity to collect health and pension contributions on governments' behalf. And even in countries where the structural transformation process has advanced enough to create a critical mass of modern firms, the limited ability of governments to monitor economic activity and enforce regulations means that mandated worker protections and social insurance rarely extend beyond the relatively small share of the

**Figure 1.3    Participation in Employment-Based, Contributory Social Insurance Remains Stagnant in Most Low- and Middle-Income Countries**

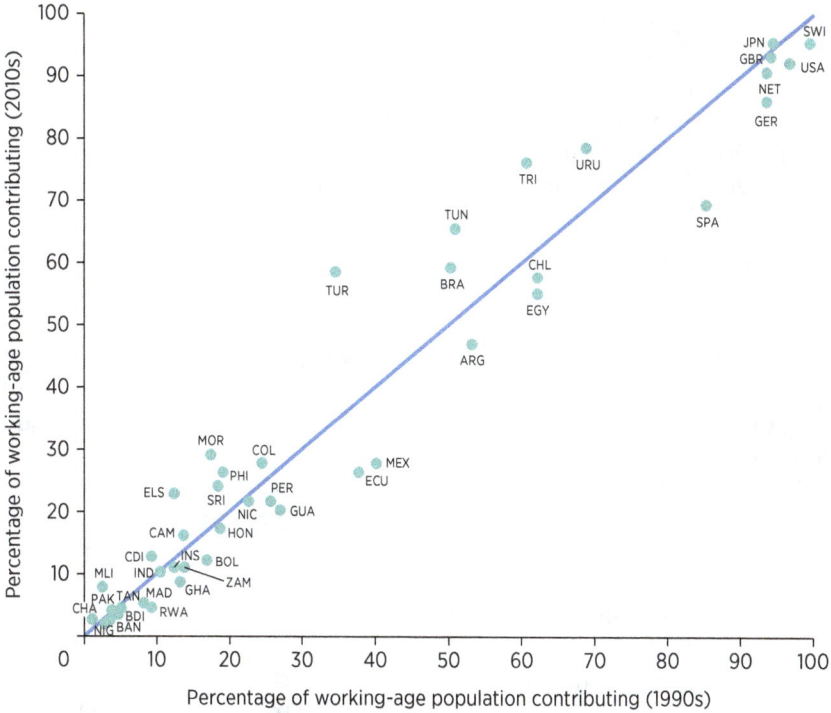

*Source:* World Bank Pensions Database.

*Note:* This figure compares the percentage of the working-age population contributing to mandated pension programs in various countries in the 1990s and the 2010s.

population that works in the civil service, state-owned enterprises, or the larger (often foreign-owned) firms of the private sector.

If the assumptions about how most people work no longer hold, are the prevailing risk-sharing policies relevant any longer? This question is being asked with greater urgency in countries at all levels of development. Even before the global financial crisis of 2008–09 and the economic contraction that followed, questions were raised about the suitability and sustainability of prevailing risk-sharing arrangements, albeit mainly in high-income countries where the services sector and digital economy had already become dominant over manufacturing (Stone 2004). Concern was growing for how to sustain economic productivity, worker protection, and social insurance in economies that were deindustrializing (Dasgupta and Singh 2006; Matsuyama 2009; and Nickell, Redding, and Swaffield 2008). Since the nadir of the global crisis, these concerns have spread from forums of discussion in high-income countries to debates on how to fire the engines of economic growth and create ample job opportunities in low- and middle-income countries, where the pace and direction of the structural transformation process is now questioned and a *premature deindustrialization* is under way (Rodrik 2016).[2] For many countries in Sub-Saharan Africa, the decline in the importance of agriculture in their economies and the structural shift of the labor force into manufacturing is not unfolding as it has for countries in East Asia (see figure 1.4).

## Global Drivers of Disruption and Their Impact on the World of Work

Regional and global economic integration; advancing technological change; and social, demographic, and climate change are reshaping product and factor markets, particularly the market for labor (see table 1.1). The steady integration of the world economy has allowed the fragmentation of production processes and the emergence of complex global value chains, leading to outsourcing of a growing range of tasks and jobs, both within and between countries. Rapid advances in technology—particularly digital technology and Internet platforms—drive down the transaction costs of organizing production through markets of many small, specialized providers. Market-based production models look cheaper than relying on large, vertically integrated, hierarchical firms, indeed challenging the very economic rationale for the firm (Coase 1937). These trends have created strong cost incentives for firms to focus on their core competencies, decentralize the production process, and disperse many of the jobs that were previously integrated in large, "top-down" organizations across many different business entities orchestrated through markets. Trade in intermediate goods has come to dominate cross-border flows of goods and services, with businesses relying heavily on the ability to organize and reorganize labor and human capital along with other inputs (Gill and Kharas 2007; World Bank 2008).

These disruptors are driving change in every country, although these changes manifest in different ways in low-, middle-, and high-income countries. In addition to propelling economic integration and dramatically expanding the reach of market arrangements, technological change and automation are also fundamentally changing the need for labor inputs and the task composition of jobs. Put simply, technological change changes the skills required at work. Most technological innovations and digital tools that are spreading quickly in the workplace are labor saving. Analyses by Akerman, Gaarder, and Mogstad (2015) and by Gaggl and Wright (2014) find that, more than automating entire jobs and affecting total employment,

**Figure 1.4**  **The Path and Direction of Structural Transformation and Economic Development Does Not Appear as Certain for African Countries as It Was for East Asian Countries**

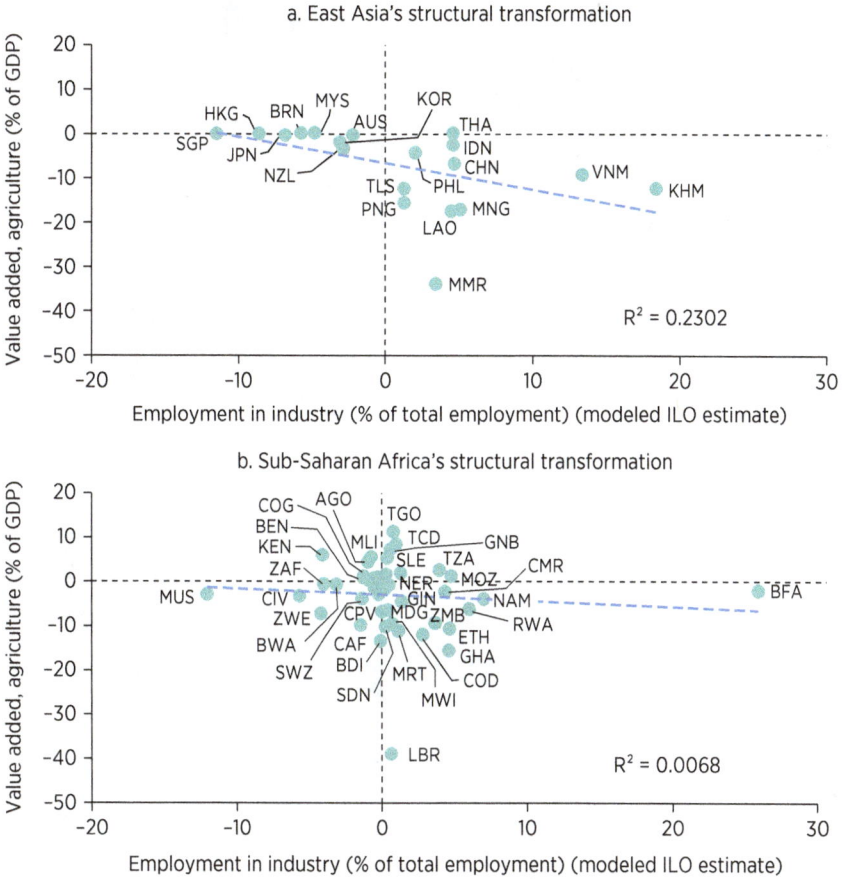

a. East Asia's structural transformation

Value added, agriculture (% of GDP)

HKG, SGP, JPN, NZL, BRN, MYS, AUS, KOR, THA, IDN, CHN, TLS, PHL, PNG, MNG, LAO, VNM, KHM, MMR

R² = 0.2302

Employment in industry (% of total employment) (modeled ILO estimate)

b. Sub-Saharan Africa's structural transformation

Value added, agriculture (% of GDP)

MUS, COG, AGO, BEN, KEN, ZAF, MLI, TGO, TCD, SLE, TZA, GNB, CMR, NER, MOZ, CIV, GIN, NAM, BFA, ZWE, CPV, MDG, ZMB, RWA, BWA, CAF, ETH, SWZ, BDI, GHA, MRT, COD, SDN, MWI, LBR

R² = 0.0068

Employment in industry (% of total employment) (modeled ILO estimate)

*Source:* Calculations based on World Development Indicators data.

*Note:* This figure shows the percentage point change in employment in industry (as a percentage of total employment) and the value added by agriculture (as a percentage of gross domestic product [GDP]) from 2000 to the most recent year for which data are available for all countries but São Tomé and Príncipe (data begins with 2001), Equatorial Guinea (data begins with 2006), and Afghanistan (data begins with 2002). Employment is defined as all persons of working age who were engaged in any activity to produce goods or provide services for pay or profit, whether at work during the reference period or not at work owing to temporary absence from a job or to a working-time arrangement. The industry sector consists of mining and quarrying, manufacturing, construction, and public utilities (electricity, gas, and water), in accordance with divisions 2-5 (International Standard Industrial Classification [ISIC] 2) or categories C-F (ISIC 3) or categories B-F (ISIC 4). Value added is the net output of a sector after all outputs are added up and intermediate inputs are subtracted; it is calculated without making deductions for depreciation of fabricated assets or depletion and degradation of natural resources. The origin of value added is determined by the ISIC, revision 3 or 4. Only Sub-Saharan countries are included. Pacific islands are not included in panel a. ILO = International Labour Organization.

**Table 1.1  Global Drivers of Disruption Are Further Diversifying the Already-Diverse World of Work and Challenging the Primacy of the Standard Employment Relationship**

*(Principal drivers of disruption in the world of work and their impact on the standard employment relationship)*

| Labor market impact | Technological change | Economic integration | Social change | Demographic change | Climate change |
|---|---|---|---|---|---|
| **Demand side** | • Urbanization<br>• Declining costs of distance and market access<br>• Declining market transaction costs<br>• Automation<br>• Artificial intelligence | • Larger, deeper, and more contestable markets<br>• Global value chains<br>• "Premature" deindustrialization<br>• Dominance of services | • Rising value of diversity in the workplace | • Rising health care demand<br>• Advent of longevity-support services | • Disruption to place-based and seasonal industries |
| **Supply side** | • Declining travel costs (migration)<br>• Connectivity<br>• Telepresence<br>• Remote work | • Cross border migration | • Women in market work<br>• Mobilization or demobilization<br>• Population flight or influx from conflict | • Youth bulge<br>• Later entry into work<br>• Falling fertility<br>• Longer life<br>• Longer healthy life | • Population flight or influx from natural disaster |
| **Market wide** | • Innovation<br>• Agglomeration (ever-narrower division of labor) | • Intermediate goods trade<br>• Fading distinction between "tradables" and "nontradables" | • From "Plan" to "Market"<br>• From majority poor to majority middle-class<br>• Changing norms and aspirations | • Rise of the "active elderly" (ages 60–80) | • Drought and soil erosion threats to agriculture<br>• Rising sea levels<br>• Severity of climate events |

*Sources:* Autor 2015; Goldberg and Pavcnik 2007, 2016; Katz and Krueger 2016; Rodrik 2016; Stone 2004; and Stone and Arthurs 2013.

technological change alters the task content of certain jobs and leads to changes in the skills sought by employers or needed by people to succeed in self-employment. For example, before the development of the spreadsheet, much of an accountant's day was spent conducting simple—but time-consuming—computations that are now automated. Consequently, the most significant impact of technological change is a change in what firms need their workers to do and what people need to learn on the job. And digital technologies favor workers with more skills, redefining the task content of occupations away from manual and routine work toward more non-routine and cognitive work (see figure 1.5). Yet when firms automate routine tasks that kept a large number of people in work, labor is displaced. If resulting gains in productivity do not translate into lower-priced or better-quality products that spur greater demand, the number displaced can be large, and the period of displacement can be painful (Acemoglu 2003a; Autor and Dorn 2011; Autor 2014; World Bank 2015).

Even in low- and middle-income countries, the shift in the content of jobs to nonroutine cognitive tasks and interpersonal tasks has enormous implications for the employability and wages of many people. In the short- and medium-term, technological change that alters the task content of jobs can constrain the job and earnings potential of those with only a basic level

**Figure 1.5**  **As More Technology Is Adopted, the Work That People Do Is Becoming More Intensive in Nonroutine Skills, Both Cognitive and Interpersonal**

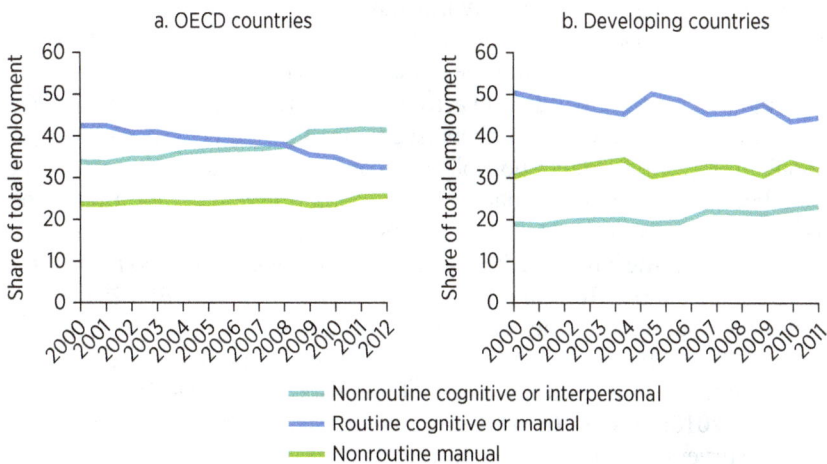

*Source:* World Bank 2016, based on International Labour Organization Laborsta data.

*Note:* This figure shows a simple cross-country average of employment composition, by type of occupation, from 2000 to 2012. The classification of skills follows Autor 2014. OECD = Organisation for Economic Co-operation and Development.

of education (Dicarlo et al. 2016; Dutz, Almeida, and Packard 2018). And although technological advances have further changed the world of work by introducing new ways to engage in the market, such as freelancing on digital platforms, and have allowed for more flexible work arrangements like telecommuting, these forms of work further challenge employer-employee risk-sharing models and the institutions that have been built on the uniform standard employment relationship (Stone and Arthurs 2013; ILO 2015a and 2015b; OECD 2018).

The standard employment relationship is losing its prominence as the pattern of structural transformation becomes less certain and the world of work grows more diverse and fluid. This change could bring about a world of work in high-income countries that is in many ways similar to how work has been for much of modern history in low- and middle-income countries. The International Labour Organization (ILO) report "World Employment and Social Outlook" (WESO) for 2015 (ILO 2015b) and the World Bank's *World Development Report 2016: Digital Dividends* (World Bank 2016) point out how these forces are causing a decline in the prominence and primacy of the standard employment relationship—the central focus of the World Bank's *World Development Report 2019: The Changing Nature of Work* (World Bank 2019b). Employment disruption is becoming more frequent. Although often overlooked in the recent policy literature, some of the most impactful disruptions changing the nature of work are social. Two disruptions in particular stand out for the effect they have had on the world of work: first, the rapid and high-volume movement of women into market work (World Bank 2011), and second, the transition from communist and socialist planning to market-driven economies (Barr 2005; World Bank 1995). Each of these changes, and the other social changes detailed in table 1.1, have had a substantial impact on both the supply and the demand sides of the labor market.

People are moving within and across industries and in and out of occupational categories in greater numbers (see figure 1.6). Career change, occupational fluidity, and holding a portfolio of incomes rather than just one full-time job is becoming the new normal for many people and setting new aspirations, particularly for young people in cities (RIWI 2019).[3] Although there is an active debate in the empirical literature as to whether *alternate working arrangements* are on the rise (Katz and Krueger 2016 and 2019; U.S. BLS 2018)[4] and trends vary substantially across countries at different levels of development (Avlijaš 2019; Chandy 2016),[5] what the ILO terms "non-standard employment" forms are a significant segment of the workforce in high-income countries (EC 2018; OECD 2018).[6] Using microdata from household and labor market surveys, Apella and Zunino (2018) note that, although there are no uniform trends across low- and middle-income countries of Latin America and Europe, a common finding is that nonstandard forms of work are more likely than in the past to be extended to people with higher levels of education and for jobs with more nonroutine cognitive tasks (see figure 1.7).

**Figure 1.6 Transitions across Employment Forms, in and out of the Labor Force, Are Becoming More Likely**

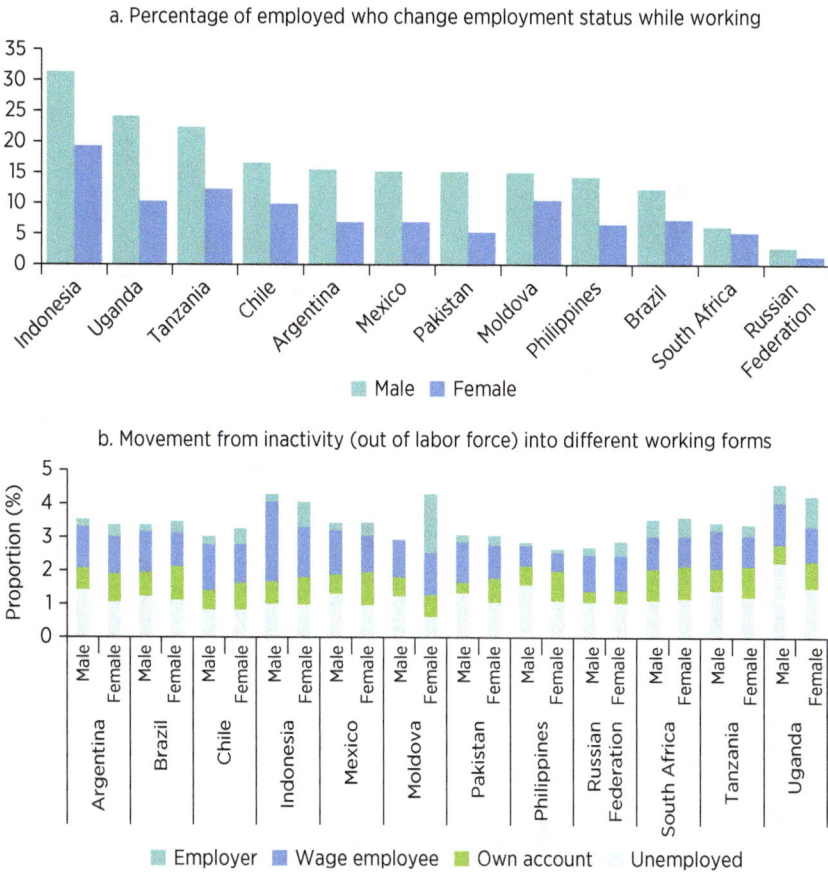

a. Percentage of employed who change employment status while working

b. Movement from inactivity (out of labor force) into different working forms

*Source:* Cho, Robalino, and Romero 2015.

*Note:* Panel a is based on unadjusted transition probability matrices. The elements of these matrices represent the probability of shifting from one state to another over the span of the panel data. In panel b, the adjusted transition matrix provides a unitless measure of the tendency of transitions, comparable across both different groups and different countries, that accounts for the propensity of job destruction and job creation in different types of work. The time span between observations is 7 years in Indonesia, 4 years in Uganda, 2 years in Tanzania, 2 years in South Africa, and 1 year in all other countries included.

Cho, Robalino, and Romero (2015) note that the scope, frequency, structure, content, and availability of data differ across the surveys. To address these differences, the variables used in their analysis were carefully harmonized across the surveys and some of the analysis was conducted separately for each country. To account for differences in frequency of data collection—the Latin American countries had monthly and quarterly observations available, while other country surveys were conducted at intervals exceeding two years—data were annualized when surveys were conducted more than once a year. Because some data sets were based on a rotational panel structure that tracked only a subsample of individuals or households, balanced panels were constructed to ensure that the same individual appeared at a minimum of two points in time.

**Figure 1.7 Nonstandard Employment Is Gaining Ground in Several Countries, Though Trends Vary Significantly**

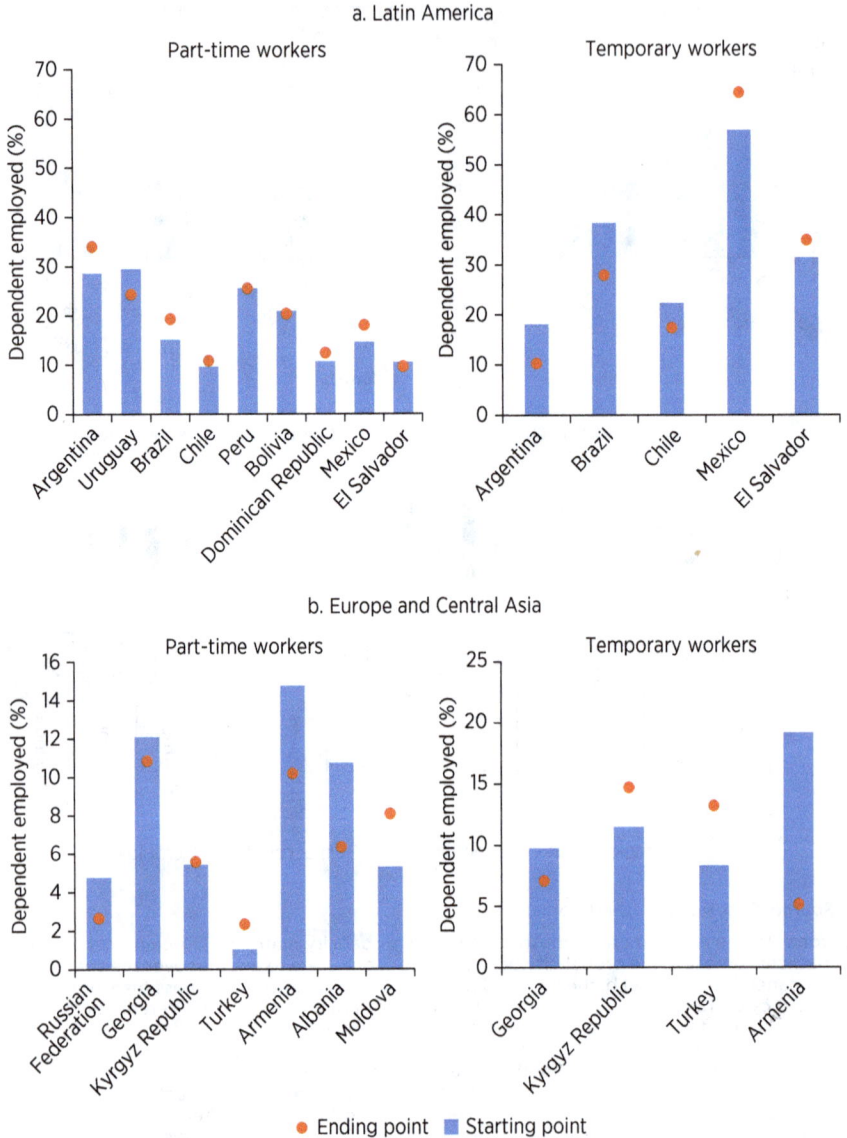

a. Latin America

b. Europe and Central Asia

● Ending point ■ Starting point

*Source:* Apella and Zunino 2018.

*Note:* This figure shows the changes in temporary and fixed-term employment in selected Latin American and European countries from the mid-1990s through the mid-2010s. "Dependent employed" refers to people employed in subordinate wage or salaried jobs with an employer or firm.

The disruption caused by demographic change has been unfolding over a much longer period than the other disruptions to the world of work, and at a notably different pace from one country to the next, but it is no less dramatic. The world has reached a critical and consequential demographic milestone: the share of the population of working age has started a steady decline (see figure 1.8). Globally, fewer births and longer, healthier lives present a formidable challenge to the social constructs of so-called working age and retirement (World Bank and IMF 2016). Despite this global trend, countries tend to sort into two increasingly extreme population profiles, sometimes with one extreme facing the other across a political border or geographic barrier: those where a bulge of young people has started to enter the labor market, and those where the fastest-growing segment of the population is 80 years and older (see figure 1.9). In each extreme, these dramatic demographic changes create different imperatives for productivity, economic growth, and fiscal sustainability. In demographically younger countries, labor markets that will soon be swamped with young job seekers will have to shift economic growth into higher gear and ensure that young people have skills that employers seek. In aggregate terms, demographic change in Sub-Saharan Africa could produce a powerful dividend (Mwabu, Muriithi, and Mutegi 2011, 2013). Many middle-income and upper-middle-income countries are in a post-dividend world where population

**Figure 1.8    The Global Share of the Working-Age Population Has Begun a Steady Decline**

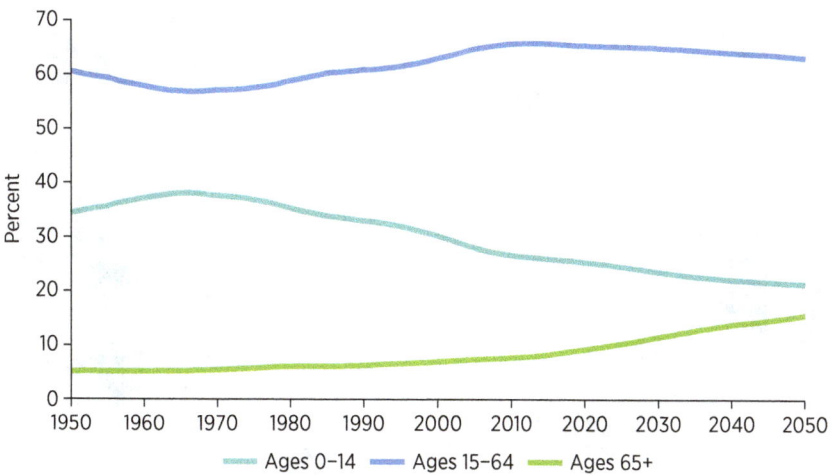

*Source:* World Bank and IMF 2016, using data from the United Nations Population Division.
*Note:* This figure shows global population shares by age cohort.

aging may lead to slower economic growth and strain public budgets but also a boost in investment and productivity (Lee, Mason, and Members of the NTA Network 2014). In rapidly aging countries, people must remain economically active for a greater (and growing) portion of their lives.

On both the supply and the demand sides of the labor market, these contrasting imperatives challenge norms and expectations and consequently strain rigid policies and social structures. In still-youthful countries, there is a growing glut of labor. The applaudable increase in access to education has raised the share of young people who complete basic education, even if learning still falls short of global benchmarks. This increase has lowered the premium of completing secondary education in labor markets and raised the stakes for young people whose transition from full-time education to full-time work is precarious or unfortunately timed (Angel-Urdinola and Gukovas 2018; Naidoo, Packard, and Auwalin 2015). In aging countries,

**Figure 1.9  Two Sides of the Same Demographic Coin? Europe's Aging Populations Stare over the Mediterranean at Youth Bulges in North Africa and the Middle East**
*(Population pyramids: Europe on left, MENA on right)*

a. 2015

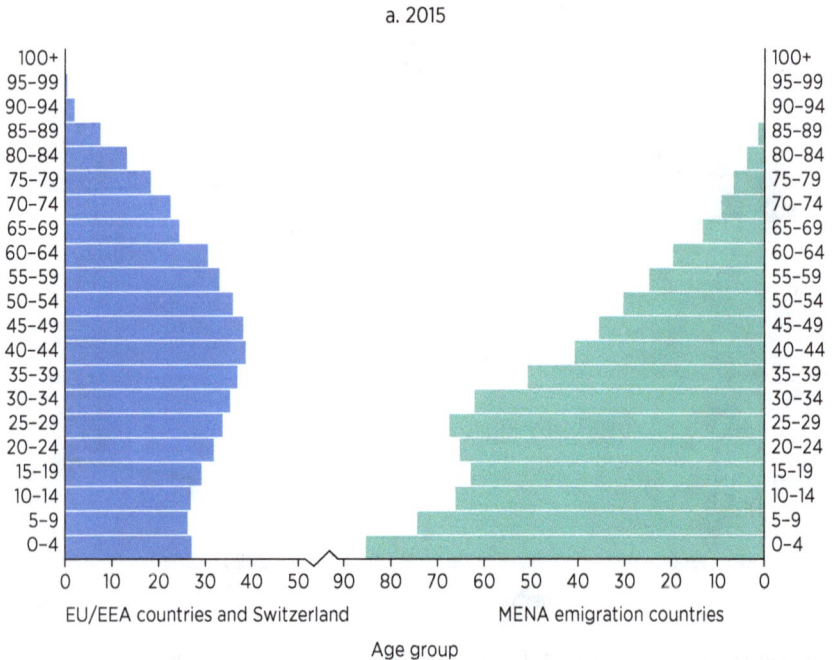

EU/EEA countries and Switzerland          MENA emigration countries

Age group

*continued next page*

**Figure 1.9** (*continued*)

b. 2040

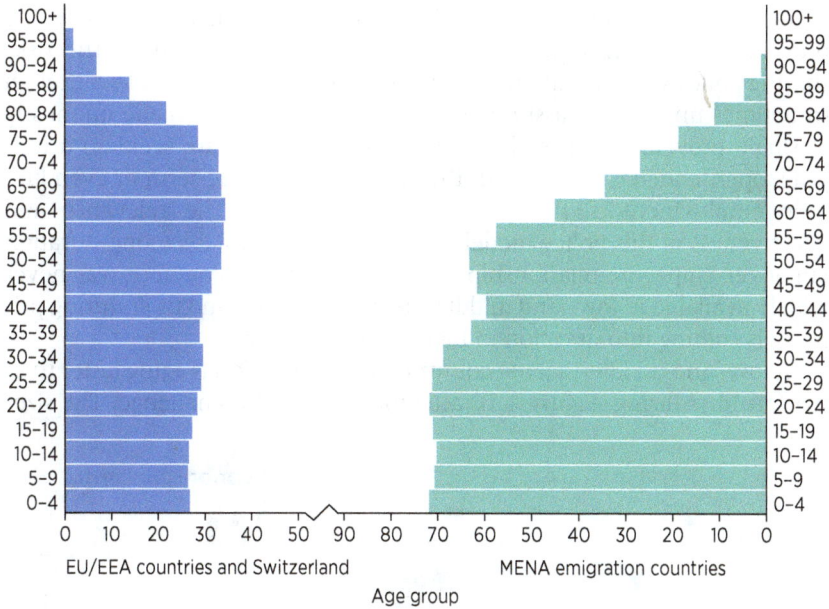

Source: United Nations, Department of Economic and Social Affairs, Population Division 2017.

Note: "EU/EEA countries and Switzerland" includes the following countries: Austria, Belgium, Bulgaria, Croatia, Cyprus, the Czech Republic, Denmark, Estonia, Finland, France, Germany, Greece, Hungary, Iceland, Ireland, Italy, Latvia, Liechtenstein, Lithuania, Luxembourg, Malta, the Netherlands, Norway, Poland, Portugal, Romania, Slovakia, Slovenia, Spain, Sweden, Switzerland, and the United Kingdom. "MENA emigration countries" includes the following countries and economies: Algeria, Djibouti, the Arab Republic of Egypt, the Islamic Republic of Iran, Iraq, Jordan, Lebanon, Morocco, the Syrian Arab Republic, Tunisia, the West Bank and Gaza, and the Republic of Yemen.

professional seniority and how it is remunerated is being redefined. Withdrawal from market activities in old age will have to become a far more gradual glide than the abrupt retirement threshold institutionalized in most social insurance arrangements. Firms and governments are looking for new ways in which the comparative advantages of older people can complement those of younger members of the workforce. New ways of working that suit the preferences of older people are emerging, by design or by older people defaulting to self-employment whether they have entrepreneurial aims and aptitude or not, and often such arrangements are in the informal economy, beyond the reach of regulation.

Even in upper-middle-income and high-income countries, anxiety is growing that the standard-employment foundations of risk-sharing policies are shifting (ILO 2015a, 2015b; OECD 2018). The pace and nature of the changes in how households and firms engage in the market present policy makers with a paradox: at a time when risks and uncertainty are rising, the prevailing risk-sharing policy models are losing their traction. The risk-sharing policies in place in most countries rest on a foundational—although sometimes unwritten—assumption that the labor force is made up mostly of single-provider heads of households who have (or are seeking) a full-time, open-ended contract, with the expectation of long-term or even life-time employment, seniority pay, and a pension. The relevance and effectiveness of this policy model rests implicitly on a stable, long-duration employer-employee relationship. Yet this form of employment was never widely available in low- and middle-income countries and its enduring primacy is coming into question in high-income countries.

In low- and middle-income countries, the population is aging faster than work is formalizing. Figure 1.10 attempts to map this challenge. The sizes

**Figure 1.10 Populations Are Aging Faster Than the Economy Is Formalizing**

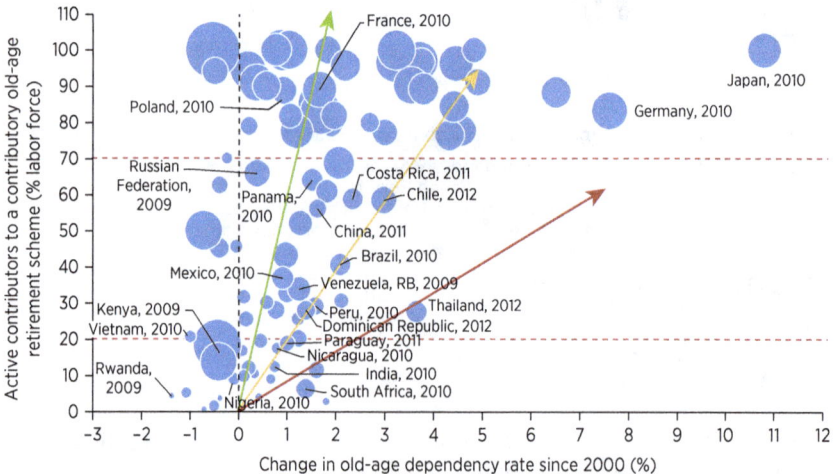

*Source:* Based on data from the World Bank Pension Database and the *World Development Indicators*.

*Note:* This figure shows the participation of the economically active population of various countries in contributory social insurance programs and changes in the countries' old-age dependency rates since 2000, by level of economic development. Arrows from the origin indicate the stylized "path" of today's high-income and upper-middle-income countries that formalized and grew wealthy before the onset of population aging (green); that of most countries, mainly middle income, where the pace of formalization has slowed and aging is rising (yellow); and that of several worrying cases in which aging is moving much faster than the pace of formalization and growth in wealth (red). Bubble size represents gross domestic product per capita at purchasing-power parity in constant 2011 international dollars.

of the spheres indicate countries' levels of development; the vertical axis measures the share of the labor force that participates in contributory social insurance, and the horizontal axis measures the percentage point change since 2000 in the countries' old-age dependency ratio. The red dashed horizontal lines show emblematic threshold levels of participation of the labor force in contributory social insurance, inspired by the *World Development Report 2013: Jobs*: at 20 percent, countries move from mainly *agrarian* or *urbanizing* economies to the *formalizing* stage of the structural transformation process, and at 70 percent and higher, countries have *formalized* (World Bank 2012). Today's high-income countries urbanized, formalized, and grew wealthy in tandem or in close concert, following a path indicated by the green arrow from the origin. Countries like Poland, Costa Rica, and Chile are aging fast but are close to the formalized threshold. There is rising concern for countries like Thailand, Brazil, and Mexico (along the yellow arrow from the origin in figure 1.10) that are aging much faster than participation in social insurance is growing. Concern is more urgent for countries that are starting to age at levels of participation nowhere near the lower threshold of the formalizing stage (along the red arrow from the origin in figure 1.10).

In conclusion, the market failures that originally motivated risk-sharing policies remain pernicious. Uneven market power between those who seek and those who sell labor, information failures on all sides, incomplete contracts, limited or weak insurance markets, and uncertainty are still critical problems (Almeida, Behrman, and Robalino 2012; Barr 2012; Kuddo, Robalino, and Weber 2015). Even where the world of work was already very diverse, the nature of work is changing (World Bank 2016; World Bank 2019b). Of the drivers of disruption that we have discussed in this chapter, technological change and global economic integration in particular are accelerating the pace of change in labor markets, requiring a more flexible workforce that can respond to these changes and possibly accelerating job creation and destruction. Digital technologies, specifically, are introducing new forms of employment and allowing for more flexible work arrangements that challenge the primacy of standard employer-employee relationships, even in high-income countries. In addition, demographic and climate changes are reconfiguring the composition of the workforce and the geography of jobs, accentuating the need for risk-sharing and labor market institutions to adapt.

More policy intervention will be required to ensure that work continues to offer people a path for economic and social advancement. It is likely that the well-known failures of the labor market will be felt more acutely, at least for a transition period of indeterminate length, as economies move from—or leap over—the industrial and early-industrial production equilibria to the next point of stability. Even the more gradually unfolding trend of demographic change motivates a new approach to labor market regulation.

## One Billion Migrants

After slowing to a meager trickle in the interwar period and for most of the remaining twentieth century, the flow of populations across national borders is surging. One in every seven people on the planet is a migrant. Fully 250 million people are international migrants, of whom just more than 17 million are refugees.[a] The largest flows of migrants (38 percent) run between low- and middle-income countries (so-called South-South migration), followed by flows from low- and middle-income countries to high-income countries (34 percent of migrants, moving South-North).

Although these large flows capture new attention, in many ways they represent a return to an ancient and constant fact of human civilization: people move mainly in pursuit of opportunity. And the disparities in opportunity between places are increasing the pressure on many to move. In 2015, the ratio of average per capita incomes in high- and low-income countries was 70:1. In the period 2015–50, the working-age population in low- and middle-income countries is expected to grow by 2.1 billion. Assuming employment rates observed in these countries in 2015 remain constant, only 1.2 billion of these people will have work. This forecast leaves 875 million people with a strong incentive to move across national borders in pursuit of jobs.

Rather than a disruptive driver in its own right, the surge in cross-border migration results from a combination of the other drivers discussed in this chapter. Technological change and economic integration are locomotives for concentration and agglomeration economies, which in turn create powerful centripetal pressures that pull more people from rural peripheries into urban centers. For many, the move to cities is the first step on a long road that can snake across borders, or onto a launch pad that propels them swiftly into a job in a new country. Social and climate changes challenge the livelihoods of many in certain places, aggravating geographic disparities in economic opportunities. And demographic changes combine with natural and political barriers on the movement of people to create a youth bulge in some countries and a dramatic scarcity of young people in others as fertility falls and longevity increases.

Migration is undoubtedly disruptive, but in overwhelmingly beneficial ways for migrants, for their countries of origin, and for the countries that receive them. Migrants can experience as much as a 15-fold increase in their incomes and gains in direct measures of well-being, including lower child mortality and better education.

*continued next page*

---

**Box 1.2** *(continued)*

The remittances they send back to their home countries dwarf flows of aid and challenge in volume even flows of foreign direct investment. These resources can have important countercyclical qualities and have been a lifeline for communities in countries hit by crises. Remittances from a diaspora can be a less risk-averse source of long-term development investment than foreign direct investment from nondiaspora sources. And in destination countries, migrants increase the pool of skills, are a source of entrepreneurial innovation, alleviate the strains of population aging, and make substantial fiscal contributions.

These benefits come at some costs. Migrants suffer the pain of being far from their families. Parents are often separated from children for long periods of time. Many who have studied hard and attained critical cognitive skills will have to struggle for years in routine work in their new countries. The specters of xenophobia and discrimination always loom. When migrants come in large surges, public services in receiving countries are strained and can become congested. Natives with the lowest skills can find a sudden increase in the supply of labor threatening. However, the bulk of empirical evidence shows that the benefits of migration far outweigh these costs and that the costs can be managed. Having the right risk-sharing policies can help.

*Sources:* World Bank 2019a; World Bank 2008.

a. This number excludes 5.3 million Palestinian refugees reported by the United Nations Relief and Works Agency for Palestine Refugees in the Near East.

---

As argued earlier in this chapter, longer, healthier lives will create a common imperative: the need to keep a larger segment of the population economically engaged for longer. Governments stand a greater chance of increasing and sustaining higher levels of market participation among women and the *active elderly* by adopting policies that support all working people, regardless of where or how they need or prefer to work. A diverse and diversifying world of work is forcing policy makers to rethink what will constitute an effective policy response.

Concern is spreading that if effective responses are not found soon, labor's share of economic activity will continue to decline or will decline at an even faster pace. Researchers have suggested myriad hypotheses for why what was once believed to be labor's stable share has been steadily declining (figure 1.11). Several of these explanations, and an accompanying body of evidence, associate the decline with drivers of disruption, such as capital-augmenting technological change and the mechanization of

## Figure 1.11 A Declining Labor Share Is Provoking Debate about Relevance of Prevailing Risk-Sharing Policies

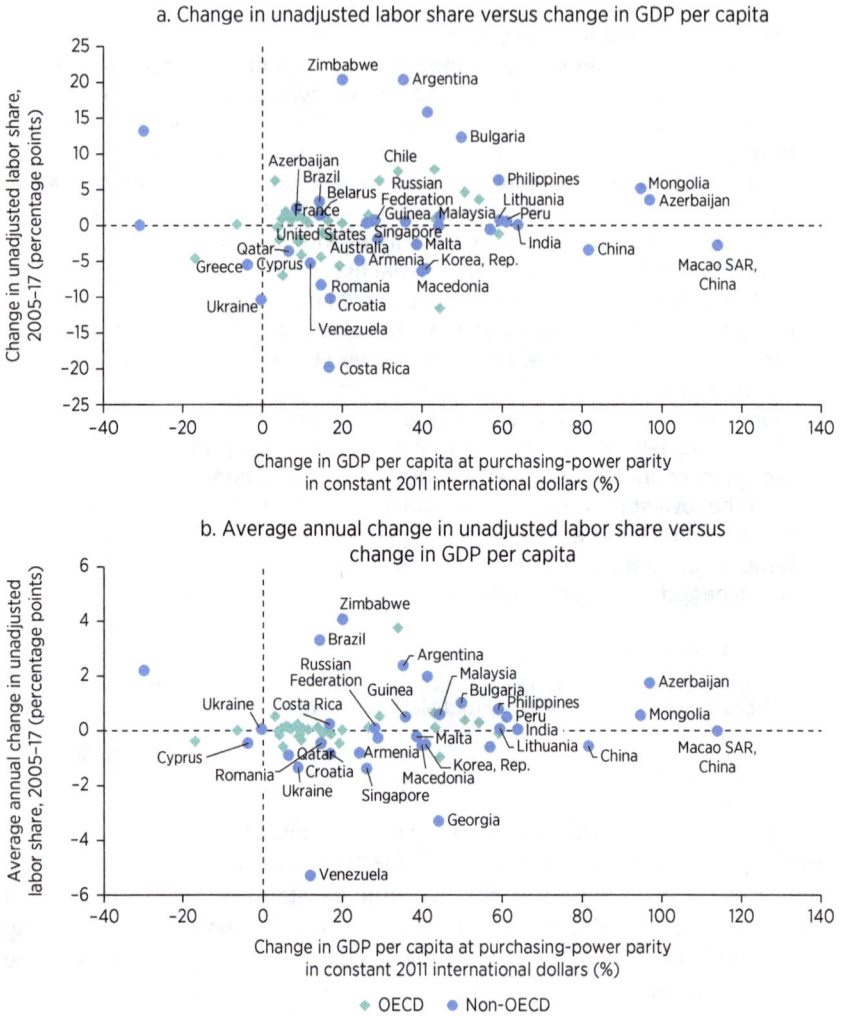

a. Change in unadjusted labor share versus change in GDP per capita

b. Average annual change in unadjusted labor share versus change in GDP per capita

◆ OECD  ● Non-OECD

*Sources:* Based on data from the International Labour Organization's *Global Wage Reports* (various years, as listed in the Note) and World Bank, *World Development Indicators.*

*Note:* The figure shows changes in GDP per capita over the period 2005–17, except in the case of Venezuela (2005–14), and changes (panel a)/average changes (panel b) in the unadjusted labor share over the same period, except in the cases of Azerbaijan (2013–15), Chile (2011–13), Colombia (2008–16), Guinea (2009–11), Iraq (2008–16), Kuwait (2010–16), Malaysia (2013–15), Moldova (2015–16), Mongolia (2007–16), Peru (2001–12), the Philippines (2009–17), Qatar (2011–15), República Bolivariana de Venezuela (2009–10), Russian Federation (2008–17), Serbia (2008–15), Ukraine (2011–17), and Zimbabwe (2009–14). In panel b, since the period covered for each country is different, the average annual change in each country is used. GDP = gross domestic product; OECD = Organisation for Economic Co-operation and Development; SAR = Special Administrative Region.

production (Acemoglu 2003a, 2003b; Acemoglu and Restrepo 2017; 2018; Brynjolfsson and McAfee 2014; Frey and Osbourne 2013; Zeira 1998); the decline in the bargaining power of labor brought about by the globalization of the labor pool; surplus labor released by the automation of many tasks (Bental and Demougin 2010; Blanchard and Giavazzi 2003; Stiglitz 2012); and industry concentration and the rise of markups (profits), at times aggravated by the market dominance of technology firms benefiting from network effects (Barkai 2016). Labor's declining share of economic output can be associated with high and rising levels of inequality (Eden and Gaggl 2015) (figure 1.12).

Intriguingly, the challenges posed by the rise of nonstandard forms of employment are, in many respects, not new to governments in the low- and middle-income countries. A likely reaction to the pressures on prevailing regulatory structures brought by global megatrends is an increase in informal economic relationships (Loayza 2016; Perry et al. 2007). Policy makers in low- and middle-income countries are very familiar with this problem, and many of them have been grappling for years with how to design mechanisms to protect the parties to these informal working relationships. The new challenge, however, is that a growing number of high-skilled, tech-savvy people could join the ranks of the informally employed and the self-employed. This new constituency of informal workers is likely

**Figure 1.12  Changes in the Labor Share in National Income Can Be Associated with Changes in Inequality**

a. Change in unadjusted labor share versus change in Gini index

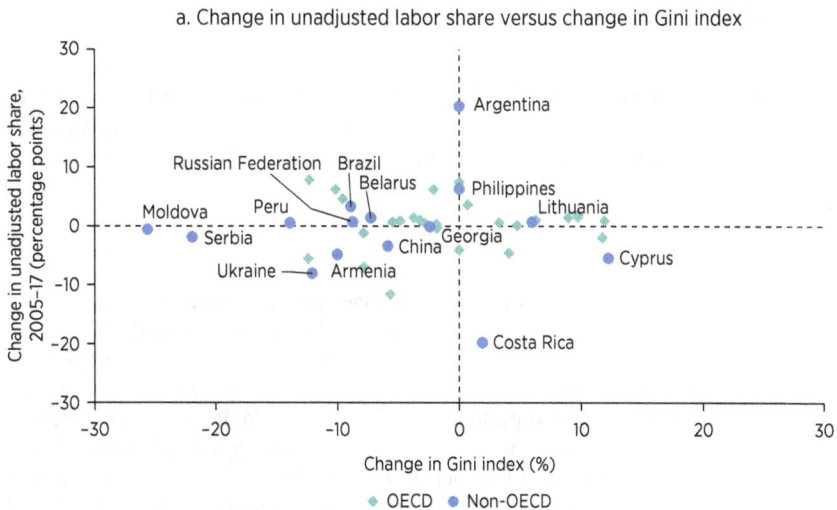

*continued next page*

**Figure 1.12** (*continued*)

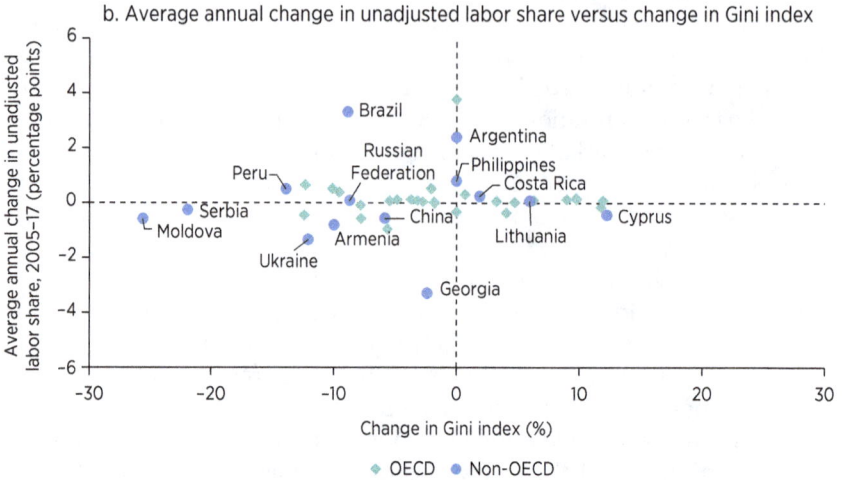

b. Average annual change in unadjusted labor share versus change in Gini index

Source: Based on Eden and Gaggl 2015.

Note: The figure shows the growth, over the period 2005–15, in the Gini index, which measures the extent to which the distribution of income/consumption expenditure among individuals or households within an economy deviates from a perfectly equal distribution (a Gini index of 0; 100 represents perfect inequality). The figure also shows the changes (panel a)/average changes (panel b) in the unadjusted labor share over the period 2005–17, except in the cases of Azerbaijan (2013–15), Chile (2011–13), Colombia (2008–16), Guinea (2009–11), Iraq (2008–16), Kuwait (2010–16), Malaysia (2013–15), Moldova (2015–16), Mongolia (2007–16), Peru (2001–12), the Philippines (2009–17), Qatar (2011–15), República Bolivariana de Venezuela (2009–10), Russian Federation (2008–17), Serbia (2008–15), Ukraine (2011–17), and Zimbabwe (2009–14). In panel b, since the period covered for each country is different, the average annual change in each country is used. GDP = gross domestic product; OECD = Organisation for Economic Co-operation and Development.

to be far more demanding of rights and protections but also may be more likely to accept a greater burden of risk and responsibility in mitigating shocks to their well-being (Apella and Zunino 2017, 2018).

## Notes

1. Here we are referring to risk-sharing policies and programs that help people manage losses from shocks that are primarily transmitted through the labor market; these policies and programs have typically been designed to rely on the place of employment, the stability of the employee-employer relationship, and the delegation of agency and key administrative functions to firms for their effectiveness. This description is, admittedly, mainly a caricature (though a useful one) that generalizes a "European model" of risk-sharing policy. It does not capture the diversity of institutional traditions and policy models that evolved in different parts of Europe.

2. Rodrik (2016) describes *premature deindustrialization* as the decline in the importance of the manufacturing sector in an economy as the provider of employment and the engine of productivity growth at a much earlier stage of a country's economic development than in higher-income countries when they transitioned into mainly service economies.

3. Motivated by the observation that conventional labor market surveys tend to underrepresent younger working people (particularly young men), RIWI—a global trend-tracking and prediction technology firm—conducted a survey of attitudes toward online-enabled "gig work." RIWI randomly surveyed people of all ages in 43 countries in all global regions. Between November 2018 and early February 2019, RIWI collected observations from more than 32,000 people, including many younger people—about 12,000 people aged 18–24, and another 12,000 aged 25–34. The RIWI methodology was more successful at reaching people who had previously not been surveyed: more than 50 percent of respondents had never before answered a survey. The firm found that the majority of young adults globally report that they take on online-enabled gigs because they want to; they see such work as an economic opportunity. RIWI found that about 60 percent of those aged 18–24 and a similar share of those aged 25–34, who are engaged in online-enabled gig work do so because they like the work, the flexibility, or the extra money. Notably, the "opportunity" signal, as RIWI refers to responses that indicate a positive attraction to gig work, is broad based and stable. The 60–40 breakdown is largely consistent across developed and developing economies, genders, age cohorts, and even types of work (location based, such as Uber or Airbnb, versus selling services or products online in a global marketplace).

4. In their 2016 paper, Katz and Krueger report analysis using the Contingent Worker Survey (CWS), part of the RAND American Life Panel, in late 2015. They show a significant rise in the incidence of "alternative work arrangements" (temporary agency workers, on-call workers, and independent contractors or freelancers) in the United States from 2005 to 2015—from 10.7 percent of the workforce in February 2005 to 15.8 percent in 2015. Their analysis shows that the percentage of workers hired out through contract companies rose the most, from 1.4 percent in 2005 to 3.1 percent in 2015. People who provide services through online intermediaries, such as Uber or Task Rabbit, accounted for 0.5 percent of all workers in 2015. A subsequent round of the CWS appears to show that the incidence of alternative work arrangements slightly declined from 10.7 percent in 2005 to 10.1 percent in 2017 (U.S. BLS 2018), driven by a decline in the share of workers classified as independent contractors. In response, the researchers returned to the topic in a National Bureau of Economic Research (NBER) working paper (Katz and Krueger 2019) in which they reconcile data from the CWS supplements to the Current Population Survey (CPS) from 1995 to 2017, the 2015 RAND-Princeton CWS, and administrative tax data from the U.S. Internal Revenue Service from 2000 to 2016. They conclude that there has been a more modest 1 to 2 percent upward trend in the share of the U.S. workforce in alternative work arrangements during the 2000s (rather than the larger increase they reported in their 2016 paper). They base this conclusion on the cyclically adjusted comparisons of the CPS CWS's measures, which use self-respondents to the CPS CWS, and

measures of self-employment and so-called 1099 workers from administrative tax data. The authors argue that the CPS question on multiple-job holding misses many instances of alternative work arrangements.

5. Avlijaš (2019) uses the European Union (EU) Labor Force Survey to show that 12.1 percent of EU-28 employees in 2016 worked on temporary contracts, 19.5 percent were in part-time work, and 14 percent were self-employed. Even in the relatively similar high-income countries of the EU, there are substantial variations: the share of temporary employment in total employment varies from almost nothing in Romania and Lithuania to 22 percent in Spain and Poland. Part-time employment is also almost nonexistent in countries such as Bulgaria and Hungary but is up to 50 percent of total employment in the Netherlands. Self-employment is as low as 8 percent of total employment in Sweden and Denmark and as high as 30 percent of total employment in Greece.

6. The Organisation for Economic Co-operation and Development (OECD) (2018) reports that, on average among OECD members, 16 percent of all workers are self-employed and a further 13 percent of employees are on temporary employment contracts. Trends in these forms of work vary substantially among the member-countries.

## References

Acemoglu, D. 2003a. "Labor- and Capital-Augmenting Technical Change." *Journal of the European Economic Association* 1 (1): 1–37.

———. 2003b. "Technology and Inequality." *NBER Reporter* (Winter). https://www.nber.org/reporter/winter03/technologyandinequality.html.

Acemoglu, D., and P. Restrepo. 2017. "Robots and Jobs: Evidence from US Labor Markets." NBER Working Paper 23285, National Bureau of Economic Research, Cambridge, MA.

———. 2018. "Artificial Intelligence, Automation and Work." NBER Working Paper No. 24196, National Bureau of Economic Research, Cambridge, MA.

Akerman, A., I. Gaarder, and M. Mogstad. 2015. "The Skill Complementarity of Broadband Internet." NBER Working Paper 20826, National Bureau of Economic Research, Cambridge, MA.

Almeida, R., J. Behrman, and D. Robalino. 2012. *The Right Skills for the Job? Rethinking Training Policies for Workers*. Human Development Perspectives. Washington, DC: World Bank.

Angel-Urdinola, D., and R. Mayer Gukovas. 2018. "A Skills-Based Human Capital Framework to Understand the Phenomenon of Youth Economic Disengagement." Policy Research Working Paper 8348, World Bank, Washington, DC.

Apella, I., and G. Zunino. 2017. "Cambio Tecnológico y Mercado de Trabajo en Argentina y Uruguay. Un Análisis desde el Enfoque de Tareas." Serie de Informes Técnicos del Banco Mundial en Argentina, Paraguay, y Uruguay, no. 11, World Bank, Washington, DC.

————. 2018. "Nonstandard Forms of Employment in Developing Countries: A Study for a Set of Selected Countries in Latin America and the Caribbean and Europe and Central Asia." Policy Research Working Paper 8581, World Bank, Washington, DC.

Autor, D. 2014. "Skills, Education, and the Rise of Earnings Inequality among the 'Other 99 Percent.'" *Science* 344 (6186): 843–851.

————. 2015. "Why Are There Still So Many Jobs? The History and Future of Workplace Automation." *Journal of Economic Perspectives* 29 (3): 3–30.

Autor, D., and D. Dorn. 2011. *The Growth of Low-Skill Service Jobs and the Polarization of the U.S. Labor Market.* Cambridge, MA: MIT Press.

Avent, R. 2016. *The Wealth of Humans: Work and Its Absence in the Twenty-First Century.* New York: St Martin's Press.

Avlijaš, S. 2019. "The Dynamism of the New Economy: Non-standard Employment and Access to Social Security in EU-28." LEQS Paper 141, London School of Economics, London.

Barkai, S. 2016. "Declining Labor and Capital Shares." Working Paper, University of Chicago.

Barr, N. 2012. *The Economics of the Welfare State.* 5th ed. New York: Oxford University Press.

Barr, N., ed. 2005. *Labor Markets and Social Policy in Central and Eastern Europe: The Accession and Beyond.* Washington, DC: World Bank.

Bental, B., and D. Demougin. 2010. "Declining Labor Shares and Bargaining Power: An Institutional Explanation." *Journal of Macroeconomics* 32 (1): 443–456.

Blanchard, O., and F. Giavazzi. 2003. "Macroeconomic Effects of Regulation and Deregulation in Goods and Labor Markets." *The Quarterly Journal of Economics* 118 (3): 879–907.

Brynjolfsson, E., and A. McAfee. 2014. *The Second Machine Age: Work, Progress, and Prosperity in a Time of Brilliant Technologies.* New York: W. W. Norton and Company.

Chandy, L. 2016. "The Future of Work in the Developing World." Brookings Blum Roundtable 2016 Post-Conference Report, Brookings Institution, Washington, DC.

Cho, Y., D. Robalino, and J. Romero. 2015. "Entering and Leaving Self-Employment: A Panel Data Analysis for 12 Developing Countries." IZA Discussion Paper 9358, IZA Institute of Labor Economics, Bonn, Germany.

Coase, R. 1937. "The Nature of the Firm." *Economica* 4 (16): 386–405.

Dasgupta, S., and A. Singh. 2006. "Manufacturing, Services and Premature Deindustrialization in Developing Countries: A Kaldorian Analysis." UNU-WIDER, United Nations University Research Paper, Volume/Issue 2006/49.

Dicarlo, E., S. Lo Bello, S. Monroy-Taborda, A. Oviedo, M. Sanchez-Puerta, and I. Santos. 2016. "The Skill Content of Occupations Across Low and Middle Income Countries: Evidence from Harmonized Data." IZA Discussion Paper 10224, IZA Institute of Labor Economics, Bonn, Germany.

Dutz, M., R. Almeida, and T. Packard. 2018. *The Jobs of Tomorrow: Technology, Productivity, and Prosperity in Latin America and the Caribbean.* Directions in Development Series. Washington, DC: World Bank.

Eden, M., and P. Gaggl. 2015. "On the Welfare Implications of Automation." Policy Research Working Paper 7487, World Bank, Washington, DC.

European Commission (EC). 2018. *Employment and Social Development in Europe: Annual Review 2018*. Brussels: European Commission.

Fenge, R., G. de Menil, and P. Pestieau, eds. 2008. *Pension Strategies in Europe and the United States*. Cambridge, MA: MIT Press.

Frey, C., and M. Osborne. 2013. "The Future of Employment: How Susceptible Are Jobs to Computerization?" Oxford University Working Paper, http://www.oxfordmartin.ox.ac.uk/downloads/academic/The_Future_of_Employment.pdf.

Gaggl, P., and G. Wright. 2014. "A Short-Run View of What Computers Do: Evidence from a UK Tax Incentive." Economic Discussion Papers, University of Essex, Department of Economics.

Gill, I., and H. Kharas. 2007. *An East Asian Renaissance: Ideas for Economic Growth*. Washington, DC: World Bank.

Goldberg, P. K., and N. Pavcnik. 2007. "Distributional Effects of Globalization in Developing Countries." *Journal of Economic Literature* 45 (1): 39–82.

———. 2016. "The Effects of Trade Policy." In *Handbook of Commercial Policy*, edited by K. Bagwell. Amsterdam: North-Holland Elsevier.

ILO (International Labour Organization). 2015a. "The Future of Work Centenary Initiative." Report of the Director General to the 104th International Labour Conference, International Labour Office, Geneva.

———. 2015b. "World Employment and Social Outlook 2015: The Changing Nature of Jobs." Flagship report, International Labour Office, Geneva.

———. 2018. "The ILO Multi-pillar Pension Model: Building Equitable and Sustainable Pension Systems." Social Protection for All Issue Brief, International Labour Organization, Geneva.

ILO (International Labour Organization) and ISSA (International Social Security Association). 1998. *Social Security Principles*. Geneva: International Labor Office.

Katz, L., and A. Krueger. 2016. "The Rise and Nature of Alternative Work Arrangements in the United States, 1995–2015." Working Paper 603, Princeton University Industrial Relations Section, Princeton, NJ.

———. 2019. "Understanding Trends in Alternative Work Arrangements in the United States." NBER Working Paper 25425, National Bureau of Economic Research, Cambridge, MA.

Kuddo, A., D. Robalino, and M. Weber. 2015. "Minumum Wages." In *Balancing Regulations to Promote Jobs: From Employment Contract to Unemployment Benefits*, edited by A. Kuddo, D. Robalino, and M. Weber. Washington, DC: World Bank Group.

Lee, R., A. Mason, and Members of the NTA (National Transfer Accounts) Network. 2014. "Is Low Fertility Really a Problem? Population Aging, Dependency, and Consumption." *Science* 346 (6206): 229–34.

Lindert, P. H. 2004. *Growing Public: Social Spending and Economic Growth since the Eighteenth Century*. 2 vols. Cambridge, U.K.: Cambridge University Press.

———. 2013. "Private Welfare and the Welfare State." In *The Cambridge History of Capitalism*, edited by L. Neal and J. Williamson. Cambridge, U.K.: Cambridge University Press.

Loayza, N. V. 2016. "Informality in the Process of Development and Growth: Toolkit for Informality Scenario Analysis." Policy Research Working Paper 7858, World Bank, Washington, DC.

Matsuyama, K. 2009. "Structural Change in an Interdependent World: A Global View of Manufacturing Decline." *Journal of the European Economic Association* 7 (2–3): 478–486.

Mwabu, G., M. Muriithi, and R. Mutegi. 2011. "National Transfer Accounts for Kenya: The Economic Lifecycle in 1994." In *Population Aging and the Generational Economy: A Global Perspective*, edited by R. Lee and A. Mason. Cheltenham, U.K.: Edward Elgar.

———. 2013. "Boosting Kenya's Demographic Dividend." National Transfer Accounts Project, Country Brief: Kenya, Bloomberg School of Public Health, Johns Hopkins University, Baltimore, MD.

Naidoo, D., T. Packard, and I. Auwalin. 2015. "Mobility, Scarring, and Job Quality in Indonesia's Labor Market." Policy Research Working Paper 7484, World Bank, Washington, DC.

Nickell, S., S. Redding, and J. Swaffield. 2008. "The Uneven Pace of Deindustrialization in the OECD." Paper produced as part of the Labour Markets and Globalisation Programmes of the Centre for Economic Performance, London School of Economics, London.

OECD (Organisation for Economic Co-operation and Development). 2018. *The Future of Social Protection: What Works for Non-Standard Workers?* Paris: Organisation for Economic Co-operation and Development.

Palier, B., ed. 2010. *A Long Goodbye to Bismarck? The Politics of Welfare Reform in Continental Europe.* Amsterdam: Amsterdam University Press.

Perry, G., W. Maloney, O. Arias, P. Fajnzylber, A. Mason, and J. Saavedraq-Chanduvi. 2007. *Informality: Exit and Exclusion.* Washington, DC: World Bank.

Ravallion, M. 1987. "Towards a Theory of Famine Relief Policy." *Journal of Public Economics* 33 (1): 21–39.

———. 2016. *The Economics of Poverty: History, Measurement, and Policy.* Oxford, U.K.: Oxford University Press.

RIWI. 2019. "The Future of Online-Enabled Gig Work." Insight of the Week series, February 13, Toronto, Canada. https://riwi.com/wp-content/uploads/2019/02/Insight-of-the-Week-Online-Enabled-%E2%80%98Gig%E2%80%99-Work.pdf.

Rodrik, D. 2016. "Premature Deindustrialization." *Journal of Economic Growth* 21 (1): 1–33.

Stiglitz, J. 2012. "Macroeconomic Fluctuations, Inequality, and Human Development." *Journal of Human Development and Capabilities: A Multi-Disciplinary Journal for People-Centered Development* 13 (1): 31–58.

Stone, K. 2004. *From Widgets to Digits: Employment Regulation for the Changing Workplace.* Cambridge, U.K.: Cambridge University Press.

Stone, K., and H. Arthurs, eds. 2013. *Rethinking Workplace Regulation: Beyond the Standard Contract of Employment.* New York: Russell Sage Foundation.

United Nations, Department of Economic and Social Affairs, Population Division. 2017. *World Population Prospects: The 2017 Revision.* DVD edition. New York: United Nations.

U.S. Bureau of Labor Statistics (BLS). 2018. "Contingent and Alternative Arrangements—May 2017." USDL-18-0942, June. https://www.bls.gov/news/release/pdf/conemp.pdf.

Willmore, L. 2007. "Universal Pensions for Developing Countries." *World Development* 35 (1): 24–51.

World Bank. 1995. *World Development Report 1996: From Plan to Market.* Washington, DC: World Bank.

———. 2008. *World Development Report 2009: Reshaping Economic Geography.* Washington, DC: World Bank.

———. 2011. *World Development Report 2012: Gender Equality and Development.* Washington, DC: World Bank.

———. 2012. *World Development Report 2013: Jobs.* Washington, DC: World Bank.

———. 2016. *World Development Report 2016: Digital Dividends.* Washington, DC: World Bank.

———. 2019a. Migration and Development Brief 31. World Bank, Washington, DC.

———. 2019b. *World Development Report 2019: The Changing Nature of Work.* Washington, DC: World Bank.

World Bank and IMF (International Monetary Fund). 2016. *Global Monitoring Report 2015/2016: Development Goals in an Era of Demographic Change.* Washington, DC: World Bank.

Zeira, J. 1998. "Workers, Machines, and Economic Growth." *Quarterly Journal of Economics* 113 (4): 1091–1117.

# 2

# The Conceptual Underpinnings of Risk-Sharing Policy and the Changing Nature of Losses

Scrutinizing current risk-sharing policies and formulating credible alternatives to them requires an appeal to first principles. Rethinking risk-sharing policies amid globally occurring disruptions and what could be a long transition out of one equilibrium and into an unknown other is challenging, to say the least. The question of relevance raised in the previous chapter has this transition dimension, but, as discussed in the opening section, there is also a salience dimension across different country types and contexts. For this reason, it may be not only difficult but also inappropriate to try to come up with *the* new risk-sharing policy model—indeed, just as inappropriate and potentially damaging as it was for the late-industrial-era, employment-based models conceived in parts of Europe to be established with little alteration in such varying country contexts. This dilemma begs a return to first principles and a conceptual framework to guide policy making rather than the formulation of detailed policy prescriptions. This section presents a framework drawn from the main conceptual underpinnings of risk-sharing policy and how, when applied to the drivers of disruption, new inferences can be drawn for policy makers.

In this section, we have used the same theoretical rationale and conceptual tools underlying the expansion of universal health coverage (UHC), a powerful policy precedent. Indeed, in a discussion of the shocks to livelihoods and losses to people's well-being and how society should respond with risk-sharing policies, it is very difficult to avoid analogies to health events and to how households, markets, and governments respond to these events.

In fact, it can seem arbitrary and even ad hoc to separate the consideration of livelihood-disrupting events from the debate on how best to help households cover the costs of health care. The policy rationale for intervention in the health-risk and medical market is intuitive and widely appreciated by non-specialists. Many people think first about health coverage when they hear the terms *social security* or *social insurance*. We want to assure readers that we have set health aside in this chapter (but drawn on it discretely), purely to demonstrate how the same motivations and concepts used in the discussion of UHC can apply to old age, disability, job loss, and other events that affect household income.

The social justice literature also provides a deep reservoir of insights that can lead to similar conclusions and policy implications (Jørgensen and Siegel 2019; Siegel and Jørgensen 2013). However, our task is to present arguments for change that are the most convincing to finance, economy, and labor ministers. For this reason, we have chosen to use a different set of tools drawn from actuarial and public economics, as presented in the remaining sections of this chapter.

## Insurance Choices in the Face of Shocks

Classical economic models of insurance and principles drawn from public economics are useful tools to guide analysis and design of risk-sharing policies.[1] Individuals, households, and societies can respond in a variety of ways when faced with the prospect of losses from shocks, whether these losses arise from job loss, sickness, death, or disability of an income earner, financial crises, or natural disasters. Classical economic and actuarial models indicate which instruments—including prevention measures—will be most effective and efficient given the nature (size and frequency) of possible losses as well as the extent to which markets fail to respond to people's need for insurance. The same models can be used to identify when coping is the most efficient course of action as well as to distinguish effective from ineffective forms of coping. Risk-sharing policies come in a variety of instruments made available by the state. Because they are designed to cover the losses that private insurance cannot cover—or to augment private coverage where it fails or falls short—risk policy instruments are not expected to strictly conform to the actuarial rules that shape market provision. That said, these rules should not be ignored. Policy-relevant insights about the nature of a loss, how it is best covered, and the degree to which the private sector should be expected to help can be drawn from the classical models on which these rules are based.

Where markets function well, insurance choices depend on the size and the frequency of losses from shocks. Figure 2.1 illustrates stylized prescriptions of the classical models on two axes, each representing a different dimension of possible losses: *size* (the amount of the loss) on the vertical axis and *frequency* (the probability of the loss's occurrence) on the horizontal axis. From a financial protection perspective, it is more efficient for individuals to cope with rather than try to insure against small, rarely occurring losses (the lowermost, left-hand corner of figure 2.1). However, as losses become more frequent, it is relatively more efficient to engage in prevention to lower the probability of losses and individual savings to cover their costs. As a probable loss becomes less frequent but increases in size, it becomes more efficient to engage in risk pooling. For many large, rare losses, households will have incentives to engage in prevention measures to further lower the probability that the loss will occur. However, for losses that are frequently occurring and catastrophic in size (the right-hand, uppermost corner of figure 2.1), there is little that individuals, households, or markets can do on their own, and measures to create a larger risk pool are required. This is the first, clear motivation for policy intervention, particularly to help manage covariate or systemic shocks, such as an economic crisis or natural disaster.

**Figure 2.1  When Risk Markets Are Available and Function Well, It Is Most Efficient to Pool the Risk of Large, Infrequent Losses**

**Complete insurance markets**

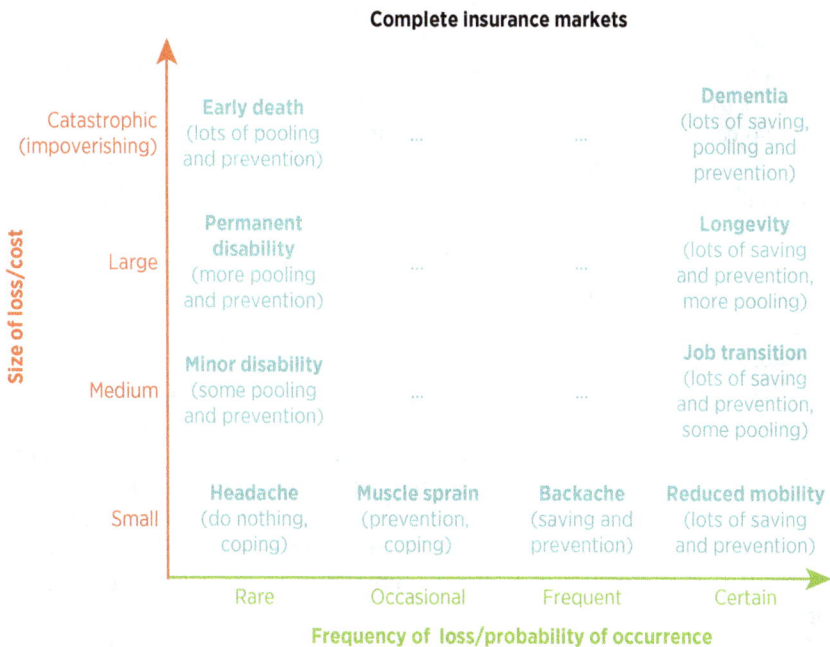

| Size of loss/cost | | | | |
|---|---|---|---|---|
| Catastrophic (impoverishing) | Early death (lots of pooling and prevention) | ... | ... | Dementia (lots of saving, pooling and prevention) |
| Large | Permanent disability (more pooling and prevention) | ... | ... | Longevity (lots of saving and prevention, more pooling) |
| Medium | Minor disability (some pooling and prevention) | ... | ... | Job transition (lots of saving and prevention, some pooling) |
| Small | Headache (do nothing, coping) | Muscle sprain (prevention, coping) | Backache (saving and prevention) | Reduced mobility (lots of saving and prevention) |
| | Rare | Occasional | Frequent | Certain |

**Frequency of loss/probability of occurrence**

*Sources:* Baeza and Packard 2006, based on Barr 2012, Ehrlich and Becker 1972, and Gill and Ilahi 2000.

*Note:* This figure shows the optimal risk instruments with which to address a given loss by the size and frequency of the loss in the absence of market failures.

Market failures on the supply and demand sides motivate policy intervention to ensure that the full set of instruments is available and efficiently provided and priced. The prescriptions of the classical models are, of course, vulnerable to many of the market failures discussed extensively in the economics literature. Of particular concern are the problems posed by "imperfect" information, which can range from problems that hinder individual consumer choice (demand-side problems) to problems that hinder market provision of savings and risk-pooling instruments (supply-side problems). An uneven distribution of information between consumers and providers leads to two problems that consistently plague private risk markets: *adverse selection* and *moral hazard*, discussed at length in appendix A. Furthermore, risk-pooling mechanisms cope badly with losses that occur frequently, that is, events whose likelihood approaches certainty or that have already occurred. Similarly, risk pooling fares poorly in situations where the probability of one member of the pool suffering a loss causes (or increases the probability of) another member suffering the loss (that is, when the probabilities of suffering the loss are not independent). In the wake of these correlated or systemic losses, too many "unlucky" members of the risk pool (those who suffer the bad state) rely on the premiums of too few "lucky" members (those who go unscathed).

*Uncertainty* is the most daunting and insurmountable challenge to insurance markets. A fundamental obstacle to market supply of insurance instruments is that of distinguishing risk from uncertainty. The difference between the two concepts is more than semantic and has profound consequences for the availability of market insurance (Barr 2001). *Risk* is measurable; that is, a probability can be assessed for the risk of a given adverse event. *Uncertainty*, on the other hand, cannot be measured—the probability of an uncertain occurrence cannot be determined. For this reason, uncertain events lie beyond the reach of the actuarial tools the market uses to price and pool risks (Barr 2001, 2012). When the uncertainty of shocks grows, the challenges to market provision of effective risk-pooling and other instruments also rise.

The role of the state in risk-sharing policy is to augment the options of households for whom any of these instruments are unavailable or out of reach. The state can pursue this role by providing risk-sharing instruments directly and by improving the workings of other markets that facilitate the function of private arrangements. The market failures on the demand and supply sides are important caveats to the prescriptions of the classical models, particularly to the availability of instruments that help people pool risk. These problems raise the price of risk-pooling instruments out of the reach of lower-income groups and even above what is economically viable, conspiring to create gaps in protection. These gaps typically occur among portions of the population that need protection the most, such as workers with lower levels of human capital, the elderly, children and expecting parents, people living with disabilities, and the chronically ill (see box 2.1 on long-term care insurance).

BOX 2.1

## Covering the Costs of Long-Term Care in the Face of Uncertainty

As rich and many upper-middle-income countries continue to age rapidly, the demand for long-term care (LTC) provided beyond informal family networks has grown. LTC provides an important example of a situation in which uncertainty has frustrated the expansion of market-based insurance. The need for LTC is subject to several forms of uncertainty, which cumulatively make LTC insurance very challenging to price.

The first form, also a concern of pension systems, is uncertainty about longevity, which is becoming greater as medicine progresses. In the past half century, United Nations projections of life expectancy have consistently underestimated the rate of longevity increase (World Bank 2016). The second, more complex, form is uncertainty around the length and intensity of the periods of functional dependency that precede death. This uncertainty is a combination of an increased expectancy of years of healthy life in most countries with shifts in medical and care technologies, which also change the degree of dependency of a given condition and severity-of-condition. The exponential likelihood of developing dementia after age 80—the costliest condition for which LTC is needed—is a particularly challenging part of the picture. A final form of uncertainty concerns policy. As the elderly's share of the population grows in better-off countries, political pressures for greater public funding of LTC have grown, with public spending on LTC now approaching 3.5–4 percent of gross domestic product (GDP) in some Organisation for Economic Co-operation and Development (OECD) member countries and social LTC insurance being introduced in several countries, such as Japan, the Republic of Korea, Germany, and the Netherlands. The interaction of publicly financed services with the demand for and the costs of privately financed services creates additional uncertainty.

This combination of factors has made private LTC insurance products unusually challenging to price because of the difficulties of assigning robust probabilities to various factors. As a result, analysis from the United States, for example, suggests that LTC insurance policies tend to have premiums well above those justified by the expected benefits and to cover relatively smaller shares of total expenditure risk (Brown and Finkelstein 2011; Cremer, Pestieau, and Roeder 2015).

The inherent challenges of such uncertainty can be seen in the low share of total LTC spending accounted for by private LTC insurance. Across the OECD, this share remains under 2 percent, and it only reaches 5 percent or higher in Japan and the United States (see figure B2.1.1).

*continued next page*

**Box 2.1** (*continued*)

**Figure B2.1.1** **The Low Penetration of Long-Term Care Insurance Reflects the Challenges of Uncertainty for Its Market Pricing**

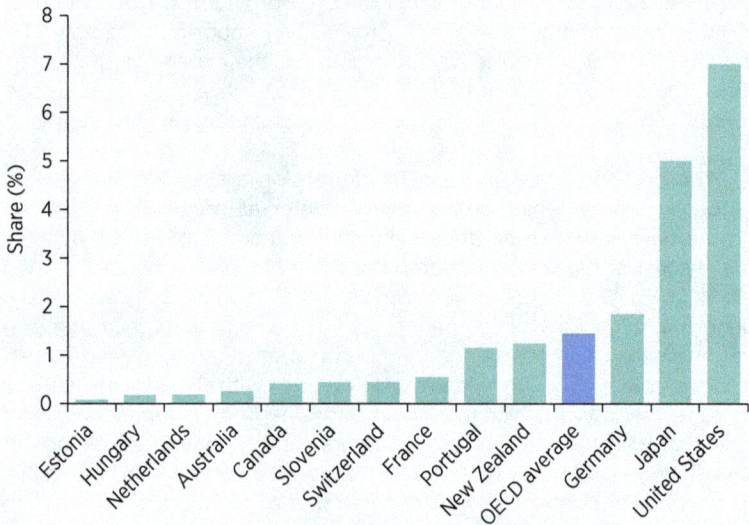

*Source:* OECD 2011, using the OECD System of Health Accounts 2010 and data from the US Department of Health and Human Services for 2010.

*Note:* This figure shows the share of total long-term care spending on private long-term care insurance. Data refer to 2008 for Canada, Estonia, France, Germany, Hungary, New Zealand, and Slovenia; 2007 for Australia and Switzerland; 2006 for Japan and Portugal; and 2005 for the Netherlands. Except in the cases of the Netherlands, New Zealand, Slovenia, and Spain, data refer to long-term nursing care only. OECD = Organisation for Economic Co-operation and Development.

Purchasers of private LTC insurance tend to be high income, reflecting the overpricing noted above. In addition, private LTC insurance is often taken as a complement to publicly financed programs (whether financed through dedicated social LTC insurance or from general revenues), with people seeking supplemental services outside the public package (OECD 2011).

From a public economics perspective, the *external*, social costs of many losses make effective coverage a public good. As is well understood and broadly accepted in public health circles, an imperative to provide coverage to those who lack it arises from the degree of externality or the extent of social benefit arising from intervening to help cover likely losses. More than the arguments about missing or malfunctioning markets presented earlier, this last market failure provides an even more powerful justification for policy intervention. Whether a risk is best covered through risk-pooling, saving, or prevention measures, to the extent that prospective losses exhibit negative externalities (that is, if the failure of an individual to take appropriate measures to address this risk imposes costs on others) and interventions yield increasing public-good characteristics, the justification for intervention to ensure optimal uptake by households will grow. We have added an axis to represent this third dimension of the nature of losses—the extent of market failures, particularly externalities—in figure 2.2.

In crafting interventions, policy makers should be guided by the nature of shocks and losses. The size and frequency of the prospective loss should determine whether a shock is best mitigated with risk pooling, individual saving, or prevention and the relative role of each instrument. But regardless of the instruments in use, as the extent of market failure or externality posed by the prospective loss grows, the justification increases for intervention by

**Figure 2.2 Market Failures—Particularly Good and Bad Externalities—Require Policy Actions to Share Risks Efficiently**

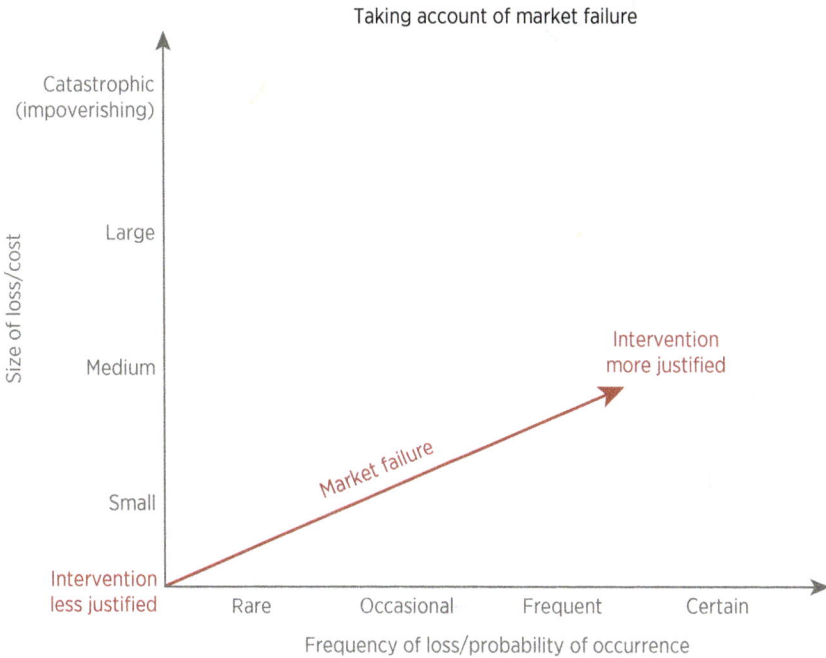

*Sources:* Baeza and Packard 2006, based on Barr 2012, Ehrlich and Becker 1972, and Gill and Ilahi 2000.

*Note:* This figure builds on figure 2.1 and shows the optimal risk instruments for addressing a probable loss by the size, frequency, and extent of market failure to cover the loss.

the state to ensure that appropriate measures are undertaken and policies are enacted to correct market failures. The rationale for risk-sharing policy actions arises when individuals or households fail to attain optimal levels of risk pooling, saving, and prevention—whether by choice or under constraints—and as the external costs of these failures grow. Such failures could occur either because one or more of the necessary instruments are not available to the individual, or, if all three instruments are available, because market inefficiencies (information problems and other market failures we have discussed) prevent individuals from using each instrument optimally. Figure 2.3 illustrates this guidance, specifying interventions, according to the three characteristics of prospective losses (size, probability of occurrence, and extent of market failure [degree of externality]) discussed above. Advances in the thinking supporting UHC have shown where important exceptions to these theoretical considerations have to be made, as discussed in box 2.2.

**Figure 2.3 Policy Options (Prevention, Saving, and Risk Pooling) Vary According to the Size and Frequency of Losses and the Extent and Ways in Which the Risk Market Fails to Cover Them**

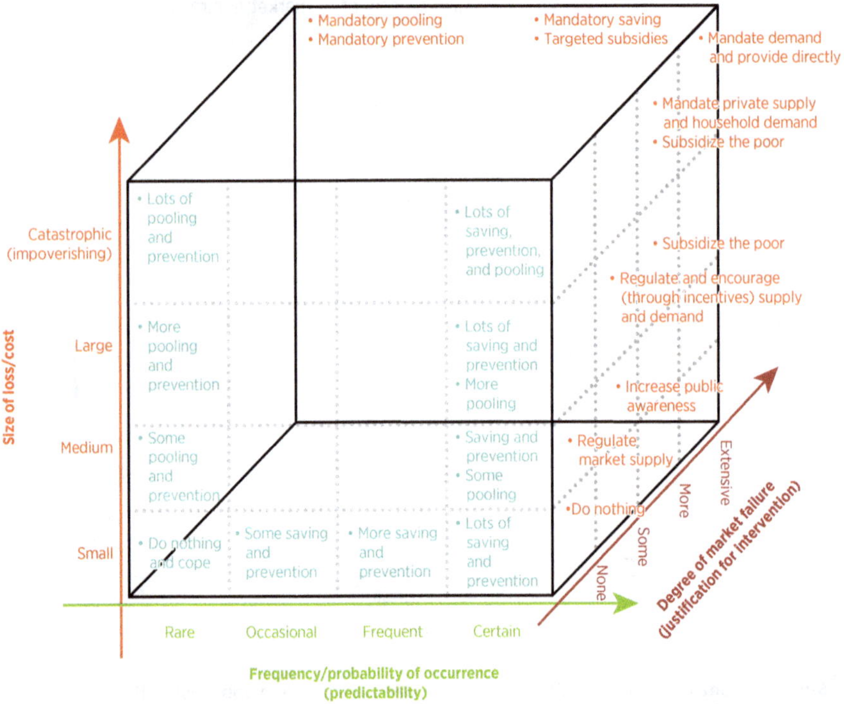

*Sources:* Baeza and Packard 2006, based on Barr 2012, Ehrlich and Becker 1972, and Gill and Ilahi 2000.

BOX 2.2

## When Are Private Goods Public Goods? Lessons from Universal Health Coverage

According to the classical definition, a public good is nonexclusive (that is, consumption of the good cannot be restricted to those who do not pay for it, or, put less awkwardly, all individuals can consume the good whether they have paid for it or not) and nonrival (that is, the consumption of the good by one individual will not imply that less of the good is available for others to consume). For example, even though it costs money to fight pollution—and government will surely pass this bill on to taxpayers—policy makers cannot prevent households who evade taxes from breathing clean air, nor does the clean air consumed by a particular household make less air available for others.

Many health interventions are private goods in the economic sense—they are only available to individuals who pay for them, and their consumption implies a reduction of the quantities of the goods available to others, such as cosmetic surgery or prescription drugs. For example, it would be relatively easy to restrict consumption of cosmetic nose surgery to those who pay for it, and a household's consumption of this treatment makes less of the surgeon's time available for others. Similarly, it would be relatively easy to restrict consumption of the hair-loss medication minoxidil to only those who pay for it, and a household's consumption of this drug makes less of it available for others.

However, in the medical market, there are numerous goods (medications, treatments, and interventions) that, although bearing all the characteristics of private goods (that is, even though they are excludable and their consumption is rival), clearly affect the welfare of individuals other than the consumer. For this reason, when left purely to the market, these private goods that have positive externalities will always be underconsumed relative to the level that is socially optimal (similarly, private goods with negative externalities will always be overconsumed from the optimal level). This is to say that the underconsumption of these goods could jeopardize the aggregate welfare.

Immunizations provide a particularly good example of a health intervention with private-good characteristics but unambiguous and powerful social benefits. When immunization coverage for a disease (such as measles, mumps, and rubella) reaches a sufficient level (usually 80 percent to 90 percent of the susceptible population), epidemics of the disease become less likely to occur. So, the benefits of children being vaccinated will be extended even to those who do not vaccinate their dependents. But this example comes with a word of

*continued next page*

**Box 2.2** (*continued*)

caution: below a sufficient level of coverage (for example, when the vaccination level is only 30 percent of the population at risk), vaccines are pure private goods, because the benefit of vaccination will most likely affect only the child who was vaccinated; it would not stop the disease from reaching those not vaccinated and thus could not prevent an epidemic. Thus, the societal importance of reaching certain threshold levels of vaccination coverage is enormous. Another obvious example of such a good is the use of condoms. There are clear advantages involved for individuals when they protect themselves from sexually transmitted infections (STIs) by using condoms. However, using condoms can also substantially slow the spread of STIs in a population. Basic education that can ensure minimum levels of literacy and numeracy in a population exhibits similar characteristics and effects on aggregate welfare.

Thus, the degree of externality posed by health and education and the public-good nature of many health treatments and education services—even those that are clearly private goods—have undeniable positive externalities. The externalities of these services would be so sorely missed that few governments believe it prudent to leave to chance or choice that households and firms will seek or receive them on their own.

*Source:* Baeza and Packard 2006.

## Poverty in a Risk Framework

A risk framework can also yield useful policy insights for helping chronically poor people manage losses from shocks. The risk framework presented in this chapter could appear relevant only to households above the poverty line faced with the possibility of impoverishing (or otherwise catastrophic) losses in the wake of a shock. But what about those individuals and households who are already poor? What about people born into poverty and those who have been living below the poverty line for years? In many countries, the correlation between economic destitution and exclusion from markets and adequate social services is so high that it is almost cavalier to think that on their own, even the best-conceived and most effective risk-sharing policies would pull these families out of poverty. As explained in the opening section of this chapter, by applying a risk framework even to the plight of chronically poor people, we do not mean to disregard or discount the vital and valuable thinking represented in the large social-justice and human-rights literature. There are many ways to motivate policy inter-ventions that provide a needed boost up the ladder of well-being, such as promoting poor people out of poverty by building vital individual, house-hold, and community assets—particularly human and social capital—that have little to do with risk.[2] We are confident that our application of a risk framework to the experience of shocks and losses of chronically poor peo-ple leads to insights and policy implications that complement rather than contradict social-justice thinking.

From a household's perspective, poverty is a state of high-frequency, even catastrophic, losses. Poverty can be brought into the risk-sharing framework in two ways. First, and most obviously, shocks are still relevant to those who are already living in poverty. The effect of shocks reduces the welfare of poor people further and can erode progress toward an escape from poverty (referring to people's distance from the poverty line rather than when they crossed the line itself). From the moment that a household falls into poverty, its members enter a state of continuous stress: losses (tending to catastrophic because of either their size or their impact relative to the household's ability to survive them) that strike with high frequency until the household emerges above the poverty line. Indeed, many anec-dotal accounts of the daily challenges faced by poor people describe poverty as a continuous series of shocks (Narayan 2000; Sen 1999). Second, in a strictly Rawlsian sense, birth into poverty can be treated as a shock in and of itself.

Policy effort on the national and even international scale is required to offer an adequate risk pool that is responsive and robust to the impact of shocks on chronically poor people. Turning once again to the illustration framework in figure 2.3, living in chronic poverty can be shown as a shock mapped to the uppermost, right-hand corner of the grid: a frequently occurring, catastrophic loss. Indeed, there is substantial empirical evidence showing that people living in poverty experience shocks with greater fre-quency and that the accompanying losses are relatively larger than even the same events and losses would be if experienced by nonpoor people. As explained above, individual effort through networks and markets is insuf-ficient to mitigate large, frequently occurring losses, and there is a clear role for outside intervention that effectively broadens the risk pool. At the aggregate level, countries with relatively low poverty rates (in which cata-strophic losses frequently occur, but only to a minority of the population) can pool this risk using direct transfers financed through broad-based tax-ation to lift the poor out of poverty. Countries where the rate of poverty is high (as a result of historical or geographic circumstance, persistent drought and famine, or a recent economic or financial crisis) are more likely to depend on international assistance—a risk-pooling device with a larger pool.

A powerful implication of this argument is that "safety net" transfers should always be in place, ready to be deployed to lower the losses of those vulnerable to poverty and the chronically poor. From a risk-sharing perspective, such transfers are another risk-pooling instrument—financed with the largest possible risk pool—at the disposal of individuals and households, should they suffer the misfortune to need them. Although safety net transfers can be a very effective instrument to eliminate poverty among the current poor, they may also be powerful in breaking the intergenerational transmission of poverty. Both the provision of income support and the frequent nudges or requirements built into transfer programs that encourage asset building—that children receive nutrition, health, and education services—heighten this effect.

## Policies Should Augment What People Do for Themselves

Lest the framework presented here be too closely associated with or confined to the consideration of formal risk-sharing instruments prevalent in upper-middle-income and high-income countries, it is worth demonstrating its relevance to the risk-sharing options most people have even where markets are severely constrained, as in the lowest-income countries. In high-income countries, most of the things households do to manage the risk of economic and financial losses lie in the private realm. In countries where the government's monitoring and regulatory capacity is great, the state can successfully limit its role to regulating formal transactions in the market. However, in most lower-income countries, governments' monitoring and regulatory capacity is limited. Not only do most household risk-mitigation activities take place privately in these countries, but also they are unregulated. Many traditional and informal arrangements in place in these countries tend to follow a similar insurance logic to formal arrangements in higher-income countries.

In low- and middle-income countries, kinship-based, community-based, and informal insurance measures are more prevalent. Table 2.1 is constructed from the point of view of a household facing a range of possible losses and examining all of its options. The table provides examples of the array of instruments households have at their disposal in almost any context, arranging these options into the "risk pooling," "saving," and "prevention" categories presented earlier. A range of "coping" measures are also presented. Additionally, table 2.1 shows how these instruments are typically provided, that is, informally (in the household or between members of a community) or formally (by the market or by government). The distinction between "informal" and "formal" used in table 2.1 merits further explanation. By "informal," we mean a strategy or an instrument taken outside the

**Table 2.1  There Are a Wide Range of Risk-Sharing Instruments: Informal and Formal, Intrahousehold and Network, and Market and Government Provided**

| | Informal | | | Formal | |
| --- | --- | --- | --- | --- | --- |
| | Intrahousehold or intrafamily | Community network–based | Provided by markets | | Provided by governments |
| **Prevention** (lowers the likelihood of a shock) | • Maintaining less-risky production technology<br>• Hygiene<br>• Nutrition<br>• Migration | • Community disaster preparation strategies, plans, and structures<br>• Community-level efforts to lower likelihood of disasters | • Privately provided education<br>• Training | | • Public education<br>• Public nutrition programs<br>• Public primary/preventive health care<br>• Workplace safety regulation<br>• Skills training that shortens unemployment spells<br>• Pollution controls |
| **Saving** (transfers resources from good times to bad times, but without pooling risks) | • Money "under the mattress"<br>• Livestock<br>• Investment in human capital | • Unregulated community-level banks | • Credit<br>• Savings accounts in regulated commercial banks<br>• Regulated microfinance<br>• Financial assets | | • Government-mandated private savings<br>• Savings instruments provided by public banks |
| **Risk pooling** (transfers resources from good times to bad times, but compensates for differences in vulnerability between individuals) | • Intrahousehold transfers<br>• Remittances from a migrant member | • Investment in social capital (rituals and reciprocal gift-giving)<br>• Funeral societies<br>• Unregulated rotating credit schemes<br>• Charity | • Private insurance<br>• Severance (job protection) schemes | | • Public pensions and unemployment and health insurance<br>• Health care provided directly by public hospitals<br>• Any cash or in-kind transfer programs<br>• Active labor measures<br>• Bankruptcy protections |
| **Coping** (measures taken to deal with a shock—including both savings and pooling—that were not originally intended for this use) | • Pulling school-age kids out of school to work<br>• Selling household assets<br>• Cutting spending on food or education (things that build human capital) | • Charity from neighbors<br>• Borrowing money from unregulated lenders | • Borrowing from commercial banks | | • Emergency disaster relief<br>• Budget reallocations |

*Sources:* Dercon 2002, Heltberg and Lund 2009, Hoddinott and Quisumbing 2010, Holzmann and Jørgensen 2000, and Siegel and Alwang 1999.

reach of regulation. For example, if an elderly parent breaks her hip and her son gives her money to pay somebody to do her shopping for her, we would classify this strategy as "interhousehold coping." If an individual is part of a funeral society or a rotating credit scheme and receives a payment from this scheme to pay for an unexpected event, this occurrence may or may not be regulated by the government. If these schemes are not regulated, they would be classified as informal "community network–based risk pooling." Such arrangements have, in many countries, grown into regulated, formal mutual societies or cooperative financial services providers. If an individual has a savings account in a bank, this strategy is indeed regulated and therefore "formal." If the bank is private, the strategy is market based.

Despite the availability of a wide array of instruments, households can still become impoverished or linger in poverty because of shocks. Gaps in effective coverage clearly remain, and market failures are a likely culprit for these gaps. Thus, in the face of uncertainty and external benefits, there is a clear role for risk-sharing policy to augment households' options.

Policy interventions should be crafted with community- and market-based measures in mind. It is vital to remember that the state is just one originator of risk-sharing instruments. Policy makers who pay close attention to the ways in which people cover risks themselves will have a better notion of where informal arrangements fall short, where and how markets fail, and thus what set of instruments is most likely to augment rather than displace or distort choices. As the established policy models are strained by the drivers of disruption, similar care must be taken in formulating reforms to these models, keeping an eye on how the same disruptions are affecting private informal and market-provided instruments.

## Options for Managing Aggregate Shocks and Losses from a Policy Maker's Perspective

The range of risk-sharing policies a government can offer to people is determined by its policy stance more generally. Just as individuals and households facing a loss can pool risks, save, or take preventive measures, or cope with losses should they fail to insure, governments face similar decisions in aggregate. Governments can "pool" the risks of a limited (but growing) range of possible losses through private market insurance and an even wider range of losses through international, multilateral risk-pooling structures (some long-standing examples of which include the International Monetary Fund, the World Bank, and more-recently-formed response funds for natural disasters and epidemics); they can "save" by accumulating surpluses in good times to spend on services during bad times (for example, by using stabilization and sovereign wealth funds and other structures that help achieve countercyclical public spending); and they can "prevent" by practicing prudent monetary and fiscal policy; investing in health, education, and disaster-resilient infrastructure; and engaging in reforms that increase the efficiency and safety of factor and product markets. These measures all lower the probability of shocks and the size of the losses they can inflict. Furthermore, by investing in increasing their information systems and their administrative capacity to collect revenue, governments improve their ability to sustain public goods and, in the wake of shocks, to deliver services to households with greater efficacy (De Ferranti et al. 2000; World Bank 2013).

Governments that fail to take precautionary prevention and insurance measures could increase the likelihood of shocks and the size of losses and will be less effective at responding to households' needs. Like households, governments can fail to insure against aggregate losses from systemic shocks and can ignore the sound economic and fiscal management that can lower the likelihood of these shocks occurring or contain the losses suffered when they occur. Systemic shocks are hitting countries in fast and furious succession. Imprudent governments are often forced to engage in coping measures. Those that prepare cope better: governments that take preventive measures through reforms that encourage fiscal and monetary prudence, invest in human capital, and eliminate distortions in product and factor markets lower the likelihood of future shocks. This averting of shocks improves the position of the state to, in turn, make more risk-pooling options available to households: the cost of premiums for pooling the risk of unemployment, for example, will be lower in countries with sound policies because the probability of bad conditions—high rates of job loss and extended periods of unemployment—will have been lowered by reforms (De Ferranti et al. 2000; World Bank 2013).

The disappointingly slow recovery of labor markets following the global economic and financial crisis has motivated a more proactive jobs policy agenda—presented in the *World Development Report 2013: Jobs* (World Bank 2012)—that fits very well with a risk-sharing framework. The objectives driving this jobs agenda are to increase investments, improve allocative efficiency, promote economic growth, and improve the performance of labor markets at matching households' supply with the economy's demand for work. Indeed, in general, when economies grow, they create jobs. And when there are fewer distortions in the allocation of productive resources— land, labor, and capital—those jobs are created in the sectors and economic activities where they generate the most value. Over time, it is expected that jobs become more productive by increasing productivity within a given job but also by shifting from lower- to higher-productivity sectors, from rural to urban areas, and from informal to formal activities. These structural transformations help to lift people out of poverty and increase standards of living.

However, prudent or preventive policy actions are required to ensure that this process unfolds as expected, such as macroeconomic policies that ensure stability and reduce uncertainty; investments in building connective infrastructure and a business environment that reduces transaction costs and promotes competition and entrepreneurship; the development of good governance and the rule of law to enforce contracts and the appropriability of returns on investments; and, of course, building human capital—people with the good health and skills that the productive economy seeks.

Beyond these fundamentals, additional action is often also required. Market failures complicate and even block the transmission mechanisms between private sector investments, growth, and job creation. Policies that increase investments and maximize the rate of return to capital, and, therefore, output, do not necessarily generate the *distribution of jobs* needed to address problems such as youth unemployment, low market participation rates among women, inequality, and poverty. In fact, at the global level, there is a large variance in the patterns of investment, growth, and job creation (Farole, Ferro, and Gutierrez 2017). The same level of investments in different sectors not only generates a different net number of jobs (which is in some cases negative[3]) but also generates a different composition of jobs with regard to age, gender, and skill level.[4] Furthermore, there is strong *path dependence* in the allocation of investments and job creation across regions. Many rural regions offer little in terms of good job opportunities, yet most poor or vulnerable workers live in these places.[5]

The social value of jobs—their value to society beyond household income and aggregate production—is substantial. Building on the concepts introduced in the *World Development Report 2013: Jobs* (World Bank 2012), Robalino, Romero, and Walker (2017) explain that job-linked externalities are important to consider when making decisions about investments. There are two specific externalities that can deviate patterns of investment and job creation from levels that would be more socially efficient.[6] First, there are *social externalities* related to jobs, most obviously for youth, women, and older people. To illustrate, in the extreme situation of a politically fragile country vulnerable to conflict and violence, there are immediately obvious social externalities linked to jobs for young men if they reduce the risks of criminality and radicalization and contribute to stability. In all contexts, young people who are employed learn critical skills on the job and build their human capital, which can make other workers more productive. Jobs for young women can also produce externalities by facilitating human capital accumulation in their children, both by reducing fecundity and by providing the women with more income to spend on early-childhood development. Second, in the face of high unemployment and underemployment, the market price of labor can deviate from the opportunity cost of labor, generating a *labor externality* (see Jenkins, Kuo, and Harberger 2011, 2). Private investors and existing firms considering a new investment will calculate the internal rate of return based on market prices, but they do not consider the social costs of leaving labor idle.

These externalities create a gap between social and private rates of return on investments and provide a strong justification for targeted subsidies to catalyze private investment. Indeed, even if policy makers succeed in tackling macroeconomic and market environment factors that undermine firms' private investment returns, the private sector *still* might not invest enough, or it might not generate the optimal portfolio of investments, from the point of view of net job outcomes. Private investments that would be socially efficient—in part because of the number and types of jobs they create—might never be made. Instead, an economy can see too much capital going into investments that are less efficient for society from a job-creation perspective. This failure is particularly harmful when there are also learning spillovers[7] and coordination failures,[8] which can further amplify the gap between social and private rates of return that emerge when job-related externalities are considered. Several challenges face policy makers keen to take such proactive measures to catalyze private investment. The first is in measuring the size of the jobs externalities accurately—quantifying these externalities and figuring out whether the benefits of creating a job after accounting for the externalities are worth the opportunity costs of the committed resources. The second is in identifying when the subsidy is no longer required and can be withdrawn. The third challenge is facing down the rent-seeking and other political interests that might resist withdrawal of subsidies when support is no longer justified or required.

## Drivers of Disruption and the Changing Nature of Shocks

Turning from the conceptual framework back to employment-based risk-sharing models, it is easy to see how these models made sense as ways to manage risks in the late industrial period and the decades that followed. At the time, most people in industrialized countries worked—or would eventually take jobs—in factories and firms. The employment-based risk-sharing model matched not only the relative homogeneity of work but also the nature (frequency and size) of probable losses from shocks. To illustrate this point, when few people lived to the age of 60—and most of them for not very long thereafter—pooling this risk by defining benefits made actuarial sense as the main instrument to cover the large but relatively rarely occurring loss of earning ability in old age. Similarly, at a time when most people could reasonably expect to work for a single employer, or at least in the same occupation or sector, for most of their active lives, job loss was a relatively rare event, and thus pooling the risks of losses from unemployment was viable among people working in the same guild, sector, and even the same firm, with employer-provided severance arrangements.

When governments developed sufficient administrative capacity to step in, a mainly risk-pooling model of defined-benefit unemployment insurance was viable and in many cases established.

In addition to a specific statutory share of financial responsibility, the classical employment-based risk-sharing models delegate essential administrative and implementation functions to the firm. These models explicitly assume stable employment relationships, rely on the workplace as a platform for risk management, and delegate enormous implementation responsibilities to employers. In the industrial era, employers were the indispensable and stalwart implementing agents of social protection and labor market policies. Although the state could pass laws and mandate such structures, it could do little else at first. Governments did not yet have extensive administrative and delivery systems and had to rely heavily on firms and their internal labor markets to provide people with career continuity. Firms' administrative structures were indispensable platforms from which risk-sharing policies were implemented. Employers were present and familiar with the day-to-day lives of their workers. They had more information about their employees and had monitoring capacities that few governments at the time could imagine wielding.

At present, however, evidence of the changing nature of work is emerging in every country and calling into question the assumed homogeneity of work and stability of the workplace. How can policy makers take account of the disrupting megatrends to create more effective risk-sharing arrangements? A good way to start is to examine whether these drivers of disruption are altering the nature of the losses that current risk-sharing policies are designed to mitigate. Table 2.2 presents an example of how such an assessment can be conducted in a given context. For each driver of disruption, we have predicted how the nature of losses (frequency, size, and extent of market failure) is changing (positively, negatively, or in uncertain ways). Note that although the drivers of disruption we have highlighted are global, the changes they imply for the natures of shocks and losses are likely to vary widely from place to place.

Many of the parametric and structural reforms to risk-sharing arrangements to date became necessary to accommodate changes to the shocks and losses they were designed to cover (such as more people reaching old age and living longer after withdrawing from full-time work, as well as the rising likelihood of unemployment spells). Changes in contribution rates, eligibility requirements, and benefit levels were one response. Payroll tax–based contributions gradually increased, reaching high and damaging levels, as defined-benefit, pay-as-you-go social insurance systems matured and populations aged. Another response was the advent of policy-mandated collective and individual savings, which were enacted along with structural reforms to national pension systems in several

# Table 2.2 Are the Drivers of Greater Diversity in Forms of Work Also Changing the Nature of Shocks?

*(Analyzing the changing nature of shocks along three dimensions: frequency, size of loss, and extent of market failure)*

| Shock/loss | Driver 1: Technological change | | | Driver 2: Economic integration | | | Driver 3: Social change | | | Driver 4: Demographic change | | | Driver 5: Climate change | | |
|---|---|---|---|---|---|---|---|---|---|---|---|---|---|---|---|
| | ρ | L | Mkt fail | ρ | L | Mkt fail | ρ | L | Mkt fail | ρ | L | Mkt fail | ρ | L | Mkt fail |
| Earnings volatility | + | + | ? | + | ○ | ○ | ○ | ○ | ○ | ○ | ○ | ○ | + | + | + |
| Job loss | + | ? | ○ | ? | ? | ○ | ○ | ○ | ○ | + | + | + | ? | ? | + |
| Long job search periods | − | − | ○ | ○ | ○ | ○ | + | ? | ? | ○ | ○ | ○ | ? | ? | + |
| Outdated/unsought skills | + | + | + | + | + | + | ○ | ○ | ○ | + | + | + | ○ | ○ | ○ |
| Impaired physical capacity | − | − | ○ | ○ | ○ | ○ | ○ | ○ | ○ | + | + | ? | ○ | ○ | ○ |
| Impaired cognitive capacity | − | − | ○ | ○ | ○ | ○ | ○ | ○ | ○ | + | ? | ? | ○ | ○ | ○ |
| Systemic (climate, political, financial) | ○ | ○ | + | + | + | + | ○ | ○ | ○ | ○ | ○ | ○ | + | + | + |

*Note:* + = expected increase; − = expected decrease; ? = change uncertain; ○ = no change expected; ρ = frequency; L = size of loss; Mkt fail = extent of market failure.

countries in Latin America and the Caribbean as well as in the countries of East and Central Europe.

It is difficult to determine how the drivers of disruption are likely to change the nature of losses from shocks. Table 2.2 shows how analysis of the impact of each driver on shocks and market conditions could be organized and applied in a particular country context. The table is intended as an illustration of an analytical approach rather than a complete or cardinal assessment of how the drivers of disruption are changing the main shocks to people's livelihoods. Shocks will vary in their frequency and in the size of the losses they inflict. The conditions that allow markets to effectively respond are obviously very different from country to country. However, as the strains on fiscal and labor markets demonstrate, what once might have been reasonable risk-sharing arrangements are now of questionable resilience, even in high-income countries. This sort of analysis is not straightforward for several reasons. First, in most cases, the drivers of disruption are changing both the downside losses and the upside gains and opportunities of shocks, sometimes simultaneously. As already pointed out, technological change is dramatically altering the task content of jobs, raising the likelihood of unemployment for many—at least in the medium term—but also raising the earnings of others with sought-after skills and opening product and labor markets to people who otherwise would find it too costly to participate. And as this change redefines and even destroys some occupations, it is creating new jobs—not only opportunities to freelance over digital platforms but also the provision of goods and services that even 10 years ago simply did not exist. Second, different drivers of disruption can alter the nature of a shock in different directions. For example, technological innovations in the workplace, such as industrial robots, can automate many routine assembly and light manufacturing jobs, raising the risk of job loss and a long job search for many people. But they can also enable people who would otherwise be constrained by age or impaired physical or cognitive ability to remain economically active.

The drivers of disruption are also changing the extent of market failures, how these failures manifest, and what is a proportionate policy response. Market failures that have always presented problems are likely to manifest in different and possibly more acute ways. Table 2.3 presents our attempt to show how. Using technological change as an example again, although the Internet and digital tools give people more information and are being actively used by many consumers to better inform their choices, the wealth of data it provides can solve some information failures and create others. Paradoxically, in the so-called information age, information failures can become more likely, given the enormous complexity that accompanies new technology and the wealth of choices with which people are presented (Barr and Diamond 2009). The decisions that working people are confronted with today are more complex than those confronted by their parents and grandparents. Many people

**Table 2.3  Are the Drivers of Disruption Also Changing the Market Failures That Policy Tries to Correct?**

*(Principal market failures that motivate risk-sharing policy intervention and likely changes to those market failures)*

| Market failures | Driver 1: Technological change | Driver 2: Economic integration | Driver 3: Social change | Driver 4: Demographic change | Driver 5: Climate change |
|---|---|---|---|---|---|
| Uncertainty (number or size of "uninsurable" prospective losses) | + | ? | + | + and − | + |
| Imperfect information | + and − | ? | ? | ? | + |
| Market power/ asymmetries between purchasers and suppliers of human capital | + and − | ++ | + | ? | ? |
| Incomplete contracts | ? | ? | ? | ? | ? |
| Missing or poorly functioning markets for risk-pooling | − | − | ? | ? | + |
| Missing or poorly functioning self-insurance | ? | ? | ? | ? | ? |
| Behavioral cognitive limitations (such as myopia, inertia, bounded rationality) | + and − | ? | ? | + | ? |
| Coordination failure and learning by doing (such as investments that boost jobs) | − | ? | + | ? | + |

*Note:* ++ = expected great increase; + = expected increase; − = expected decrease; ? = change uncertain.

react to the abundance of choice with bafflement and inaction. Thus, many information market failures may become more acute, motivating a proportionate risk-sharing policy response, albeit a different response than would have been reasonably considered proportionate in the past.

Furthermore, in many of today's disruptions lie solutions. The same disruptive driver can augment policy responses to itself. To illustrate, technology allows us to make very complex computations of the likelihood and nature of events, extending with each technological advance the frontier of probabilistic analysis. A greater number of uncertainties are in this manner becoming risks (that is, shocks with an observed, measurable probability) with which markets have more (though by no means complete or perfect) ability to contend. This change, in turn, shifts the proportionate policy response from one extreme of direct provision to the other extreme of merely regulating market provision and nudging household demand. An illustration of this shift can be found in how the market for longevity insurance (annuities) and long-term care has been evolving in the last two decades. Despite a deluge of data and exponential increases in computational capacity and technical know-how, the market for longevity risk still struggles and requires careful regulation and even outright state provision, including inflation-indexed financial assets in the most advanced countries (Barr and Diamond 2008; World Bank 2016).

## Conceptual Insights and Immediate Policy Implications

The analysis proposed in the previous section need not be comprehensive or conclusive to be useful for policy making. A fully rigorous analytical assessment of the changing nature of losses from shocks and the ability of markets to cover them effectively is too ambitious a task for most countries to undertake. Furthermore, in the time that it would take to complete a comprehensive and conclusive assessment, the nature of the shocks will likely have changed. As discussed earlier, what makes the drivers we are discussing so disruptive is the speed at which they bring about fundamental shifts. That said, there are some global tendencies and common manifestations of these drivers of disruption, many of which have been presented in earlier sections: more frequent changes in employment and occupation, automation of routine tasks, concentration of human settlement in cities, more people crossing national borders for economic reasons, fewer births, and longer and healthier lives.

The general orientation of policy action is already becoming clear. There is sufficient evidence of common trends that point in the same general direction to allow useful and impactful shifts in current policies to be discussed and pursued with confidence. Indeed, there are some policy changes for which an impressive consensus—at least among specialists—has already formed, namely:

- *To mitigate disruption from technological change:* Give greater emphasis in primary and secondary school curricula to development of nonroutine cognitive skills (including socioemotional skills) and start intentional instruction at earlier ages (through purposeful play and other age-appropriate means), when key behaviors of enduring and increasing value in the labor market are more likely to form (Almeida, Behrman, and Robalino 2012; World Bank 2018b).

- *To mitigate losses from greater economic integration*: Provide labor market adjustment assistance in the form of retraining and psychological and placement support—including support for relocation—to people whose skills and experience are no longer sought after or need to be updated and augmented (World Bank 1995; World Bank 2012).
- *To mitigate the impact of demographic change:* Keep people economically active longer by eliminating mandatory retirement thresholds, and formalize less-than-full-time and other flexible contracting arrangements (Bussolo, Koettl, and Sinnott 2015; World Bank 2016).

However, there is vast room for reasonable debate on how to implement such policies to best help households manage risk and uncertainty. This debate is well under way, spurred by the concerns of voters, policy makers, academics, think tanks, and international organizations.

On a broad range of other topics, there is much less consensus, and, indeed, very active debate. If most economically active people are no longer working full time in a long-term, subordinate standard employment relationship, what defining features of the prevailing employment-based risk-sharing policy model are challenged? Clear and crisp distinctions of time use over the life cycle, such as "study," "work," "unemployment," and "retirement" are blurred. Firms' incentives to invest in employees' human capital are changed; the promise of internal labor markets for workers' career continuity and advancement is fading. The reliability of the employer as a stalwart intermediary implementing agent and the firm as a stable implementation platform (the channel of financing, monitoring, information management, enforcement, and so forth) for risk-sharing policies can no longer be taken for granted.

Sustained or increasing diversity of work forms has profound implications for risk-sharing policies designed for—or in anticipation of—a homogenous world of work. Disruptions to people's livelihoods, whether from involuntary separations (cyclical and structural) or geographical or occupational mobility, becomes the "new normal." Many (and in some places, most) working people are in multiple, fluid, and short-term forms of market engagement. Even in high-income countries, it is increasingly likely that a person's earnings come from a portfolio of activities, including selling labor and receiving profits from capital at the same time. It is also not unusual for an individual to change market status from employee to employer to contractor to sole proprietor (in any order or combination) in a span of 10 years. If the share of working people outside of standard employment relationships approaches even 30 percent, society will struggle to rely on employers and firms as a platform for effective policy implementation. Indeed, the social costs of this delegation will outweigh benefits that were once obvious. Any implicit or explicit limitations on access to publicly financed (or subsidized) risk-pooling arrangements based on where and how people work will be distortionary and could become regressive.

A comprehensive policy package of protection can be designed using the insights drawn from the insurance framework presented in this chapter. The once politically convenient mingling of social objectives—enabling actuarial risk pooling, eliminating poverty, and pursuing equity through wealth redistribution—will probably require more explicit distinction and financing channels. To prevent people from falling into poverty, for example, the largest and most effective risk pool is a country's national budget financed from broad-based taxes. Ideally, the decisions about financing alternatives would follow a consideration of the appropriate policy instrument to deploy (risk pooling, saving, prevention) and the proportionate policy response given what risk-pooling mechanisms and other instruments are available through markets. Figure 2.4 presents a stylized package of protection against losses from livelihood shocks. The innermost core represents the guaranteed minimum support to cover the most catastrophic losses, for which there are no viable or effective market alternatives and which ideally—but not always—are relatively rare. Interventions to cover more frequently occurring, lower-loss events that have obvious and substantial external social benefits from coverage could pragmatically and efficiently be included in this guaranteed

**Figure 2.4 A Conceptually Comprehensive Package of Risk-Sharing Instruments Can Be Designed According to the Nature of Losses and Market Failures**

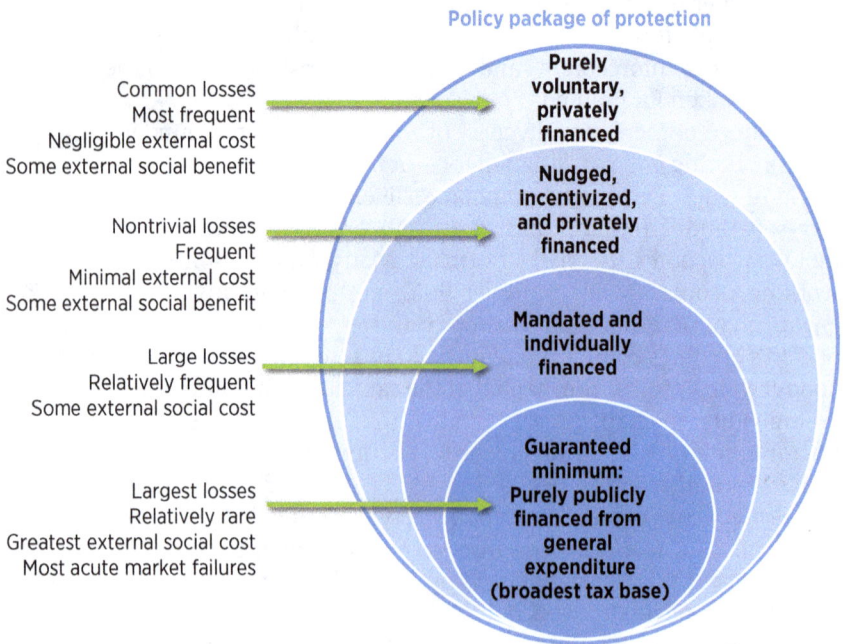

minimum support. In the three remaining segments of the stylized package of protection, responsibility for financing and provision shifts gradually away from purely public resources and direct government provision to household or individual financing and market provision. The specific contents of this package are developed in greater detail in later chapters.

## Notes

1. Based on Barr (2012), Ehrlich and Becker (1972, 1992), and Gill and Ilahi (2000). A fuller presentation of our conceptual framework, underpinned by economic and actuarial principles, is provided in appendix A.
2. See, for example, Dreze and Sen (1989) for an early and seminal discussion of social policy objectives. For an extension of a risk management framework to include assets, see Jørgensen and Siegel (2019).
3. For a discussion of the indirect jobs and general equilibrium effects, see Robalino, Romero, and Walker (2017).
4. For more information on this effect, see the *Tunisia Systematic Country Diagnostic* (World Bank 2015).
5. For more information on this effect, see Merotto (2017).
6. The *World Development Report 2013: Jobs* (World Bank 2012) points to some of the sources of social externalities related to jobs: (i) women who have a job invest more in the human capital of their children; (ii) youth who have a job learn on the job and make other workers in society more productive; and (iii) jobs can contribute to peace and social stability.
7. Investments in new technologies and products can push the technological frontier forward and facilitate future innovation. They also can increase firms' absorptive capacity (their ability to assimilate knowledge from their environment) and therefore help firms identify further opportunities for investment and job creation (Aghion and Jaravel 2015).
8. Coordination failures emerge when economic agents are unable to achieve coordination among complementary activities. Coordination failures can lead the market to an outcome inferior to the situation if resources could be allocated efficiently. Job social externalities can amplify coordination failures (see, for instance, Rodrik 2006).

## References

Aghion, P., and X. Jaravel. 2015. "Knowledge Spillovers, Innovation and Growth." *The Economic Journal* 125 (583): 533–573.

Almeida, R., J. Behrman, and D. Robalino. 2012. *The Right Skills for the Job? Rethinking Training Policies for Workers.* Human Development Perspective Series. Washington, DC: World Bank.

Baeza, C., and T. Packard. 2006. *Beyond Survival: Protecting Households from Health Shocks in Latin America.* Stanford, CA: Stanford University Press.

Barr, N. 2001. *The Welfare State as Piggy Bank.* New York: Oxford University Press.

————. 2012. *The Economics of the Welfare State,* 5th edition. New York: Oxford University Press.

Barr, N., and P. Diamond. 2008. *Reforming Pensions: Principles and Policy Choices.* New York: Oxford University Press.

————. 2009. "Reforming Pensions: Principles, Analytical Errors, and Policy Directions." *International Social Security Review* 62 (2): 5–29.

Brown, J. R., and A. Finkelstein. 2011. "Insuring Long-Term Care in the United States." *Journal of Economic Perspectives,* 25 (4): 119–42.

Bussolo, M., J. Koettl, and E. Sinnott. 2015. *Golden Aging: Prospects for Healthy, Active, and Prosperous Aging in Europe and Central Asia.* Washington, DC: World Bank.

Cremer, H., P. Pestieau, and K. Roeder. 2015. "Social Long-Term Care Insurance with Two-Sided Altruism." *Research in Economics* 70: 101–109.

De Ferranti, D., G. Perry, I. Gill, and L. Serven. 2000. *Securing Our Future in a Global Economy.* World Bank Latin American and Caribbean Studies. Washington, DC: World Bank.

Dercon, S. 2002. "Income Risks, Coping Strategies and Safety Nets." *World Bank Research Observer* 17 (2): 141–166.

Dreze, J., and A. Sen. 1989. *Hunger and Public Action.* Oxford: Clarendon Press.

Ehrlich, I., and G. Becker. 1972. "Market Insurance, Self-Insurance, and Self-Protection." *Journal of Political Economy* 80: 623–48.

————. 1992. "Market Insurance, Self-Insurance, and Self-Protection." In *Foundations of Insurance Economics: Readings in Economics and Finance,* edited by G. Dionne and S. Harrington. Boston: Kluwer Academic Publishers.

Farole, T., E. Ferro, and V. M. Gutierrez. 2017. *Job Creation in the Private Sector: An Exploratory Assessment of Patterns and Determinants at the Macro, Sector, and Firm Levels.* Washington, DC: World Bank.

Gill, I., and N. Ilahi. 2000. "Economic Insecurity, Individual Behavior, and Social Policy." Office of the Chief Economist, Latin America and Caribbean Region, World Bank, Washington, DC.

Heltberg, R., and N. Lund. 2009. "Shocks, Coping, and Outcomes for Pakistan's Poor: Health Risks Predominate." *Journal of Development Studies* 45 (6): 889–910.

Hoddinott, J., and A. Quisumbing. 2010. "Methods for Microeconometric Risk and Vulnerabilty Assessment." In *Risk, Shocks, and Human Development: On the Brink,* edited by R. Fuentes-Nieva and P. Seck, 62–100. Basingstoke, UK: Palgrave Macmillan.

Holzmann, R., and S. Jørgensen. 2000. "Social Risk Management: A New Conceptual Framework for Social Protection and Beyond." Social Protection Discussion Paper No. 6, World Bank, Washington, DC.

Jenkins, G. P., C.-Y. Kuo, and A. C. Harberger. 2011. "Cost-Benefit Analysis for Investment Decisions: The Integrated Analysis of Investment Projects." Development Discussion Paper 2011-1, Queens University, Kingston, Canada.

Jørgensen, S., and P. Siegel. 2019. "Social Risk Management 2.0: Social Protection in an Age of Global Disruption." Social Protection and Jobs Global Practice, World Bank, Washington, DC.

Merotto, D. L. 2017. "Zambia—Jobs Diagnostic (English)." Job Series no. 7, World Bank, Washington, DC.

Narayan, D. 2000. *Can Anyone Hear Us? Voices of the Poor.* Washington, DC: World Bank.

OECD (Organisation for Economic Co-operation and Development). 2011. "Help Wanted? Providing and Paying for Long-Term Care." Health Policy Studies, Organisation for Economic Co-operation and Development, Paris.

Robalino, D., J. Romero, and I. Walker. 2017. "Guidance Note on the Economic Analysis of Jobs Investment Projects." Jobs Working Paper No. 7, World Bank, Washington, DC.

Rodrik, D. 2006. "Goodbye Washington Consensus, Hello Washington Confusion? A Review of the World Bank's *Economic Growth in the 1990s: Learning from a Decade of Reform.*" *Journal of Economic Literature,* 44 (4): 973–987.

Sen, A. 1999. *Development as Freedom.* Oxford, UK: Oxford University Press.

Siegel, P. B., and J. Alwang. 1999. "An Asset-Based Approach to Social Risk Management: A Conceptual Framework." SP Discussion Paper 9926, Social Protection Unit, Human Development Network, World Bank, Washington, DC.

Siegel, P., and S. Jørgensen. 2013. "Global Climate Change Justice: Toward a Risk-Adjusted Social Floor." IDS Working Paper Volume 2013 No. 426, Institute of Development Studies, London.

World Bank. 1995. *World Development Report 1995: Workers in an Integrating World.* Washington, DC: World Bank.

———. 2012. *World Development Report 2013: Jobs.* Washington, DC: World Bank.

———. 2013. *World Development Report 2014: Risk and Opportunity—Managing Risk for Development.* Washington, DC: World Bank.

———. 2015. *Tunisia Systematic Country Diagnostic,* Washington, DC: World Bank.

———. 2016. *Live Long and Prosper: Aging in East Asia and Pacific.* World Bank East Asia and Pacific Regional Report, Washington, DC.

———. 2018a. *The State of Social Safety Nets 2018.* Washington, DC: World Bank.

———. 2018b. *World Development Report 2018: Learning to Realize Education's Promise.* Washington, DC: World Bank.

# 3

# From an Employment-Based to a Comprehensive Model of Risk Sharing

To be relevant and effective in a diverse and diversifying world of work, risk-sharing policies must be fundamentally rethought. As argued in chapter 1, a powerful combination of persistent challenges and new disruptions to the world of work requires this scrutiny. Its motivating circumstances may differ between high-, middle-, and lower-income countries (Chandy 2016; IPPR 2018; OECD 2018). However, reassessments seem to converge on the need for the state to provide people with guaranteed minimum protection that is more extensive, accessible, and responsive and is financed from a broader base than most countries' prevailing social insurance and social assistance programs. Although its prospect can seem daunting, the establishment of a guaranteed minimum of protection may require of many countries only that they continue to move along a path they have already started down, albeit with more deliberate and ambitious rethinking (per arguments laid out in Gill, Packard, and Yermo 2005; Grosh et al. 2008; Holzmann, Robalino, and Takayama 2009; Ribe, Robalino, and Walker 2012; Rofman, Apella, and Vezza 2014).

To be effective, risk-sharing instruments should be accessible to people no matter how they engage in the market to earn a living and pursue prosperity. An immediate observation following this statement is that to achieve the specific objectives of preventing poverty and covering potentially impoverishing losses, the de jure distinction between *contributory* social insurance and *noncontributory* social assistance will have to be blurred and possibly eventually abandoned altogether. Through the lens of public economics, the distinction between the two is secondary and cosmetic, if not largely irrelevant to how benefits are de facto financed. Indeed, the current distinction between "contributory" and "noncontributory" social programs has little meaning in countries where the largest, most consistent, and often the fastest-growing source of financing for social insurance benefits is transfers from governments' general budgets and revenues. In the worst case, maintaining the distinction can be a source of exclusion, causing regressive distribution and perpetuating inequality (Gill, Packard, and Yermo 2005; Lustig 2018).

Because the majority of working people go without coverage or are underinsured, the most vital of these risk-sharing instruments is a publicly financed risk-pooling mechanism. The largest risk-pooling mechanism in any country is typically the public finance system of taxation and expenditure, because almost all residents and citizens contribute to this system through one tax channel or another. Thus, all transfers financed from this risk pool can be considered *insurance*.[1] Furthermore, direct transfers from the risk pool will be more effective when complemented with the judicious use of obligations and inducements for people to take additional measures and thus to insure themselves and their families as comprehensively as possible against shocks and losses. In pursuit of better risk-sharing policy, social assistance and social insurance programs (as they have come to be known in all countries), along with accompanying mandates and incentives to save and insure through regulated quasi- or pure-market mechanisms, are *all* ways that the state can provide *insurance assistance*.

In this chapter, we describe a comprehensive policy package of protection from shocks and losses that relies little, to be effective, on where or how people work. The package has a publicly financed guaranteed-minimum risk-pooling mechanism at its core, along with additional layers of mandated, nudged, and wholly voluntary market insurance. Building on the conceptual discussion in chapter 2, this chapter describes the most salient and broadly applicable features of this package, as shown in figure 3.1. In some countries, what is described in the broadest terms in figure 3.1 is generally, if perhaps not intentionally or coherently, already in place. And the fiscal and administrative capacity to offer what we are proposing is within the reach of many countries, putting aside the formidable political obstacles that would undoubtedly arise from groups with a vested interest in the current employment-based risk-sharing models. For other countries, where the fiscal and administrative capacity to realize the comprehensive package is still lacking and will take many years to build, the approach shown in figure 3.1 may be only aspirational for the foreseeable future. But in many of these countries—the

**Figure 3.1  Governments Should Aspire to Offer People a Comprehensive Package of Insurance Assistance**

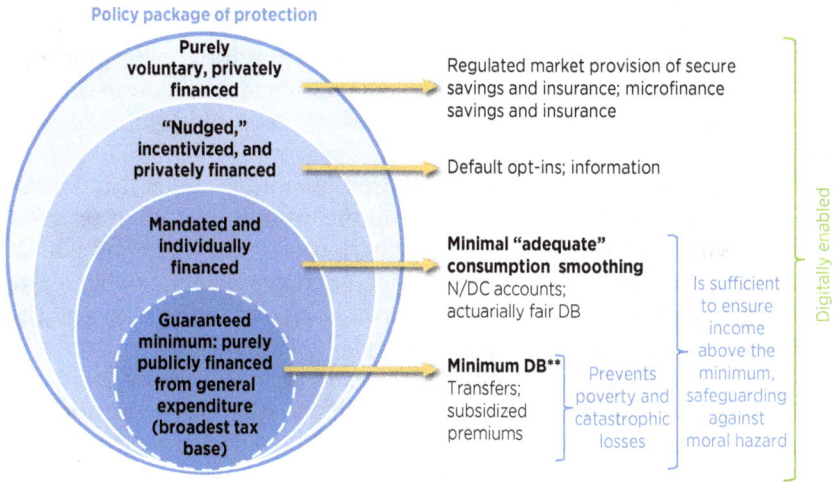

Policy package of protection

Purely voluntary, privately financed → Regulated market provision of secure savings and insurance; microfinance savings and insurance

"Nudged," incentivized, and privately financed → Default opt-ins; information

Mandated and individually financed → **Minimal "adequate" consumption smoothing** N/DC accounts; actuarially fair DB

Guaranteed minimum: purely publicly financed from general expenditure (broadest tax base) → **Minimum DB**\*\* Transfers; subsidized premiums

Prevents poverty and catastrophic losses

Is sufficient to ensure income above the minimum, safeguarding against moral hazard

Digitally enabled

*Note:* DB = defined benefit; N/DC = notional or defined contribution. \*\* Replaces contributory minimum guarantees and tax incentives.

lowest-income countries in particular—the legacy employment-based approach is *also* aspirational. Aspirations encourage and bring about policy choices with consequences that unfold over long time spans. So, for these countries, we believe that the proposed package of comprehensive insurance assistance is a better aspirational goal to work toward.

To be broadly applicable in a diverse set of countries, our proposal gives greater weight to policy objectives than to specific instruments or programs. For example, to provide effective and affordable coverage, the core of the package includes two indispensable components of public risk-sharing policy: transfers to prevent poverty and subsidies to cover the premiums for contingent coverage of catastrophic losses. Both components draw resources from the national general-expenditure budget. These two elements of the core are discussed first, then the "layers" around the core: mandated, nudged, and purely voluntary forms of insurance (risk pooling and individual savings). A dashed border separates the core guaranteed minimum from the next layer, "mandated consumption smoothing." This border is intended to represent specific design features that (a) provide protection from losses that would exhaust even the most generous flat benefits and (b) ensure integration of instruments that primarily benefit the poorest people with instruments designed for the entire population. This integration is a safeguard against ghettos of exclusion in risk-sharing systems. A similar dashed line might be drawn between the mandated layer of the package and the nudged layer, to reflect the limits on most governments' abilities to observe people's work and to compel participation in consumption smoothing. After the concepts are discussed, simple simulations are provided to illustrate some of the magnitudes of the costs and the trade-offs between different design parameters.

In the risk-sharing sense, the proposed guarantees extend universal coverage, but benefit payments are contingent and should be progressive. As with the public policy and provision of health care and education, *universality* does not necessarily mean that every person will receive a payout in a given period or, equally, from each part of the package. The essential, inalienable meaning of universality in many policy arenas is that a benefit or service is available *when and where it is needed* to all citizens, and, in many cases, even to all residents. Many benefits and services will not be needed by many people in a given period, or even at all, or people might choose to forgo receipt of goods or services to which they are entitled. In a discussion of risk-sharing policy, what is vital is the *universality of entitlement* to coverage of impoverishing losses. Those who do not suffer such losses may be covered by the guarantee but never receive a payout.

## The Core of Insurance Assistance: Guaranteed Minimum Poverty Prevention

The policy objective of the core minimum guarantee is to prevent poverty and further impoverishment of people who are already poor. Social protection policy instruments are deployed to promote people out of poverty as well as to make up for missing or exclusionary markets for credit and insurance (Dreze and Sen 1989; Holzmann and Jørgensen 2000; World Bank 2012). The distinction between these objectives is important. Emphasizing the objective of helping people manage risk does not discount the promotion objectives (Grosh et al. 2008). And, as pointed out in chapter 2, the two objectives are closely intertwined. Furthermore, even the best-designed minimum consumption support programs, which draw on resources from the broadest and deepest risk pools, will have more effect when supported by other policies to loosen constraints on people.[2] Nonetheless, a minimum guarantee is a powerful instrument to allow people to take appropriate risks and reach for opportunities. The innermost circle of the comprehensive package of insurance assistance depicted in figure 3.1 consists of transfers financed from general revenue, as motivated by the risk-sharing principles presented in chapter 2.

The notion that there should be some sort of minimum protection is also congruent with other perspectives that motivate social protection programming. A human-rights perspective would examine how well a legislated minimum standard of living is realized. A social-justice perspective might be concerned both with the absolute status of the poor and with inequalities in either income or other outcomes between groups of people. A human-capital orientation would examine how well people (particularly children and youths) are achieving full health and a high standard in learning.

The core minimum can be shaped in different ways. At one extreme of this continuum, a guaranteed minimum income (GMI) program (such as those found in many European countries) can be characterized as a *minimal-minimum* model: strict, means-based targeting intended to prevent poverty with the lowest possible draw on the budget, albeit with a higher risk of undercoverage of poor people and significant work disincentives. At the other extreme of the continuum, universal basic income (UBI) could be considered a *maximal-minimum* option when set generously. A UBI would have fewer errors of exclusion and would provide fewer work disincentives but would also require substantially more government resources to finance. An intermediate option on this continuum is, when tax systems are functional, a negative income tax (NIT) with a relatively high eligibility threshold and a gradual withdrawal of benefits as people's market incomes rise. Another intermediate option is a smallish targeted poverty benefit supplemented with age-categorical transfers, such as a child allowance or a social pension, or combined with an earned income tax credit (EITC). The variety of now-familiar social assistance programs—poverty-targeted and "categorical" cash transfers, food stamps and in-kind food transfers, payments made to participants in labor-intensive public works, and so on—are all parts of current social protection programming that help fill the conceptual space of a guaranteed minimum.

The most viable options for providing guaranteed minimum protections will vary across countries and in the same country over time as it develops. Figure 3.2 compares, in a stylized way, some common designs of poverty prevention instruments, with reference to the poverty line.[3] In the left panel, child allowances may be (but are not always) available to all children up to a set age threshold and are fairly low in value. They are meant to provide a minor income supplement to parents of the children. Social pensions (again, sometimes but not always available to all elderly people) usually have higher levels of benefits, meant to substitute for earnings of former workers. In the right panel, guaranteed minimum income programs often are very tightly targeted to the poorest families; have fairly high benefits, as they are income substitution programs; and have steep benefit withdrawal rates as income increases. Conditional cash transfer (CCT) programs are often designed to reach

### Figure 3.2 Minimum Guarantee Programs Have the Same Basic Function but Take Many Forms

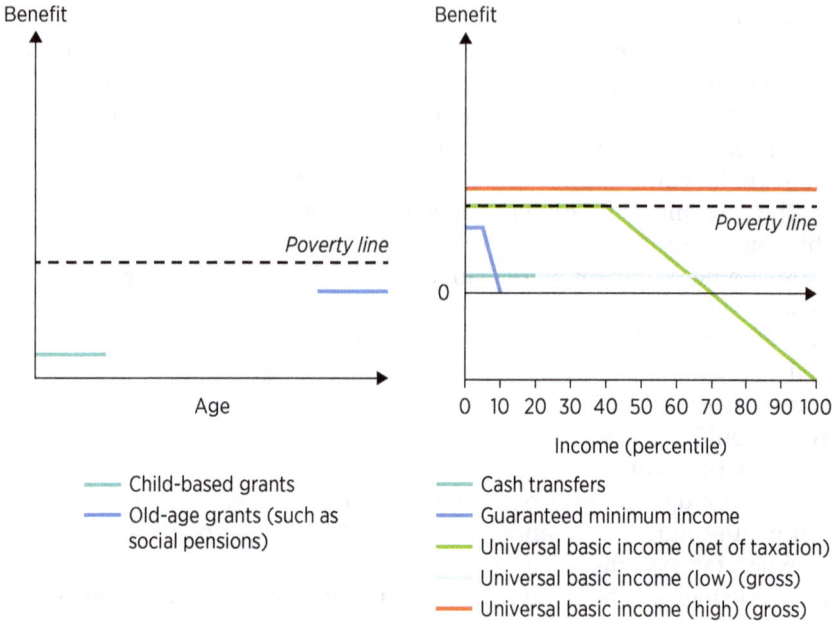

- Child-based grants
- Old-age grants (such as social pensions)

- Cash transfers
- Guaranteed minimum income
- Universal basic income (net of taxation)
- Universal basic income (low) (gross)
- Universal basic income (high) (gross)

*Note:* The figure presents a stylized representation of alternative benefit and eligibility structures for minimum guarantee programs.

more households with lesser benefits and tend to have sharp withdrawal functions as households pass their eligibility thresholds (usually defined by an asset-based proxy of welfare and by the ages of children in the household). A UBI—as the term has come to be used—is a flat amount paid to all people regardless of their means. However, if the amount is considered part of taxable income, the net benefit can be withdrawn from the wealthiest people through a progressive tax system (and becomes equivalent to a NIT). A vital consideration when determining eligibility and delivery of benefits is whether entitlement is granted to individuals or to households (see box 3.1).

The direction of travel we propose is away from a minimal minimum and toward a more substantial minimum, or even a maximal minimum. As is evident from the still pervasive problems of poverty and low human capital, the current core minimum is insufficient. How far countries choose to move in the proposed direction, or how quickly they can accomplish such moves, will vary, a theme we pick up in chapter 5.

BOX 3.1

## The Individual or the Household as the Unit of Analysis?

When discussing risk-sharing schemes, it is important to consider whether to use the individual or the household as the unit of analysis. From a human-rights or social-justice perspective, one obviously wants all individuals to enjoy at least the prescribed minimum protections. Workers' rights and benefits also pertain most clearly to individual workers. But the household or family is the most basic unit of risk management in society, with workers providing for dependent children, at least, and often for nonworking spouses, parents, or other relatives. Also, most poverty analysis is based on survey data in which the household is the unit of observation for many (though not all) descriptors of welfare. In fact, the household is usually defined around eating from a common pot and sharing a dwelling, which implies pooled resources for the largest consumption streams. Thus, discourse in social protection commonly moves back and forth between individual-centric and household-centric perspectives.

To understand appropriate benefit designs and implementation arrangements and the expected impacts of social protection programming, it is important to think about the degree to which the individual and the household can or should be separated. To what degree will benefits nominally directed toward one family member be shared? Will benefits for one family member encourage or discourage the work of other family members? Are some family members (perhaps girls or women, the elderly, or those with disabilities) systematically less favored in family decision making or in the sharing of household resources, and can benefit design affect this? Can individuals or households be identified, in practice, and can their welfare levels or enrollment in various benefits or services be tracked? Individuals are increasingly covered by countries' foundational identity systems. Households, however, have no equivalent common enumeration system and change their composition as individuals are born or die, or move in or out of the household. Despite this complication, the household is often the unit of eligibility for benefits.

With our focus on changes in the world of work, we are predominantly concerned with individual workers. Yet, since our discussion is also about risk sharing, we recognize that the (usually family-based) household is often of first-order importance. To the degree that current social protection policy is defined sometimes around individuals and sometimes around families, we switch fluidly from one perspective to the other.

Many countries, including those at the lowest levels of income and institutional development, are already moving in the direction of providing a viable guaranteed minimum. Three key approaches are consistent with a progressive realization of a guaranteed minimum: (i) new and increasingly popular single national flagship interventions, a few of which are quite large; (ii) an aggregation of many separate interventions that, combined, take the shape of a substantial minimum guarantee that tapers away gradually as market income rises; and (iii) an increasingly blurred distinction between social insurance and social assistance, whether by default or by design, that results in a core guaranteed minimum. These three trends, hereafter discussed, are mutually compatible and are often combined.

National flagship interventions anchor a core minimum, though not necessarily a guaranteed one. From their origins in Latin America, such national, poverty-targeted, conditional cash transfer programs have now spread to more than 60 countries. Coverage of these flagship programs varies from just a few percent of the population to well over 20 percent. An even larger number of countries offer unconditional cash transfer programs. Labor-intensive public works programs have grown just as common. By 2014, about 101 economies had old-age social pensions, some universal and some poverty-targeted. Food-oriented safety nets (targeted food rations, subsidies, or food vouchers) reach about 1.5 billion people. In Africa, more than 20 safety net programs a year have been launched in nine of the past eleven years (considering all types of safety net programs).

A combination of programs can resemble a guaranteed minimum when aggregated. In Europe, most countries have an explicit GMI. However, these programs tend to be small and only one part of the social policy that helps build the provided minimum package. Child allowances (universal in some cases, targeted in others), heating allowances (targeted), and minimum pensions are also important for poverty prevention (and reduction) and have much larger budget allocations. Similarly, in Brazil, the Bolsa Família program's minimum guarantee is complemented by a smaller benefit for those who are somewhat less poor and by social pension programs for the elderly poor (the *Benefício de Prestação Continuada* [BPC] and the quasi-contributory Rural Pension in the *Regime Geral de Previdência Social* [RGPS]) and for the disabled poor (the BPC *Benefício assistencial ao idoso e à pessoa com deficiência*). Figure 3.3 illustrates the social assistance transfer *landscape* of Poland and Brazil on the basis of the largest programs in those countries.[4] The jagged, sometimes steep cliffs in these landscapes present households with disincentives either to work or to work in jobs that can be observed, lest they lose eligibility for benefits. Together, the GMIs and the other programs form a policy package that has a larger footprint than the small GMIs alone, though a smaller one than universal coverage would

**Figure 3.3** **When Aggregated, Safety-Net Programs in Brazil and Poland Begin to Resemble a Minimum Poverty-Prevention Guarantee**

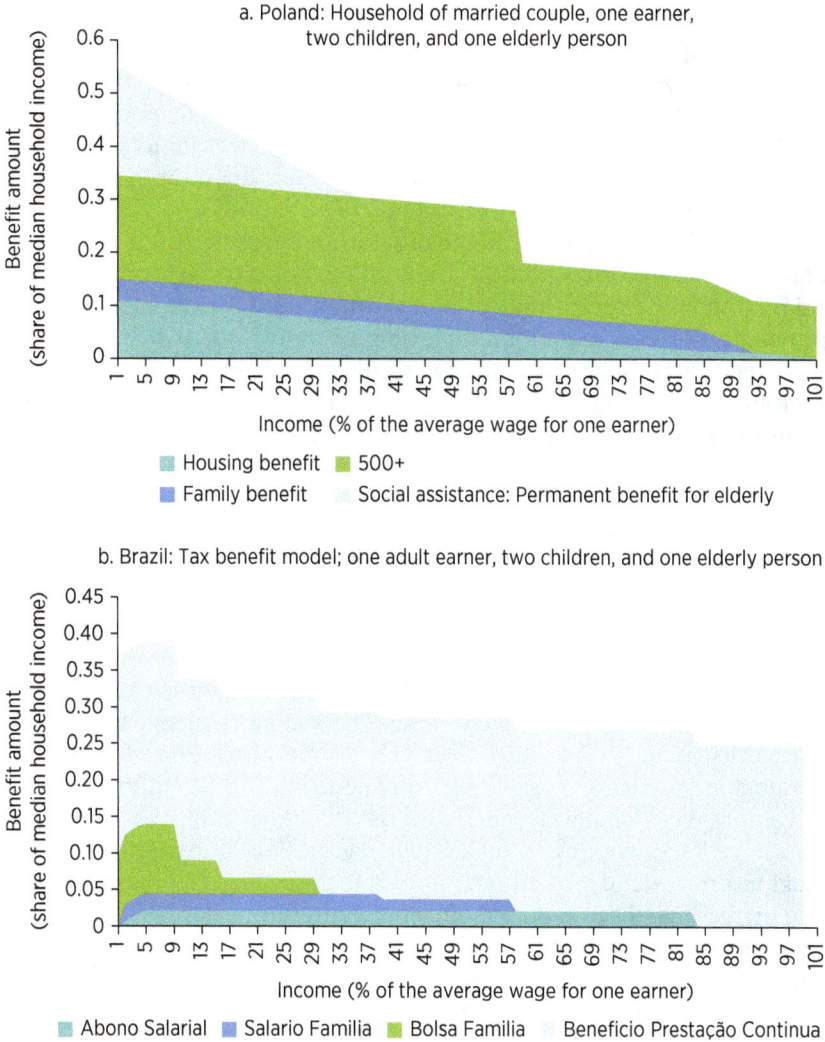

a. Poland: Household of married couple, one earner, two children, and one elderly person

Income (% of the average wage for one earner)

- Housing benefit
- Family benefit
- 500+
- Social assistance: Permanent benefit for elderly

b. Brazil: Tax benefit model; one adult earner, two children, and one elderly person

Income (% of the average wage for one earner)

- Abono Salarial
- Salario Familia
- Bolsa Familia
- Beneficio Prestação Continua

*Source:* Bargu and Morgandi (2018) for Poland and application to Brazil.

*Note:* This figure shows the de jure amount of poverty-prevention benefits a representative household is eligible for, by income (measured as a percentage of the average wage of one-earner households). In Brazil the Beneficio Prestação Continua (Brazil's social pension) is awarded according to the individual recipient's market income. The family income of the adult child of the elderly person is not included in the income assessment for the benefit, and thus in panel b, the benefit amount does not decline as the market income of the adult earner rises. Abono Salarial is a wage top-up, Salario Familia is a child allowance, Bolsa Familia is a targeted family conditional cash transfer, and Beneficio Prestação Continua is a targeted social pension for the elderly.

have, and with progressive incidence of benefits, though with more stepped benefits than the smooth taper of a GMI. A similar benefit topography can be observed in many more countries, where some benefits are narrowly targeted and others apply more broadly.

Achieving a smoothly declining benefit slope is challenging in systems of multiple benefits and administration structures. Although the composite benefit structure may imply on paper that, on average, poorer households receive larger benefits, the structure imperfectly mimics a smoothly declining share of benefits as income (or another indicator of household means) increases. Various peaks and notches occur as people fit eligibility criteria for different benefits, some of which are welfare based, but others of which are categorical (that is, given out according to age, family composition, disability, work status, or homeownership, for example). Multiple programs may also require multiple administrative systems. Shared eligibility registries or shared information systems that feed data from programs back into a coordinated system can attenuate the problem of redundant administrative efforts, but such systems are still being built in many countries. Countries with fewer programs could focus on these programs' essential features in order to more effectively deliver a guaranteed poverty-prevention benefit.

An important feature of the core guaranteed minimum we propose is precisely the guarantee, but this aspect of such programs has proven difficult for countries to deliver. The first and most fundamental challenge of a guarantee, of course, is collecting and assigning enough fiscal resources to the task and maintaining a fiscal stance that can handle the risk of cyclical increases in costs from time to time. The second challenge is in fostering participation. People must be aware of the program(s), face low or reasonable transaction costs to securing benefits, and be willing and able to comply with whatever paperwork or conditions apply. Several countries have been working to make their registration processes more agile, making on-demand procedures more widely available. Countries have also increasingly been working on active outreach by devising communication strategies, working to extend official identity documents to those without them, and the like. However, these barriers are endemic, and such work is rarely complete. The final challenge is to enable program administrators to clearly determine who meets eligibility criteria. Income is hard to observe and volatile, making assessments of eligibility for poverty-prevention programs difficult and error-prone. Governments are using a variety of techniques, often simultaneously, to get the best assessments feasible at manageable operational costs. As discussed at greater length in chapter 5, improvements in the coverage and use of unique personal identification numbers and digital technologies could bring about more agile data checking across various sources and improve eligibility determination. It will take years to get these systems working on a mass scale, and many countries are just beginning the adoption process, but the worldwide trend is toward more powerful and accessible data systems.

Interest is growing in the potential and limits of offering more extensive and ambitious guarantees against poverty, which could greatly reduce the risk of exclusion. As societies have grown more comfortable with formal safety net programs and governments have gotten better at reaching the poorest, concern has risen for the exclusion and perverse incentives caused by tight targeting. These concerns are motivating a growing interest in universal child grants and may have informed a number of social pension initiatives (ILO and UNICEF 2019). Such concerns seem also to contribute to the ubiquitous discussion of UBI, the boldest of the guarantees depicted in figure 3.2. NIT proposals—shown in figure 3.4—make fewer headlines today but, like the UBI, offer (under specific design parameters) a guarantee to all people.

**Figure 3.4    The Merits and Drawbacks of More Extensive Poverty Prevention Guarantee Instruments Have Been Debated for Years**

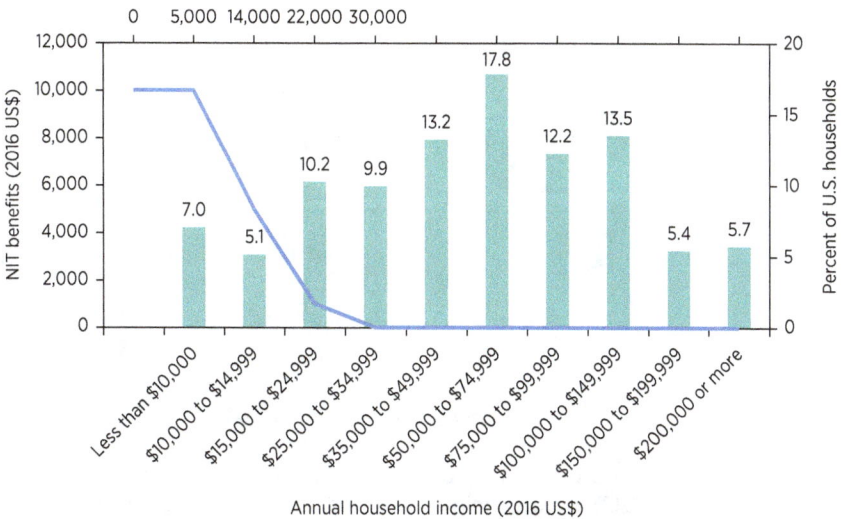

Annual household income (2016 US$)

*Source:* Based on data from the U.S. Census Bureau's 2012–2016 American Community Survey 5-Year Estimates to update Friedman 1987.

*Note:* This figure shows the benefit structure of a negative income tax (NIT), as proposed in Milton Friedman's 1970 Family Assistance Plan (Friedman 1987), updated to reflect the 2016 U.S. household income distribution. The U.S. median household income in 2016 was US$57,617.

The UBI is an instrument proposed in pursuit of numerous policy objectives, including preventing poverty.[5] In the generally accepted lexicon of the social assistance community and the evolving taxonomy of assistance transfer instruments, a program needs to meet five criteria in order to be accepted as a UBI. First, a UBI is universal, that is, meant for everyone living in a polity independently of need, income, or employment status. Second, it is provided in the form of cash, as opposed to in-kind transfers and services. Third, it is rendered unconditionally of activities such as training or work. Fourth, it is paid on a regular and permanent basis and at uniform amounts for everyone. And fifth, it is meant for individuals, not households or communities. NITs function similarly, except that their benefits decline as recipients' incomes rise. The rate of decline can be designed to result in the ideal gradual slope discussed earlier. This structure has two implications. First, it generates a marginal tax rate (MTR) on earned income (for example, in the U.S. experiments cited, the MTR for the target population was on average 50 percent—that is, 50 cents of benefits were taken away for each dollar earned). Second, at a certain break-even point, program benefits would be zero: at that threshold, the costs of the program, such as taxes to finance it, would outweigh the benefits of program participation (for example, in the U.S. pilot programs, this point was reached at an income level 1.8 times the poverty line). These instruments are not new, per se—their merits and drawbacks have been the subject of significant debate for decades—but they are largely untested at scale (see box 3.2). As such, they are both intriguing and risky.

---

**BOX 3.2**

### Experiences with Universal Basic Incomes and Negative Income Taxes

Mongolia had a fully fledged universal basic income (UBI) that covered its entire population, although only for a short period. The program provided US$16.60 per month to 2.8 million people and lasted for two years (2010–2012) before being unwound when resource revenues proved an unstable financial support. The Islamic Republic of Iran also had a program that closely resembled a UBI for a short period: in 2011, energy subsidies were replaced by cash transfers for the entire population, with subsequent gradual downsizing from 21 million households

*continued next page*

**Box 3.2** *(continued)*

at the start of the program to about 17 million today. The program currently provides about US$45 per month per person. In Iraq, the national Public Distribution system for subsidized food is universal and contributes to about 75 percent of the caloric intake of people in the poorest quintile.

Supplementing these three national experiences are a wealth of ongoing small-scale experiments. Finland undertook a randomized controlled trial that provided 2,000 unemployed citizens with nearly US$600 per month over two years; in Oakland, California, in the United States, 100 families were provided with up to US$2,000 per month over a year; and 250 Dutch households in Utrecht and nearby municipalities will receive US$1,100 per month over two years. The Canadian province of Ontario is preparing a test that will provide 4,000 people with US$13,300 per year. In Kenya, a pilot is underway to provide a UBI to 11,500 people over two years (plus a second group of 6,000 people covered for twelve years). Except for the Kenya pilot, these schemes do not test a pure UBI but rather variants of targeted schemes.

Similarly, a range of subnational resource-dividend schemes are in place. The Alaska Permanent Fund in the United States, for example, is designed to redistribute oil revenues to all Alaska residents. In 2016, the Fund distributed about US$2,000 each to 660,000 individuals. A conceptually similar program in the United States involves sharing dividends from casinos: for instance, since 1997, the tribal government of the Eastern Band of the Cherokee Nation has distributed a portion of its profits to 16,000 adult members of the tribe. An analogous scheme is now under way in Macao SAR, China.

Past negative income tax (NIT) trials can also help illuminate some empirical questions. In the United States, the Nixon administration had considered an NIT as part of its Family Assistance Plan (which passed one chamber of the country's legislature but not the other). To inform the bill, a set of experiments were conducted between 1968 and 1974 that reached nearly 8,700 households across 7 U.S. states (Colorado, Indiana, Iowa, New Jersey, North Carolina, Pennsylvania, and Washington). The U.S. experience was mirrored by Canada's "Mincome" scheme in Manitoba: running from 1975 to 1979, this scheme covered 1,300 households in the cities of Winnipeg and Dauphin. Appendix B provides a summary of such experiences.

*Source:* Gentilini et al. 2019.

In countries with a progressive tax system and where all income is subject to tax, such as a progressive income tax, a UBI and an NIT can be the same policy in different guises. The two interventions can result in the same outcome in terms of net income distribution (Tondani 2009). However, they differ substantially in how they are implemented. First, a UBI requires a larger fiscal commitment than an NIT in terms of expenditure and taxes. Second, when a UBI can be financed from a revenue source other than the personal income tax, some equivalence to an NIT is foregone.

A key difference between an NIT and a UBI lies in administrative requirements, specifically, the government's ability to observe income or other measures of well-being. In a country where incomes are observable, an NIT is a more progressive way than a UBI to deliver the minimum poverty prevention guarantee. Although such observation of income is not yet an option in most low- and middle-income countries, the substantial and rapid increase in digital information available to governments is making it ever more possible to rank households based on income proxies in a way that allows governments to mimic a progressive tax system. Rather than collect taxes, however, the government could reduce the amount of benefits the UBI program pays out to more affluent households. This *tapering* of the UBI as wealth rises—a tapered UBI (TUBI)—is similar to how the old-age "solidarity" pension in Chile has been offered since 2009. For this program, households are ranked from poorest to richest based on administrative data. Households in the bottom 60 percent of the distribution that have an elderly member are eligible for the noncontributory pension (the *Pensión Básica Solidaria* [PBS]). The amount of this benefit is reduced, however, for each peso of that person's contributory pension income. The result is a gently tapering benefit.

To serve as the core of a comprehensive package of protection, the guaranteed minimum would ideally be available to all those in need, provide adequate benefit levels, incentivize work, respond to changing circumstances, and be fiscally sustainable. These are the ambitious, accepted, and sought-after attributes of the ideal safety net. However, a growing body of experience and evidence shows how difficult it is to attain these attributes (Grosh et al. 2008; Fiszbein et al. 2010). There are obvious tensions among them—high coverage and generous benefits, for example, raise spending and make fiscal sustainability difficult to achieve. Tightly targeting benefits will contain costs but will also raise the risk of exclusion and might increase disincentives to work. For these reasons, individual programs or combinations of programs rarely realize all desirable attributes simultaneously. Yet years of experience, trial, and error have yielded lessons that governments can use to provide a more robust minimum than they previously have, probably through using an expanded and more coordinated combination of existing instruments. These lessons build upon observed practices but also ambitiously extend them in fundamental ways:

- *Entitlement guarantee.* To fully meet the goals of the guaranteed minimum, programs need to operate as entitlements. Entitlements entail budget allocations that respond to observed needs rather than rigidly rationed beneficiary numbers. This characteristic, for instance, makes programs countercyclical and part of a country's automatic stabilizers. To meet the entitlement principle, programs would also need to have continuous eligibility processes (sometimes called "open enrollment").
- *Inclusive definition of beneficiaries.* All citizens (and, indeed, all residents) who are in need should be eligible for the guaranteed minimum. Currently, many programs focus only on children of a certain age, the elderly, or the disabled, leaving all those who live in households without such members ineligible. Even households that indirectly benefit because they have an eligible member often receive benefits designed for the needs of that individual and not the full household. Countries need a program or set of programs that keeps even able-bodied adults of working age out of poverty.
- *Work incentives.* Eligibility for programs like GMIs or those with categorical targeting can be discontinuous with income because of sharp, abrupt phase-out or phase-in rules, which can induce disincentives to work. A guaranteed minimum would desirably have a "gentler" benefit structure that tapers out more smoothly. The eligibility and benefit parameters of the minimum can vary, but they should avoid discontinuities and align with a country's wealth distributions. The ideal form could be visualized as a downward hill slope rather than a cliff face. Fewer "cliffs" and gentler, tapering "slopes" would induce more positive work incentives. Although not addressing the income effect, continuous tapering would considerably attenuate substitution effects. It may be too complex to customize benefits for each household and adjust them every time the household's income changes, but a gradually descending "staircase," with different levels of benefits for different ranges of welfare and periodic reassessments, may sufficiently approximate a slope.
- *Net eligibility thresholds set relatively high.* Today, many programs are designed with eligibility thresholds near or sometimes even below the country's extreme poverty level. But in many low and middle-income countries, the distribution of the population by welfare measures may be relatively dense at lower levels. This distribution results in households with very similar levels of welfare being treated differently across the threshold of eligibility. Small inaccuracies in eligibility decision-making processes can result in more errors of inclusion or exclusion in these contexts than where fewer households are poor.

Moreover, many social assistance interventions are designed to address chronic poverty, with eligibility criteria that are insensitive to short-run changes in household welfare, such as those that tend to follow shocks. There is substantial movement of people in and out of poverty, including in the poorest countries. Higher eligibility thresholds can keep these programs from excluding the newly or temporarily poor. This change would reduce the risk of undercoverage and hollow guarantees.

The guaranteed minimum poverty prevention benefit would, in most cases, reduce the importance of mandatory individual contribution–based social insurance. In the case of old-age pensions, for example, a guaranteed minimum income would allow for a reduction in the replacement rate target, which in turn would allow for a lower statutory contribution rate. The implications of this change are discussed and modeled later in this chapter. This change does not, however, address the coverage gap that persists for insurance. Under the current rules of many social insurance systems, those outside formal employment are not part of the risk pool for the losses that accompany insurable events such as death, disability, and functional dependency in old age. To cover all people against catastrophic losses, further subsidized risk-pooling instruments will be needed.

## Coverage against Catastrophic Losses and Further Mandated Arrangements

Many shocks result in losses that would overwhelm even very generous minimum income guarantees. An important part of the current employment-based, risk-sharing model of social insurance is the mechanism that addresses losses that are "insurable" in a strictly actuarial sense, as described in chapter 2. Such losses include costs from health events (lost working time and earnings and the costs of medical treatment and medication), disability, premature death, extended longevity, functional dependency in old age, and the need for long-term (nonmedical) care. The losses from these still relatively rare events are large and can quickly grow to catastrophic size,[6] and their impact can impoverish households all along the welfare distribution. Yet despite being eminently insurable in strictly actuarial terms, myopia and market failures have left a gap that government-mandated—social—insurance is meant to fill. Social insurance interventions—direct public provision, mandated market provision, and market-augmenting and -enabling policies—aim to reduce or eliminate adverse selection and moral hazard. The policy challenge is to provide coverage to all and overcome the shortcomings of risk markets. Principal among these shortcomings is the markets' inability to cope with uncertainty.

The greatest progress in policy making toward addressing these shocks has been made by countries that have moved toward universal health insurance. In at least two dozen countries, the government pays part or all of the health insurance premium for people in the lower part of the income distribution. In the best-designed cases, governments establish a benefit package of health care as an entitlement, determine the actuarially fair premium for the package, and then subsidize those who cannot afford to pay the premium by their own means (Baeza and Packard 2006). People who receive premium subsidies are mostly workers without a history of making statutory contributions that would entitle them to traditional social health insurance (SHI) (Cotlear et al. 2015). This approach of subsidizing actuarially fair premiums effectively blurs the distinction between contributory and noncontributory social insurance. In doing so, it extends contingent coverage against catastrophic losses by integrating people who cannot afford to pay actuarially fair premiums into the risk-pooling systems with everybody else. Figure 3.5 presents the "slopes and cliffs" of benefit topography that households in Indonesia face, including the subsidized health coverage received by poorer households—the *Program Indonesia Sehat* (PIS) (formerly known as PBI-JKN), the largest single source of coverage for health costs.

Other than health coverage, there are few examples of a universal social insurance approach being taken to cover large contingent-variable losses. Although some countries have subsidized contributions for pensions, to the best of our knowledge, none have done so for the entire population. Costa Rica's government pays part of the pension contributions of self-employed workers. In addition to an almost-universal, flat old-age pension, Thailand pays part of the premium for a variable old-age, survivor, and disability pension for working-age people who are working informally. This defined-benefit plan yields in an annuity and thus provides insurance against death, disability, and longevity. China has implemented a contributory rural pension plan in which the incentive for people to contribute is both a matching contribution and a noncontributory pension for the elderly parents of the contributor (see box 3.3).

Recently proposed changes in social insurance financing aim to provide universal contingent coverage. The most prominent among these recent proposals promises to "end informality," to paraphrase the title of a recent book on social protection and labor market policies in Mexico (Anton, Hernandez, and Levy 2013). Frustration with the low and stagnant percentage of working people who participate in social insurance has long been evident in Mexico, as in many countries in Latin America, a region where the institutional history of Bismarckian social insurance is almost as old as it is in Europe. Mexico's informal economy and its share of people working beyond the reach of regulation and taxation are larger than those

**Figure 3.5** **Along With Targeted Transfers, Indonesia Provides a Declining Subsidy of Social Health Insurance Premiums**

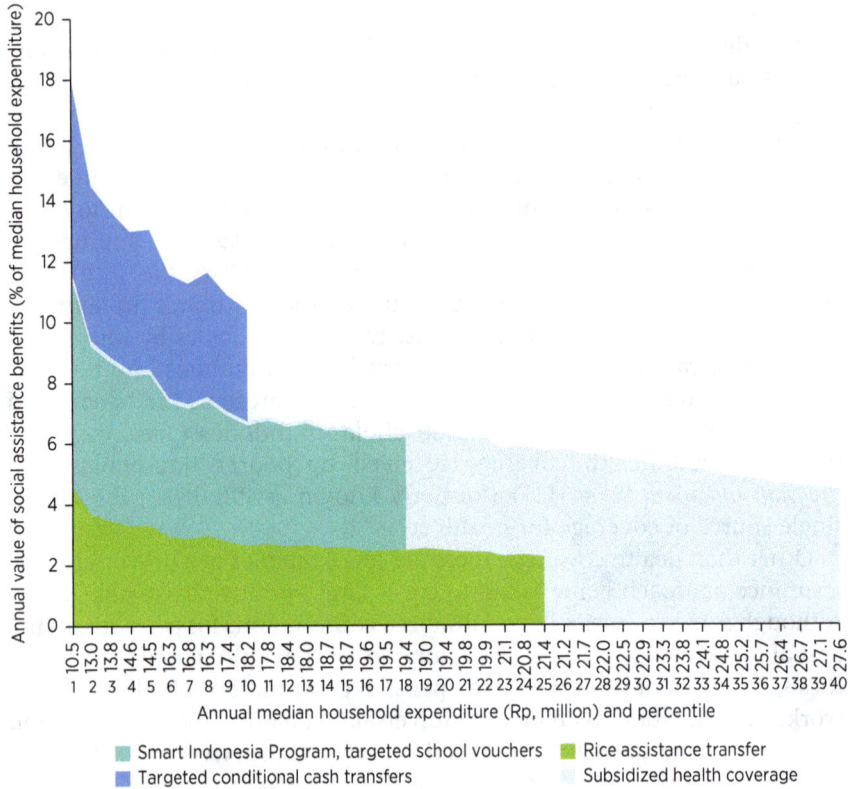

*Source:* Pinxten 2019.

*Note:* This figure shows de jure benefit entitlements for a representative household, by percentile of household expenditure, in Indonesia in 2016.

of other countries at its level of development. Strong evidence shows that the extent of economic informality has had serious negative effects on the country's productivity (Levy 2018; Pages 2010). A novel approach to providing contingent coverage is proposed by Anton, Hernandez, and Levy (2013), whereby the statutory payroll-tax contributions applied to earnings below a certain threshold would be replaced with a consumption tax.[7] The revenues from this new tax would finance the contributions for health and pension coverage for lower-income workers and reduce the required statutory payroll tax for workers with above-average incomes, who are mostly in formal work. The authors characterize their proposal as universal social insurance, or USI. After shifting spending on existing programs, the authors

## Blurring the Distinction between "Contributory" and "Noncontributory": Social Pensions in China

Like many countries, China had struggled for years to expand coverage of its contributory pension system to workers outside formal employment. Although some progress had been made between 1997 and the late 2000s, coverage of rural workers had stalled at around 55 million. In response (and informed by lessons from extensive subnational pilot programs), the central authorities designed a scheme for informal workers which went national for rural workers in late 2009 and for urban informal workers in 2011. The plan's design is an innovative, and successful, example of blurring of the lines between contributory social insurance and social assistance.

The basic design, common to the rural and urban plans—and, more recently, the basis for a merged rural and urban plan—is as follows. It is a voluntary plan in which informal workers are required to make a modest annual contribution to an individual account (when introduced, the minimum annual contribution was around US$15, though workers could choose to contribute at higher levels). This contribution is matched at a rate of 30 percent by the local government and is typically invested in low-return term deposits. After a minimum of 15 years of contributions, the worker is entitled at age 60 to a basic monthly pension benefit, currently a minimum of around US$11 per month, though many prefectures provide a higher payment. In the design, though seemingly less in practice, there was a provision for "family binding," whereby those 60 and over with no formal sector pension could receive the basic benefit if their children contributed on their behalf or if the individual paid 15 years of minimum contributions in a lump sum. The basic benefit is financed entirely by the central government in western and most central provinces, with a higher share of subnational financing in coastal and some other central provinces.

In effect, the system acts as a contributory social pension—in other words, a hybrid of a matching defined-contribution (MDC) pension in the accumulation phase and a social pension with a modest funded-pension portion in the payout phase. The financing for the average retiree is around 80 percent subsidy, considering contributions, a basic rate of return on the individual account accumulation, and the basic benefit flow (Wang, Chen, and Gao 2011).

The increase in coverage among informal sector workers because of this plan has been impressive. Currently, around 360 million rural and

*continued next page*

---

**Box 3.3** (*continued*)

urban informal workers are contributing to the plan, and around 150 million elderly people are receiving payments. This is an extraordinary increase in participation for a voluntary scheme. At the same time, concerns remain with the adequacy of the benefit, especially when compared to wage replacement rates of around 40 percent in the formal sector pension plan for urban workers and considerably higher replacement rates in the pension plans for civil servants and public-service units (PSUs).

Even so, the hybrid plan is an interesting case which cannot be characterized by the standard terms of social insurance or social assistance. The plan represents a blurring of the lines which goes beyond the MDC approach seen in other countries.

*Sources:* Dorfman et al. 2013; Wang, Chen, and Gao 2011.

---

estimated that an additional 2.7 to 3.2 percent of Mexico's gross domestic product (GDP) would be required to finance the USI, requiring the proposed increase in consumption tax revenues.

As with the guaranteed minimum poverty-prevention transfer, the subsidy for contingent coverage can be withdrawn gradually as people's income or consumption rises. The USI proposed by Anton, Hernandez, and Levy (2013) applies to insurance premiums rather than to a cash transfer and is aimed at workers, or adults of working age, rather than the entire population. This is an important distinction: although the amount of a minimum flat benefit does not change to cover the size of its recipient's losses, subsidized premiums allow all people access to risk-pooling arrangements that can cover catastrophic losses. As with market insurance, the size of the payout from the USI is determined by the size of the losses covered by the plan. The proposal recognizes that what may be deemed an adequate minimum for a certain set of circumstances is not the same amount as for individuals who have experienced shocks that entail larger losses. Tapering this subsidy as income rises is analogous to the TUBI discussed earlier. Turkey provides one example of such a program: the amount of the subsidy for risk-pooling health insurance premiums is reduced gradually as incomes (as proxied by administrative data) rise. Building on Anton, Hernandez, and Levy's USI proposal for Mexico, in the remainder of this chapter, we refer to a tapered subsidy for risk-pooling premiums as *tapered* universal social insurance (TUSI).

By consolidating poverty prevention and any other redistributive objectives in the core of the policy package of protection, governments can increase coherence and reduce perverse incentives and evasion. A pervasive problem in prevailing social protection systems is the segmentation and lack of coherence between social assistance and the redistributive elements of employment-based, contributory social insurance programs. As mentioned previously, the pursuit of redistribution objectives—"vertical" income redistribution as well as "horizontal" risk redistribution—is implicitly combined in the design of most contributory social insurance arrangements. However, the mingling of policy objectives is often done with little reference to other income-transfer programs. This lack of coherence can distort individuals' labor supply decisions, increase the costs to employers of making formal employment offers, and ultimately result in inequitable outcomes. Greater coherence can be achieved by tapering subsidies for insurance premiums, as with the tapered guaranteed minimum income. In the lexicon we have introduced in this chapter, a UBI or TUBI would be combined with a USI or TUSI. Given their demonstrated higher impact on poverty, the combination of a TUBI and a TUSI is likely to be superior where governments' administrative and implementation capacities allow them to observe people's means. The tapered subsidy for risk-pooling premiums could purchase contingent coverage for longevity, health, and long unemployment spells.

With reference again to figure 3.1 at the start of this chapter, although adding subsidized coverage of large and catastrophic losses to the core package would require expansion of this core, it can lower the size of the mandated savings and insurance segment (the next-closest layer to the center, discussed later in this chapter). This reduction of the mandated segment is made possible through two channels. First, to the extent that a TUBI has provided a minimum income guarantee to keep all people out of poverty, a large component of redistribution can be stripped out of mandated plans, leaving only consumption smoothing or actuarially fair insurance in its place. For example, a minimum pension currently financed by statutory contributions would be replaced with a social pension or TUBI financed by taxes unrelated to labor market activities. In cases where the traditional contributory minimum pension guarantee is higher than the social pension or TUBI, or if the premium needed to finance the basic package of health services (including catastrophic insurance) is not affordable even with increased social assistance or a TUBI in place, additional subsidies can be mobilized with the TUSI. However, unlike in traditional, contributory social insurance, these subsidies would be *explicit* and would be financed by a broader-based levy than statutory payroll tax contributions.

Second, by eliminating implicit redistribution, remaining mandatory contributions would be linked entirely and explicitly to the benefits a participant receives, reducing the pure-tax component (in other words, the economic ration) created by the mandate to contribute. As an example, in Panama, the public pension system pays pensioners in its social insurance scheme a minimum pension of US$185 per month, and anyone without a contributory pension receives a social pension worth US$100.[8] Following the approach described here, both pensions would be replaced fully or partially by a TUBI and a TUSI. This change would allow the government to reduce the level of statutory contributions that finance the traditional minimum pension.

The remaining mandatory contributions from working individuals (and their employers) serve two primary purposes. First, mandatory, actuarially fair arrangements reduce the risk of moral hazard that naturally arises from the government providing the minimum guaranteed core of protection (Kotlikoff 1987). Second, the remaining mandatory contributions provide a vehicle for consumption smoothing that may not be available in the market; this consumption smoothing can also protect people from their own improvidence or myopia. Due to adverse selection, annuity markets, for example, have not developed organically; this has been cited as one of the rationales for government intervention (Walliser 2002). However, the remaining mandatory contributions can be both smaller and less distortionary with a TUBI-and-TUSI scheme in place than they would be otherwise. In a defined-contribution (DC) plan, the annuity to be paid out is, by definition, a direct result of the savings that have been accumulated. Either a notional DC (NDC) or an actuarially fair defined-benefit (DB) plan achieve this goal through appropriate parameters, including increments or decrements for late or early retirement ages, respectively.

In the last section of this chapter, we illustrate how a UBI or TUBI could be combined with a USI or TUSI, and we simulate the potential impact of this approach on taxes, benefits, and spending compared with the prevailing employment-based approach. The starting point for our calculations is a typical Bismarckian DB pension plan financed by statutory contributions levied on firms' payrolls. The calculations consider how long an individual would receive the pension benefit in order to calculate the contribution rate that would be required to finance the pension on an actuarially fair basis. In this way, it is possible to calculate the reduction in statutory contributions that would be possible. We simulate these changes for a traditional contributory pension plan, but the results can be generalized to coverage of other losses, such as those from health events or from unemployment.

## Nudged and Purely Voluntary Insurance

If minimum guaranteed protections are in place, it is reasonable to expect nonpoor people to rely mainly on their own efforts to achieve consumption smoothing, particularly where relatively foreseeable losses are concerned. For example, as a population ages and average life expectancy improves, a greater share of people are likely to reach old age and to live relatively longer thereafter than those who preceded them. As the loss of earning ability from aging becomes more common and predictable, it becomes more difficult to pool the risk of this loss effectively between generations and more efficient to rely on individual savings, actual or notional. However, within any given generation, there will always be some who are longer-lived than others. Even if these individuals can form reasonable expectations about their longevity based on that of their parents, many will still underestimate the remaining period of life they will need to finance without being able to work. Similarly, in most labor markets, the likelihood of job separations caused by routine churn and transitions is more predictable than the likelihood of job losses because of the sudden bankruptcy of a firm or in the wake of a financial crisis. Although a spell of unemployment is relatively foreseeable, some unemployed face a costly, protracted search period before they can find a new job or start their own business. For many people, the market can respond with appropriate saving and pooling instruments. But where markets struggle to respond, policies can help to mimic or coax market provision.

Although reasonable, mandates to save and insure can be disproportionate, given people's preferences and alternative options, and difficult to enforce for governments with limited information and administrative capacity. Earlier sections described the policy rationale for these mandates: from society's and the policy-maker's perspective, mandating that individuals save—whether through defined contributions, notional defined contributions, or actuarially fair defined-benefit plans—lowers the risk of moral hazard and helps to ensure that the resources in the risk pool that finances the core guaranteed minimum protections will be available to the people who need them most when they are needed most. From individuals' perspectives, the mandate to save or take up risk-pooling can help them achieve prudent management of resources in the face of imperfect information about their future needs, irrational time-inconsistent behavior, and other market failures. The capacity to mandate contributions is improving, and technology can accelerate gains in this area considerably. The task is made easier with actuarially fair instruments in place.

The mandatory contribution amounts currently observed in employment-based social insurance systems are likely to have been established when those systems were the *only* way people had to insure, or with little regard to the alternative instruments that were made available by markets. In recent years, in which the employment-based, contributory social insurance model has been adopted in low- and middle-income countries, the sizes of mandatory contributions appear similarly set, with little regard for alternative arrangements, including traditional family- or community-based risk-pooling mechanisms. Many of these informal or market arrangements can be displaced by new, statutory contribution requirements.

With the core of guaranteed minimum protection in place, there will be room to lower the size of contribution mandates and to allow people to save and insure voluntarily. Relaxing the mandate could take the form of a percentage-point reduction in statutory contributions or a lowering of the ceiling on earnings subject to these statutory contributions. Either measure could lower the "costs" of participation in the system and encourage greater uptake, even among individuals with higher discount rates and stronger liquidity preferences. With the core of the benefits package firmly in place, governments should proceed with a lighter touch and with an eye to alternative informal and market options available to individuals and households. Policy makers must strike a balance between protecting the effectiveness of the publicly financed risk pool from moral hazard, limiting the size of the mandate required to achieve consumption-smoothing goals, and helping people make better use of market-provided instruments to manage their own myopia and achieve their aspirations.

Purely voluntary uptake of market instruments has been disappointing in countries at all levels of development, reflecting people's cognitive and behavioral limitations. Despite the many measures governments have taken to lower costs and to improve investment performance incentives, people are slow to insure. People are confronted with an increasingly diverse array of investment options, each of which offers sophisticated combinations of risk and return. The household response to growing choices at varying price points and performance levels has been underwhelming. People's ability to grasp even simple financial concepts has been shown to be very limited, even in mature, high-income economies (Lusardi and Mitchell 2014). Faced with a growing number of investment options, many people respond with bewilderment and paralysis (Barr and Diamond 2009).

Most successful policy innovations to expand the uptake of voluntary insurance draw on insights from behavioral economics. With mainstream recognition of the social and cognitive limitations of people's ability to make rational choices (Kahneman 2011; World Bank 2015), policy makers have been increasingly resorting to behavioral "nudges" to coax people to save and insure. For example, in many countries that mandate saving and insurance, employers and people who are self-employed are statutorily free to choose whether to participate in such programs. Periodically, there is interest in extending mandates to cover these groups, but in low- and middle-income countries where this has been tried, it has often had the opposite effect of increasing incentives to evade. As such, policy makers have experimented intensively with an alternative to a mandate: making participation the lowest-effort, default option that people can take at key moments of contact with government. Some measures that have been tried include adding an opt-in default on business registration and income tax returns that lowers the transaction costs of participating for employers and the self-employed. Such use of opt-in defaults accords well with research on retirement savings behavior in high-income countries, which shows that when participation in voluntary company pension plans (such as the 401(k) plans in the United States) is made the default option, worker enrollment doubles (Benartzi and Thaler 2004).

Carefully crafted default options and other "nudges" have increased voluntary savings in low-income countries as well. In Kenya, giving people a gold-colored coin with numbers for each week to keep track of their weekly deposits doubled their savings rate (Akbas et al. 2016). Another form of nudging is a commitment device, a strategy whereby people agree to incur a loss if they do not reach a savings goal. Evidence from the Philippines shows this strategy increased savings by 81 percent (Ashraf, Karlan, and Yin 2006). Digital technology vastly increases the types of nudges that are possible. For example, it facilitates setting a default to round up individual financial technology (fintech) and credit-card transactions and store the extra money in savings—shifting money from bank accounts into longer-term savings instruments.

Behavioral economics and the design of default options also form the basis of larger national efforts to nudge people to make more effort to save and insure. The KiwiSaver plan in New Zealand is one such program. As one of the few countries that has never established a system of mandatory consumption-smoothing and which relies solely on a general-revenue financed flat pension to prevent old-age poverty, New Zealand leaves much responsibility for old age in the hands of its inhabitants. Their low rates of private savings and insurance uptake alarmed policy makers, who were concerned that the country's poverty-prevention benefit would come under too much strain. Yet in a 1997 referendum on whether to establish a mandatory retirement savings scheme, 91.8 percent of voters (with a turnout of over 80 percent) rejected the proposal. The eventual response was the establishment of

KiwiSaver, which came into full operation in 2007. Although voluntary and available to all residents and citizens, the program relies on automatic enrollment (Thaler and Sunstein 2008). People from the ages of 18 to 64 who start a new job are automatically enrolled in KiwiSaver. Between 14 and 56 days after starting their new job, they can choose to opt out. Participants choose how much to save and are offered a very limited set of investment choices. The program relies on limited and simple investment options and centralized account management to keep costs very low. The United Kingdom's National Employment Savings Trust, or UK NEST, operates on similar automatic enrollment principles. Although people can withdraw from both programs, incentives are structured to strongly dissuade them from doing so. Other voluntary pension arrangements with automatic enrollment are in place in Brazil, Chile, Poland, the Russian Federation, and Turkey and act as important complements to guaranteed minimum and mandated coverage, requiring the active regulatory oversight of governments (Rudolph 2019).

In countries that have actuarially fair, mandatory consumption-smoothing already in place, the burdens of their mandates could be lightened by allowing people to access a portion of their savings for key life events. With the aim of increasing participation in Chile's mandatory individual savings plan, Beyer and Valdes (2004) show how participants could be allowed to "borrow" up to a certain amount from their individual account. The interest on this loan from their future selves could be set at market rates and paid back into their own accounts. Interest could also be set at higher-than-market rates to encourage even quicker repayment. Participants could also be restricted from taking a second loan from their accounts until the first had been paid back. Singapore grants workers access to their mandatory savings for specific aspirational investments, such as housing and education. In New Zealand's KiwiSaver program, individuals are allowed access to their savings to purchase their first home or to further their education. Similarly, Brazil allows workers access to their *Fundo de Guarantia do Tempo de Serviço* (FGTS) for housing investments. These measures make the relatively large mandates to save imposed by these countries' social protection systems more tolerable for participants. In the United States, individuals can draw on their 401(k)s and IRAs, although the rates of taxation then applied dissuade most from doing so. The challenge for policy makers is to balance individuals' liquidity preferences with their long-term consumption-smoothing objectives. Access to individual savings has to be limited: many participating workers in Singapore exhaust their account balances before reaching retirement. Allowing participants' present selves to borrow and repay their future selves with interest can be a way to achieve this balance.

## Simulations to Inform a Prudent Debate of Policy Options

A prudent consideration of policy options requires some quantification—however imperfect—of alternatives, using conservative assumptions. In this section, we present the results of simple simulation exercises to help quantify the fiscal costs and welfare impact of the proposed package of protection. The simulations are not comprehensive, nor are they meant to be prescriptive—any policy makers seriously considering the options presented in this chapter would be wise to conduct their own extensive simulations using assumptions and parameters appropriate to their contexts. Rather, in presenting these simulations, our intent is to convey to readers the relative magnitudes of the ideas we have presented, in terms of both public expenditures and poverty impact. We hope the simulations give a more palpable sense of the possibilities, decisions, and challenges governments would face if they were to adopt the policies we have discussed. We start with simulations of the alternative UBI and TUBI guarantees to set outer-bound estimates of the costs and benefits of offering these ambitious poverty-prevention benefits. We then simulate the introduction of subsidies financed from the general budget for purchasing contingent, catastrophic coverage—the USI and TUSI alternatives. In these latter simulations, we reserve financing through statutory employer and employee contributions only for an individual's (and their covered dependents') own, actuarially fair coverage (such as for old age, whether pure defined-benefit or funded or unfunded defined-contribution). We use these simulations to show how governments can rely less on statutory contributions, further tighten the link between remaining statutory contributions and benefits, and thus make participation in mandatory consumption-smoothing plans less of a burden for all concerned.

All else being equal, tapering the guaranteed minimum poverty-prevention benefit lowers its fiscal costs and increases its impact on poverty. As discussed earlier, tapering refers to decreasing people's benefits as their observable income or consumption increases, whether through a progressive tax system or with resort to other administrative means of assessing households' income or wealth. Tapering provides a more fiscally viable way to offer universal coverage: a TUBI. To compare the UBI and the TUBI, a simulation exercise conducted for this volume by Majoka and Palacios (2019) uses household survey microdata from 52 low- and middle-income countries. For simplicity, the benefit level for the UBI is set at 5 percent of the average per capita consumption. The same budget allocation is then applied as a TUBI in which each decile receives a 1 percentage-point lower transfer, as shown in figure 3.6. A third option shows a lower budget allocation, a TUBI set at half the value (2.5 percent of average per capita consumption) with a steeper taper to zero by the 60th percentile. In all

**Figure 3.6 Tapering a Universal Poverty Prevention Benefit Makes It More Affordable**

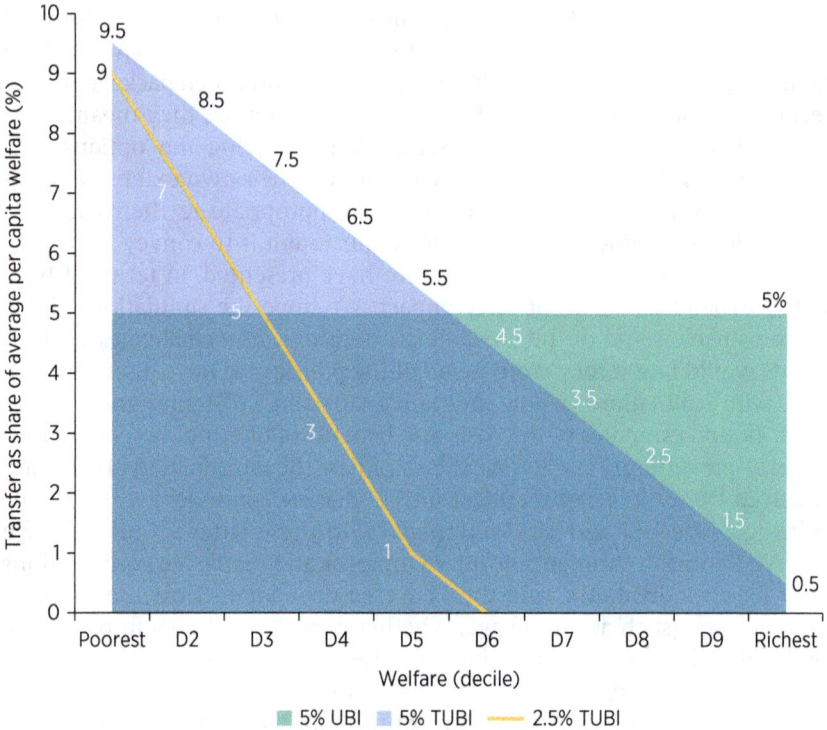

*Source:* Majoka and Palacios 2019.

*Note:* This figure shows a comparison of a universal basic income (UBI) and tapered universal basic incomes (TUBIs) of various benefit amounts.

simulations, a relative poverty line is set at half of the median per capita level of welfare.[9] Similar findings emerge from tax-benefit microsimulations presented in Gentilini et al. (2019) that compare a UBI to existing targeted interventions. Overall, these findings are most important if poverty reduction is the core objective, although, as mentioned earlier, in several contexts UBI (and TUBI) can be used to pursue policy goals unrelated to poverty (such as a more efficient and equitable transfer of natural resource rents in countries where governance is poor).

A tapered benefit is likely to have a greater impact on poverty for the same level of expenditure as a flat UBI. Ignoring behavioral changes, figure 3.7 shows the range of estimated reductions in poverty

**Figure 3.7  A Tapered Benefit Has a Greater Impact on Poverty for the Same Level of Expenditure**

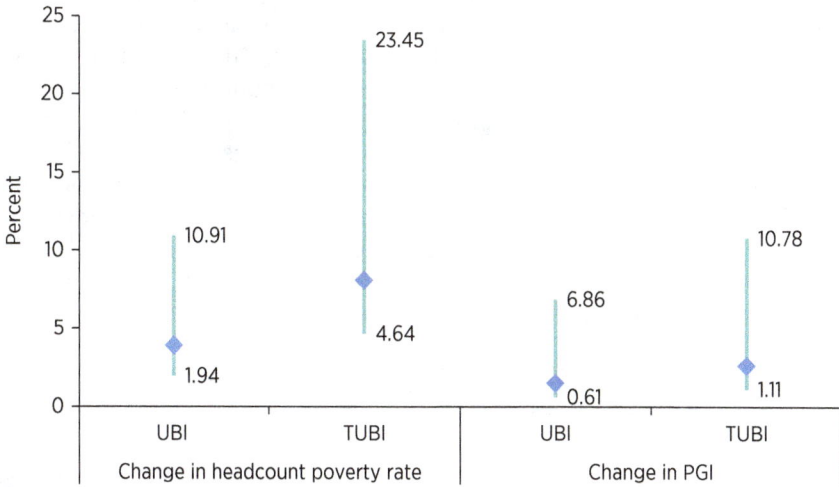

*Source:* Majoka and Palacios 2019.

*Note:* This figure shows the reduction in headcount poverty and poverty gap index (PGI) from a universal basic income (UBI) and a tapered universal basic income (TUBI) with the same budget. Blue diamonds indicate mean values.

(by head count) as well as in the poverty gap caused by a UBI or TUBI. With the same budget allocation, a TUBI reduces headcount poverty as well as the poverty gap by more than twice as much as a UBI.[10] Note that the differential impact varies widely among countries: the maximum reduction in headcount poverty is five times the minimum. This result reflects different distributions of income and consumption across countries. For the lower benefit/lower budget scenario, by sharply increasing the slope of the taper, the poverty impact remains largely unchanged, but the benefits go to zero by the sixth decile. The trade-off in this case is that the marginal tax on earnings increases sharply and may reduce the labor supply. How large this trade-off will be is an empirical question, and the answer will undoubtedly vary across countries and over time.

To capture the impact of new transfers more fully, however, the sources of revenue to fund them must also be considered. Among the options for taxation to finance the proposed benefits—corporate, personal income, property, wealth, inheritance, carbon, or excise taxes—the value added tax (VAT) is likely to be the least progressive (we return to this issue in chapter 5) and therefore serves as a reasonable lower bound when simulating the amount of redistribution that could be achieved with these alternative poverty prevention instruments. Figure 3.8 shows the impact of levying a VAT to finance the UBI or TUBI simulated above, on the basis of the average of all 52 countries in Majoka and Palacios's sample. The simulations show that, after considering taxation, the transfer to the bottom part of the distribution remains positive, with only minor reductions in the amounts received by people in the poorest deciles. The net transfer becomes slightly negative by the seventh decile and sizably negative for the top quintile. The top decile pays twice as much as the bottom decile receives. The consumption tax required is around 5 percent. Using any other tax instrument to finance the same amount of spending would almost certainly result in a more progressive net incidence.

**Figure 3.8** **Taking Taxation into Account Shows a Promising Level and Distribution of Costs**

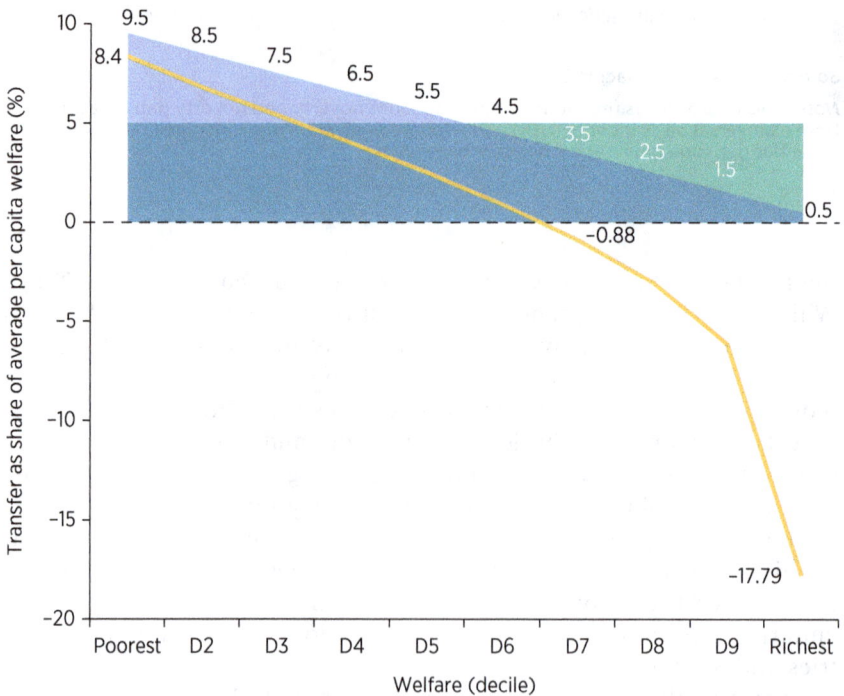

*Source:* Majoka and Palacios 2019.

*Note:* This figure shows the net transfer of a tapered universal basic income (TUBI) after value added tax (VAT) financing (yellow line). The other component segments are the same as those shown in figure 3.6.

The simulations in the remainder of this section, conducted by Palacios and Robalino (2019) for this volume, show the gains from financing poverty prevention and other redistribution subsidies from broader-based sources than statutory payroll contributions. We simulate four scenarios—presented in figures 3.9 through 3.12—to show how a new guaranteed minimum, mandated, and subsidized contributory social insurance could fit together. These scenarios assume two levels of generosity of the contributory pension plan: (i) a target replacement rate of 40 percent of lifetime consumption and a minimum pension guarantee of 15 percent of average consumption, and (ii) a target replacement rate of 70 percent of lifetime consumption and a minimum pension guarantee of 25 percent of average consumption.[11] For the introduction of a UBI or TUBI, three scenarios are considered: (i) a UBI of 5 percent of average per capita consumption; (ii) a TUBI of 5 percent of average per capita consumption with a reduction of 10 percent per decile; and (iii) a TUBI of 10 percent of average per capita consumption with a reduction of 10 percent per decile. In all cases, we assume that benefits received upon retirement do not change as a result of the integration. Essentially, the pension plan pays the difference between the prereform targeted income and the benefits received from the UBI or TUBI. We also assume that in the reformed system, workers in the first four deciles receive subsidies to cover the premiums for contingent coverage for catastrophic losses (a TUSI component): these participants can pay contributions below the actuarially fair contribution rate, and the government pays the difference from general revenues. As a result, there are no statutory contributions required from people in the first consumption decile and the maximum contribution is 5 percent, 10 percent, and 15 percent of income for the second, third, and fourth deciles, respectively. The illustration uses the Philippines' distribution of consumption (see Palacios and Robalino 2019 and details of the simulations in appendix C). Note that, for simplified and clearer presentation of results, in figures 3.9 through 3.12 the top-left panels, "Source of Benefits," show only the first 5 deciles of the income distribution, where the measures simulated are likely to have a greater impact.

The first set of simulations focuses on the UBI with a supplemental TUSI. From the starting point of a less-generous prereform pension system, introducing a new 5 percent UBI would allow the minimum pension guarantee to be reduced to 10 percent of average consumption and the target replacement rate to be reduced to less than 35 percent (see figure 3.9, top right panel). This change is feasible because part of the pension benefits would be replaced by the UBI for all workers (see the top-left panel). Because the minimum pension guarantee is higher than the UBI, the pension system would continue to provide subsidies to workers in the first three deciles in the form of a TUSI (a declining subsidy for the actuarially fair risk-pooling premiums).[12] Thus, for the first decile, the UBI would replace 31 percent of earnings and the TUSI

## Figure 3.9 Can Statutory Contribution Rates Be Lowered?

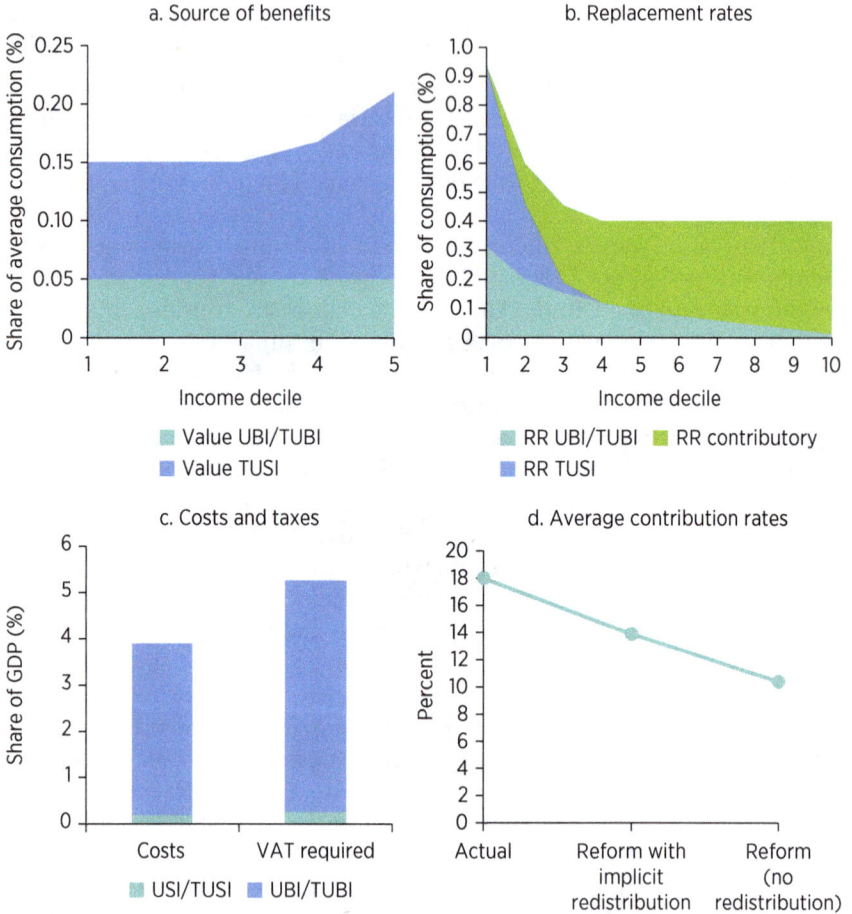

a. Source of benefits

b. Replacement rates

Value UBI/TUBI
Value TUSI

RR UBI/TUBI    RR contributory
RR TUSI

c. Costs and taxes

d. Average contribution rates

USI/TUSI    UBI/TUBI

*Source:* Palacios and Robalino 2019.

*Note:* This figure shows the integration of a new guaranteed minimum package of protection into an existing employment-based contributory pension plan with a 40 percent replacement rate and a 15 percent contributory minimum guarante. See details in appendix C. GDP = gross domestic product; RR = replacement rate; TUBI = tapered universal basic income; TUSI = tapered universal social insurance; UBI = universal basic income; USI = universal social insurance; VAT = value-added tax.

would replace 62 percent, while for the third decile, the UBI would replace only 15 percent of earnings and the TUSI would replace only 3 percent (see the top-right panel). Starting in the fourth decile, subsidies would come only from the UBI and would represent a declining share of the pension paid. The subsidies embedded in the TUSI would be lower than in the prereform system, explicit, and financed out of general revenues.

Broader coverage can be achieved at reasonable, though substantial, additional fiscal costs. The main fiscal cost of the integration would be from the new UBI (3.7 percent of GDP) and would require revenues equivalent to a 5 percent consumption tax.[13] The cost of the TUSI—the cost of the remaining redistribution in the pension system—would be about 0.2 percent of GDP. This figure assumes full coverage of the working-age population in each decile and therefore should be considered an upper-bound estimate. The assumption of full coverage of the contributory system is optimistic. But note that with the proposed design, workers do not lose the UBI (or TUBI) when they enroll and contribute. On the contrary, they become entitled to receive additional subsidies. For workers in the first decile, these additional subsidies require only enrollment, because for these people there are no statutory contributions from earnings.

The new poverty-prevention benefit and subsidized coverage of catastrophic losses would allow mandatory contributions to savings and insurance for consumption smoothing to be significantly lowered. For workers participating in traditional, employment-based social insurance, a substantial component of their mandatory contributions purchases benefits they will eventually receive. For this reason, much of the mandatory contributions are perceived as deferred compensation, valued by the covered worker. However, as discussed in earlier sections of this chapter, the mingling of consumption-smoothing with income redistribution in traditional social insurance plans, along with individuals' preferences and their myopia, can make contributions for a future benefit feel like a tax to many (Corsetti 1994; Summers 1989). The "pure tax" element perceived by workers can be even greater in countries with poor governance and low administrative capacity, because the firms and workers who are required to contribute may have little confidence that they will receive quality, publicly provided benefits in return (Packard, Koettl, and Montenegro 2012). Thus, an additional benefit of the proposed reform is the reduction of the statutory contribution rate from 18 percent to 10 percent. Four percentage points of this reduction is explained by the presence of the UBI, which, as discussed above, allows for a lower mandate (replacement rate) in the actuarially fair pension plan. In addition, shifting additional redistribution from the pension plan into a TUSI financed from general revenues allows a further reduction of the contribution rate from 14 percent to 10 percent (see equations (C.19) through (C.22) in appendix C). A total 8-percentage-point reduction in the statutory contribution rate is substantial and can help reduce distortions in the labor market (particularly where the parameters of related wage and worker-protection regulations are set at reasonable levels, as discussed in chapter 4).

As with the poverty-prevention transfer, tapering the subsidized premiums for contingent coverage makes the package more fiscally affordable. Substantial cost savings can be achieved by relying on a TUBI. Tapering the

UBI by 10 percent of average consumption per capita for each decile above the first, for instance, would reduce fiscal costs from 3.7 percent of GDP to around 1 percent (see figure 3.10). Clearly, this change implies that except for the very poor, the level of the cash transfer would fall, and therefore the pension system would need a larger mandate and a larger TUSI. Still, the cost of the TUSI would remain manageable at 0.26 percent of GDP, requiring a consumption tax of 0.35 percent. The net savings of a TUBI comes mainly from lower costs in the top five deciles of the consumption distribution.

Even where an existing employment-based contributory pension plan is very generous, this new approach allows significantly lower statutory contributions. With a more generous prereform pension plan, the role of a modest UBI would be less important, but the TUSI would still play an important part in reducing statutory contribution rates. For instance, consider the case of a prereform pension plan with a 70 percent replacement rate and a contributory minimum pension guarantee equivalent to 25 percent of consumption (see figure 3.11). The UBI would represent only 20 percent of the pension paid to people in the first decile and 17 percent of the pension paid to people in the fourth decile. For those in the top deciles, the UBI would represent less than 10 percent of their pension. As a result, the mandate of the pension system would not change much, and the possible reduction in the statutory contribution rate would be more modest, from 30 to 27 percent (figure 3.11, bottom-right panel).[14] In the more generous pension system considered here, the equilibrium contribution rate would be around 30 percent. Still, by adopting a TUSI and financing redistribution through general revenues, the remaining statutory contribution rate could still be reduced significantly, to 18 percent. This 12 percentage-point reduction is even more substantial than the reduction achieved with reform to the less generous pension plan. A reform in this case would require a more generous and higher-cost TUSI (0.62 percent of GDP) and consequently a higher, but still manageable, consumption tax of 0.8 percent (see figure 3.11, bottom-left panel).

In countries where employment-based contributory pension systems impose a large mandate, covering the poorest workers is likely to entail a lower fiscal cost. In this context, a TUBI that offers a higher level of benefits to poorer people would cost less and require a less generous TUSI. For instance, a TUBI that offers a benefit equivalent to 10 percent of consumption (with a 10 percent clawback) could replace 60 percent of earnings for workers in the first decile and provide 40 percent of the pension. Because of the taper, the cost of the TUBI would be lower than that of the UBI—2.9 percent of GDP versus 3.7 percent. The more generous TUBI would also reduce the level of redistribution required in the

**Figure 3.10  Tapering the Poverty Prevention Benefit Increases the Affordability of the Proposed New Arrangements**

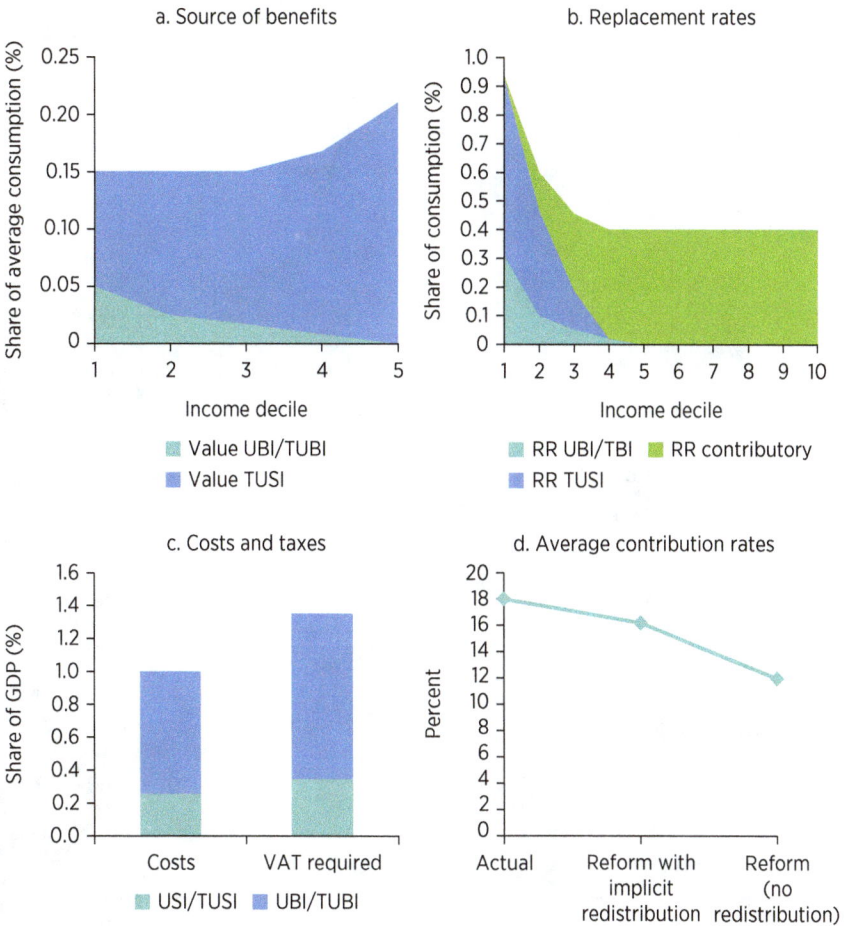

a. Source of benefits

b. Replacement rates

c. Costs and taxes

d. Average contribution rates

*Source:* Palacios and Robalino 2019.

*Note:* See details in appendix C. GDP = gross domestic product; RR = replacement rate; TUBI = tapered universal basic income; TUSI = tapered universal social insurance; UBI = universal basic income; USI = universal social insurance; VAT = value added tax.

actuarially fair part of the pension system through the TUSI. Thus, the TUSI would cost 0.5 percent of GDP instead of 0.6 percent. As a result, the level of consumption tax needed to finance the reform would fall from 5.8 percent to 4.6 percent (see difference in the bottom-left panels of figures 3.11 and 3.12).

**Figure 3.11 Statutory Contributions Can Be Lowered Even When Providing a More Generous Pension Plan**

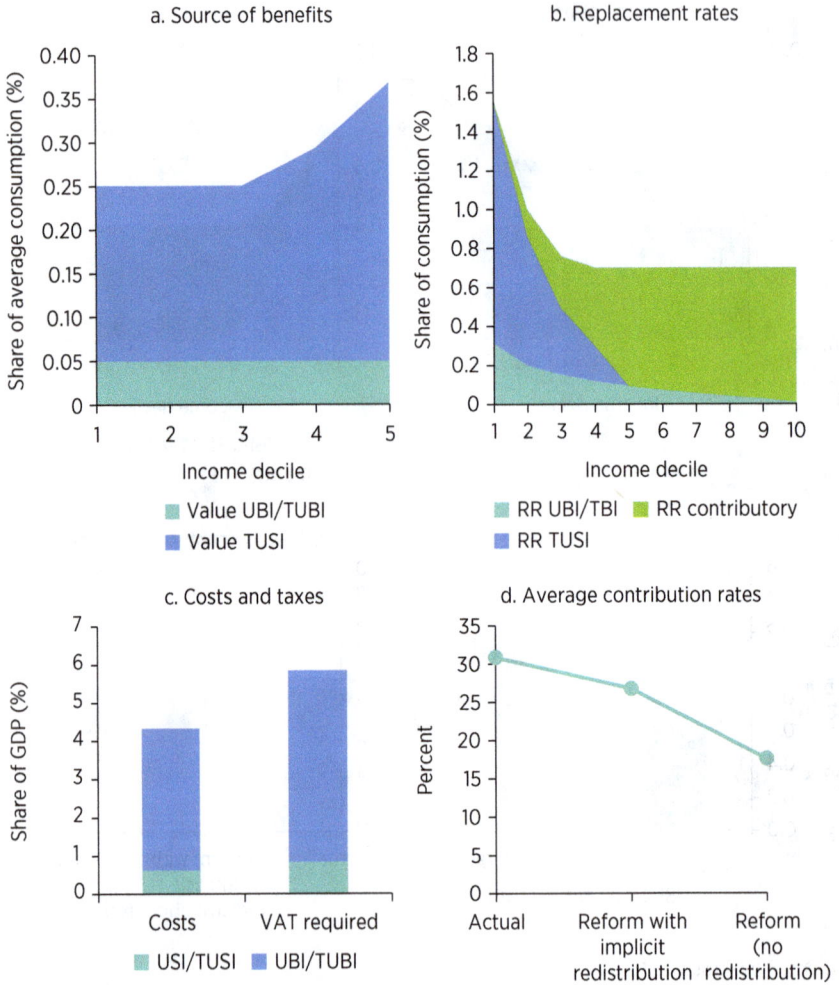

a. Source of benefits

b. Replacement rates

Value UBI/TUBI
Value TUSI

RR UBI/TBI     RR contributory
RR TUSI

c. Costs and taxes

d. Average contribution rates

USI/TUSI     UBI/TUBI

*Source:* Palacios and Robalino 2019.

*Note:* This figure shows the results of simulations with a 70 percent replacement rate and a pension guarantee of 25 percent of average consumption. See details in appendix C. GDP = gross domestic product; RR = replacement rate; TUBI = tapered universal basic income; TUSI = tapered universal social insurance; UBI = universal basic income; USI = universal social insurance; VAT = value added tax.

**Figure 3.12 The Integrated Model Can Provide a More Generous Pension Plan with a More Generous Tapered Universal Social Insurance**

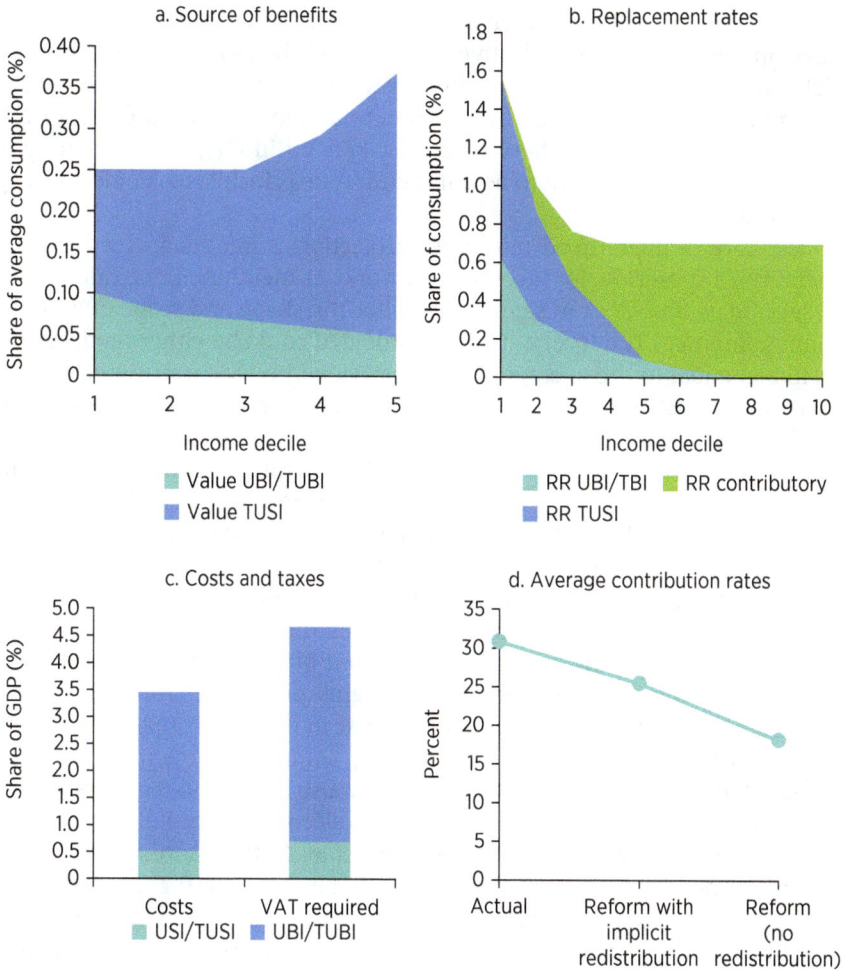

a. Source of benefits

b. Replacement rates

c. Costs and taxes

d. Average contribution rates

*Source:* Palacios and Robalino 2019.

*Note:* See details in appendix C. GDP = gross domestic product; RR = replacement rate; TUBI = tapered universal basic income; TUSI = tapered universal social insurance; UBI = universal basic income; USI = universal social insurance; VAT = value added tax.

## Key Principles for Designing the Core Minimum of Guaranteed Protections

How different the current risk-sharing arrangements are from these notional scenarios differs widely across countries according to their level of development, their administrative capacity, and the coverage and acquired rights of people participating in their prevailing employment-based social insurance systems. The discussion of potential reform paths and countries' readiness to embark on these paths is taken up in chapter 5 in earnest. Meanwhile, it is important to bear in mind some principles to guide consideration of policy options.

The core of guaranteed minimum protection is intended as a complement, not a substitute, for income from work. As mentioned, the calibration of specific parameters can significantly alter the shape and scope of a minimum guarantee. The level of benefits provided could be either modest (for example, equal to the average amount provided under current social assistance programs), the amount required to close the poverty gap, or more generous in order to meet wider needs (such as housing expenses and tuition fees). These modalities are intended to complement employment income and to enhance current social protection systems. However, as examined in Gentilini et al. (2019), a more radical perspective on UBI envisions the instrument as a possible *substitute* for work, one providing a livable income. Advocates for this perspective often propose a UBI as a response to the needs of people whose jobs have been eliminated by automation, as a way of empowering the "precariat" to opt out of work (Standing 2011), or as a way to adhere to broader human rights provisions. Although well-meaning, these objectives may not be realistic in the next couple of decades, the broad time horizon of this volume. By some standards, the vision of deliberately replacing work with leisure may also be interpreted as a societal declaration of surrender, in terms of our collective ability both to govern technology and to generate jobs (Gentilini et al. 2019). Moreover, because of the foundational nature of work in shaping societal values—offering pathways out of poverty and related externalities—we consider the version of UBI complementary to employment, that is, universal cash transfers for modest amounts as part of a social protection system.

The steps governments take toward establishing guaranteed minimum protections should be along a progressive path. Poor people should gain in distributional terms, or at least should not be negatively affected by the establishment of guaranteed minimum protection. There are always trade-offs—less spending elsewhere, more taxes, or lower benefits—and these should be assessed ex ante. If guaranteed minimum protection from poverty and impoverishing losses is the direction to take, the trajectories to achieve it matter. A guaranteed minimum will not be put in place overnight, and, in the absence of existing broad-based assistance programs to replace or extend, choices need to be made as to where (urban or rural areas) and with whom (informal workers, the disabled, or other groups) to start. The concept of *progressive universalism*, borrowed from the push for universal health coverage, places much weight on ensuring that the poorest benefit from the expansion of protection before, or at least in tandem with, other groups. For such prioritization to happen, systems to identify those most in need are vital. We return to this point in chapter 5 and again in chapter 6.

The pace of implementation will have to match the growth of administrative and taxation capacity to ensure sufficient fiscal space and minimize distortions. As chapter 5 makes clear, a solid core of guaranteed minimum protection will entail additional fiscal costs. Countries must pace the introduction of guaranteed minimum protection with their capacity to tax and deliver on that guarantee. This pacing is paramount, considering the role that the tax system plays not only for financing but also as a vehicle through which benefits are determined and beneficiary information is gathered. In this regard, the development of social registries should at some point converge with the development of the broader public administration, particularly the information platforms managed by the tax authorities. The model of setting up information systems and providing benefits based on proxies for wealth will likely present the same advantages and limitations as current proxy measures used to target social assistance.

## Notes

1. Quoting Barr (2001, 18), "The term 'insurance' is used by different people to mean different things: as a device that offers individuals protection against risk, or as an actuarial mechanism. The first defines insurance in terms of its objective, the second in terms of the mechanism by which that objective might be achieved. Even where institutions are not insurance in the second sense, they might still be regarded as insurance in that they offer protection against risk."

2. As an example, policies that help improve the functioning of land and capital markets can facilitate the functioning of labor markets, allowing households more mechanisms by which to reduce risk through their private actions. We take up this point later in this chapter when discussing the nudged and purely voluntary segments of the insurance assistance package. Improving land tenure security may facilitate diversification into migrant employment (see, for example, de Brauw and Mueller 2012), and facilitating migration may free up liquid forms of precautionary savings for other productive investments (see, for example, Giles and Yoo 2007; Kinnan, Wang, and Wang 2018).

3. The minimum guarantees depicted in figure 3.2 most commonly provide income support via cash, though, as alluded to in the opening paragraph of this section, "near cash" or even food, in some circumstances, may be a reasonable way to

provide the same function. In general, cash-based approaches have the important advantage of allowing recipients maximum flexibility in the use of benefits, and they can be provided at lower administrative cost than other forms of benefits, but their appropriateness and effectiveness should be carefully gauged, especially in lower-income settings, and alternative forms of provisions could be allowed in specific circumstances. For example, some evidence shows that cash may be less effective for specific goals such as improving nutrition (Gentilini et al. 2019). In the United States, the Supplemental Nutrition Assistance Program (SNAP) food voucher is two to ten times more effective than an equivalent cash transfer at increasing nutrients consumed by households. Experimental evidence from Niger shows that the highest impact on child malnutrition is attained by combining cash and in-kind transfers rather than by implementing individual interventions. From a different perspective, a quantitative study in Yemen found that large-scale in-kind interventions can be more cost-efficient than cash when markets are weak and inflation is high. "Universal basic income (net)" data in the figure refer to universal basic income when financed through the tax system.

4. To underscore how benefit levels shape labor-supply decisions (as well as for ease of comparison across countries), we use the share of the average wage rather than the share of autonomous (or total) income.

5. See Gentilini, Grosh, Rigolini, and Yemtsov (2019), offering a comprehensive analysis of UBI theory, evidence, experiences, financing, political economy, and delivery.

6. In health policy circles, out-of-pocket payments for health care are considered "catastrophic" when they amount to 30 percent or more of a household's disposable income.

7. The actual proposal made by Anton, Hernandez, and Levy (2013) is to eliminate exemptions that reduce the tax effort of the VAT.

8. The parameters here are from 2012. The eligibility age for the latter pension is set at 70, while the eligibility age for the contributory pension depends on contribution history.

9. The welfare measure was based on consumption, except in the Latin American countries, where it was based on reported incomes. See Majoka and Palacios (2019) for methodology and data sources.

10. Majoka and Palacios (2019) also provide evidence that the additional administrative costs of targeting would not significantly alter the result with regard to the poverty impact of a TUBI or a UBI.

11. This positive correlation between minimum pension guarantees and target average replacement rates is very common in pension systems around the world.

12. As discussed in appendix C, the simplifying assumption here is that individuals in the lowest levels of the income distribution face the same mortality rates as those in the upper levels.

13. It is important to note that the UBI or TUBI would also replace existing social assistance programs, so the required financing could be lower, depending on how much the country in question had been spending on social assistance prior to the reform.

14. The initial statutory contribution rate in this example is higher, 30 percent versus 20 percent, because the pension system is more generous.

# References

Akbas, M., D. Ariely, D. Robalino, and M. Weber. 2016. "How to Help Poor Informal Workers to Save a Bit: Evidence from a Field Experiment in Kenya." IZA Working Paper 1024. Bonn, Germany.

Anton, A., F. Hernandez, and S. Levy. 2013. *The End of Informality in Mexico? Fiscal Reform for Universal Social Insurance*. Washington, DC: Inter-American Development Bank.

Ashraf, N., D. Karlan, and W. Yin. 2006. "Tying Odysseus to the Mast: Evidence from a Commitment Savings Product in the Philippines." *Quarterly Journal of Economics* 121 (2): 635–72.

Baeza, C., and T. Packard. 2006. *Beyond Survival: Protecting Households from Health Shocks in Latin America*. Latin American Development Forum. Stanford, CA: Stanford University Press.

Bargu, A., and M. Morgandi. 2018. "Can Mothers Afford to Work in Poland? Labor Supply Incentives of Social Benefits and Childcare Costs." World Bank Policy Research Paper No. 8295. Washington, DC: World Bank.

Barr, N. 2001. *The Welfare State as Piggy Bank*. Oxford: Oxford University Press.

Barr, N., and P. Diamond. 2009. "Reforming Pensions: Principles, Analytical Errors and Policy Directions." *International Social Security Review* 62 (2): 5–29.

Benartzi, S., and R. H. Thaler. 2004. "Save More Tomorrow: Using Behavioral Economics to Increase Employee Saving." *Journal of Political Economy* 112 (1): S164–S187.

Beyer, H., and S. Valdes. 2004. "Propuestas para aumentar la densidad de cotizaciones." Paper presented at the seminar "Competencia y Cobertura" hosted by the Centro de Estudios Publicos (CEP) and the Superintendency of the AFP system (SAFP), Santiago, November 11–12.

Chandy, L. 2016. *The Future of Work in the Developing World: Brookings Blum Roundtable 2016 Post Conference Report*. Washington, DC: Brookings Institution Press.

Corsetti, G. 1994. "An Endogenous Growth Model of Social Security and the Size of the Informal Sector." Revista de Analisis Economico 9 (1): 57–76.

Cotlear, D., S. Nagpal, O. Smith, A. Tandon, and R. Cortez. 2015. *Going Universal: How 24 Developing Countries Are Implementing Universal Health Coverage Reforms from the Bottom Up*. Washington, DC: World Bank.

de Brauw, A., and V. Mueller. 2012. "Do Limitations in Land Rights Transferability Influence Low Mobility Rates in Ethiopia?" *Journal of African Economies* 21 (4): 548–79.

Dorfman, M., D. Wang, P. O'Keefe, and J. Cheng. 2013. "China's Pension Schemes for Rural and Urban Residents." In *Matching Contributions for Pensions*, edited by R. Hinz, R. Holzmann, D. Tuesta, and N. Takayama. Washington, DC: World Bank.

Dreze, J., and A. Sen. 1989. *Hunger and Public Action*. Oxford: Clarendon Press.

Fiszbein, A., N. Schady, F. H. G. Ferreira, M. Grosh, N. Keleher, P. Olinto, and E. Skoufias. 2009. *Conditional Cash Transfers: Reducing Present and Future Poverty*. World Bank Policy Research Report. Washington, DC: World Bank.

Friedman, M. 1987. "The Case for the Negative Income Tax." In *The Essence of Friedman*, edited by K. Leube, 57–68. Stanford, CA: Hoover Institution Press.

Gentilini, U., M. Grosh, J. Rigolini, and R. Yemtsov, eds. 2019. *Decoding Universal Basic Income: Evidence, Choices, and Practical Implications in Low- and Middle-Income Countries.* Washington, DC: World Bank.

Giles, J., and K. Yoo. 2007. "Precautionary Behavior, Migrant Networks and Household Consumption Decisions: An Empirical Analysis Using Household Panel Data from Rural China," *The Review of Economics and Statistics*, 89 (3): 534–51.

Gill, I., T. Packard, and J. Yermo. 2005. *Keeping the Promise of Social Security in Latin America.* Stanford, CA: Stanford University Press.

Grosh, M., C. del Ninno, E. Tesliuc, and A. Ouerghi. 2008. *For Protection and Promotion: The Design and Implementation of Effective Safety Nets.* Washington, DC: World Bank.

Holzmann, R., and S. Jørgensen. 2000. "Social Risk Management: A New Conceptual Framework for Social Protection and Beyond." Social Protection Discussion Paper No. 6, World Bank, Washington, DC.

Holzmann, R., D. A. Robalino, and N. Takayama. 2009. *Closing the Coverage Gap: The Role of Social Pensions and Other Retirement Income Transfers.* Washington, DC: World Bank.

ILO (International Labour Organization) and UNICEF (United Nations Children's Fund). 2019. "Towards Universal Social Protection for Children: Achieving SDG 1.3." ILO, Geneva, and UNICEF, New York.

IPPR (Institute for Public Policy Research). 2018. *Prosperity and Justice: A Plan for the New Economy.* The Final Report of the IPPR Commission on Economic Justice, Institute of Public Policy Research. Cambridge, UK: Polity Press.

Kahneman, D. 2011. *Thinking, Fast and Slow.* New York: Farrar, Straus & Giroux.

Kinnan, C., S.-Y. Wang, and Y. Wang. 2018. "Access to Migration for Rural Households." *American Economic Journal: Applied Economics.* 10 (4): 79–119.

Kotlikoff, L. 1987. "Justifying Public Provision of Social Security." *Journal of Policy Analysis and Management* 6 (4): 674–96.

Levy, S. 2018. *Under-Rewarded Efforts: The Elusive Quest for Prosperity in Mexico.* Washington, DC: Inter-American Development Bank.

Lusardi, A., and O. S. Mitchell. 2014. "The Economic Importance of Financial Literacy: Theory and Evidence." *Journal of Economic Literature* 52 (1): 5–44.

Lustig, N. 2018. *Commitment to Equity Handbook: Estimating the Impact of Fiscal Policy on Inequality and Poverty.* Washington, DC: Brookings Institution Press.

Majoka, Z., and R. Palacios. 2019. "Targeting versus Universality: Is There a Middle Ground?" Technical Background Note for Social Protection and Jobs White Paper on Risk Sharing, World Bank, Washington, DC.

Organisation for Economic Co-operation and Development (OECD). 2018. "The Future of Social Protection: What Works for Non-Standard Workers?" Policy Brief on the Future of Work, Organization for Economic Cooperation and Development, Paris.

Packard, T., J. Koettl, and C. E. Montenegro. 2012. *In From the Shadow: Integrating Europe's Informal Labor.* Directions in Development: Human Development. Washington, DC: World Bank.

Pages, C., ed. 2010. *The Age of Productivity: Transforming Economies from the Bottom Up.* Washington, DC: Inter-American Development Bank.

Palacios, R., and D. Robalino. 2019. "Integrating Social Insurance and Social Assistance for a Future World of Labor." Technical Background Note for Social Protection and Jobs White Paper on Risk Sharing, World Bank, Washington, DC.

Pinxten, J. 2019. "De Jure Benefit Entitlements for Indonesian Families." Technical Background Note for Social Protection and Jobs White Paper on Risk Sharing, World Bank, Washington, DC.

Ribe, H., D. A. Robalino, and I. Walker. 2012. *From Right to Reality: Incentives, Labor Markets, and the Challenge of Universal Social Protection in Latin America and the Caribbean.* Latin America Development Forum. Washington, DC: World Bank.

Rofman, R., I. Apella, and E. Vezza, eds. 2014. *Beyond Contributory Pensions: Fourteen Experiences with Coverage Expansion in Latin America.* Directions in Development Series. Washington, DC: World Bank.

Rudolph, H. 2019. "Pension Funds with Automatic Enrollment Schemes: Lessons from Emerging Economies." World Bank Policy Research Working Paper No. 8726, World Bank, Washington, DC.

Summers, L. H. 1989. "Some Simple Economics of Mandated Benefits." *American Economic Review* 79 (2): 177–83.

Standing, Guy. 2011. *The Precariat: The New Dangerous Class.* London: Bloomsbury Academic.

Thaler, R. H., and C. R. Sunstein. 2008. *Nudge: Improving Decisions about Health, Wealth, and Happiness.* New Haven, CT: Yale University Press.

Tondani, D. 2009. "Universal Basic Income and Negative Income Tax: Two Different Ways of Thinking Redistribution." *Journal of Behavioral and Experimental Economics* 38 (2): 246–55.

Walliser, J. 2002. "Adverse Selection in the Annuities Market and the Impact of Privatizing Social Security." *Scandinavian Journal of Economics* 102 (3): 373–93.

Wang, D., J. Chen, and W. Gao. 2011. "Social Security Integration: The Case of Rural and Urban Resident Pension Pilot in Chengdu." Unpublished, World Bank, Washington, DC.

World Bank. 2012. *World Development Report 2013: Jobs.* Washington, DC: World Bank Group.

———. 2015. *World Development Report 2015: Mind, Society, and Behavior.* Washington, DC: World Bank Group.

# 4

# Labor Policy for a Diverse and Diversifying World of Work

Human capital is the most important asset in which people invest, and the labor market is where they seek the return on that investment as well as a place where most people experience shocks and losses. Like all markets, the labor market has imperfections and failures that motivate actions by governments to improve people's prospects (Boeri and van Ours 2014). These policy actions vary widely across countries both in form and in the combination and the intensity with which they are deployed. There are also sizable differences in the capacity of governments to implement, monitor, and enforce policies; to limit the unintended effects of their interventions; and to make these measures amount to more than just pages in the labor code (Kanbur and Ronconi 2018; Kuddo, Robalino, and Weber 2015; Packard and Van Nguyen 2014; World Bank 2012). However, the objectives of most governments are similar: to ensure that the labor market is safe, fair, and a place where people's skills and enterprise are rewarded. These objectives are particularly important to achieve so that the newest entrants to the labor market—either coming fresh from full-time education or having never previously had market work—have the best chances of success.

This chapter presents ideas to motivate and inform a new generation of labor market policies better suited to a diverse and diversifying world of work. In earlier chapters, we argued that the drivers of disruption—technological change and economic integration, in particular—are challenging the primacy of the archetypal standard employer-employee relationship as a formal institution, and even as an aspirational norm.

But other drivers of disruption are also felt in the labor market. Social, demographic, and climate changes are reconfiguring the composition of the workforce and the geography of work. More women are engaging in market work than ever before, broadening the set of expectations and preferences for how work is done and what prosperity means. In countries managing a youth bulge, there is a wealth of increasingly better-educated and urbanized young people competing for jobs, acting on new goals and ideas about the directions they want their career paths to take. In demographically aging countries, a clear policy imperative has emerged to keep people productively engaged for longer portions of their lives, and a new generation of active elderly expect more choice and flexibility when deciding how to use their time. Global climate change is threatening to force, or has already forced, people to relocate to pursue their livelihoods, and it is challenging the viability of many industries and forms of work.

In this chapter we discuss five key implications of these disruptions for labor market policies:

1. *There is a rising premium on adaptability.* The social costs of rigidity—so-called labor market sclerosis—and of protecting certain firms and jobs from changing market forces is rising. More than ever, for countries to capture the benefits of disruption, firms and working people need to adapt quickly to the changing structures of production and nature of work. Recent World Bank reports (Kuddo, Robalino, and Weber 2015; World Bank 2012) have advocated a moderated approach to labor market policy to balance the needs of market participants (working people and firms) and society. However, the regulatory stance of many governments, especially those of low- and middle-income countries, is neither moderate nor balanced and tends, de jure, toward greater restriction of the decisions of firms and people. There appears to be a growing tendency to use regulation as the primary policy instrument for redistribution and risk sharing, in lieu of better-articulated social protection and tax systems. However, this tendency is observed even in countries where national social protection and progressive tax systems are quickly developing and where governments and markets can offer superior instruments with fewer adverse consequences.

2. *Labor market policies should reflect a diverse and fluid world of work.* Labor market policies in most countries do not accommodate diversity and fluidity of working forms well. As argued in chapter 1, this flaw probably reflects the contexts in which these policies were conceived as well as the aspirations of past and present governments in low- and middle-income countries for how their economies should develop. In today's low- and middle-income countries, the world of work has long

been characterized by diversity and fluidity, and that is likely to remain the case. Diversity and fluidity are now becoming characteristics of work in high-income countries too. Yet labor policies—particularly employment protection and labor regulation—assume homogeneity and stability and that employers are effective and reliable agents for the implementation of social protection. If guarantees against poverty, catastrophic losses, and other protections were instead defined in a way that is neutral to where and how people work, greater diversity and fluidity could be embraced, not feared. The exclusion at present of many working people from these protections is more often than not an artifact of how the protections are designed. Where and how a person works need no longer be either a de jure or a de facto obstacle to coverage.

3. *Greater effort is required to help people manage labor market transitions and dislocation.* Rather than allocating the bulk of resources to protecting people *from* change, governments should protect people *for* change. The volume, coverage and efficiency of active employment assistance measures and income protection arrangements will have to increase to facilitate more frequent livelihood disruptions, labor market transitions, and changes in how people engage with the economy (for example, from unemployment or inactivity into work and from lower- to higher-quality jobs) and to meet the needs of people who have been dislocated by structural changes such as trade liberalization and automation. "Flexicurity" is now an old idea for how to intervene in the labor market, but it is still a very good one that was only ever fully achieved in a handful of countries. Its underlying principles can be applied more broadly than they have been, even in countries with extensive informal employment and a large informal economy. But in any country, flexicurity requires that much greater public expenditure, effort, and expertise be allocated to active employment policies, including skill development. Too many governments that enthusiastically loosened labor regulations have yet to bring these resources to bear. This is a grave mistake that can be corrected.

4. *Even with the best policies in place, targeted interventions will be required to stimulate demand and increase productivity.* Labor policies will need to better integrate and coordinate with targeted interventions to address government and market failures that still constrain job creation and the quality and productivity of existing jobs.

5. *Measures to counter the concentration of market power and institutions that give all working people greater voice are more vital than ever.* The structural and political decline of labor unions has removed an important accountability instrument that was once available to many working people.

The fundamental problem with labor unions is that even when they were at their prime, these institutions were not available to enough working people. The same is true of employer and professional associations with respect to small-business owners and the self-employed. New structures are needed for dialogue and bargaining and to hold all market participants accountable. These structures should represent the diversity of interests in the labor market. This representation can foster greater inclusion, since women and low-skilled workers are more likely to work informally and in nonstandard formal work. Traditional labor and employer organizations will remain relevant when they embrace that diversity and seek out new membership or make room for working people who historically have not been represented in the prevailing tripartite dialogue between workers, employers, and government. And at the national level, the structures of dialogue may have to be reshaped to reflect the diversity of work and to give interested parties their own seat at the table. The ability to observe, record, report, and mobilize, which has been so radically atomized by digital technology and social media, may ultimately prove a far more powerful check on market power than traditional measures as well as the most effective instrument to encourage greater social responsibility from all market participants.

Policy actions are more likely to be effective when they are appropriately *prioritized* and *sequenced*. This chapter uses the policy pyramid of the *World Development Report 2013: Jobs* (World Bank 2012) to organize its response to the challenges of a diverse and diversifying world of work (see figure 4.1). As the core business of the World Bank's Social Protection and Jobs Global Practice, the policy categories represented by the top two segments of the pyramid are treated in detail in this chapter. Many of the risk-sharing policies already discussed in chapter 3—those that support household consumption in the wake of shocks—are part of the middle segment of the pyramid, "Labor policies" (such as income support during unemployment spells). Furthermore, we have a more specific interpretation than does the *World Development Report 2013* of what belongs in the top segment, "Priorities"; namely, measures targeted to isolated or excluded groups for whom the social benefits of jobs are highest (according to the *World Development Report 2013*, these groups are women, young people, and people in conflict-affected or otherwise fragile contexts) and whose job options are the most constrained even when the best policies are in place. However, the foundational role of the bottom segment of the pyramid—policy "Fundamentals"—is a vital priority in every country that cannot be ignored. Following the logic of the *World Development Report 2013*, we start this chapter with a brief discussion of policies at the base of the pyramid and then work our way to the top. A strong base of policy fundamentals provides the support for policy actions in the top two segments.

**Figure 4.1    In the Face of Uncertainty, a Resilient Pro-work Strategy Starts by Eliminating Policies That Bias Firm Choices against Labor**

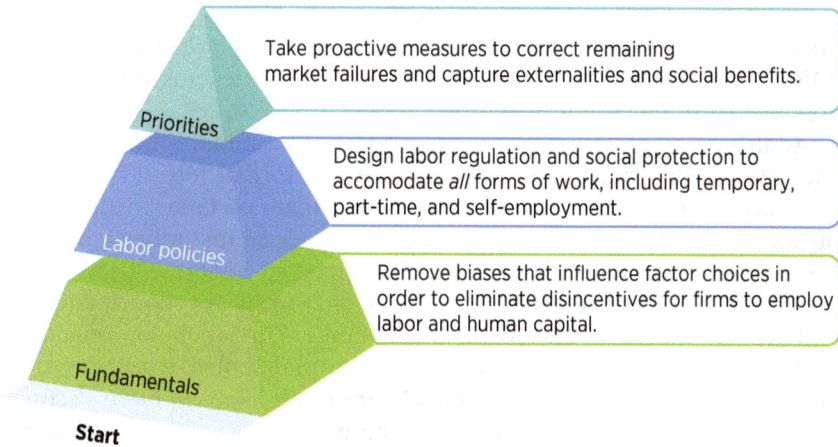

Take proactive measures to correct remaining market failures and capture externalities and social benefits.

Priorities

Design labor regulation and social protection to accomodate *all* forms of work, including temporary, part-time, and self-employment.

Labor policies

Remove biases that influence factor choices in order to eliminate disincentives for firms to employ labor and human capital.

Fundamentals

**Start**

*Sources:* Adapted from World Bank 2012 and Packard and Van Nguyen 2014.

## Fundamentals: Remove Policy Biases That Put Working People at a Disadvantage

With growing uncertainty about the changing nature of work, a more adaptive and resilient policy stance starts by removing policy-induced biases on firms' factor choices. There is an inconsistency between the growing consensus around the social value of work (that is, that work holds a value to society greater than the earned income paid to workers, the profits paid to firms, and the production added to the economy) and policies that implicitly discourage employment creation and formal job offers. Borrowing from well-accepted (if not always applied) principles of taxation (see Furman 2008; Piketty and Saez 2012), policy makers should seek a more neutral stance with respect to the factors of production than what is currently observed in many countries (Packard and Van Nguyen 2014). A more neutral policy stance is one that avoids explicit or implicit incentives that shape the choices of market participants or that systematically—sometimes only implicitly—favor one factor of production over others. Yet, globally, since 2004 the burden of taxation has shifted away from profits and toward labor earnings. Taxes on earnings from labor are now set at higher rates than are those on most other sources of income. Furthermore, in almost every country, inherited wealth, land, and pollution are undertaxed (World Bank 2013) despite the ample orthodox economic arguments for more intensive use of these levies. The European Commission (EC) recently encouraged member countries of the European Union (EU) to lower the tax burden on labor, which it concluded was very high (European Union 2015), and to shift to more growth-friendly levies (as discussed in greater depth in chapter 5).

Additionally, governments in many low- and middle-income countries levy high explicit and implicit taxes on formal jobs. The explicit taxes are easier to identify: relatively higher taxes on labor income than on income from other sources and statutory social insurance contributions which are only loosely linked to expected benefits. These taxes create a wedge between the cost of labor that firms are required to pay and the remuneration that workers take home. This labor-tax wedge can be very large, and even larger for low- to mid-skilled workers (Arias et al. 2014; Pagés 2017). These people are more likely to be in occupations intensive in routine tasks and, therefore, most vulnerable to the disruptive impact of automation. There is evidence that a large tax wedge can contribute to a reduction in the number of formal employment offers (Heckman and Pagés 2004; Kugler and Kugler 2009). This reduction occurs as firms replace labor with capital but also as lower-productivity firms exit, or as new firms choose not to enter, the formal economy in order to avoid payroll taxes, other taxes, and nontax compliance costs. Tax exemptions and special tax treatment of small firms can also create an implicit tax on scale and the creation of formal jobs (Bird and Smart 2014; Levy 2008 and 2018). From a household perspective, overtaxing labor earnings can create disincentives to work or to work formally, especially among younger and older workers, lower-skilled workers, and women (Arias et al. 2014; Koettl and Weber 2012). As discussed in the previous chapter, reducing the size of tax wedges involves rethinking both the design and the financing of publicly provided risk-pooling arrangements with poverty prevention and other redistributive objectives.

There are also significant policy biases in nontax laws that distort labor costs for specific population subgroups. This is often the case for women, for example (World Bank 2018, 2019). Some of these laws affect preferences for hiring men over women because they make women's labor de facto more expensive: laws that prohibit women from doing certain types of work; those that restrict the ability of women to inherit productive assets; those that require provision of childcare services by employers according to the number of employees or of women employees; those that relate to maternity- and paternity-leave policies; and those that concern public childcare financing.[1] A similar lack of neutrality in laws affects, for example, informal household enterprises by restricting or punishing these types of businesses.

Beyond fiscal policies and taxation choices, governments could pay closer attention to other powerful levers of macroeconomic and regulatory policy that affect the demand for labor. There is nothing deterministic about the path that the drivers of disruption are taking and the changes they are making to the nature of work. Firms and households react to their policy environment. Exchange-rate and monetary policy have intended and unintended impacts on the choices that firms make. The pace of technology adoption and automation may be rapid, but it also can be unduly hastened by relatively inexpensive capital. A policy stance that biases firms' decisions one way or the other may accelerate and aggravate disruption in ways that are unfavorable to people who depend on work for their livelihood. Such a stance can lead to structural imbalances: too much capital and not enough labor in certain sectors of the economy, or vice versa. Over time, these imbalances can become embedded economically and even politically as interest groups form and become accustomed to policy-enabled favorable treatment in factor and product markets (Packard and Van Nguyen 2014).

Finally, threats to competitive and contestable product and service markets are growing and hindering the labor market, requiring a far more robust response from governments, particularly to curb the concentration of market power. The market power of firms is growing in many parts of the world. Ensuring competitive and contestable markets has long been a challenge in low- and middle-income countries where governance institutions are weak and can be especially vulnerable to oligopolistic pressures. However, many of the same pressures, and the dangers of market concentration, are increasing in high-income countries as well (Aznar, Marinescu, and Steinbaum 2017; Stiglitz 2019; Dube et al. 2018). A growing body of research from the United States, the United Kingdom, and other high-income countries shows that as local-level employer concentration grows, wages remain persistently low, and that the negative impact for a given level of concentration is increasing (Benmelech, Bergman, and Kim 2018). Concentration is often accompanied by restrictive practices, such as the proliferation of local licensing requirements or the extensive use of non-compete clauses and no-poaching agreements even in industries that hire mostly lower-skilled people (Krueger and Posner 2018; Naidu, Posner, and Weyl 2018). These restrictions to competition combine with declining labor mobility to erode labor's bargaining power, put downward pressure on earnings (Konczal and Steinbaum 2016), and limit the opportunities for working people to prosper.

## Labor Market Regulation in Low- and Middle-Income Countries: Off the Plateau?

Labor market regulations are important instruments in the policy maker's toolkit to ensure people's talent and effort are rewarded fairly. Reflecting the anxiety that accompanies the drivers of disruption in many countries, long-running debates over the benefits and costs of labor market regulations are once again rising in volume and pitch. The *World Development Report 2013* argued that on a broad *plateau* between extreme *cliffs* of too little and too much regulatory intervention, the impact of these instruments matters less to aggregate employment and earnings outcomes than the strident tone of much of the debate suggests (see figure 4.2). However, this conclusion does not mean that labor market regulations are of no consequence. The core labor standards of the International Labour Office (ILO), for example, represent vital

**Figure 4.2  To Minimize Adverse Labor Market Outcomes, Countries Should Avoid Regulatory Extremes**

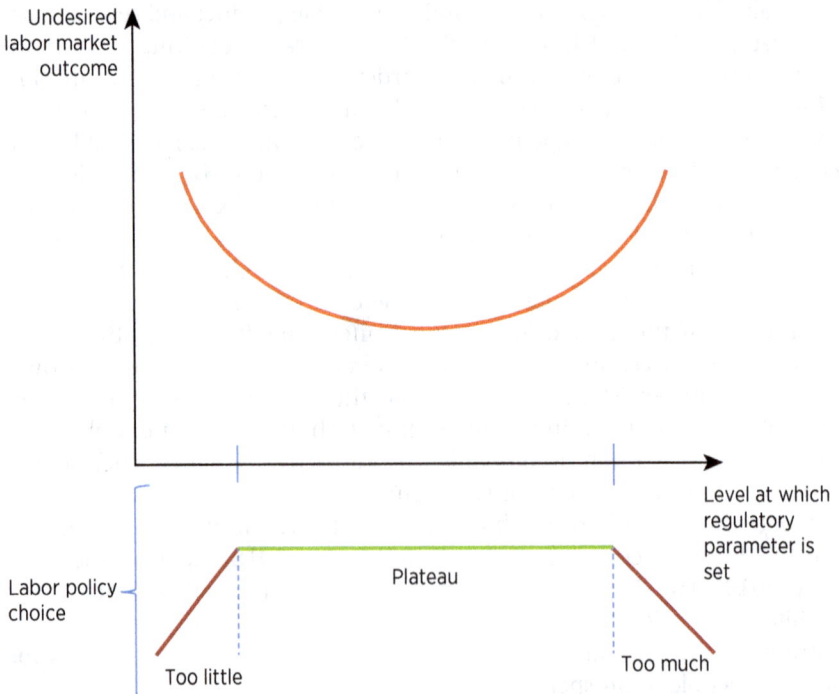

bulwarks that safeguard hard-won advances in human well-being and that remain a key development benchmark used in the World Bank's annual *Country Policy and Institutional Assessment.*

The vital principle for policy makers to follow when setting labor regulation is to avoid extremes. The topographic reference to a plateau is a compelling and powerful metaphor. But this plateau has not yet been sufficiently developed to provide actionable policy guidance. More analytical effort is required to empirically and convincingly identify its features, most importantly the inflection points—where "too little" stops and "too much" starts—and at what levels between the two extremes regulation is relatively beneficial and benign. It is safe to assume that these features of the "topography" of regulation and outcomes will vary significantly according to countries' economic and institutional development: setting a national minimum wage at a certain level—relative to the median wage or average worker productivity—in Chile or Turkey, for example, will have a very different impact on outcomes than it will in Brazil or the Philippines, all of which have similar ratios of the statutory minimum wage to the median wage. Furthermore, the plateau metaphor was originally presented with reference to a limited set of market outcomes: aggregate employment and earnings. On distributional outcomes— that is, differences in outcomes between groups of working people—and on firms' ability to adjust to cyclical and structural changes, the evidence presented in the published literature is more ambiguous. To extend the metaphor, the safe plateau level for beneficial distributional outcomes could lie at a different "altitude," or it may not be as broad. In a diverse and diversifying world of work, all of these matters become equally important.

Despite the call for moderation in labor market regulations, the stance of many governments in the labor markets of low- and middle-income countries is becoming more restrictive, even as restrictions are being eased in higher-income countries, as illustrated in figure 4.3. The *World Development Report 2013* and subsequent prominent World Bank publications (Kuddo, Robalino, and Weber 2015) show how the parameters of labor regulations are often set at relatively extreme levels: either scant and barely enforced or restrictive and applied partially or even opportunistically to choke off competition. In many low- and middle-income countries, the de jure parameters of labor regulation—restrictions on protections that can be extended to people working less than full time, restrictions on when and where work can take place, restrictions on firms' hiring and dismissal choices and on what jobs can be done by women (World Bank 2018)—may indeed lie on the extreme "cliffs" of the plateau (Kuddo 2015 and 2018; World Bank 2012).

**Figure 4.3 Off the "Plateau"? The Regulatory Stances of Many Governments of Low- and Middle-Income Countries Regarding Their Labor Markets Appear Extreme**

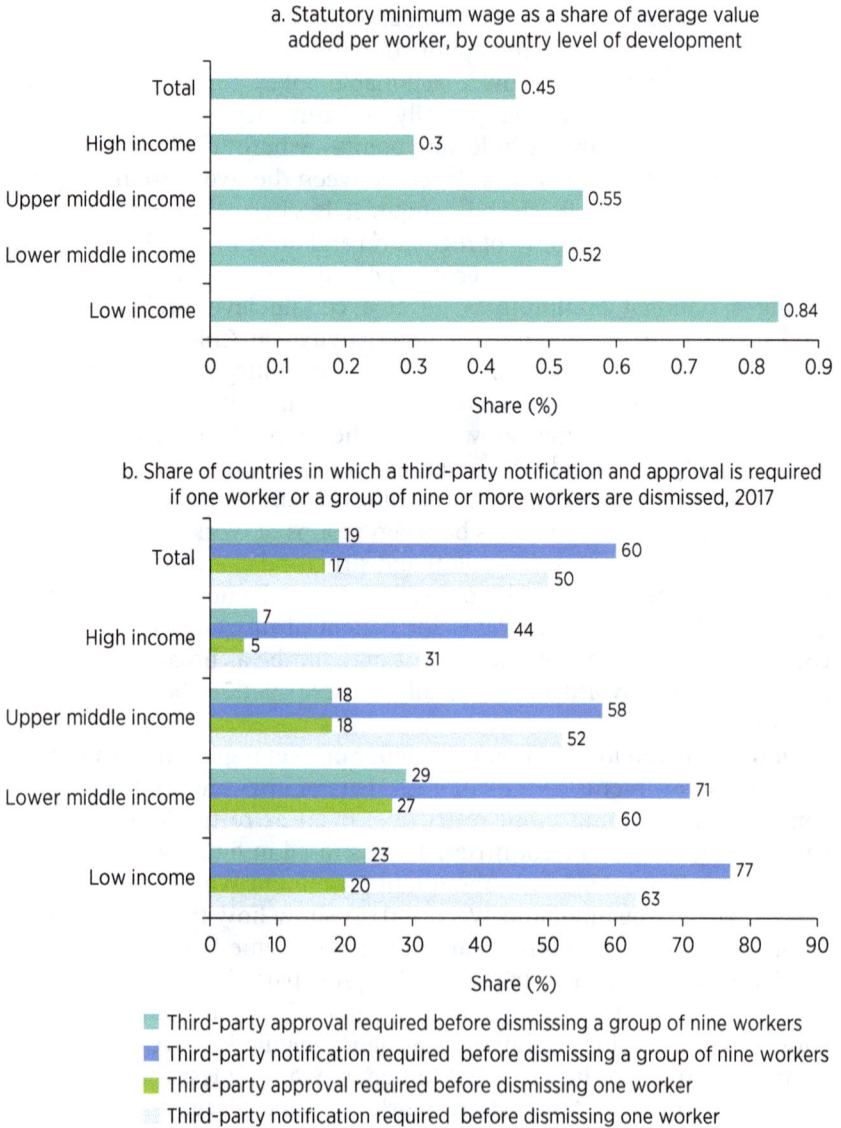

a. Statutory minimum wage as a share of average value added per worker, by country level of development

b. Share of countries in which a third-party notification and approval is required if one worker or a group of nine or more workers are dismissed, 2017

■ Third-party approval required before dismissing a group of nine workers
■ Third-party notification required before dismissing a group of nine workers
■ Third-party approval required before dismissing one worker
  Third-party notification required before dismissing one worker

*Source:* Kuddo 2018, using data from World Bank 2017.

*Note:* Panel a excludes Liberia (with a ratio of 2.54) and República Bolivariana de Venezuela (with a ratio of 5.99) as outliers.

The flurry of labor market reforms in the past two decades are taking countries in different directions. Many high-income countries are liberalizing, while many low- and middle-income countries are increasing restrictions (Duval and Loungani 2019; Kuddo 2018). The regulatory extremes in the labor codes of many low- and middle-income countries, including those in Central and Eastern Europe, become more starkly apparent when compared with how parameters of labor regulation have been shifting in the countries of Southern and Western Europe in the past two decades (Gill, Koettl, and Packard 2013; Bussolo et al. 2018; Packard, Koettl, and Montenegro 2012). Between 2007 and 2017, fully 99 countries passed reforms to their labor regulations. The most common changes made were to (i) procedural requirements in case of contract termination and changes in notification arrangements (51 cases); (ii) the use of fixed-term contracts (42 cases); and (iii) severance pay requirements (24 cases). Approximately 60 percent of the reforms made labor legislation more flexible, and 40 percent made regulation more restrictive and protective of jobs (Kuddo 2018). Many low- and middle-income countries of Southeast Asia that only recently introduced their first labor codes have opted for very restrictive regulations (Packard and Van Nguyen 2014; Schmillen and Packard 2016).

Low- and middle-income countries may be using strict labor regulations to make up for absent or nascent risk-sharing and other social protection arrangements. A general hypothesis to explain this extreme stance is that labor regulation is still being deployed by policy makers as the principal instrument of redistribution and risk-sharing policy. In the mid- and late industrial era, when most governments lacked the fiscal and administrative capacity to develop other risk-sharing and redistribution instruments, this approach probably made sense. However, as discussed for a broad range of poverty-prevention and consumption-smoothing objectives in chapter 3, this is no longer the case even in low- and middle-income countries, where the capacity to deliver timely cash and other transfers has grown exponentially. This is a point we will return to in chapter 5.

Society need no longer place as much reliance on the place and stability of employment to extend reliable and resilient protection from shocks and losses, or even to pursue greater equity. Readers will recall from the opening chapter that when the prevailing models were put in place, the employer and firm were the assumed superior providers of protection and continuity, primarily through seniority-based advancement or internal labor markets. Partly due to the nonexistence or inadequacy of government-provided risk-sharing arrangements such as formal social protection systems, firms were reasonably expected to be the platform for delivery of social protection, whether in the form of risk pooling, mandatory precautionary saving, or skill renewal mechanisms. Labor regulations and mandates on firms were used to provide more than just basic protections; they were the tools at hand to prevent in-work poverty, keep unemployment relatively rare, smooth consumption in the wake of shocks, and help people make market transitions. However, the advances in government capacity in many countries since then have made available alternative and more reliable instruments that pose a much lower risk of collateral damage to job opportunities.

The statutory minimum wage remains prevalent and popular, but as an instrument for broad poverty prevention and achieving greater earnings equality, its effectiveness and efficiency is increasingly unclear. The original purpose of setting a statutory floor on earnings was to ensure a fair remuneration to workers that reflected their marginal labor product (Boeri and van Ours 2014). By setting a statutory floor on earnings, the minimum wage protects working people from an abuse of market power by employers. Most countries and economies now legislate a minimum wage. The policy practice has expanded in the past decade to Bhutan; Cabo Verde; Germany; Hong Kong SAR, China; Kiribati; Kosovo; Malaysia; Myanmar; and West Bank and Gaza. However, rather than deploy the instrument for its original purpose, most countries and economies try to use the minimum wage as a minimum income guarantee or to pursue redistribution objectives. This approach may have made sense when governments were fiscally or administratively unable—or politically reluctant—to offer social transfers. However, now that most can, a legislated wage floor is a second-best tool for guaranteeing an income, especially where it is set too high relative to labor productivity. Rather, the statutory minimum wage should be increasingly seen as complementary to other approaches that increase households' incomes, help them smooth consumption, and support a fairer distribution of labor's marginal product. As an increasing number of governments become adept at delivering social transfers to prevent poverty, as well as at deploying other public services to ameliorate the inequities of pure-market outcomes, the social costs of distortions imposed by the statutory minimum wage are rising.

The effectiveness of the statutory minimum wage in low- and middle-income countries is even more uncertain. In developing-country labor markets where the informal economy is sizeable and the largest share of the labor force works informally, statutory wage floors are relatively blunt instruments to combat poverty and inequality that can inflict considerable collateral damage. A statutory minimum wage can raise the earned income of families at the bottom of the wage distribution. Key to this outcome, however, is that people who earn close to the imposed minimum remain employed. Whether and in what circumstances firms are likely to retain lower-productivity workers when a statutory minimum is imposed or raised has long been disputed, with appeals to a large body of empirical literature that continues to grow (Card and Krueger 1995; Dube 2018; Neumark and Wascher 2008). The main limitations of a statutory floor on earnings as a tool of social policy in low- and middle-income countries are weak governance and the severe limitations on monitoring and enforcement capacity that create an environment of evasion and abuse (Almeida and Carneiro 2011; Cunningham 2007; Del Carpio and Pabon 2017; Kanbur and Ronconi 2018). For example, in a recent report on wage inequality in Latin America, Messina and Silva (2018) find that noncompliance with the statutory minimum wage rises linearly with its level as a share of median earnings.[2] In the same report, the authors argue that although a rise in the statutory minimum wage can compress the earnings distribution, the contribution of this policy to more equitable earnings outcomes has been markedly procyclical and relatively minor compared with other factors, such as rapid expansion of education, shifts in aggregate domestic demand, and the impact of exchange-rate appreciation on nontradable services. By the time that many of the countries in Latin America cycled out of the recent commodity boom–fueled, high-growth years, increases in statutory minimum wages had priced many workers out of formal jobs.[3] In an analysis of a large increase in the national minimum wage in Turkey, Acar, Bossavie, and Makovec (2019) found that the increase raised firms' exit rates from the formal economy by 12 percent. Firm exits attributable to the minimum wage increase accounted for up to one-third of the total formal employment destruction that occurred between 2015 and 2016.

Even as a tool to correct uneven market power between employers and workers, the statutory minimum wage as it is designed and administered in many countries can be a relatively blunt instrument. The way that statutory wage floors are designed and implemented in most countries assumes that the uneven market power, and any resulting unfair distribution of marginal labor product, is the same across sectors or geography. Where governments have attempted to take account of the variation across sectors or geography, even greater distortions and administrative burdens arise from the resulting complexity of myriad statutory wage levels. If the statutory minimum is set relatively low, these issues are likely to affect job outcomes less. However, in many countries, the statutory minimum wage can rise with little relationship to differences in market power or productivity in different sectors and locations. In some cases, the resulting minimum wage is too high given workers' labor productivity. Where the minimum wage is too high, governments' enforcement capacity is limited; and where compliance is poor, minimum wages can be unintentionally distortive and cause many of the work relationships with the greatest social benefits—such as jobs for young people—to be informalized or destroyed. Statutory minimum wages are also slow or unresponsive to changes in market power.

The foregoing arguments notwithstanding, statutory wage floors are still a vital instrument of social policy. The important policy debate is no longer *whether* a statutory minimum wage should be imposed but rather *how*: at what level, and how that level should be adjusted over time. The key principle to follow in reforming statutory minimum wages is to contain market distortions by strengthening the link between the level of the minimum and changes in productivity. Where a comprehensive package of risk-sharing instruments (as described in the previous chapter) is in place—or can be approximated by aggregating and coordinating traditional safety nets and other social protection instruments—the market power of working people is strengthened. They will have greater agency with which to decline abusive job offers. Robust social protection instruments with broad coverage, such as the tapered universal basic income (TUBI) and tapered universal social insurance (TUSI) discussed in chapter 3—and eventually other instruments that similarly use a country's public finance system rather than the employment relationship as a delivery platform—would relieve much of the social and political upward pressures on the statutory minimum wage. Indeed, with these measures in place, the original objective of protecting workers against abuses of employer market power and ensuring that they are paid according to their productivity could be given priority. A positive and powerful incremental reform to how statutory minimum wages are currently structured is to give greater weight to changes in average productivity in the formulas used to determine how the level of the minimum is adjusted (see box 4.1). But, as stressed at the beginning of this chapter, enforcing competition laws and other curbs on concentration and market power are even more vital.

Strong institutions for dialogue and negotiation can help keep the statutory minimum wage at reasonable levels. As important as, or even more important than, the specific parameters of the level-adjustment formula are the accompanying institutional structures that encourage a more continuous and systematic engagement of stakeholders. The results of a level-adjustment formula should ideally be used as the starting point in frequent, regularly occurring, and mundane negotiations to set the statutory minimum wage rather than being predetermined and unquestionable outcomes that could mechanically depart dramatically from the economic cycle and market outcomes.

Ultimately, the best way to align the incentives of firms and their workers is to encourage more firms to offer employees a stake in the success of their enterprise. Recognizing that it is becoming increasingly difficult in many sectors to clearly identify and price workers' marginal labor product, a complementary—but far more ambitious—approach would be to align firm and worker interests explicitly with policies that incentivize greater use of profit-sharing and employee-ownership structures. Profit-sharing is

## BOX 4.1

## Minimum Wage Formulas: Renewed Respectability, with a Productivity Argument

The debate on how the level of the minimum wage should be adjusted has evolved from arguments as to *whether* to arguments as to *how*. The old debates pitted ardent proponents of discretion and flexibility in the face of uncertain future economic circumstances against equally passionate advocates for transparency and predictability in how wage policy is carried out. The latter argued for clear, undiscriminating adjustment formulas and their technical value in places with weak or opaque governance institutions, vulnerable to capture by one or another party. The former feared the hand of policy on the level of statutory wage floors would be pushed or pulled mechanically and with little reference to circumstances. In countries prone to price instability, critics of formulas warned of wage-price spirals. Adjustment formulas are newly in vogue.

The current debate is duller but also more useful. In this debate, the value of a transparently designed and managed adjustment formula is clearly recognized, but just as important to the adjustment process are the voices of stakeholders and government, interacting regularly through permanent institutions. The debate is now over the relative weights of stakeholder and government input and over formula outcomes. Del Carpio and Pabon (2017) conclude that it is best to have a clear formula that avoids excessive rigidity in the process and that is easy for all stakeholders to understand, apply, and discuss. The formula should be constructed to reflect policy objectives agreed upon by stakeholders and government (for example, to ensure that workers in uncompetitive labor markets are fairly remunerated per their contribution to firms' and the economy's productivity), and that the resulting levels should serve as a technically derived starting position in regular negotiations.

Additionally, in this new debate, productivity and growth appear to sit equally alongside risk-management and social-justice objectives. When adjustment formulas include arguments to reflect labor's marginal product, a large part of the distortion imposed by a wage floor can be mitigated. Cunningham et al. (2016) present wage-setting and adjustment formulas that they use to calculate an adjustment path for minimum wages that takes better account of economic conditions, including the extent of informal employment. Their methodology starts with a formula to set the level of a basic minimum wage as a function

*continued next page*

**Box 4.1** *(continued)*

of the median wage and the poverty line. The outcome is adjusted for labor productivity, the unemployment rate, and the cost-of-living index. A second formula is defined to annually adjust the level by the cost of living, labor productivity, the employment rate, and the rate of informal employment.

*Setting the level:* The starting level of the minimum wage is a simple average of the poverty line per worker (*P*) and the median salary of workers in the lower half of the wage distribution. This calculation ensures that the minimum wage is always above the poverty line. The second argument in the formula takes account of productivity (*PR*), the consumer price index (*CPI*), and the rate of unemployment (*U*). This term allows the minimum wage to keep pace with salaries in the rest of the economy.

$$MW_i = \left[ Average\left(P_i, (Median\ wage)\right)\right] * \left[ 1 + \left(\frac{PR_i}{100}\right) + \left(\frac{CPI_i}{100}\right) - \left(\frac{U_i}{100}\right)\right]$$

(B4.1.1)

*The annual adjustment:* A second formula determines the annual adjustment using four arguments: the *CPI*, workers' productivity (*LPR*), the share of workers in the informal sector (*INF*), and the employment rate (*EMP*).

$$\Delta\%MW_{t-t_{-1}} = +\beta_1\%CPI_{t-t_{-1}} + \beta_2\%\Delta LPR_{t-t_{-1}}$$
$$- \left(\beta_3\right)\%\Delta INF_{t-trend} + \left(\beta_4\right)\%\Delta EMP_{t-trend}.$$

(B4.1.2)

The coefficients $\beta_1$ and $\beta_2$ are set by negotiation between stakeholders. The coefficients $\beta_3$ and $\beta_4$ are calculated using elasticities of employment with respect to the minimum wage and the rate of informal employment. The positive sign on the CPI reflects the increases required to maintain workers' purchasing power. Productivity also enters the formula positively, reflecting a greater contribution of workers to gross domestic product (GDP). The positive sign on the employment parameter is associated with the possibility of raising the minimum wage when doing so contributes to employment growth. The coefficient on the rate of informality is negative, reflecting the observation that increases in the minimum wage tend to increase rates of informal work.

*Sources:* Cunningham et al. 2016; Del Carpio and Pabon 2017.

an expanding practice in many countries that can deliver gains in worker well-being as well as in firm performance (Blasi, Freeman, and Kruse 2013; Doucouliagos et al. 2018; Estrin et al. 1997). A growing number of firms—including many outside the high-tech sector in high-income countries, where this is relatively common practice—offer profit-sharing and employee-ownership plans as a motivation to their workforces and in order to attract the best talent.[4] What would it take to make profit-sharing and employee-ownership practices the rule rather than the exception? Can market-friendly policies give working people a larger stake in the productivity upside of structural changes in the economy? We return to these questions in chapter 6.

## Flexibility and Greater Neutrality with Respect to Where and How People Work

Stringent restrictions on firms' hiring and dismissal decisions can create structural rigidities and obstacles to inclusion that will incur higher social costs as worker diversity increases and market disruption becomes more frequent. Reforming the most stringent restrictions on firms' hiring and dismissal decisions should be a priority. Once a buzzword of labor policy in Europe in the 1990s (European Commission 1997) and a pillar of the European Social Model in the years prior to the Global Financial Crisis (Council of the European Union 2007), the so-called flexicurity approach has lost its allure. But the idea maintains a strong logic and is being reconsidered as the nature of work changes (Bekker 2018): in contexts where regulation makes it very difficult and costly for firms to dismiss workers, employers will hesitate to make formal job offers, particularly to younger job seekers. However, many governments still favor protecting jobs over protecting working people, and many low- and middle-income countries are still setting these regulations at extreme levels. In Bolivia, Oman, and the República Bolivariana de Venezuela, for example, the labor code does not allow contract termination for economic reasons (such as poor performance or market downturns), limiting grounds for dismissal to disciplinary and personal reasons. In 32 countries, employers need approval of a third-party agency even in the case of individual redundancies. For example, in Indonesia, an approval from the Industrial Relations Dispute Settlement Board is required; in Mexico, the employer must notify and obtain approval from the Conciliation and Arbitration Labor Board. In Sri Lanka, the employer must obtain prior written consent of the employee or approval of the Commissioner of Labor, and in Suriname, the employer must receive consent from the Ministry of Labor. If there is a requirement to give employees reasonable advance notice of dismissal, firms should be given more flexibility in their human resource decisions. To prevent abuse or discrimination, ministries of labor can implement risk-based, ex post audits and apply severe penalties in cases of abuse or discrimination.

Flexicurity may have lost its allure because many reforming governments have pursued flexibility but have been slow to deliver the promised security. As discussed later in this chapter, flexible hiring and dismissal procedures need to be balanced with increased and more effective protections outside of the employment contract. Without these support measures in place—reemployment support measures to meet the income and other needs of people who lose jobs—lifting restrictions on hiring and dismissal decisions would shift an unreasonable risk burden onto working people. The prevailing approach to labor policy in most countries is to place too much of this burden on firms. However, many nongovernment organizations that advocate for working people express justified skepticism that governments who want to loosen restrictions on firms' hiring and dismissal decisions will devote their energy and public resources to providing reliable income and job-search support, particularly the sustained support required to meet the needs of low-productivity workers or those displaced by structural changes.

Some core principles of a flexicurity approach are broadly applicable even in low- and middle-income countries. Four vital features of flexicurity can be successfully translated even to settings of high informality and limited government enforcement capacity. First, protection must be accessible not only to people who work in the conventional sense but also, and mostly, to those who work outside of labor contracts. Protection cannot be linked to any specific job, so that losing a job no longer necessarily entails catastrophic losses. Second, an assumption that people who can work should work, as well as assume other social responsibilities and obligations, is important to ensure that effort is encouraged and free-riding incentives are minimal. Third, stakeholders (social partners and others) should have a clear responsibility for and an interest in the success of the approach. In the Nordic countries, where flexicurity has been a success, this observation mostly means that governments, employers, and trade unions should all be interested in making the system work and work well. In low- and middle-income countries, this institutional cast of interested actors would also need to include the self-employed and family workers (who often work informally) and others in nonstandard forms of work. Finally, the assignment of responsibility for financing protections is just as important as the design of benefits and services and their delivery. Figure 4.4 attempts to benchmark countries from a flexicurity perspective, adopting a more expansive definition of protection that includes public spending on health and education as well as on

# Figure 4.4 A "Flexicurity" Approach to Labor Policy Requires That Governments Invest More in Protection Than Most Do Currently

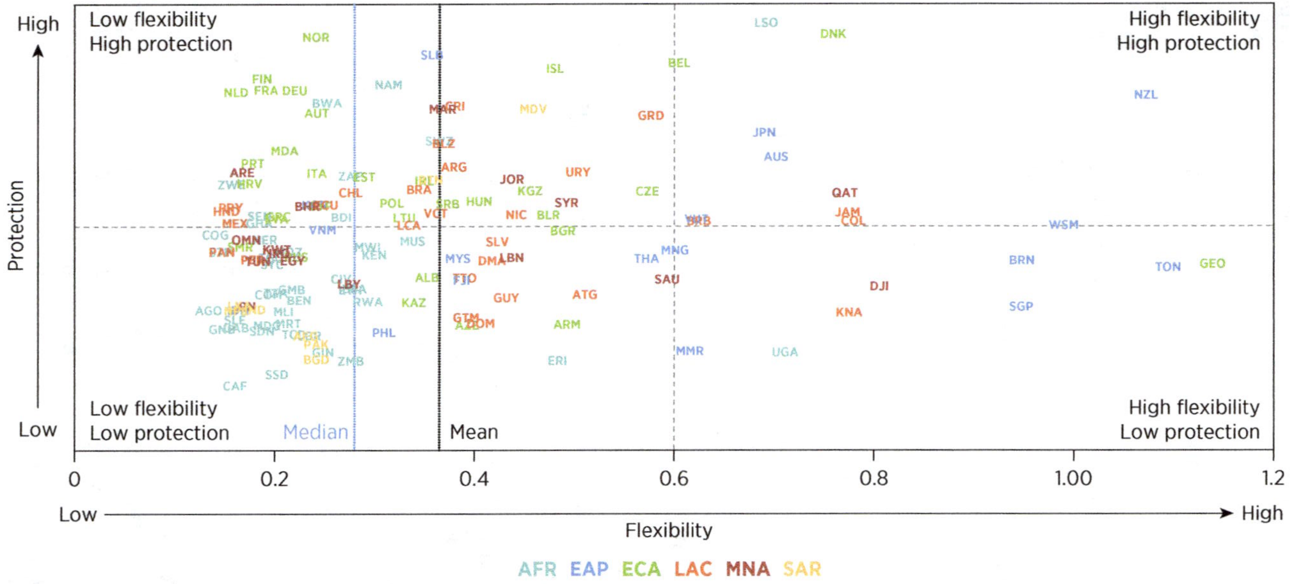

*Source:* Based on World Bank, Doing Business Employing Workers (Labor Market Regulation) indicators; World Bank, *World Development Indicators*; and indicators from World Bank, *The Atlas of Social Protection Indicators of Resilience and Equity.*

*Note:* This figure shows indices of labor market flexibility and protection, derived through principal component analysis as defined in Packard and Montenegro 2017, for various countries. "Flexibility" is defined as the inverse of rigidity of hours, restrictions on hiring, financial cost of dismissals, and procedural requirements for dismissals. "Protection" is defined as public spending on health, education, income support, and employment services as a percentage of GDP (using the latest data available for the country). Higher index values indicate more flexibility and protection. AFR = Africa; EAP = East Asia and Pacific; ECA = Europe and Central Asia; LAC = Latin America and the Caribbean; MNA = Middle East and North Africa; SAR = South Asia.

income support and employment services. Countries mapped to the upper right-hand quadrant, such as Denmark and New Zealand, place fewer de jure restrictions on firms' human resource decisions and spend generously on services that build human capital and assist working people through market transitions. Countries in the lower left-hand quadrant still attempt to protect working people from change by restricting firms' choices and spend relatively meager amounts to support labor market transitions.

Even very recent labor reforms in low- and middle-income countries are designed to preserve specific jobs and rely heavily on inefficient and unreliable employer-administered and -financed protection (Duval and Loungani 2019). Employer-financed and -administered severance plans are a prime example. Income support for unemployment organized as employer-provided severance is the instrument least resilient to shocks or to the sustained disruptions that are driving changes to the labor market. Severance pay is the most prevalent form of unemployment income protection in most low- and middle-income countries. From a legal perspective, severance is supposed to compensate an employee for the damage caused by the employer ending the assumed or de jure specified indefinite labor contract. Severance is, in this way, a perfect example of an instrument conceived for a world of work when open-ended, permanent dependent employment was the norm. But in addition to this compensatory function, severance came to be the most commonly available consumption-smoothing instrument. Mandated, firm-financed severance was the only way that governments could provide consumption support for unemployment before they developed the capacity to administer national risk-pooling and saving systems. However, as more governments gain this capacity, the inefficiency and unreliability of severance has become dramatically apparent. Because severance pools risk at the level of the firm, it is inefficient and unreliable; firms rarely fund or insure contingent liabilities. The firms that dismiss workers are in many cases also experiencing financial difficulties and might not have the funds to honor severance pay. As a result, lengthy legal procedures usually must precede the payment of severance. Data for Mexico shows that fewer than 20 percent of workers eligible for severance pay after dismissal have received the payment one year after the fact. Severance is thus both an inefficient and an unreliable risk-sharing instrument from the worker's point of view (Holzmann et al. 2012). Furthermore, some countries have extremely generous severance pay schemes, at least on paper. For example, after 10 years of continuous employment, the statutory severance entitlement equals 132 weeks of salary in Sierra Leone, 130 weeks of salary in Mauritius, and 120 weeks of salary in Bahrain (Kuddo 2018).

Even when set at levels that do not affect aggregate outcomes, as currently designed, many instruments of labor regulation can compromise the work opportunities of young people, women, and older people. The *World Development Report 2013* pointed out that even if the impact of reasonable, plateau levels of labor regulation on aggregate employment outcomes might be negligible, their adverse impact on working women, youth, and older workers could be substantial, as observed in a large body of empirical literature (Betcherman 2014; Heckman and Pagés 2004). What all three groups often have in common is a preference, and even a need, for greater flexibility than full-time, subordinate wage or salaried employment typically provides (see box 4.2). As we have argued in previous chapters, full-time, subordinate wage or salaried employment is the form of work that prevailing regulations in most countries assume is preferred by most people. As with traditional employment-based social insurance, these prevailing models of labor regulation were conceived of and established in countries where and at a time when most working people were prime-age men and the social norm was that just one—usually male—adult family member was the primary breadwinner.

A more diverse workforce will have more diverse preferences for when, where, and how its members work. As women venture into market work in greater numbers, as young people delay the transition from study into full-time work, and as older people delay full withdrawal from work, there is a growing mismatch between the labor code and how substantial segments of the labor force engage in the market. The labor codes in many countries also assume that most people maintain a clearly defined and stable market status for long periods or even throughout their working lives—as employer, worker, self-employed, and so on—in a way that ignores the multiplicity and fluidity of the market engagements of many working people. In low- and middle-income countries, these assumptions were always questionable, and the resulting mismatch between de jure labor policies and de facto working forms was always glaringly apparent. The unconventionally employed groups in low- and middle-income countries are now joined by a substantial share of workers in high-income countries in nonstandard employment arrangements.

Placing greater reliance on nationally organized arrangements and the efficiency and resilience of the broadest possible risk pool gives working people more reliable and resilient protection. Now that governments are able to provide instruments that rely less on the agency of employers and the platform of stable, long-term employment, severance will ideally be replaced by income-support structures that can be accessed no matter where or how people have worked. The policy principles

BOX 4.2

## When More Women Work, People Work Longer

The policy responses of most governments to the systemic shock of population aging fall into two categories: encouraging people to have more children and encouraging people to remain in productive activities for a longer portion of their lives. The propensity for women to work is vital to both approaches. Why? Women's time-use choices can determine the speed of demographic changes; women's natural lifespans stretch further than those of men in almost every country and context; and whether very young, of child-bearing and parenting age, or in later life, women take or are assigned default responsibility for work in the home, whether or not they hold jobs.

Globally, the share of the population of working age has peaked and will continue a steady decline. Although the picture varies substantially across regions, older countries are already facing significant challenges in how to mitigate shrinking working-age populations. This phenomenon involves policies across the life cycle as well as challenges concerning the behavioral change of employers and workers.

The most powerful measure to mitigate labor force decline in an aging population in most countries is to increase the labor force participation of women. This strategy involves policies that facilitate balancing work and family life. Public subsidies for childcare have proven an important tool, but so has public financing of aged care, since women members of a household usually take up this task. Measures that can free women caregivers in the household to pursue other work have a twofold benefit: women with talent and interests other than providing long-term care can pursue their passions, and this pursuit creates demand for market home-care service providers.

For many families, paid parental leave, up to a reasonable maximum, has also proven an effective instrument for supporting the market aspirations of parents, and of mothers in particular. Where paid parental leave is a well-established institution, people's preferences for work are reinforced. This policy increases the likelihood that the primary caregiving parent—typically a woman—will return to market work. In contrast, direct measures to stimulate fertility, such as baby bonuses, have rarely had significant impacts on fertility or on women's labor force participation.

*continued next page*

**Box 4.2** (*continued*)

Migration policies have a similar double benefit, increasing the participation of women in market work and keeping older people working longer. In countries with below-replacement fertility rates, migration is a major potential source of workforce supplementation and can allow many women into market work who might otherwise stay home to take care of dependent household members. Migration is also likely to have beneficial effects for sending countries (World Bank 2016).

Public awareness efforts to offset employer bias against women and older workers are also necessary. Employer bias, and internalization of such bias by women and older workers themselves, has proven a major hurdle to increased workforce participation of older people in aging economies. Although financial incentives are important, attitudinal change is equally so, and more experimentation is needed in this area in order to see what works. At the macro level, one important misconception to overcome is the "lump of labor" fallacy, under which it is assumed that increased participation of older workers negatively affects participation rates of younger workers. In fact, across the member countries of the Organisation for Economic Co-operation and Development (OECD)—and in developing countries such as China—this has not proven to be the case; higher participation of older workers has at worst a neutral effect on participation of younger workers and on average a modestly positive effect (Gruber, Milligan, and Wise 2010).

In sum, looking at the potential impacts of various measures to mitigate labor force declines due to aging, increasing the labor force participation of women appears to be the most effective.

*Source:* World Bank 2016.

for designing income support for unemployment are the same as those presented in chapter 3, although because individuals can more easily affect the probability of their unemployment, moral hazard is a much greater concern. Given the risks of moral hazard and the principles presented in earlier chapters, a more incentive-compatible instrument for consumption smoothing is a nationally organized system of unemployment savings accounts that could be drawn upon, for example, in case of unemployment or for retraining purposes (Robalino and Weber 2014).

One advantage to this plan is that workers would be able to access the funds irrespective of their employers' financial status. In addition to several Latin American countries, Jordan and Turkey also have individual savings accounts for unemployment.[5] Singapore has individual accounts as part of its provident fund that can be used for precautionary purposes (such as unemployment) as well as for aspirational saving and investment objectives (such as housing and education). Workers without enough savings would be able to rely on publicly provided risk pooling—the minimum income guarantee financed through general revenues discussed in chapter 3. If an individual never needed to draw on these savings, or only drew on a portion of the savings, they would accumulate and be available upon retirement.

The indispensable role of labor policy—to ensure transparent and fair contracts that are respected and enforceable—will also have to change. As economies and labor markets evolve, a wide variety of employment contracts have emerged. These contracts differ significantly in the degree of employment security, the associated working and living conditions, and the types of benefits that they provide to workers. Full-time employment contracts of indefinite duration are still an aspirational gold standard for many people and remain a common form of employment relationship in high-income countries, although, as pointed out in chapter 1, their primacy is being challenged (OECD 2018). However, variations on this standard, including temporary employment contracts (fixed-term contracts, including project- or task-based contracts), seasonal work, casual work (including daily work), part-time contracts, on-call contracts (including zero-hours contracts), contracts for workers hired through temporary employment agencies, subcontracted labor, civil law contracts, and freelance contracts, have become established features of modern labor markets. Emerging and increasing forms of atypical contracting also include employee sharing, job sharing, and online work.

As the world of work becomes more complex, governments should avoid regulating the *types* of contracts and focus instead on creating a base of standards and protections that apply to *all* contracts. A uniform set of protections could be defined in a way that is neutral with respect to the duration of the contract and does not create incentives to avoid open-ended contracts. For instance, contributions to actuarially fair segments of social insurance plans should be part of all contracts regardless of their duration. If dismissal procedures are simplified, as discussed above, this change should be possible. This is the spirit of recent reforms to labor market regulation in Italy and Slovenia, for example.[6] Workers and employers would then negotiate, bilaterally, any benefits above those specified in the base contract.

Otherwise, the result would be labor market segmentation and inequities in policy-provided protection. Youth and women are disproportionally likely to be hired on temporary contracts, which lack access to many benefits and protections against dismissals (Gatti, Goraus, and Morgandi 2014; Kuddo 2015). Yet if more flexible work contracts are regulated just like permanent contracts, there can also be large inefficiencies, and some of these more flexible jobs may cease to exist. Although flexible work contracts are controversial, it is no coincidence that many countries have introduced them in recent years, such as "mini-jobs" in Germany or zero-hours contracts in the United Kingdom. The response to these new developments is to protect all working people rather than the particular jobs they happen to be in, as discussed later in this chapter, as well as to level the playing field in terms of regulations and taxation across all forms of market work. If effective risk-sharing instruments are available and accessible regardless of how people are engaged in the market, a level playing field can be achieved, either by having one universally applicable way to contract dependent employment, or by having the ability to extend rights and protections on a pro rata basis proportional to time worked. This change will also mean that firms and people seeking work would make their decisions in the labor market based on firms' variable skill needs and people's ability to meet those needs according to their own preferences and within their own constraints.

A good starting point is to do away with regulations that explicitly or implicitly prohibit flexible work arrangements. In Montenegro, contracts for part-time employment cannot be less than 10 hours per week.[7] Ecuador's constitution prohibits remunerated work by the hour. Just as ripe for reform are tax systems that tax part-time work at higher per-hour rates than full-time work. In Serbia, the reference wage that determines the statutory minimum social contribution is not adjusted for hours worked, meaning that social contributions are disproportionately high for part-time workers (Krstic and Schneider 2015).

In countries with strict definitions of remuneration and contributions in monthly terms, these de facto higher costs for social insurance coverage create a tax on firms providing covered employment to anybody who prefers or needs to work less than full time or to work hourly. Reforms are also necessary in terms of working time arrangements. The traditional five-day schedule of 8 hours of work per day starting somewhere between 6 and 9 a.m. and ending between 3 and 6 p.m. is no longer desirable for many workers (Kuddo 2015). The standard workday in most countries around the world is 8 hours, but it varies between 6.6 hours in Italy, 7 hours in France and the Republic of Congo, and 7.4 hours to 9 hours in Chile, India, Israel, Lesotho, Norway, Oman, Pakistan, Switzerland, and Tanzania.

Working hours above these thresholds are considered overtime and are regulated separately. Ten countries limit the number of days worked per week to five. Relaxing these regulations should be accompanied by a strengthening of workers' protections, decoupled from their work contracts, as discussed elsewhere in this chapter.

As industrial-era employment protections are scrutinized, so too should be rigid and possibly outdated legal specifications of market engagements. The assumptions about the duration of employment relationships, the homogeneity of work, and the stability and exclusivity of how people engage in the market—for example, as employer, employee, sole trader, entrepreneur, equity partner, and so on—that underlie prevailing labor regulation in many countries are being challenged. These assumptions have never accurately reflected work in low- and middle-income countries, and they are now being stretched and challenged even in high-income countries. Some new forms of work blur the distinction between being an employee and being a "dependent" self-employed worker: is an Uber driver an Uber employee? As a matter of urgency, labor codes should define more clearly what it means to be an employee to ensure that all receive the basic set of protections discussed above. This exercise should be based on the extent to which an individual has true choice over working conditions (for example, in determining not just when and how to work but also the remuneration for a service rendered). Courts and legislators are doing their best to keep up with new arrangements. The industrial-era approach to labor market regulation assumes and assigns rights and responsibilities to clearly defined categories of market engagement that are assumed to be single and stable. A new approach is needed to match the diverse and diversifying world of work. In the medium term, rather than incremental extensions to the labor code to reflect this diversity in detail and ensure that each category of work is protected, it is arguably more efficient and resilient to ensure that the most vital protections—of core labor standards, from catastrophic losses—are accessible to all people, no matter how they engage in the market. Following this approach also means that workers and firms in one area of the economy should also have the same set of responsibilities—including in terms of taxation—as workers and firms in other areas.

Once vital protections are ensured, government can then focus on the essential role that only government can play: clearly defining and enforcing the law and ensuring fair and safe conditions at work (see table 4.1). Countries need to adapt policies to enforce adequate working conditions, relying less on labor inspectors and more on civil society and new technologies. Digital technologies themselves can be useful, especially in reducing costs related to enforcement. In many

**Table 4.1 There Are Promising Alternatives to Prevailing Labor Regulations, Interventions, and Institutions**

| Prospective loss | Market failure | Current interventions | Problems | Further or alternative interventions |
|---|---|---|---|---|
| **Abuse/ hazardous conditions** | Monopsony | • Labor standards<br>• Contracts<br>• Occupational safety and health conditions | • New occupations and interactions of capital and labor<br>• Legal restrictions on labor supply and use of "noncompete" contracts<br>• Need to better capture firm-specific needs above the nationally uniform standard | • Antitrust measures<br>• Enforcement of labor standards, harnessing benefits of third-party enforcement |
| **Exploitation (workers paid less than their marginal product)** | Monopsony | • Statutory minimum wages | • Relatively blunt instrument with multiple de facto objectives, but inefficient at providing a living wage<br>• Can discourage formal hiring of lower-productivity workers when set too high | • Antitrust measures<br>• Enforcement of labor standards, harnessing benefits of third-party enforcement<br>• Closer alignment of wage floors with productivity<br>• Encouragement of transparent and monitored profit-sharing plans<br>• Elimination of barriers to formation of cooperatives/shared ownership enterprise models |
| **Unfair dismissal/ arbitrage by contract forms** | Monopsony<br>Information asymmetry | • Contracts<br>• Severance pay<br>• Procedural restrictions on dismissals and hiring decisions | • Question of who is an employee<br>• Acts as taxes on adjustment, constraining technology adoption and innovation (affecting both firms and workers)<br>• Reduces hiring among particular groups, such as youths | • Single contract with uniform basic protections<br>• Individual savings to finance consumption during structural–churn unemployment…<br>• …underpinned with the guaranteed minimum benefit to prevent poverty<br>• Easing of dismissal procedures<br>• Prorated benefits |
| **More frequent job loss (or longer searches) resulting in disengagement** | Information asymmetries (plus behavioral/ cognitive limitations) | • Counseling<br>• Training<br>• Intermediation and search assistance<br>• Wage subsidies | • Not enough scale<br>• Often ignores labor demand<br>• Not well-targeted to beneficiaries<br>• No appropriate incentives for private providers<br>• Insufficiently evaluated and adjusted | • Active labor market support, augmented by ID and monitoring systems, profiling, integrated service provision, and contracting and payment to reward performance |

developing countries, there is an important gap between de jure and de facto labor regulations and enforcement of labor regulations (Kanbur and Ronconi 2018), although increasing workers' effective protection on the job, also imposes significant costs on firms (Almeida and Carneiro 2011). Digital technologies can bring down enforcement costs by more cheaply and effectively monitoring compliance with laws. In Brazil, the Annual Social Information Report (digital administrative records from social security covering information about all workers, including their wages, their occupations, and the types of firms they work for) is used to monitor compliance with the Apprentice Law and, increasingly, other labor laws (Silva, Almeida, and Strokova 2015). Oman is implementing a worker protection scheme that allows for monitoring wage payments, which could be useful in countries with frequent wage-payment delays. The governance structures to allay concerns as to whether technology and data are being used appropriately are taken up in chapter 5.

Digital technologies can further reduce the costs of enforcing labor laws by shifting the paradigm from top-down to bottom-up accountability. Technology can help provide governments with the information they need to monitor compliance. For instance, in-work collective bargaining agreements can be presented and discussed bit by bit, enhancing understanding and discussion. Governments and workers themselves can harness the power of digital technologies to empower workers and unions with mechanisms to convey complaints and violations and resolve conflicts. Coworker.org, for example, is a website where workers can convert their demands into petitions, which then get spread via social media. In the United States, workers can anonymously file online complaints and requests for inspection of their workplace if they believe there is a serious hazard or labor law violation; they can also access information about their rights.[8] Workers could also check online whether their employers have paid their contributions to pension plans and other risk-sharing schemes. This way, workers could have simple, direct access to an independent assessment of claims. Similar tools could be used to outsource enforcement of at least some regulations to third parties, including trade unions and other nonprofits. For example, governments could, through results-based contracts, outsource to third parties the development of online applications, the management of complaints, and the resolution of conflicts. These tools to increase workers' agency have the potential to balance the loss of bargaining power that workers in nontraditional work arrangements—such as independent contractors in the sharing economy or online work—can experience.

More representative structures are essential to give working people a voice and to hold all market actors accountable. In a diverse and diversifying world of work, tripartite institutions may not be enough. In the past, traditional labor unions have tried to exercise a monopoly in representing working people in dialogue with the government and employers' associations and have failed to represent the views of many who do not work in dependent wage or salaried employment relationships. An analogous concern can be raised about employers' associations and their shortcomings in representing small businesses or the self-employed.

Labor unions and other nongovernment organizations have been at the forefront of efforts to build just, equitable, civil societies and to ensure human rights and the rule of law (Farber et al. 2018; World Bank 2012). In transitioning economies, where governance institutions are still weak, union membership is associated with smaller informal sectors (Packard, Koettl, and Montenegro 2012). However, in countries with weak governance structures, labor market institutions that only allow the participation of a narrow group of stakeholders—whether labor unions on the supply side or industry associations on the demand side—can become fiefdoms in which selected interests become entrenched and decisions are taken that make labor and human capital markets less, rather than more, contestable, threatening productivity and sustained well-being from work.

In a diverse and diversifying world of work, the institutions of voice, accountability, and dialogue must evolve beyond "tripartite," particularly when discussing national and international policies. When the labor force was more homogeneous and the roles and interests of parties were more stable and clearly defined, the tripartite institutions (as shown in figure 4.5) were very effective. They may still be, within sectors and firms where the interests of parties are clearer. However, at the economy-wide level, many legitimately interested parties do not have a seat at a tripartite table. Admittedly, the number of "sides" at the dialogue table may have to be contained to avoid an unproductive cacophony of interests and to enable a productive space for dialogue that facilitates decision making. There is also value in maintaining an odd number of interests to prevent stalemates. An incremental step in a more progressive direction might be to grow tripartite institutions into the next-highest odd number: "pentapartite." Whatever the optimal number of sides may be, the institutions of industrial relations and social dialogue should be modernized and made more representative than they are currently.

As the diverse world of work diversifies further, the profile of organized labor is changing slowly and organically but dramatically. A key factor that has sapped the strength of organized labor in many

**Figure 4.5  From "Tripartite" to "Pentapartite"? A Diverse and Diversifying World of Work Requires a More Representative Negotiating Table**

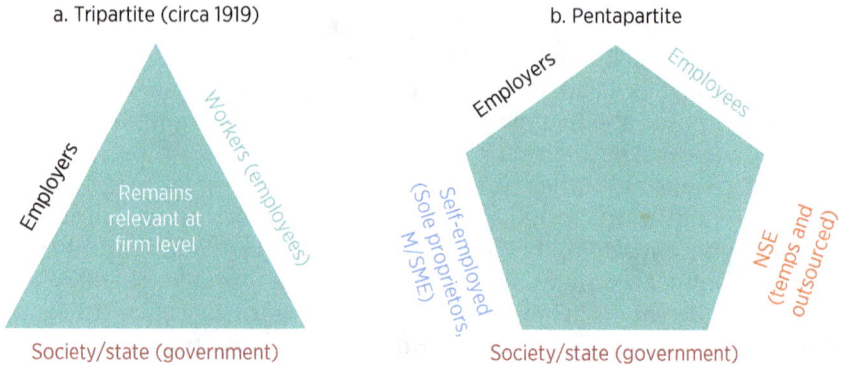

a. Tripartite (circa 1919)

b. Pentapartite

Employers

Workers (employees)

Remains relevant at firm level

Society/state (government)

Employers

Employees

Self-employed (Sole proprietors, M/SME)

NSE (temps and outsourced)

Society/state (government)

*Note:* M/SME = micro-, small, and medium enterprises; NSE = nonstandard employment.

countries, particularly in low- and middle-income countries of South and East Asia, is the tendency of labor unions to be narrowly aligned with sectors where full-time, dependent-wage or salaried employment is the dominant form of work. The inclusion of groups that mobilize people in other forms of work—such as India's Self-Employed Women's Association and, globally, Women in Informal Employment: Globalizing and Organizing and the Service Employees International Union—is still rare in the organized labor movements of most countries. Thankfully, this gap in representation is changing. Labor unions around the world are facing similar existential threats. People in self-employment, irregular employment, and migrant work, particularly working women, are often overlooked by organized labor as a significant source of grassroots mobilization. The bargains that labor unions strike for their members can come at the expense of unrepresented workers. However, labor unions in high-income countries and economies with large, fast-changing service sectors have begun to reach out enthusiastically to working people with more heterogeneous profiles. In East Asia and the Pacific, migrant labor organizations and associations sponsored by nongovernmental organizations in Indonesia and in Hong Kong SAR, China, are a part of this trend and are providing a wider segment of working people with opportunities to engage in labor institutions (Ford 2004). In Indonesia, the digital ride-hailing platforms Go-Jek and Grab now face formidable mobilization by the

Alliance of Online Taxi Drivers. This evolution can be enabled more actively by national labor policies.

## Augmented and Assertive Employment Assistance

The rise in flexibility and ongoing changes in the world of work are increasing the importance of active labor measures to facilitate transitions and improve matches between workers and jobs. People are increasingly moving from job to job in a world of short-term contracts and gigs, from inactivity or unemployment into a job, or from lower- to higher-productivity jobs. As a larger portion of risk shifts from employers to workers, the need for government intervention that is unrelated to the type or place of employment will increase. This is already the case for most workers in low- and middle-income countries, but it will be a significant change for formal workers. Many groups in the labor market can cope with higher levels of responsibility for risk. However, certain constrained groups simply cannot, which requires that governments prioritize proactive interventions to help them into productive work. This observation is a clear, but also clearly justified, departure from the principle of neutrality that has guided our consideration of current and alternative policy responses up to now. The departure is based on the strong positive externalities associated with raising employment and productivity among these priority groups, as discussed in the *World Development Report 2013*.

Working people can face different kinds of shocks, and active labor measures to help them back into work should be deployed according to the shock that caused their displacement. Public employment services in many countries are deployed only partially or indiscriminately, with little regard for the shocks and losses workers have experienced. Figure 4.6 presents a range of shocks and corresponding interventions. The segments on the left of the diagram represent transient shocks. The segments on the right represent permanent shocks. The top segments show systemic—that is, industry-wide or economy-wide—shocks, and the bottom segments show shocks that affect only a given individual or household. On the top left, there is the case of correlated shocks that affect an entire country, such as the 2008–2009 financial crisis (a transient systemic shock), the frequency of which is likely to increase because of economic integration and the connectivity of markets. On the bottom left, increased competition and more flexible dismissal procedures, structural churn, and cyclical fluctuations (transient idiosyncratic shocks) can lead to more frequent separations and reemployment or to variations in earnings. Disruption drives structural transformations

**Figure 4.6  Specific Active Labor Measures Should Be Deployed According to the Nature of the Shocks That Created the Need for Assistance**

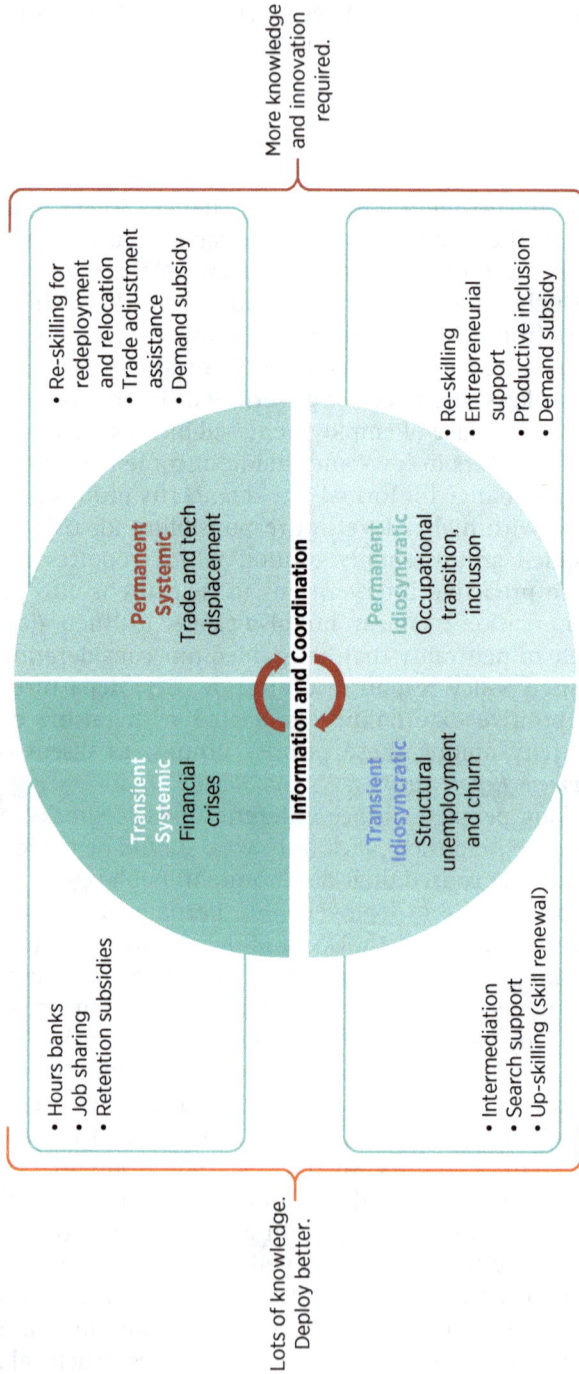

More knowledge and innovation required.

- Re-skilling for redeployment and relocation
- Trade adjustment assistance
- Demand subsidy

- Re-skilling
- Entrepreneurial support
- Productive inclusion
- Demand subsidy

**Permanent Systemic**
Trade and tech displacement

**Permanent Idiosyncratic**
Occupational transition, inclusion

**Information and Coordination**

**Transient Systemic**
Financial crises

**Transient Idiosyncratic**
Structural unemployment and churn

- Hours banks
- Job sharing
- Retention subsidies

- Intermediation
- Search support
- Up-skilling (skill renewal)

Lots of knowledge. Deploy better.

(permanent systemic shocks, shown on the top right) that cause the destruction of certain occupations and the emergence of new ones with different skill sets. Conflict and climate change, in addition to techno-logical change and trade, also generate this type of disruption. And finally, on the bottom right are permanent idiosyncratic shocks, which call for policies to facilitate more slowly unfolding transitions from lower- to higher-productivity jobs, particularly in lagging areas and regions, or from long-term unemployment or inactivity to employment.

There is better knowledge about how to help working people manage transient shocks versus permanent shocks. A general observation is that the body of empirical evidence indicating what can be done, and done better, to help people recover from transient shocks is far larger and more rigorous than the knowledge about helping people recover from more permanent, structural shocks. Even in the case of transient shocks, however, there are still significant knowledge gaps in terms of the optimal implementation and tailoring needed to address the multiplicity and variety of constraints that different population groups face in the labor market.[9] For example, there is some evidence that mentoring or self-efficacy training may have more impact for women than more conventional training to grow the profits of a business (Campos et al. 2017). Hence it is vital to follow an evidence-based iterative approach, grounded in careful evaluation, when expanding the scope of employment programs.

Across countries, the types of services needed to support individuals affected by certain types of labor market shocks are likely to be similar, but the combination and intensity of these services required to get people back to work could be different. Standard services, dealing with information and skill constraints, will continue to include counseling, various types of train-ing, job-search assistance, intermediation, and various forms of wage subsidies. But the combination of services required to support those in transition between similar types of jobs when an individual firm downsizes will be different from the combination needed to support people displaced by trade liberalization or technological changes affecting whole industries and places. Probably the most difficult interventions are those needed to facilitate transitions out of very low–productivity activities (for example, out of substance agriculture or own-account work in household enterprises). In these cases, when and where ensuring access to quality public services and adequate connective infrastructure is not enough, traditional active labor measures may need to be combined with demand-side interventions to mobilize investment and create new job opportunities (Robalino 2018). This approach is being followed, and evaluated, in a number of countries. The Kenya Youth Employment and Opportunities Project is an apt example (box 4.3).

## Kenya's Youth Employment and Opportunities Project

The Kenya Youth Employment and Opportunities Project (KYEOP) is an example of an active employment intervention that recognizes key labor market characteristics in low- and middle-income countries and makes use of digital technologies. KYEOP addresses multiple constraints to employment and includes interventions to improve skills and support self-employment in multiple ways as well as competitions to identify promising employment-creation initiatives. KYEOP's interventions both build on evidence from recent research—including the impact evaluation of the Kenya Youth Empowerment Project, a pilot project (Honorati 2015)—and introduce new interventions that will be rigorously tested with randomized controlled trials.

*Addressing socioemotional skills and general work skills.* KYEOP recognizes the importance of socioemotional skills and of broad business skills for success at work—and the increasing need to build skills that are transferable across occupations, given accelerated technological change. Hence, for those youth who elect to receive support for employability, the training starts with one month of life skills and core business skills training. Although only anecdotal evidence of this training's effectiveness exists for the time being, participants express appreciation for the life skills training, as it allows them to become more self-confident, speak in public more effectively, and better manage relationships with others.

*Accepting that the informal economy will remain the arena of engagement for many working people.* In KYEOP, youth who choose to receive support to improve their employability can choose between two options: (i) the classic option of training with formal training providers followed by an internship with a formal employer, or (ii) training in the informal economy with master craftsmen. Kenya has adopted legislation that allows informal-sector workers to be protected from some life shocks. Informal workers can benefit from health insurance, and pensions have also been extended to them, although the amounts are small. A key challenge is to ensure quality training in the informal sector. The master craftsmen receive two weeks of pedagogical training, during which they develop a training plan for the youth that apprentice with them. However, there is need for more work, both at the due diligence stage and in the monitoring of master craftsmen, including better use of technology to collect and analyze data.

*continued next page*

## Box 4.3 *(continued)*

*Supporting self-employment but recognizing that not everyone can be self-employed.* In KYEOP, youth can choose either to receive business support directly or to first go through skill training and then apply to receive business support. Thus, recognizing that constraints to employment are multifaceted, the program provides some youth with a full package of support. However, the program also recognizes that not everyone can be successfully self-employed. Thus, KYEOP youth who want to receive business support start by taking the Entrepreneurship Aptitude Test (EAT). The EAT includes cognitive questions—numerical and logic—as well as personality questions. The latter type of question, in addition to recognizing the importance of socioemotional skills for entrepreneurs, is also included to give a better chance to qualify to women, who tend to have less schooling than men and thus may do worse than men on numerical questions. Implementing the EAT is a logistical challenge, however, with high costs so far. The high costs may be worth it, however, given that attrition after the EAT is very low, and that low completion is a challenge in many other self-employment support programs (McKenzie and Woodruff 2014). In addition, the employability component of KYEOP also faces considerable attrition, particularly in large urban centers, where youth have higher opportunity costs and better chances from pursuing multiple opportunities at once.

*Addressing capital, knowledge, and behavioral constraints to self-employment.* When youth choose to apply for support for small businesses, they are randomly allocated to receive business grants, business development services (BDS), or a combination of the two. In KYEOP, BDS will include a short, simple training session and give more weight to follow-up visits in which the youth are counseled directly in their businesses. This arrangement was decided upon using evidence from research that shows that theoretical financial and business training, which rely on high literacy levels, do not work well in developing countries (Drexler, Fischer, and Schoar 2014). In addition, KYEOP includes behavioral interventions that aim to support women's entrepreneurship. Although these interventions are still being piloted, they will likely include supporting women to network with other entrepreneurs as well as a potential intervention to help with goal setting and planning for the future.

*Using digital interventions.* All business development services and behavioral interventions will eventually be done either fully or partly using cell phones. In the case of business development services, train-

*continued next page*

---

**Box 4.3** *(continued)*

ing via phone allows more flexibility in the time at which training takes place and the duration of a given session, potentially increasing uptake of the training. This may be particularly helpful to women with children, who may need more flexibility in terms of time use. Similarly, behavioral interventions will be conducted using phones. If found successful—these interventions will be subject to a randomized controlled trial—these interventions could easily be scaled up at a low cost.

*Using competitions to select the most promising ideas, both for job creation and for hard-to-serve youth.* To identify promising firms, KYEOP includes a business plan competition (BPC). Inspired by the Nigeria YouWin! Program, the KYEOP BPC will be subject to a rigorous impact evaluation that will examine how to increase cost-effectiveness by evaluating the extent to which the screening and the business plan support matter to business success. For hard-to-serve youth, such as street youth and vulnerable and marginalized groups, KYEOP will also include a competition and fund the most promising proposals.

*KYEOP implementation challenge: implementing with high quality at a large scale.* An overall challenge for KYEOP is to implement all of the above interventions at a large scale while maintaining quality. This challenge is where the use of digital technologies to monitor the project will hopefully improve results compared with previous employment projects.

***Source:*** Safir 2019.

---

To meet the challenges of low-productivity employment and the changing nature of work, countries will need to expand the coverage of and improve the design of active labor measures. Most low- and middle-income countries spend very little on active labor measures: about 0.5 percent of GDP, on average. But even the countries that spend at a higher level have a rather poor performance record (McKenzie 2017). The number of evaluations of these programs has grown over time, and the results are often disappointing. For instance, among 90 rigorously evaluated youth employment programs, only 30 percent had a positive impact on employment rates or earnings, and their effect was small (Kluve et al. 2016; Robalino and Romero 2019). Moreover, there were no significant differences in effectiveness between types of programs (for example, training versus job-search assistance). Most active labor measures managed by public employment offices have not been evaluated. But the measures' institutional capacity is usually lacking, they face severe constraints in terms of human and financial resources, and their existing staff have weak incentives to respond to the needs of job seekers and employers.

Several lessons from international experience can be used to guide the reform of active labor measures. First, the evidence shows that it is important to move away from single interventions and toward providing an integrated package of services. Even individuals affected by the same type of shock seldom face identical constraints to accessing new jobs. This observation implies that the success of a program depends on its ability to adapt services to very different profiles and to the demands of different workers. To do this, reemployment assistance services have to benefit from registration and statistical profiling systems that help identify the constraints facing individuals. Also, modern monitoring and evaluation practices are key to assessing the results of programs and introducing corrections when they are needed.

A second important element of improving labor measures is to rethink delivery of reemployment assistance to better align the incentives of the provider with those of the people receiving support. To this end, there is a growing role for private nonprofit and for-profit organizations in providing a full suite of active labor services, depending on their assessments of needs. A promising approach is to split the role of provider from that of purchaser of services. In a model analogous to how services are structured in many health care systems, the role of government can be limited to providing financing. Private providers, paid for employment results, can assume a role analogous to general practitioner physicians and diagnose individual employment challenges and prescribe treatments that increase the likelihood of reemployment (see box 4.4).

Maintaining the fiscal sustainability of larger, more effective programs will also require diversifying their sources of financing. Where governments make risk pooling structures more widely available to cover shocks with uncertain and catastrophic losses, it is reasonable to expect resources from people and firms to fill the needs created by more foreseeable and less costly shocks. Today, most active labor measures are financed from general budget expenditures. Given the nature of shocks and losses and the degree of market failures, this arrangement is appropriate for some needs, but not necessarily for all. Reemployment assistance is probably the most difficult to design and finance for people who have suffered dislocation from permanent systemic shocks (see box 4.5).

BOX 4.4

## A Purchaser-Provider Split in Provision of Active Labor Measures

Active labor measure (ALM) systems will need to be resilient to new risks stemming from the growing presence of nontraditional forms of employment. For several decades, health care systems have evolved to respond to a wide range of constantly changing health risks. There are valuable lessons from this experience that can strengthen public employment services. Both ALMs and publicly funded health care systems have the same basic function: balancing equity in access to services with financial sustainability. Equity in access is strategically important in order for an economy to maximize the social and economic returns of its public expenditures. However, as in the health sector, benefits from ALMs may not be realized in the short term, and achieving financial sustainability through the right risk-pooling scheme and organizational structure are necessary to make ALMs fiscally feasible. ALM systems can benefit from experience of health care systems and can be structured along similar lines to them, as detailed below.

*The public sector as purchaser rather than provider:* In many of the best-performing health care systems, most practitioners and specialists are private sector actors who render services purchased by the public sector. Australia was the first large economy to reform its ALM systems in this direction by creating the Job Network in 1994. Service delivery and mainstreaming of employment services were fully outsourced to a competitive market of about 300 for-profit and nonprofit organizations (OECD 2012).

*A strong role for service gatekeepers:* In many health systems, the costs of general practitioner (GP) physician services are covered by central risk pooling structures, and specialist fees are covered contingent on GP referral. Similarly, service providers in ALMs can serve the role of diagnosing beneficiary needs and providing referrals to specialists within a network of providers. As in health and life insurance, this arrangement would encourage adoption of improved risk assessment tools, such as statistical profiling, and increase financial planning ability. The idea of gatekeepers in ALMs is not new; it is often a function performed in public employment services offices by job-search counselors and caseworkers, though sometimes only for the very limited

*continued next page*

## Box 4.4 (*continued*)

purpose of assessing unemployment benefit eligibility. A gatekeeper function like that of the GP in many health systems would be far more expensive.

*Cost sharing to mitigate client moral hazard*: As in health care, there are information asymmetries regarding the type of risk that an unemployed individual represents. Funding some ALM services through cost sharing (for example, requiring a co-pay for a dedicated job-search coach or mentor) would lead to self-selection that aligns ALM support with needs. To the best of our knowledge, no ALM systems have adopted this type of policy.

*Balancing incentives of service providers through payment methods*: The efficiency of the ALM system relies on balancing service quality (and depth) with the number of people served. Capitation (fee-per-beneficiary) and fee-for-service, the two most common payment methods in health care in the European Union, are examples of how this problem is addressed. Capitation provides incentives to keep costs low and not to overprescribe, while fee-for-service discourages skimming of low-risk/low-cost individuals. A full typology suggested in Benreson et al. (2016) illustrates the range of methods used in health care, with categories according to provider incentives that include fixed payments, fee-for-service, case rates, population-based payments, and incremental payments.

*System-level quality and performance monitoring*: As a purchaser rather than a provider, the public sector's role would be to manage the system to enforce quality standards, analogous to medical practice licensing, and to track resource flows and corresponding outputs. Most countries have public sector entities in charge of identifying and upholding quality standards that service providers are required to abide by. France, after seeing poor performance from its skill-training system, recently implemented a reform whereby individual workers were given personal training accounts with budgets of €500 to €800, replenished annually. Also, as part of the reform, training centers were required to become accredited in order to be paid with funds from the training accounts.

*Source:* Robalino and Romero 2019 (for this volume).

BOX 4.5

## Permanent, Systemic Shocks: Responses to Job Dislocation Caused by Structural Changes

Even the best-performing, most generously funded modern public employment services will struggle to meet the needs of people who have lost jobs in the wake of permanent systemic shocks. Examples of such shocks include changes brought about by regional and global economic integration that can make businesses or entire industries unviable in certain places—even in places where the industry might have employed most people; technological changes that make the skills held by many obsolete faster than a skill-training system can renew their human capital; and climate changes that render barren entire swaths of a country formerly bountiful with a profitable cash crop. The large losses from this category of shocks and their after-shocks, which can ripple through an economic system, are of a magni-tude that most intermediation and job-search assistance programs are not designed to bear.

Many middle-income countries have a diverse set of labor market programs, predominantly including passive labor measures but also some active labor measures. However, in these countries, active labor measures typically are poorly funded, are purely publicly provided, and rely on outdated practices. Even when effective, these public employ-ment services can seem paltry, given the extent of dislocation from systemic shocks. Additional resources and programs may be needed, particularly for older working people who have been displaced by structural changes. Workers displaced by structural changes such as economic integration and technological change will need to upgrade their skills. They may also require support to change their location and active encouragement and coaching to learn about and take advan-tage of opportunities for redeployment and reinsertion into work. Helping them take advantage of new opportunities in growing indus-tries is more effective than protecting them in uncompetitive jobs. But the latter is a considerably higher-cost, higher-intensity intervention than that required by people who have suffered transient shocks.

Thankfully, there are experiences from countries that have responded to people who bore the brunt of immediately disruptive but ultimately beneficial structural changes. These experiences include tar-geted labor adjustment assistance programs that created appropriate incentives to minimize mobility costs and accelerate employment transitions. The United States' Trade-Adjustment Assistance program

*continued next page*

## Box 4.5 *(continued)*

is a federal program that helps workers through job-search assistance and training and provides wage subsidies to prospective new employers, health insurance to the unemployed, and reallocation allowances. The program helps workers who have been displaced due to trade liberalization or to firm relocation to another country (both for workers in the import-competing industry and for those employed by downstream or upstream producers).

Evaluations of this program show mixed results, including limited effectiveness at helping trade-affected workers obtain reemployment at a suitable wage (D'Amico and Schochet 2012). Critics of the program emphasize that the best reskilling is delivered on the job and have proposed the alternative of "wage insurance"—time-bound payments made directly to workers to reduce the difference between what they earned in the job just lost and their salary in the new job, up to a ceiling. Wage subsidies instead of class training could encourage workers to reenter employment rapidly while improving their access to on-the-job learning.

The Austrian Steel Foundation program has helped displaced workers find new work since the privatization of the steel industry by offering a wide range of services, including vocational orientation programs, small business start-up assistance, extensive training and retraining, formal education, and job-search assistance. The foundation is financed by all participants: the trainees themselves, the firms, local governments (through unemployment benefits), and the remaining workers in the steel industry, who pay a *solidarity share* of their gross wages to the foundation. The program has been successful at increasing the probability of participants being employed (Winter-Ebmer 2000).

The German moving subsidy for unemployed job seekers has been effective at promoting labor mobility, with beneficiaries receiving higher wages and finding more stable jobs mainly due to improvements in their job matches (Caliendo, Künn, and Mahlstedt 2017). Similarly, Romania's program of reimbursement to unemployed individuals of expenses associated with migration has been effective at improving labor market outcomes (Rodríguez-Planas and Benus 2006). And the Moving to Opportunity USA experiment, which offered randomly selected families housing vouchers to move from high- to low-poverty neighborhoods, increased college attendance and earnings and reduced single parenthood rates, provided the families moved while the children were still young (Chetty et al. 2016).

*Source:* Based on Vijil et al. 2018.

## Targeted Measures to "Crowd In" Private Investment for Jobs and Productivity

The global drivers of disruption could be limiting the structural shift of labor out of low-productivity agriculture into more productive sectors. In high-income countries and leading regions, much of the concern with technological progress has been about job destruction. In the lowest-income countries, the jobs that could be destroyed may not yet exist. New technologies can halt or disturb the process of structural transformation: the movement of labor from agriculture into manufacturing and services and from lagging rural regions to leading urban areas. This disturbance can occur if new technologies reduce the comparative advantage that low-income countries once had in the form of lower-cost labor and therefore reduce the need for multinational employers to create jobs abroad in traditional sectors such as manufacturing and tradable services.

In some regions, and for some population groups, job opportunities can be very limited, requiring more proactive policies to create jobs or improve the quality of existing jobs. More than 60 percent of workers in low- and middle-income countries are self-employed; they are farmers or own-account workers in small household enterprises, involved in low-productivity activities, often with no pay (Fields 2011). Even in urban areas, there can be important job shortages: in many cases, the economy simply does not create enough jobs to absorb new entrants to the labor market. In Tunisia, for instance, youth unemployment rates have surpassed 30 percent, and given the rate of new entrants to the labor force, there is a deficit of close to 20,000 jobs each year. Migration is an obvious coping strategy, but not everybody is able to move to another town or country. In these settings, the impact of reemployment assistance measures discussed above will be feeble. Other types of proactive interventions that focus on mobilizing private investments for job creation or improving the productivity, earnings, and working conditions of existing jobs may be required.

The social externalities of work discussed in chapter 2 justify policies that stimulate private investments conditional on improved jobs outcomes for certain population groups. These externalities can create a gap between private and social rates of return on investments. Essentially, even after having addressed macro and regulatory policies that constrain employment creation by the private sector, certain investments that are important to improve job opportunities and resilience for certain population groups might not take place because expected private rates of return are not sufficiently high. A classic example of this phenomenon is the geographic concentration and path dependence in the distribution of private investments. These investments tend to flow to regions that generate the highest expected rates of return, in part due to agglomeration externalities. Provided that governments have made every effort to extend common institutions to all areas particularly the services essential to building human capital) and have invested in connective infrastructure to help link people to agglomerations (such as roads, rail, bridges, telephony, and broadband Internet), there may still be a need for targeted interventions in regions where geography presents the most formidable obstacle to shared prosperity (World Bank 2008). In these extreme cases, there is a role for policy to provide incentives to realign expected private and social rates of return on investments. Subsidies to catalyze investment can take different forms: matching grants for capital investments, including for the adoption of new technologies; below-market interest rates on loans; public investments in basic infrastructure and social services to support the development of secondary towns; or simply free training, advisory services, and market research. The beneficiaries of these measures include subsistence entrepreneurs as well as start-up enterprises.

The idea of subsidizing demand for job creation is not new and has motivated many costly mistakes, but the approach proposed here is fundamentally different. Labor-intensive public works and wage subsidies are well-known and widely deployed instruments to spur employment. Most public works programs operate more like safety nets that create jobs for very low-skilled workers, in low-productivity activities, paying less than the minimum wage. The jobs they create are, by design, temporary. As for wage subsidies, the experience has been mixed at best. Employers often substitute workers who receive wage subsidies for workers who do not, or they use the subsidy to hire workers they would have hired anyway. In general, subsidized jobs tend to come and go with the subsidy. More importantly, when employers cannot expand their productive capacity (for example, because of lack of demand or capital), taking on additional workers, even with a subsidy, does not pay off.[10] In contrast, the approaches described below target the creation or expansion of enterprises and, through this channel, the creation of more permanent jobs, or more sustainable improvements to labor productivity, earnings, and working conditions.

*Economic inclusion programs.* These programs, targeted to poorer workers, provide continuous coaching and training and an asset transfer to support household enterprises, and they have proven effective in increasing earnings. They can be considered part of the more assertive deployment of active employment and reemployment services advocated earlier in this chapter. On average, these programs can increase consumption in a household by US$5 per capita per month.[11] Most such programs, however, have been relatively small in scale, and there are concerns about the fiscal costs of expanding their size and coverage. In addition, programs to date have financed investments for the production of nontradable goods that are consumed by the household or sold in local markets. This limits their potential in terms of job creation and labor productivity growth. There are, nonetheless, ongoing initiatives to reduce the costs of such programs. There are also innovative program designs in which traditional interventions are complemented by other services to link program beneficiaries to markets and value chains.

*Support to entrepreneurs and small and medium enterprises (SMEs), including social enterprises.* Traditional programs of this type have focused on promoting the creation of new businesses and improving the productivity and competitiveness of existing ones. They offer common services, including different types of training (technical, management, and behavioral), advisory services, access to finance, networking support, and access to markets and value chains. The results of current evaluations of these programs have been mixed, particularly in terms of their impact on employment and earnings (see Buba 2018 and Cho, Robalino, and Watson 2014). One of the key challenges to these programs is their ability to select business ideas or existing enterprises that have the potential to succeed and grow. This requires them to be able to distinguish among at least three types of enterprises that require very different types of support: (i) subsistence enterprises that have little potential on their own but that can produce goods and services for other investment projects receiving government support; (ii) vocational enterprises that can be sustainable and profitable even if they remain small; and (iii) transformational enterprises (so-called gazelles) that have a high potential for growth. There are, nonetheless, recent innovations to adapt these programs to maximize their impact on jobs. Among these innovations is the use of psychometric tests to screen large numbers of participants in order to identify those with entrepreneurial and managerial aptitude (Buba 2018).

A key innovation to such programs is the mechanism used to select investment projects that receive matching grants in order to maximize the program's impact on jobs. Traditional programs focus on the private, or "internal," rate of return (IRR) on investments. However, in the presence of jobs externalities, the IRR is a poor indicator (see Robalino and Walker 2017; Robalino, Romero, and Walker 2019). Instead, from a normative point of view, projects should be ranked by the level of job-linked externalities they generate per dollar of subsidy.[12] It is also important to have entrepreneurs and investors define the level of matching grant they require; the matching grant does not have to be defined ex ante and need not be the same for all projects. Given a fiscal envelope, this type of selection mechanism equates the private and social benefits of the investment and is more likely to maximize the number of jobs created. Investment projects selected in this way would receive lower subsidies and at the same time create more jobs. The trade-off is that such projects would have a lower level of aggregate labor productivity than if they had been selected on the basis of private rates of return (see figure 4.7). Essentially, it becomes socially efficient to reduce average output per worker in order to reduce unemployment or underemployment and promote structural transformation.

Social rates of return can be particularly high for social enterprises. In these cases, governments can improve job outcomes while increasing the supply of social services such as child- and eldercare; education, training, and health services; environmental protection; or waste management, clean water, and sanitation. These services generate social externalities of their own accord, and, therefore, there is cause for the government to sub-sidize their provision beyond job-related externalities.

*Value-chain development programs.* Programs that support the develop-ment of value chains, particularly in agriculture and agribusiness, have the potential to increase the productivity of informal jobs and link

**Figure 4.7 Job-Linked Externalities Are a Rationale for Catalytic Subsidies**

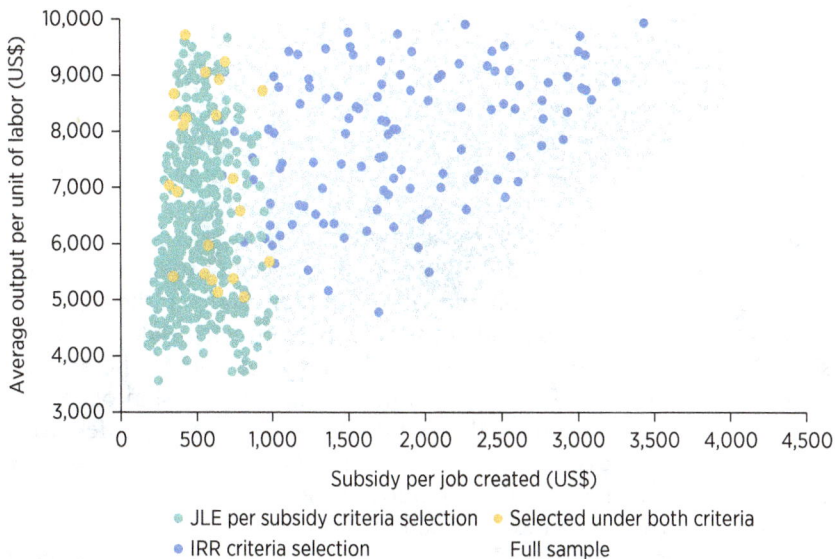

*Source:* Based on Robalino, Romero, and Walker 2019.

*Note:* This figure shows the jobs created and labor productivity under different selection mechanisms of business projects. IRR = internal rate of return; JLE = job-linked externalities.

workers to wage employment. They can target the types of economic actors described above (subsistence entrepreneurs and start-ups) and offer similar types of services. Their main difference with the stand-alone programs described previously is that their interventions are chosen and organized around the development of a given product or set of products. Their objectives are usually (i) to increase the quality and output of a product to increase market share or to enter new markets, (ii) to support the development of transformational activities linked to this product, and (iii) to facilitate the emergence of enterprises that offer services and inputs at different levels of the value chain. Because of the need to solve coordination problems between different participants in the value chain, these programs operate at the group level and minimize interventions that focus on individual participants, thus reducing costs. For the same reason, programs also often involve investments in basic infrastructure, such as storage facilities (Buba 2018).

*Access to new technologies.* As discussed earlier, new digital and other information and communication technologies create risks but also open new opportunities in terms of job creation. First, new technologies provide access to jobs that are not available locally. For example, the new Women in Online Work (WOW) program in Kosovo encourages women to pursue online employment by providing them with online-work employability training. Beneficiaries compete in the global market for jobs in information technology (IT) and related services, such as graphic design, data entry, and virtual assistance.[13] Second, new technologies support entrepreneurship by facilitating access to information (for example, about prices or the weather) as well as access to regional and foreign markets. There are many examples of farmers who now can check the weather or spot prices for their crops on their smartphones. Producers can also now export their products through e-trade platforms, greatly increasing their prospective demand and the potential scale of their enterprises. In Morocco, for instance, women working on handcrafts in the country's northwest region have expanded foreign sales of their products tenfold since 2010. Finally, online platforms can help producers in the agricultural sector reduce capital costs by outsourcing the provision of certain services (such as preparing and clearing the land) to third parties using online platforms. Governments can play an important role in facilitating the diffusion and adoption of these new technologies.

Of course, when it comes to targeting public subsidies to stimulate job creation, the proverbial devil is in the details. It is reasonable to ask what distinguishes the approaches described in this section from the questionable and costly industrial policy of the past—so-called picking-winners policies. There are four such distinguishing features: (i) these policy measures follow *only* when the more neutral policy stance described earlier in this chapter is clearly not enough to encourage work; (ii) the rationales for the subsidies are measurable jobs externalities; (iii) the subsidies are one-off, and only a catalyst for "crowding in" private investment; and (iv) ventures that receive the subsidies are expected to compete fairly in the market, to meet and sustain market standards of competitiveness, and to be allowed to fail if they prove uncompetitive. These criteria set a very high bar, but one that is vital to maintain to avoid rent-seeking and capture by elites.

## Crafting Labor Policy in a Risk-Sharing Framework

Labor policies are risk-sharing policies too. Work is arguably the most widespread and most effective way for individuals and households to manage risks. At the same time, the world of work, as discussed throughout this volume, can be a risky and uncertain place, in which most people face shocks and losses. Long-term unemployment, for example, can be a catastrophic loss for individuals and their families. In this sense, labor policies—just like assistance or insurance services and instruments—provide tools and protections that help workers and their families prevent, save, and pool to mitigate risks and to cope better with losses in the wake of shocks. Chapter 3 presented a package of comprehensive insurance assistance aimed at making risk-sharing mechanisms available to everyone, no matter how they engage in work. This chapter concludes by presenting proposals for labor market policies that follow the same risk-sharing framework, which is based on the principles of actuarial and public economics outlined in chapter 2 (see figure 4.8).

Here, as in chapter 3, we describe a package of labor policies aimed at protecting workers from labor-market- and work-related risks and losses that depends less than prevailing models on where or how people work in order to be effective. Just like the package of insurance assistance presented in chapter 3, this policy package has a publicly financed, guaranteed minimum of protection at its core and supplementary layers of mandated, nudged, and fully voluntary segments. Importantly, this package is to be seen in conjunction with the comprehensive insurance assistance package presented in chapter 3.

The core of this labor policy package is guaranteed minimum protection designed to mitigate catastrophic losses, address areas where market failures are likely to be significant, and reap the most external social benefits. These aims justify public financing from general revenues. The protections afforded under this guaranteed minimum would be available to everyone who needs them regardless of people's specific work arrangements.

**Figure 4.8  A Comprehensive Package of Labor Policies Can Also Be Derived from Risk-Sharing Principles**

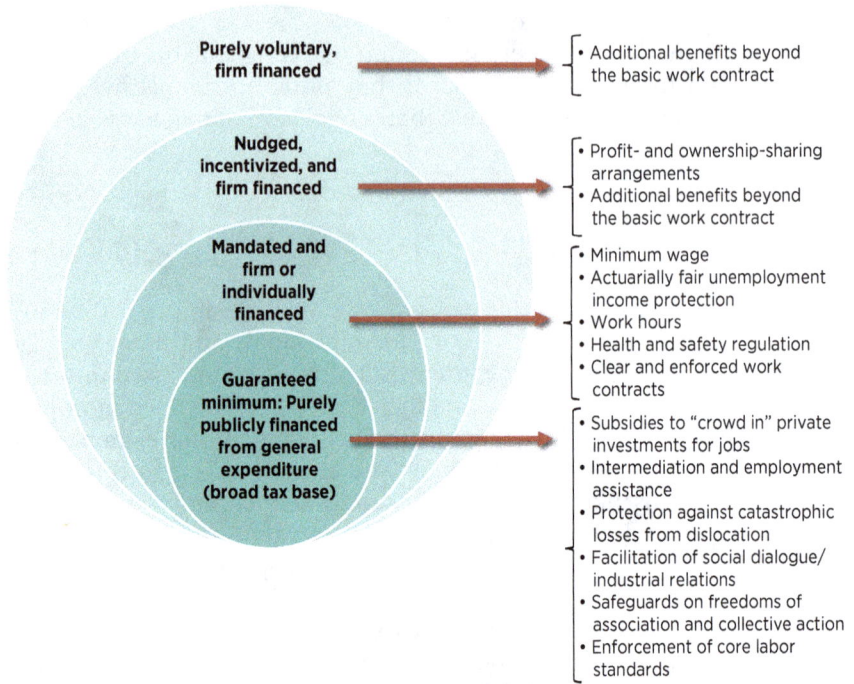

The core guaranteed minimum addresses the rarest events, the largest losses, and the problems presenting the greatest social externalities. Of greatest priority among these are relatively permanent shocks that affect many individuals or entire sectors, such as structural displacement. Skill programs, entrepreneurial support, and intermediation are types of employment assistance aimed at helping workers navigate transitions in the labor market: from inactivity into work, from one job to another, from unemployment to employment, and so on. When well designed, such programs can play an important role in helping workers both mitigate and manage job-related risks by improving the speed and quality of labor market transitions. These policies are today mostly financed from general revenues. Because, especially for vulnerable populations, public financing is still required, employment assistance is considered part of the core guaranteed minimum. That said, this chapter discusses the conditions under which some of these policies may be co-financed by firms, industries, or individuals themselves. Additionally, this chapter has presented demand-side measures—economic inclusion programs, support to entre-preneurs and SMEs, and subsidies for the development of value chains and access to technology. These programs are justified on the grounds that many investments that could greatly improve job opportunities and resil-ience would not otherwise take place because their private returns would not be high enough to match their social returns (Robalino, Romero, and Walker, 2019).

Countries can also consider including parental benefits as part of the minimum guaranteed protection financed from general taxation. As discussed earlier, jobs for women, especially young women, can have significant positive externalities. Parental leave is an effective instru-ment for supporting the market aspirations of parents. Income security during maternity also shields women and children from economic hardships and health risks. Moreover, employer liability models whereby employers directly or indirectly bear the cost of paid (usually) maternity leave may lead to discrimination against women in the (formal) labor market.[14] Finally, financing parental benefits from gen-eral taxation can help expand these benefits beyond a narrow set of formal-sector workers. Hence, there are several arguments for includ-ing parental leave (at least partially) in a minimum guaranteed package of protection.

The minimum guaranteed segment of the package includes effective mechanisms for enforcing labor laws and increasing workers' voice, with the goal of preventing catastrophic losses in the form of abuse or discrimi-nation, trafficking, or hazardous working conditions. As this chapter explains, weak enforcement of labor laws and protections often leaves workers (even those with formal contracts) de facto unprotected. Informality makes enforcement even more challenging in most settings, leaving without legal recourse precisely the workers who are most likely to need the protection of labor inspectorates or the judicial system. This agenda also includes mechanisms to increase the influence of workers, especially those in the informal sector, who are often not organized and whose voices are not always heard in policy debates. The government's role in this context is to ensure that all working people, including those in the informal economy, are represented in the social dialogue that informs and shapes labor policy.

Beyond the core guaranteed minimum, additional layers of mandated, nudged, or fully voluntary labor policy protections are needed. These additional policies recognize the limits—especially in terms of fiscal sustainability—of minimum labor policy guarantees. Just as importantly, these additional layers aim to decrease adverse selection and moral hazard. Some of the risks discussed here are also insurable, by individuals acting either alone or in combination with employers.

Labor market regulations—mandated, by definition—are critical in several areas. Core labor standards are part of the guaranteed segment of the package. But additional mandated protections, in terms of hours worked or notice and due process for dismissals, are vital. This chapter also discusses the relevance of the mandated minimum wage, noting, however, that the instrument can inflict high collateral damage, particularly in low- and middle-income countries. Although minimum wage policies aim to ensure a fair wage for workers that reflects their marginal product of labor, if set too high, they can impose distortions and costs that become less justifiable if social protections outside of the work contract are strengthened along the lines discussed in chapter 3. In addition, nudged mechanisms can also complement the minimum wage to achieve its original objective of preventing firms from abusing their market power in setting wages.

Although some protections would remain tied to the job under the proposed package, such protections would be fewer than in prevailing models. A case in point relates to severance pay. In this chapter, we propose to increase reliance on national, mandated unemployment savings accounts (actual or notional/actuarial) underpinned by risk-pooling arrangements instead of severance pay. These savings accounts would be complemented by additional nudged or voluntary savings. Used in this manner, a mandate would safeguard the fiscal sustainability of the core minimum by reducing moral hazard. It would also rebalance responsibilities between firms and workers concerning risks for which individual savings can be an appropriate risk management instrument. This mandate would be, consequently, smaller and less distortionary than what is typically required for severance pay requirements in many countries.

Finally, there is also a role for nudged and voluntary measures in a comprehensive package of labor policy protections. If a core guaranteed minimum is in place, workers and firms can rely more on their own efforts to cover losses that are foreseeable and self-insurable and to achieve private arrangements for risk management. As discussed above, precautionary savings for unemployment can be incentivized and nudged beyond the mandate. This chapter discusses ways in which this has been done. Examples discussed in chapter 3 aimed at increasing individual savings are also relevant here. Nudged and voluntary arrangements to extend profit sharing and ownership sharing are a relatively niche practice that holds enormous promise and could help give working people a greater stake in the productive upside of innovation and growth. Lastly, this chapter argues that governments, firms, and workers would be well served by a uniform set of basic protections that are part of all labor contracts, but once such protections were in place, additional protections and benefits beyond those that are mandated could be negotiated between workers and firms. These agreements could be left to be made on a purely voluntary basis or could be proactively incentivized and nudged.

## Notes

1. See the World Bank's Women, Business, and the Law indicators and publications at https://wbl.worldbank.org/.
2. Lotti, Messina, and Nunziata (2016) find that a higher minimum wage is associated with a larger self-employment share. The effect is approximately linear with the relative level of the minimum wage, even in contexts where higher levels of minimum wages are associated with higher levels of noncompliance. The estimated impact of the minimum wage on informality is economically significant: a 1 percentage point increase in the minimum wage ratio is associated with a 0.204 percentage point increase in the self-employment rate.
3. Minimum wage policies can encourage firms to provide training or adopt technology that will raise the value added by their workers. Indeed, some of the theoretical literature supports this expectation (Katz 1986; Levine 1992; Raff and Summers 1987), and governments in low- and middle-income countries thinking of introducing or raising their statutory minimum wage often cite this argument. In a recent empirical analysis of minimum wage increases in China, Mayneris, Poncet, and Zhang (2014) find substantial increases in the productivity of firms that survived the statutory hike in labor costs. The authors argue that the policy had a "cleansing effect" that not only has raised aggregate productivity but also has led to increased compliance with labor standards. Despite the inability of many firms to survive with the higher statutory floor on wages and the job losses that these failures entailed, the overall gains to the economy are clear. Importantly to these positive outcomes, however, the minimum wage increase the authors study occurred during China's high-growth period, and the increases tended to keep the statutory minimum wages (which differed across locations) at about 40 to 60 percent of median wages. Similar gains in productivity might be had with more employment-friendly policies, such as improvements in the coverage and quality of education, tighter links between firms and providers of skill training, or easier access to credit for investment.
4. In the United States and the United Kingdom, profit-sharing and shared-ownership plans have been offered by market leaders such as Southwest Airlines and John Lewis & Partners department stores and supermarkets.
5. See Reyes, van Ours, and Vodopivec (2011) for a discussion of the Chilean unemployment savings accounts and their impact on job-finding rates.
6. For information on the Italian reform, see Pinelli et al. 2017. For information on the Slovenian reform, see Vodopivec, Laporšek, and Vodopivec 2016.
7. See Arias et al. (2014)'s analysis of Montengro's labor law.
8. For more information on this online portal, see https://www.osha.gov/as/opa/worker/complain.html.
9. This paragraph gives a general characterization of a very large empirical literature that evaluates a very diverse set of programs deployed in a wide range of country contexts. Card, Kluve, and Weber (2017) synthesize the findings of more than 200 recent studies of active labor market programs. The authors distinguish among three different post-program time horizons and develop

regression models for the estimated program effect (for studies that model the probability of employment) and for the sign and significance of the estimated effect (for all the studies in the sample). They conclude from this review that average impacts are close to zero in the short run but become more positive 2 to 3 years after the completion of programs; that the time profile of impacts varies by the type of program, with larger average gains for programs that emphasize human capital accumulation; that there is systematic heterogeneity of impacts across groups, with larger impacts for women and participants who come from long-term unemployment; and that programs are more likely to show positive impacts in a recession.

10. A consensus is emerging that wage subsidies have an important role to play in building and improving human capital by allowing first-time job seekers to gain work experience. In this sense, wage subsidies are not very different from subsidies to finance training. On-the-job training can be added to the menu of active labor measures discussed in the previous section of this chapter (see Almeida, Beherman, and Robalino 2011). That said, the programs are no panacea, as Groh et al. (2016) show in a randomized trial in Jordan.

11. Per capita consumption increases by 0.12 standard deviations ($q$-value 0.001), which is equivalent to US$4.55 per capita per month at purchasing power parity (PPP), or roughly 5 percent of the control group mean of PPP US$78.80 (Banerjee et al. 2015).

12. A risk inherent in such programs is that in the absence of a sound measurement approach, the "job-linked externalities" argument could be deployed to support almost any jobs program. However, it is also necessary to determine whether social expenditures are an optimal use of scarce resources. As discussed in chapter 2, Robalino and Walker (2017) argue that job-linked externalities have two dimensions: (i) the difference between the market wage and the economic opportunity cost of the workers who get the jobs, which is called the *labor externality*; and (ii) the social value that the jobs generate, such as the positive impact on child welfare of better jobs for women and the impact on social stability of better jobs for young men, which is called the *social externality* (Robalino, Romero and Walker 2019).

13. After two pilot phases in 2016 and 2017, 85 women—most of whom had been under- or unemployed—from five municipalities finished the program, with collective earnings reaching approximately $30,000 on 335 competitively gained online contracts, while an additional 5 participants had found jobs in the local IT market (and generated approximately US$9,000). Some WOW graduates began earning more than the country's average salary while enjoying flexible and few work hours. In addition, some of the beneficiaries transitioned to entrepreneurship, forming three start-ups. The program is now moving toward scale-up as part of a planned investment project that could potentially cover up to 2,000 men and women over the coming few years.

14. Both of these supply-and-demand effects of parental leave have been shown to be at play. See, for example, Sarin (2016) for the case of the state of California in the United States.

# References

Acar, A., L. Bossavie, and M. Makovec. 2019. "Do Firms Exit the Formal Economy After a Minimum Wage Hike?: Quasi-Experimental Evidence from Turkey." Policy Research Working Paper No. 8749, World Bank, Washington, DC.

Almeida, R., J. Beherman, and D. Robalino. 2011. *The Right Skills for the Job? Rethinking Training Policies for Workers*. Washington, DC: World Bank.

Almeida, R., and P. Carneiro. 2011. "Enforcement of Labor Regulation and Informality." IZA Discussion Paper 5902. Bonn, Germany.

Arias, O., C. Sanchez-Paramo, M. Davalos, I. Santos, E. Tiongson, C. Gruen, N. de Andrade, G. Saiovici, and C. Cancho. 2014. *Back to Work: Growing with Jobs in Europe and Central Asia*. Washington, DC: World Bank.

Aznar, J., I. Marinescu, and M. I. Steinbaum. 2017. "Labor Market Concentration." NBER Working Paper No. 24147, National Bureau of Economic Research, Cambridge, MA.

Banerjee, A., E. Duflo, N. Goldberg, D. Karlan, R. Osei, W. Parienté, J. Shapiro, B. Thuysbaert, and C. Udry. 2015. "A Multifaceted Program Causes Lasting Progress for the Very Poor: Evidence from Six Countries." *Science* 348: 1260799.

Bekker, S. 2018. "Flexicurity in the European Semester: Still a Relevant Policy Concept?" *Journal of European Policy* 25 (2): 175–92.

Benmelech, E., N. Bergman, and H. Kim. 2018. "Strong Employers and Weak Employees: How Does Employer Concentration Affect Wages?" NBER Working Paper No. 24307, National Bureau of Economic Research, Cambridge, MA.

Benreson, R., D. Upadhyay, S. Delbanco, and R. Murray. 2016. "Payment Methods and Benefit Designs: How They Work and How They Work Together to Improve Health Care." Urban Institute and Catalyst for Payment Reform, Washington, DC.

Betcherman, G. 2014. "Labor Market Regulations: What Do We Know about Their Impacts in Developing Countries?" Policy Research Working Paper No. 6819, World Bank, Washington, DC.

Bird, R., and M. Smart. 2014. "Financing Social Expenditures in Developing Countries: Payroll or Value Added Taxes?" In *Social Insurance, Informality and Labor Markets: How to Protect Workers while Creating Good Jobs*, edited by M. Frolich, D. Kaplan, C. Pagés, J. Rigolini, and D. Robalino. Oxford: Oxford University Press.

Blasi, J., R. Freeman, and D. Kruse. 2014. *The Citizen's Share: Reducing Inequality in the 21st Century*. Yale University Press: London.

Boeri, T., and J. van Ours. 2014. *The Economics of Imperfect Labor Markets*. 2nd ed. Princeton, NJ: Princeton University Press.

Buba, J. 2018. *Disclosable Version of the ISR - Youth Economic Inclusion Project - P158138 - Sequence No: 02 (English)*. Washington, DC: World Bank Group.

Bussolo, M., M. E. Davalos, V. Peragine, and R. Sundaram. 2018. *Toward a New Social Contract: Taking on Distributional Tensions in Europe and Central Asia*. Washington, DC: World Bank.

Caliendo, M., S. Künn, and R. Mahlstedt. 2017. "The Return to Labor Market Mobility: An Evaluation of Relocation Assistance for the Unemployed." *Journal of Public Economics* 148: 136–51.

Campos, F., M. Frese, M. Goldstein, L. Iacovone, H. C. Johnson, and D. McKenzie. 2017. "Teaching Personal Initiative Beats Traditional Training in Boosting Small Business in West Africa." *Science* 357 (6357): 1287–90.

Card, D., J. Kluve, and A. Weber. 2017. "What Works? A Meta-Analysis of Recent Active Labor Market Program Evaluations." NBER Working Paper No. 21431.

Card, D., and A. Krueger. 1995. *Myth and Measurement: The New Economics of the Minimum Wage.* Princeton, NJ: Princeton University Press.

Chetty, R., N. Hendren, P. Kline, and E. Saez. 2016. "Where is the Land of Opportunity: The Geography of Intergenerational Mobility in the United States." *Quarterly Journal of Economics* 129 (4): 1553–1623.

Cho, Y., D. Robalino, and S. Watson. 2014. "Supporting Self-Employment and Small-Scale Entrepreneurship." Policy Note No. 92629, World Bank, Washington, DC.

Council of the European Union (Council of Europe). 2007. "Towards Common Principles of Flexicurity—Council Conclusions." Council Document No.16201/07, December 6, Council of the European Union, Brussels.

Cunningham, W. 2007. *Minimum Wages as Social Policy: Lessons from Developing Countries.* Washington, DC: World Bank.

Cunningham, W., X. V. Del Carpio, L. Iacovone, J. M. Moreno, L. M. Pabon Alvarado, E. Perova. 2016. *El salario mínimo y la productividad empresarial, laboral, y general con un enfoque en el caso de México.* Washington, DC: World Bank.

D'Amico, R., and P. Schochet. 2012. *The Evaluation of the Trade Adjustment Assistance Program: A Synthesis of Major Findings; Final Report Prepared as Part of the Evaluation of the Trade Adjustment Assistance Program.* Washington, DC: US Department of Labor.

Del Carpio, X. V., and L. M. Pabon. 2017. "Implications of Minimum Wage Increases on Labor Market Dynamics: Lessons for Emerging Economies." Policy Research Working Paper No. 8030, World Bank, Washington, DC.

Doucouliagos, H., P. Laroche, D. Kruse, and T. Stanley. 2018. "Where Does Profit Sharing Work Best? A Meta-Analysis on the Role of Unions, Culture, and Values." IZA Discussion Paper No. 11617.

Drexler, A., G. Fischer, and A. Schoar. 2014. "Keeping It Simple: Financial Literacy and Rules of Thumb." *American Economic Journal: Applied Economics* 6 (2): 1–31.

Dube, A. 2018. "Minimum Wages and the Distribution of Family Incomes." NBER Working Paper No. 25240, National Bureau of Economic Research, Cambridge, MA.

Dube, A., J. Jacobs, S. Naidu, and S. Suri. 2018. "Monopsony in Online Labor Markets." NBER Working Paper No. 24416, National Bureau of Economic Research, Cambridge, MA.

Duval, R., and P. Loungani. 2019. "Designing Labor Market Institutions in Emerging Market and Developing Economies: Evidence and Policy Options." IMF Staff Discussion Note, SDN/19/04, May, International Monetary Fund, Washington, DC.

Estrin, S., V. Pérotin, A. Robinson, and N. Wilson. 1997. Profit-Sharing in OECD Countries: A Review and Some Evidence." *Business Strategy Review* 8 (4): 27–32.

European Commission. 1997. "Partnership for a New Organization of Work: Green Paper." COM(97)128 Final, November 22, Commission of the European Communities, Brussels.

European Union. 2015. "Tax Reforms in EU Member States 2015: Tax Policy Challenges for Economic Growth and Fiscal Stability." European Economy Institutional Paper 008, European Commission.

Farber, H., D. Herbst, I. Kuziemko, and S. Naidu. 2018. "Unions and Inequality Over the 20th Century: New Evidence from Survey Data." NBER Working Paper No. 24587, National Bureau of Economic Research, Cambridge, MA.

Fields, G. 2011. *Working Hard, Working Poor: A Global Journey*. Oxford, UK: Oxford University Press.

Ford, M. 2004. "Organizing the Unorganizable: Unions, NGOs, and Indonesian Migrant Labour." International Migration 42 (5): 99–119.

Furman, J. 2008. *The Concept of Neutrality in Tax Policy*. Washington, DC: Brookings Institution Press.

Gatti, R., K. Goraus, and M. Morgandi. 2014. "Balancing Flexibility and Worker Protection: Understanding Labor Market Duality in Poland." Washington, DC: World Bank.

Gill, I., J. Koettl, and T. Packard. 2013. "Full Employment: A Distant Dream for Europe." *IZA Journal of European Labor Studies* 2: 19.

Groh, M., N. Krishnan, D. McKenzie, and T. Vishwanath. 2016. "Do Wage Subsidies Provide a Stepping-Stone to Employment for Recent College Graduates? Evidence from a Randomized Experiment in Jordan." *The Review of Economics and Statistics* 98 (3): 488–502.

Gruber, J., K. Milligan, and D. Wise. 2010. *Social Security Programs and Retirement around the World: The Relationship to Youth Employment*. Chicago: University of Chicago Press.

Heckman, J., and C. Pagés, eds. 2004. *Law and Employment: Lessons from Latin America and the Caribbean*. National Bureau of Economic Research. Chicago: University of Chicago Press.

Holzmann, R., Y. Pouget, M. Vodopivec, and M. Weber. 2012. "Severance Pay Programs around the World: History, Rationale, Status, and Reforms." In *Reforming Severance Pay: An International Perspective*, edited by R. Holzmann and M. Vodopivec. Washington, DC: World Bank.

Honorati, M. 2015. *"The Impact of Private Sector Internship and Training on Urban Youth in Kenya."* Policy Research Working Paper no. 7404. World Bank, Washington, DC.

Kanbur, R., and L. Ronconi. 2018. "Enforcement Matters: The Effective Regulation of Labour." *International Labour Review* 157 (3): 331–56.

Katz, L. F. 1986. "Efficiency Wage Theories: A Partial Evaluation." *NBER/ Macroeconomics Annual* 1 (1): 235.

Kluve, J., S. Puerto, D. Robalino, J. R. Romero, F. Rother, J. Stöterau, F. Weidenkaff, and W. Witte. 2016. "Do Youth Employment Programs Improve Labor Market Outcomes? A Systematic Review." IZA Discussion Paper No. 10263, Institute for the Study of Labor, Bonn, Germany.

Koettl, J., and M. Weber. 2012. "Does Formal Work Pay? The Role of Labor Taxation and Social Benefit Design in the New EU Member States." *Research in Labor Economics* 34: 167–204.

Konczal, M., and M. Steinbaum. 2016. "Declining Entrepreneurship, Labor Mobility, and Business Dynamism: A Demand-Side Approach." Roosevelt Institute Working Paper, July, Roosevelt Institute, New York.

Krstic, G., and F. Schneider. 2015. *Formalizing the Shadow Economy in Serbia: Policy Measures and Growth Effects.* New York: Springer International Publishing.

Krueger, A., and E. Posner. 2018. "A Proposal for Protecting Low-Income Workers from Monopsony and Collusion." Policy Proposal, The Hamilton Project, Brookings Institution, Washington, DC.

Kuddo, A. 2015. "Labor Regulations and Institutions for the New Economy." Background paper for the World Development Report 2016, World Bank, Washington, DC.

———. 2018. "Labor Regulations Throughout the World: An Overview." Social Protection and Jobs Global Practice, World Bank, Washington, DC.

Kuddo, A., D. Robalino, and M. Weber. 2015. *Balancing Regulations to Promote Jobs: From Employment Contract to Unemployment Benefits.* Washington, DC: World Bank Group.

Kugler, A., and M. Kugler. 2009. "Labor Market Effects of Payroll Taxes in Developing Countries: Evidence from Colombia." *Economic Development and Cultural Change* 57: 2.

Levine, D. I. 1992. "Can Wage Increases Pay for Themselves? Tests with a Production Function." *The Economic Journal* 102 (414): 1102–15.

Levy, S. 2008. *Good Intentions, Bad Outcomes: Social Policy, Informality, and Economic Growth in Mexico.* Washington, DC: Brookings Institution Press.

———. 2018. *Under-Rewarded Efforts: The Elusive Quest for Prosperity in Mexico.* Washington, DC: Inter-American Development Bank.

Lotti, G., J. Messina, and L. Nunziata. 2016. "Minimum Wages and Informal Employment in Developing Countries." World Bank and Inter-American Development Bank, Washington, DC.

Mayneris, F., S. Poncet, and T. Zhang. 2014. "The Cleansing Effect of Minimum Wages: Minimum Wage Rules, Firm Dynamics and Aggregate Productivity in China." Working Papers 2014–16, CEPII, Paris.

McKenzie, D. 2017. "How Effective Are Active Labor Market Policies in Developing Countries? A Critical Review of Recent Evidence." *World Bank Research Observer* 32 (2): 127–54.

McKenzie, D., and C. Woodruff. 2014. "What Are We Learning from Business Training and Entrepreneurship Evaluations around the Developing World?" *World Bank Research Observer* 29 (1): 48–82.

Messina, J., and J. Silva. 2018. *Wage Inequality in Latin America: Understanding the Past to Prepare for the Future.* Latin America Development Forum. Washington, DC: World Bank.

Naidu, S., E. A. Posner, and E. G. Weyl. 2018. "Antitrust Remedies for Labor Market Power." Research Paper No. 850, University of Chicago Coase-Sandor Institute for Law & Economics, Chicago.

Neumark, D., and W. Wascher. 2008. *Minimum Wages.* Cambridge, MA: MIT Press.

Organisation for Economic Co-operation and Development (OECD). 2012. *Activating Jobseekers: How Australia Does It.* Paris, OECD Publishing.

———. 2018. "The Future of Social Protection: What Works for Non-Standard Workers?" Policy Brief on the Future of Work, Organisation for Economic Co-operation and Development, Paris.

Packard, T., J. Koettl, and C. E. Montenegro. 2012. *In from the Shadow: Integrating Europe's Informal Labor.* Washington, DC: World Bank.

Packard, T., and C. E. Montenegro. 2017. *"Labor Policy and Digital Technology Use: Indicative Evidence from Cross-Country Correlations.* Policy Research Working Paper no. WPS 8221, World Bank, Washington, DC.

Packard, T., and T. Van Nguyen. 2014. *East Asia Pacific at Work: Employment, Enterprise, and Well-Being.* World Bank East Asia and Pacific Regional Report. Washington, DC: World Bank.

Pagés, C. 2017. "Do payroll tax cuts boost formal jobs in developing countries?" Article 345, IZA World of Labor, Institute for the Study of Labor, Bonn, Germany.

Piketty, T., and E. Saez. 2012. "A Theory of Optimal Capital Taxation." NBER Working Paper No. 17989, National Bureau of Economic Research, Cambridge, MA.

Pinelli, D., R. Torre, L. Pace, L. Cassio, and A. Arpaia. 2017. "The Recent Reform of the Labor Market in Italy: A Review." European Economy Discussion Paper 072. European Commission, Brussels.

Raff, D., and L. Summers. 1987. "Did Henry Ford Pay Efficiency Wages?" *Journal of Labor Economics* 5 (4): 557–86.

Reyes, G., J. C. van Ours, and M. Vodopivec. 2011. "Incentive Effects of Unemployment Insurance Savings Accounts: Evidence from Chile." *Labor Economics* 18 (6): 798–809.

Robalino, D. 2018. "New Ways to Tackle the Global Jobs Crisis." *Akzente GIZ Magazine*, March 18.

Robalino, D., and J. Romero. 2019. "A Purchaser Provider Split in Public Employment Services? Lessons from Healthcare Systems." Social Protection and Jobs Global Practice, World Bank, Washington, DC.

Robalino, D., J. Romero, and I. Walker. 2019. "Allocating Matching Grants for Private Investments to Maximize Jobs Impacts." Unpublished, World Bank, Washington, DC.

Robalino, D., and I. Walker. 2017. "Economic Analysis of Jobs Investment Projects: Guidance Note." Jobs Issue Paper no. 7, World Bank, Washington, DC.

Robalino, D., and M. Weber. 2014. "Designing and Implementing Unemployment Benefit Systems in Middle and Low Income Countries: Key Choices between Insurance and Savings Accounts." Social Protection and Labor Discussion Paper No. 1303, World Bank, Washington, DC.

Rodríguez-Planas, N., and J. Benus. 2006. "Evaluating Active Labor Market Programs in Romania." IZA Working Paper no. 2464, Institute for the Study of Labor, Bonn, Germany.

Safir, A. 2019. "Kenya's Youth Employment and Opportunities Project." In R. Sundaram and J. Pape Utz, *Kenya Social Protection and Jobs Programs: Public Expenditure Review.* Report No. 139735. Washington, DC: World Bank Group.

Sarin, N. 2016. "The Impact of Job-Protected Leave on Female Leave-Taking and Employment Outcomes." University of Pennsylvania Law School, Philadelphia.

Schmillen, A. D., and T. G. Packard. 2016. "Vietnam's Labor Market Institutions, Regulations, and Interventions: Helping People Grasp Work Opportunities in a Risky World." Policy Research Working Paper no. WPS 7587, World Bank, Washington, DC.

Silva, J., R. Almeida, and V. Strokova. 2015. *Sustaining Employment and Wage Gains in Brazil: A Skills and Jobs Agenda*. Directions in Development. Washington, DC: World Bank.

Stiglitz, J. 2019. *People, Power and Profits: Progressive Capitalism for an Age of Discontent*. New York: Norton.

Vijil, M., V. Amorim, M. Dutz, and P. Olinto. 2018. "Productivity, Competition and Shared Prosperity." In *Jobs and Growth: Brazil's Productivity Agenda*, edited by Mark Dutz. Washington, DC: World Bank.

Vodopivec, M., S. Laporšek, and M. Vodopivec. 2016. "Levelling the Playing Field: The Effects of Slovenia's 2013 Labour Market Reform." IZA Discussion Paper No. 9783, Institute for the Study of Labor, Bonn, Germany.

Winter-Ebmer, R. 2000. "Long-Term Consequences of an Innovative Redundancy-Retraining Project: The Austrian Steel Foundation." Economics working paper 2000-29, Department of Economics, Johannes Kepler University, Linz, Austria.

World Bank. 2008. *World Development Report 2009: Reshaping Economic Geography*. Washington, DC: World Bank Group.

———. 2012. *World Development Report 2013: Jobs*. Washington, DC: World Bank.

———. 2013. *Paying Taxes 2014*. Washington, DC: International Finance Corporation, PriceWaterhouseCoopers, and World Bank.

———. 2016. *Live Long and Prosper: Aging in East Asia and Pacific*. World Bank East Asia and Pacific Regional Report. Washington, DC: World Bank.

———. 2017. *Doing Business 2018: Reforming to Create Jobs*. Washington, DC: World Bank.

———. 2018. *Women, Business, and the Law 2018*. Washington, DC: World Bank.

———. 2019. *Women, Business, and the Law 2019: A Decade of Reform*. Washington, DC: World Bank.

# 5

# Charting the Course for a Challenging Transition

Redefining risk-sharing policies as we advocate in the previous chapters requires political vision and will. But just as importantly, it requires greater public resources and administrative capacity than are currently applied by most governments to social protection. To put in place the approach to risk sharing outlined in the previous two chapters demands that governments—and supporting development partners—bring to bear substantial additional financial and technological resources to augment their capacities. This chapter discusses both types of resources and makes a preliminary attempt to assess the relative readiness of countries to embark on—or move further along—the path that we have proposed. Some countries are already in a good position to move forward. Others will have to undertake deeper reforms of their current risk-sharing arrangements, significantly increase their tax revenues, or build their administrative and delivery systems—or a combination of all three.

The transition path is also shaped by the salience of current risk-sharing institutions to most working people and whether countries can leapfrog directly to newer policy models. In addition to identifying possible fiscal and technological options for reform-minded governments, this chapter addresses the constraints imposed by legacy commitments of the risk-sharing institutions currently in place. The most formidable among these constraints is the fiscal cost of covering contingent liabilities of employment-based social insurance plans. These commitments can be a formidable obstacle, even in many low- and middle-income countries where population aging has not yet begun in earnest. The chapter also argues that—somewhat ironically—countries where participation in pre-vailing social insurance programs is low and where the effective reach of labor regulation and institutions is limited are at an advantage: they are more easily able to leapfrog into new institutional forms. As has been the case with telephony and financial services in many low-income countries, especially those in Sub-Saharan Africa and emerging East Asia, the limited coverage of legacy, analog models left the ground fertile for new digital approaches to germinate, take root, and spread rapidly. New technologies such as digital identification and mobile payments that bypass rich-country legacy institutions can also facilitate the shift in risk-sharing policy that we have proposed.

## How Can Countries Finance the New Protections Proposed?

Risk-sharing policies and programs are embedded in the broader system of government spending and taxation, the impact of which on poverty and inequality must be simultaneously and comprehensively considered. What matters to people's well-being is the *net* impact of *all* public spending and taxes (Lustig 2018). Revenue sources and the way taxation instruments are deployed must be given as careful consideration as benefit expenditures.[1] A growing body of evidence from analysis of low- and middle-income countries confirms the generally positive impact of social spending—that is, public expenditure on social protection, education, and health services—on reducing poverty and inequality. For most countries, the net impact of transfers and taxes—at least from an accounting perspective—is to reduce inequality. However, in many countries, the overall impact is to impoverish some people because transfers are not large enough to offset tax payments made by lower-earning households; in some countries, this is because transfers are low, while in other countries it is because taxes are very high. Two important conclusions emerge. First, the effects of taxes and expenditures should be examined jointly to fully understand their impact. Second, in countries that have public finance systems where the net impact of the cash part of the budget is to push some people into poverty, there is a need for fundamental change. In Lustig's (2018) words, "If the policy community is seriously committed to eradicating. . . poverty, governments will need to explore ways to redesign taxation and transfers so that the poor do not end up as net payers."

It follows, then, that proposals for financing an expanded set of guaranteed protections must be considered from a holistic fiscal perspective. A reasonable starting point is to work within the existing revenue and expenditure envelopes, looking for opportunities to better use resources that are already available. Then the possibilities for gathering additional resources can be considered, keeping in mind the many competing demands upon any new revenue and balancing the potential negative effects of new taxes against the gains of more accessible and robust risk-sharing institutions. Analysis of these tradeoffs at the country level is an essential step to making our policy proposals specific and relevant to each country.

## Improved Allocation of Resources within the Existing Budget Envelope

An obvious source of financing for the proposed new protections described in chapters 3 and 4 is to redirect spending from existing programs with nominally similar objectives but that have been proven to be less effective or even regressive. Specifically, existing social assistance spending and spending on price subsidies could be redirected toward the kind of transfers outlined in chapter 3 and the employment services and subsidies described in chapter 4. Figure 5.1 provides the range and magnitude of spending on these policy instruments in 83 low- and middle-income countries. The orange portion of each bar in the figure is based on International Monetary Fund (IMF) estimates of the cost of energy price subsidies, while the blue portion is based on World Bank estimates of social assistance "safety net" spending. The median spending level in the sample is 2.1 percent of gross domestic product (GDP), but there is significant variation. Public spending on energy price subsidies is exceptionally high in the Islamic Republic of Iran and Zimbabwe; in contrast, Georgia and Lesotho have unusually high levels of social assistance spending. Ukraine is exceptional in that its spending on the two categories of assistance is relatively high and evenly divided between them. In almost a third of the countries, the combined resources are similar to what would be required to finance a new set of guarantees of the type simulated in chapter 3. The remaining countries in the figure would need to find additional resources or to scale their new poverty-prevention guarantees to be smaller or less generous than the illustrative simulations.

The government resources already allocated to programs with stated objectives of preventing poverty and inequality could be consolidated and used more effectively. There is still plenty of room to improve the incidence of existing safety net programs. Among more than 90 countries for which data are available, in only 15 countries did more than half of safety-net spending reach the bottom quintile in the income distribution. None of these countries manages to cover more than two-thirds of those households (World Bank 2018). Although a number of these cases reflect the de jure-universal or quasi-universal nature of some programs, many programs that are explicitly targeted to households in the poorest decile

**Figure 5.1 Many Governments Already Allocate Substantial Resources to Prevent Poverty and Inequality, Even if the Net Impact of This Spending Can Be Regressive**

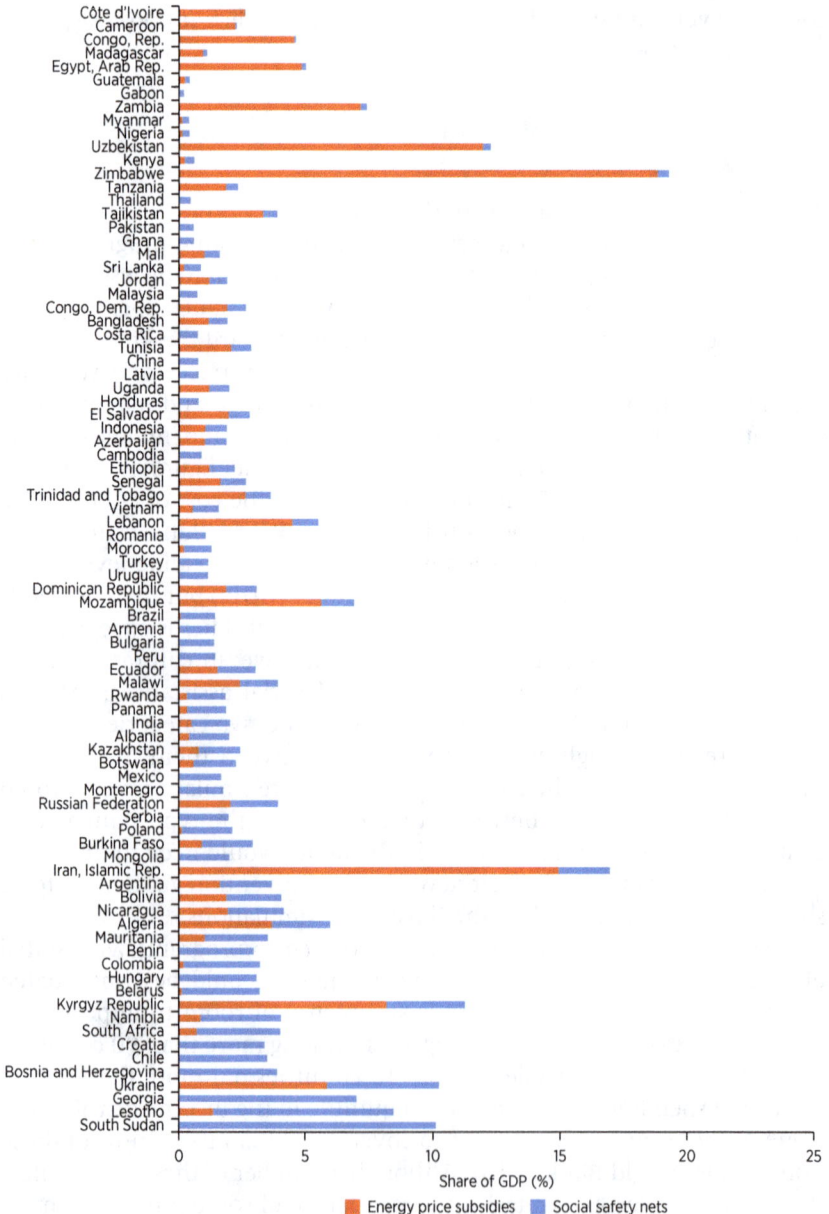

*Sources:* Arze del Granado, Coady, and Gillingham 2012; World Bank 2018.

*Note:* This figure shows the safety net and energy subsidy spending for 83 countries.

or quintile nonetheless continue to channel a large proportion of benefits to the top half of the distribution. Notwithstanding the performance shortfalls in these countries, the fact that there are many countries with much better, progressive performance outcomes suggests that significant improvement is possible even within existing expenditure envelopes.

Some programs are designed to be universal in the conventional sense and therefore would be expected to have about equal proportions of beneficiaries in each income quintile. This is the case, for example, in social pensions programs such as those of Mauritius and Timor-Leste. In some richer countries, such as New Zealand, the progressive income tax is applied to benefits received by high-income individuals, while in Australia and South Africa, affluence tests make benefits more progressive by excluding the rich. These offset or "claw-back" mechanisms can be phased in gradually, as described proposed in the case of tapered benefits proposed in chapter 3. Benefit withdrawal rates should be determined while taking into account incentives on both the spending and revenue sides of the equation (Chomik and Piggot 2013).

Redirecting resources allocated to energy price subsidies is an even more appealing way to finance new poverty-prevention guarantees. Reforming energy price subsidy programs is intrinsically attractive, given the highly regressive incidence of below-market pricing of fuel, especially gasoline and electricity. The regressive incidence of these subsidies is well documented and uncontested (World Bank 2018). For example, according to Arze del Granado, Coady, and Gillingham (2012), on average across low- and middle-income countries, the poorest quintile benefits from only 7 percent of fuel price subsidies, while the richest quintile benefits from 43 percent. Figure 5.2 shows the incidence of fuel price subsidies in India as reported in a more recent IMF report.[2] Moreover, there are indirect costs to energy price subsidies, including pollution, congestion, and even global climate change, that could be reduced with subsidy reform. These indirect costs of energy price subsidies are often of a similar order of magnitude as the subsidies themselves.

By harnessing technology, a growing number of countries have successfully shifted away from broad price subsidies to cash transfers. Aside from the public-economics case for price subsidy reform, a shift in approach is becoming more administratively feasible. In the wake of technological advances, it is increasingly possible to transition away from these programs if mechanisms are in place to convert a substantial portion of the fiscal savings into cash transfers to individuals and households. This transition took place in the Islamic Republic of Iran and in Jordan, where governments withdrew fuel price subsidies in 2009 and 2013, respectively. In each instance, population registries with extensive coverage were combined with substantial and concerted efforts

**Figure 5.2** **Despite Stated Objectives of Poverty Alleviation, in Many Countries the Benefits from Fuel Price Subsidies "Taper Away" toward the Bottom of the Welfare Distribution**

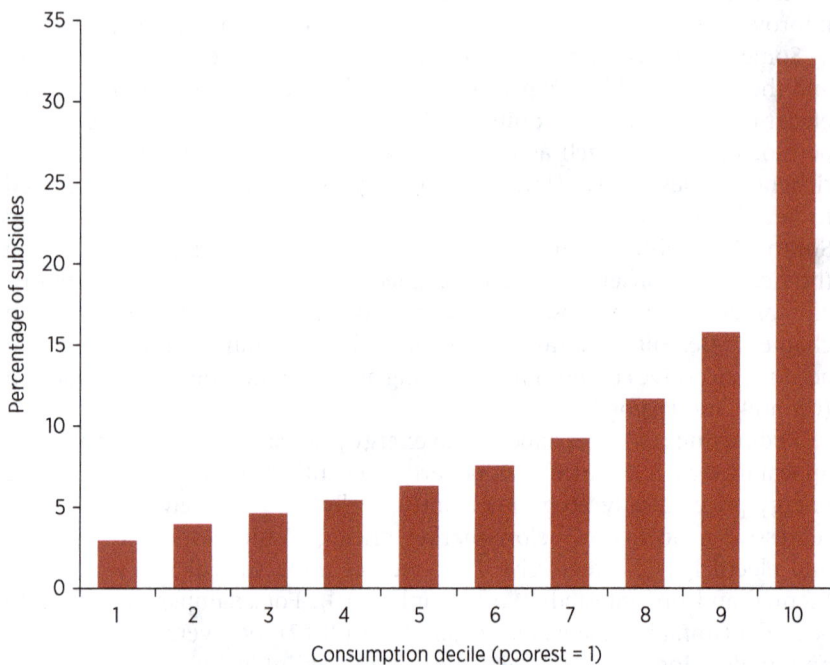

Source: Coady and Prady 2018, based on IMF staff calculations using data from India's 2011–12 National Sample Survey.

Note: This figure shows the percentage of fuel price subsidies in India received by each consumption decile (poorest = 1).

to increase financial inclusion, which allowed the rise of fuel prices to be offset by simultaneous transfers to households' bank accounts. Currently, the Arab Republic of Egypt is in the process of a large expansion in its cash transfer program financed by savings from the reduction of fuel price subsidies.

In short, although it is still difficult for governments to shift away from price subsidies, it can be done. But the shift requires implementation capacity that may not always be in place.[3] Without sufficient compensation to poorer households, the elimination of these price subsidies can increase and deepen poverty, including through indirect effects such as higher transportation costs. The transition must be handled with care, because

BOX 5.1

## More Resources for Public Policy from Better Balance-Sheet Management

The International Monetary Fund's (IMF's) October 2018 *Fiscal Monitor* (IMF 2018) makes an enticing case for better management of public sector balance sheets. Few governments know how much they own, or how they can use those assets to generate more resources for the public's well-being. Revenue gains from nonfinancial public corporations and government financial assets alone could be as high as 3 percent of GDP a year, which the IMF estimates is equivalent to the annual corporate tax collections across advanced economies.

Public sector balance sheets provide the most comprehensive picture of public wealth. They bring together all the accumulated assets and liabilities that the government controls on citizens' behalf, including public corporations, natural resources, and pension liabilities. Better balance-sheet management is an important national-level risk-management tool, enabling countries to increase revenues, reduce risks, and improve fiscal policymaking. Stronger balance sheets—statements of what a government owes and owns at a given point in time—allow governments to boost spending in a downturn. This boost cushions the impact of shocks and results in shorter and shallower recessions. Take Kazakhstan in 2014, which faced a halving of oil prices and a slump in external demand for oil. The government responded by using part of its financial assets in the National Fund to ease the downturn. Chile similarly responded to a sharp downturn in the world copper price, releasing funding for labor-intensive public works programs and other safety-net support structures.

The *Fiscal Monitor* draws on analysis of a new database that shows comprehensive estimates of public sector assets and liabilities for a broad sample of 31 countries, covering 61 percent of the global economy. These countries' public assets amount to $101 trillion, or 219 percent of the sum of their GDPs. The countries' net worth—the difference between their assets and their liabilities—is positive on average, although about one-third of the countries in the sample are in negative territory, including most of the G-7 economies. However, the report's authors point out that net worth does not account for the state's ability to tax in the future, which is why intertemporal balance sheet analysis—which combines current wealth with future revenue and expenditure—is important.

*continued next page*

**Box 5.1** (*continued*)

The report underlines that balance-sheet strength is not an end in itself but rather a tool to support the objectives of public policy. The balance-sheet approach reveals a more nuanced picture than what deficits and debt alone show. It recognizes that public investment creates assets, and it accounts for valuation effects, which are particularly large on the asset side.

There are substantial challenges to compiling reliable balance sheets. But the benefits of basic balance-sheet analysis are within reach of many countries, not just advanced economies with high-quality data. Only a handful of countries currently undertake a public sector balance-sheet approach, yet balance-sheet estimates can be developed even in data-constrained environments such as The Gambia or complex emerging economies such as Indonesia.

Balance-sheet analysis enriches the policy debate by focusing on the full extent of public wealth. Public assets are a significant resource, and how governments use and report on them matters, not just for financial reasons, but also in terms of improving service delivery and preventing the misuse of resources that often results from a lack of transparency.

*Sources:* Gaspar, Harris, and Tieman 2018 and IMF 2018.

many countries do not yet have the population information and banking coverage necessary to undergo such a shift without creating significant exclusion, especially of poorer households.

## Expanding the Budget Envelope

A second source of financing is to broaden the base of existing taxes and to deploy new revenue instruments. Although much can be gained by increasing allocative efficiency and by governments using their existing wealth more effectively (see box 5.1), more intensive use of existing taxes and the deployment of new levies will be required in most cases to fund the proposed new risk-sharing models. Although most countries now collect a significant amount of their revenues from value added taxes (VATs) or less-efficient sales taxes, substantial resources are not collected because of statutory tax exemptions. Exemptions to VATs are common and variously motivated. In some cases, governments recognize that enforcement is very difficult and would, counterproductively, encourage activity to shift to the informal economy. Similarly, the cost of complying with a VAT could be prohibitive or infeasible for small firms. Most important, however, is the equity argument that leads to the exemption of basic foodstuffs, certain types of fuel (such as kerosene), and other goods and services used by poor people and otherwise vulnerable groups and of items that encourage socially desirable behaviors (such as exemptions on certain foods to encourage more nutritious diets, children's clothing to reduce the burden on families, and printed matter to encourage the purchase of books). However, although often well intended, these exemptions can have a blunt and even regressive impact, just as price subsidies can.

Although some tax exemptions can reduce poverty, the *tax expenditures* (the forgone revenue to the government) that they imply can disproportionately benefit wealthier households. Analysis by Harris et al. (2018), at the Institute for Fiscal Studies (IFS) in conjunction with the World Bank, used household data to simulate the impact of VAT exemptions on absolute poverty rates in four countries: Ethiopia, Ghana, Senegal, and Zambia. The government revenue forgone from these exemptions can reach as high as 50 percent of total potential VAT revenues.[4] The authors found that the incidence of the tax expenditure, although progressive in these cases, was not well targeted. The social assistance programs in each country are relatively well targeted, but their coverage is not sufficient, nor are benefits adequate to compensate many of the poor people that would be affected by the elimination of exemptions. The authors conclude that by transferring at least three-fourths of the fiscal savings from reducing VAT exemptions back to households in the form of a universal basic income, most people living in absolute poverty would be better off. In short, eliminating VAT exemptions and using the fiscal savings to finance a broad-reaching cash transfer program is a better way to reduce poverty.

Figure 5.3 shows the impact of this change on consumption for the four African countries analyzed by Harris et al. (2018). The pattern of incidence resembles closely the simulations of minimum guarantees for poverty prevention shown in chapter 3. This observation underlines the point made by Lustig (2018) on the need to consider the *net* effect of all taxes and transfers rather than any individual instrument in isolation, a vital point when considering a shift in policy. The elimination of VAT exemptions alone would very likely increase poverty, but when combined with the introduction of a broad-reaching cash transfer, the change unambiguously reduces poverty.

A related area of research looks at the effects on the labor market and income distribution that arise from shifts in how public risk-pooling instruments are financed, specifically shifts from statutory levies on firms' wage bills to consumption taxes. In a general equilibrium analysis of Chile's 2008 pension reform, Santoro (2017) compared the impact of

**Figure 5.3 Eliminating Value Added Tax Exemptions to Finance a Broad Cash Transfer Can Be a More Progressive Policy**

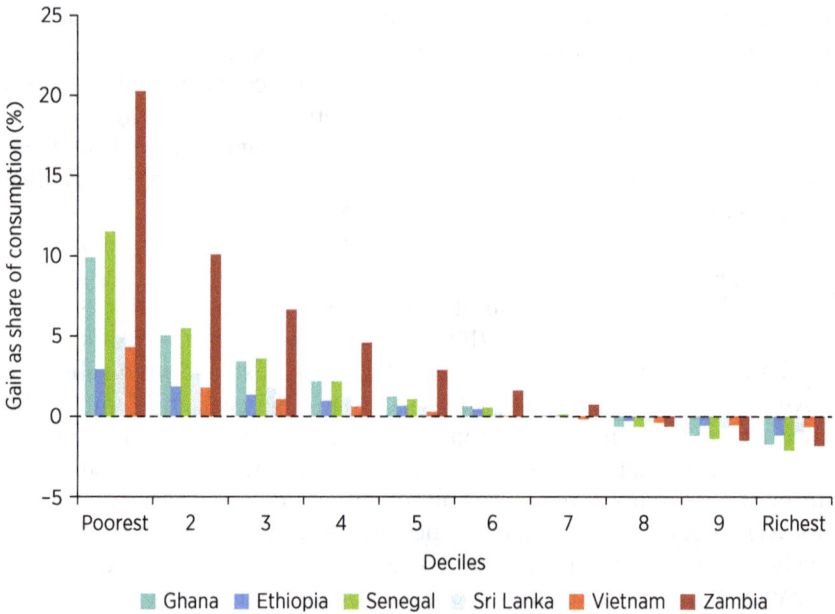

*Source:* Harris et al. 2018, using GHATAX, ETHTAX, and CEQ/World Bank fiscal incidence analysis.

*Note:* This figure shows the distributional impact of implementing a uniform value added tax (VAT) and using 100 percent of revenue gains to fund a universal basic income (UBI). Population deciles are ranked by per capita consumption; the UBI is funded with the full revenue gain from implementing the VAT (which excludes only public services, financial services, and hotel lodgings) at the standard rate in each country and is distributed per capita.

financing new "solidarity" pensions with a VAT rather than a new statutory payroll tax. The positive indirect effects of taxing consumption relative to taxing labor made the former a better option in terms of increasing formal employment, productivity, and growth. The empirical literature tends to find that positive, albeit small, increases in formal sector employment follow the shift from payroll to consumption taxes (Pestel and Sommer 2017). However, without a compensating transfer, this shift will generally be regressive, especially in low- and middle-income countries (Antón, Hernandez, and Levy 2013).[5]

Additionally, there are sources of revenue and taxation instruments that most countries have not yet exploited fully and that tend to have a progressive impact. Calls for the comprehensive reform of taxation and for tax policy to be modernized and tailored to the globalized, digitized economy are growing louder. Profit shifting, tax competition, and the worldwide decline in corporate tax rates have come under increased scrutiny (IMF 2019; OECD 2018; World Bank 2019). Prominent global institutions now advocate concerted action by governments and international agencies to increase tax revenues, motivated especially by the resources required to meet the Sustainable Development Goals (IMF, OECD, World Bank, and UN 2015). The equity and efficiency case for deploying taxation of land, other property, and inherited wealth more intensively than is currently done in most countries was presented in chapter 4, and a jobs-supportive case was argued for the long-standing revenue policy principle of *neutrality* to be put into broader practice, particularly in regard to how income from different sources is taxed (Packard and Van Nguyen 2014).

In addition, more intensive use of underutilized levies will be especially vital to increasing the tax revenue as a share of GDP in low- and middle-income countries, which still lag far behind wealthier countries in this regard. One study found that property tax revenues as a share of GDP in middle-income countries averaged 0.8 percent, or about half of the rich-country average (Norregaard 2013). In most low-income countries, the share is even less; for example, in 2015, the figure was 0.05 percent in Senegal and 0.02 percent of GDP in Cabo Verde and Rwanda (Goodfellow 2016). Recent technological innovations, including the use of satellite imagery to create property tax maps, make it possible at a low cost to levy broader and more progressive property taxes (Ali et al. 2016). Taxing property effectively is an enormous undertaking, fraught with political-economy and governance issues. There are many ways, even in higher-income countries, for property owners to underrepresent the value of real estate and other wealth, and these ways multiply in developing-country settings. However, as in many areas of public policy, advances in technology and the growing capacity of governments can make avoidance and evasion more difficult.

For many countries, then, a combination of better management of existing assets, improved allocation of existing safety-net spending, compensation for price subsidy reform, and broadening the tax base would be sufficient to finance a significant part of the new guaranteed minimum protection. However, in middle-income countries, particularly those at an advanced stage of the demographic transition, projected spending on health and pensions combined with a shrinking labor force equate to formidable social insurance deficits. This scenario is already the case in much of Europe, and the magnitude of the liability is becoming clear in other developing regions. Without reforms, "contributory" pension systems struggling to run on a pay-as-you-go basis in some countries will consume the resources that might otherwise be available for the core guaranteed minimum protections proposed in chapters 3 and 4, as well as other spending on services that build human capital. This tradeoff is already evident in parts of Central and Eastern Europe and in some countries in Latin America.

## Reducing Unfunded Social Insurance Liabilities

Many middle-income countries are already struggling to keep the promises of their employment-based social insurance systems, and these struggles must be considered in charting a course for transition. As discussed in chapter 1, traditional contributory social insurance programs became common in most fully industrialized and partially industrialized countries by the 1970s. Today, many of these plans operate in deficit, drawing on transfers from the general budget or other earmarked taxes to finance a significant part of the benefits they promise. Pay-as-you-go plans promised pensions in the future in exchange for statutory employer and employee contributions today. Given the demographic changes that accompany development and the parameters of these plans, the implied rate of return for contributors typically exceeded the sustainable rate of return. The situation worsened as fertility fell fast and as statutory minimum retirement ages failed to keep pace with lengthening life expectancy. Today, the estimated value of pension promises exceeds the explicit public debt in most European countries, Japan, and several other countries, such as Argentina, Brazil, and China. Figure 5.4 illustrates this pattern in Argentina. The surpluses of the national pension system's early years eventually turned into deficits, which continue to this day (Centrangolo and Grushka 2004). By 2010, more than 40 percent of pension spending was covered with revenue from earmarked consumption taxes (Bertranou et al. 2012).

The situation is especially acute in the countries of Central and Eastern Europe, where coverage was close to universal until the collapse of planned economies in the 1990s. During the past 30 years, coverage rates have fallen to levels typical for countries at similar income levels. The informal economy and informal employment grew dramatically in countries such as Albania, Bulgaria, Romania, and Serbia as well as in most of the countries that emerged from the former Soviet Union. Growing informalization of work dramatically exacerbated the imbalance between contributors and pensioners. This imbalance resulted in large deficits even when statutory contribution rates were set at levels above 20 percent. Rather than increase minimum retirement ages, most countries in the region simply did not index pensions for inflation, while periodically raising the contributory minimum pension. The result was that in many countries, pension payouts bore little or no relation to workers' historical contributions.

**Figure 5.4  The Pace of Demographic Change Combines with Rigid Parameters to Make Most Defined-Benefit, PAYGO Pension Plans Unsustainable**

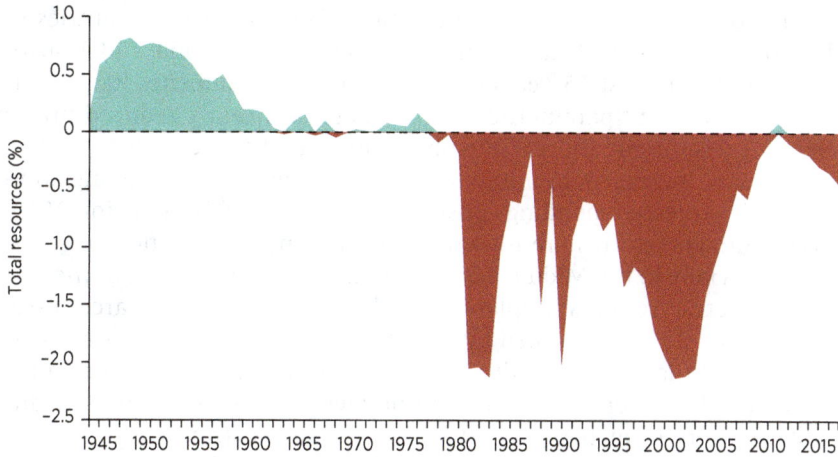

*Sources:* Based on and updating Bertranou et al. 2012 and Centrangolo and Grushka 2004.

*Note:* This figure shows the balance of contribution revenues minus benefit expenditures for Argentina's pension plan from 1944 to 2017.

In Georgia, by 2006 almost half of pension spending was financed with transfers from the general budget, and most people received the contributory minimum pension. Projections suggested that an increasing proportion of the elderly would not qualify for even the contributory minimum pension. In 2008, the government finally recognized that the old system was no longer viable. The contributory pension was replaced by a universal flat benefit. The link between statutory payroll tax contributions and benefits from the national pension system had been eliminated. This episode in Georgia was not the first time that a defined-benefit, pay-as-you-go pension plan had been closed. But it was the first time that a de jure contributory plan was replaced by a noncontributory plan. It is unlikely to be the last case; several other formerly planned-economy countries could soon face a similar choice as their population pyramids continue to invert. Managing the tradeoff between adequate consumption-smoothing and maintaining a reasonable minimum standard of living for all the elderly is a continuing struggle in the countries of Central and Eastern Europe (Schwarz and Arias 2014).

The long-run challenge of population aging for fiscal policy faced by most high-income countries is just as formidable. In 2016, average pension spending in European Union (EU) countries exceeded 10 percent of GDP; this rate is very high when compared to the levels observed in low- and middle-income countries other than in several of the countries in the Southern Cone of Latin America (such as Argentina and Brazil). However, in the past 15 years or so, most of these countries have managed to implement parametric reforms that significantly reduced future spending requirements. EU member countries have reduced pension benefits and increased minimum pensionable ages and, in so doing, lowered their projected spending considerably (European Commission 2015, 2018). Similar reforms are now debated in many middle-income countries, especially in the Middle East and in Latin America. Without the sort of parametric reforms implemented by EU countries, scarce fiscal resources could be consumed by increasing deficits of contributory pension plans. In low- and middle-income countries, where covered workers tend to be better off than those not covered, bailing out these plans with transfers from the general budget—financed from taxes paid by people whether or not they are entitled to the contributory coverage— has a clearly regressive impact. Although intergenerational equity is the focus in richer countries, this structural "diagonal redistribution" from younger, lower-income people to older, higher-income people threatens to exacerbate inequality in most low- and middle-income countries.

At the other end of the development spectrum, a small number of countries have never mandated statutory contributions for social insurance from workers and firms in the private sector. In Africa, this group of countries includes Botswana, Lesotho, Namibia, Somalia, South Sudan, Sudan, and South Africa. In Asia, it includes Bangladesh and Bhutan.[6] Other Asian countries—Cambodia, the Lao People's Democratic Republic, Myanmar, and Nepal—recently passed legislation to introduce mandatory employment-based, contributory social insurance but have not implemented these plans. Indonesia's employment-based, contributory social insurance system is only a few years old and will mature only after several decades. Aside from the Southern African countries that have funded plans for civil servants, the rest of these countries all have unfunded pension liabilities linked to civil servants.

Many low- and middle-income countries have a long enough history of employment-based social insurance that a substantial number of people have some claim to future pensions that will have to be financed. Unfortunately, there is no standard set of financial projections of these obligations for low- and middle-income countries, as there now is for countries in the EU.[7] Nor is there an agreement on the best way to measure unfunded pension liabilities or the financing gap across countries.[8] What is clear, however, is that liabilities are lower in countries with low levels of partici-pation and where pension plans were introduced later. Ethiopia and Indonesia, for example, have only recently introduced their employment-based, contributory social insurance plans and still have relatively low lev-els of coverage of the working population. In contrast, most of the plans in Middle Eastern countries, as well as many in Latin American countries, have higher levels of worker participation and are now maturing. In East Asia, the unprecedented pace of population aging will hasten this process relative to that observed in other regions, most dramatically in Thailand and Vietnam. Along with China, these countries will lose the race between coverage and aging and will have to resort to noncontributory programs as the primary policy instrument to support the consumption of the elderly (World Bank 2016).

It will be more difficult for this last group of countries to reduce their dependence on the statutory contribution—an earmarked payroll tax—as the primary financing channel for their social insurance plans (see box 5.2). However, their transitions will be easier to the extent that parametric reforms that reduce their social insurance obligations are started early and phased in gradually. Korea reformed its pension system early in the life of the plan with a view toward delaying deficits until beyond 2050, a formi-dable feat in such a rapidly aging country. Increasing retirement ages in line with life expectancy and reducing replacement rate targets are measures that can and should be phased in gradually. The political challenge of reduc-ing the value of pension commitments cannot be overstated, because the potential losers tend to be politically powerful. Meanwhile, shifting redistri-bution to noncontributory "social pensions" (financed by general revenues) reduces the need to raise earmarked payroll taxes to balance systems' finances in the short run (see box 5.3).

Countries with higher levels of coverage and more mature pension systems will find it more difficult to transition to a new model because of the overhang of their unfunded pension liabilities. A handful of coun-tries in Africa and Asia could still largely avoid the path toward an industrial-era, employment-based contributory social insurance model. However, many low- and middle-income countries have substantial unfunded liabilities from their prevailing employment-based contribu-tory social insurance, despite low levels of worker participation. More ambitious parametric reforms of the type implemented over the past two decades in the EU countries and Japan will be needed to reduce future liabilities. The current deficits of these plans already consume resources that would be better deployed to build and protect human capital, particularly that of most lower-means households which they fail to cover. In extreme cases where employment-based contributory social insurance plans are no longer viable (that is, the plans are unable

BOX 5.2

## The Puzzling Persistence of the Payroll Tax

The proposals for a comprehensive package of insurance assistance presented in chapter 3 and the suggestions for how to finance each segment are built on the argument that a country's public finance system is the largest, most effective and efficient risk pool that the government can offer to households to redistribute risks, manage uncertainty, and pursue greater equity. Although larger risk pools with regional and even global breadth are increasingly available, in most contexts a country's public finance system will remain the largest and most efficient mechanism for pooling risks and managing uncertainty.

In the approach proposed in chapter 3, statutory employer and worker contributions have an important role. But this role is more limited than the role they are assigned in prevailing employment-based, contributory social insurance. The so-called Bismarckian approach to risk sharing that prevails in many countries (and which is still being considered in several countries) is to use statutory employer and worker contributions, and the benefits they nominally finance, as an instrument for "vertical" and "horizontal" redistribution— that is, to prevent poverty and redistribute wealth within and between generations *as well as* to redistribute exposure to risks and uncertainty. We argue that for the purposes of poverty prevention and other wealth redistribution objectives, the traditional approach offers households a relatively inefficient and ineffective instrument where and when the superior alternative of a larger risk pool, financed with a range of tax instruments with a much broader base, is available.

Traditional social insurance plans were designed to take advantage of the *relative observability* of wages and salaries and to use the workplace as a platform and the employer as an agent for collecting contributions and information about when employment started and stopped, and under what circumstances. However, the very essence of economic informality is the *unobservability* of whether and where economic activity—including work—is taking place. Diversity in how people work challenges the assumed presence of the employer. Thus, the shortcomings of using a workplace-related contribution mechanism are becoming apparent regarding not only individuals who are employed informally but also nonsalaried workers operating within the framework of the law.

*continued next page*

## Box 5.2 (*continued*)

As payroll contribution–financed social insurance plans mature and covered populations age, the statutory rates that are required to sustain these plans can rise, reaching high and damaging levels. They have reached double digits in most countries in Europe and Latin America and can often exceed 20 percent. At these levels, and when combined with hidden wealth redistribution and stringent labor market regulations like a binding minimum wage and high severance mandates, payroll taxes have a negative impact on formal sector employment. The result is a vicious cycle in which rates increase, firms and workers have a greater incentive to evade contribution, and the tax base narrows.

When the policy objective is to prevent poverty and redistribute wealth, the broader public-finance system is a far more effective, efficient, and equitable mechanism for risk pooling, assuming the progressivity of tax collection instruments and subsequent public spending (Mossialos et al. 2002; Savedoff 2004). The most important gain from financing minimum guaranteed protection through general tax revenues is that the risk of losses is effectively pooled across the *entire* taxpaying population— a larger share of the population than might otherwise be the case, particularly where employers and workers can evade statutory payroll contributions. Shifting to general revenue financing can also be less regressive if the revenue from property, rents, capital gains, and profits is appropriately taxed. Of all the sources of financing, general taxation entails the lowest transaction costs for allocating poverty-prevention and equity subsidies, because the entire society becomes a single risk pool (Savedoff 2004).

Yet, despite clear advantages, efforts to move away from statutory contributions structured as a payroll tax are often resisted by most policy makers, administrators of social insurance agencies, labor unions, and even affiliated workers. Three main arguments are typically made against a shift to general-tax financing. First, the providers of employment-based social insurance see the statutory-contribution payroll tax as a relatively independent and secure revenue source that is safe from annual political budget discussions. Second, the statutory-contribution payroll tax is perceived to be less cyclical than general revenue sources in the sector. Third, statutory-contribution payroll-tax financing makes it more difficult for governments to cut benefits, because it gives workers a sense of entitlement that they will defend, which creates a powerful political deterrent.

*continued next page*

**Box 5.2** (*continued*)

Counterarguments include that although independent, earmarked sources of revenue such as a statutory payroll tax can give consider-able autonomy to the social insurance administrator, they can limit the extent to which these institutions respond to public questioning of their performance and their use of resources. Furthermore, although all public expenditure can come under pressure during eco-nomic downturns that lower governments' overall revenue, financing through payroll contributions and employment can have an even more severe procyclical pattern—particularly employment in sectors that comply with the mandate to contribute. Finally, although payroll taxes certainly confer a strong sense of entitlement and a political deterrent to cuts in services, this phenomenon may translate into capture by elites rather than protection of services, particularly those intended for the poorest people.

*Source:* Baeza and Packard 2006.

to provide an effective consumption-smoothing mechanism), priority should be given to ensuring a minimum guaranteed benefit (Lindeman, Rutkowski, and Sluchynskyy 2000).

## How Can the New Package of Protection Be Implemented?

The policies that we propose can only be implemented if there is a fundamental shift in the way governments harness the advances of digital technology to implement risk-sharing programs. Many of the features of traditional risk-sharing models reflect not only the way most people were expected to work in the past but also technological constraints on government capacity to interact with citizens that have since been overcome. Today, advances in digital technologies are rapidly broadening what governments can do without the intermediation of employers or reliance on easy-to-observe formal-sector payrolls.

Three areas of technological progress are especially transformative. The first two—digital identification and digital payments—are closely related. The ability to comprehensively and robustly verify the identity of the individual combined with the power of cashless payments to and from the government (referred to as person-to-government [P2G] and

BOX 5.3

## How "Contributory" Are Pension Systems, Really?

Financing guaranteed minimum protections from taxes with a broader base can strike many as utopian and too administratively daunting. Yet a transition away from relying on statutory contributions levied as payroll taxes is already well underway. Unfortunately, this shift is too often being made by default rather than by design and having a regressive impact.

General revenue and other channels of earmarked revenue are playing a gradually more significant part in financing nominally "contributory" pensions across countries at various levels of economic development. In some cases, this change is a result of initial design decisions; in others, the change is an explicit adaptation of originally purely contributory social insurance plans. In most countries, reliance on the general budget is becoming a public-finance default, as changing demographic and economic realities challenge the viability of rigid pension-system parameters, leading to increasingly regressive outcomes. For example, in Latin America, especially in the countries of the Southern Cone, a large share of purportedly contributory pension plans is being financed from general budget transfers (Bird and Smart 2011).

In a small number of countries, the shift from statutory contributions to general-budget financing or alternative earmarked taxes is an intentional policy strategy, although this is not widely known. In some cases, the systems started as purely contributory social insurance plans. In Japan, rapid population aging over the past 50 years has made a purely contributory model increasingly difficult to sustain without economically and politically untenable increases in statutory contribution rates. Instead, the Japanese authorities have earmarked sales-tax revenue to fund the basic pension (and other forms of risk sharing, such as social long-term care insurance). The system matches the contribution revenue one to one, so that the basic pension is 50 percent funded from general revenues. Germany is now facing similar demographic pressures to Japan and is adapting the financing of its social insurance system accordingly.

The oldest examples of countries that chose to finance their core pension systems from the general budget are Australia and New Zealand. New Zealand introduced a flat and universal basic pension in 1891 and has retained it, while Australia has taken a similar approach to financing its pension but means-tests the basic benefit. In Australia, around 40 percent of people of pensionable age receive

*continued next page*

**Box 5.3** (*continued*)

a full basic pension, and the pension tapers to zero by around the 60th percentile of the income distribution. Although both countries have subsequently added individual contributory consumption-smoothing plans to their systems (Australia with a mandatory defined-contribution plan and New Zealand with a nudged savings plan with an auto-enrollment default and matching-contribution incentives), the general-revenue funding of their core old-age benefit has prepared them well for population aging and changes to the nature of work and has resulted in systems that are rated among the most robust in the world. Among low- and middle-income countries, Bangladesh, Lesotho, Namibia, Somalia, and Sudan also finance their core pension benefits from general revenues.

General-revenue financing has also played a major and growing role in countries that seek to expand coverage by providing a safety net or a social pension. Around 80 countries at all levels of income have "social pensions"—that is, a flat, age-based transfer to the elderly financed by general expenditure. The number of countries offering this instrument has more than doubled since 1990, largely driven by uptake in developing countries (HelpAge International 2019; Rofman, Apella, and Vezza 2015). Some countries use this instrument as a core element of the pension system (such as Bolivia, South Africa, and Timor-Leste), others as a poverty-prevention program for the elderly (such as Bangladesh, India, Kenya, and Vietnam), and still others as a tool to address (sometimes large) coverage gaps in their contributory plans (such as Chile, China, the Republic of Korea, Mexico, and Thailand).

government-to-person [G2P] payments) can greatly facilitate implementation of the new risk-sharing model by reducing the cost of payments on both sides of the equation[9] while simultaneously reducing the potential for corruption. The same principle applies to the expansion of social insurance coverage described in chapter 3 as the flow of funds is reversed. For example, these technologies are put to use in the Mbao informal sector pension plan in Kenya, a private retirement scheme established in 2009 by the Kenya National Federation of Jua Kali Associations and the Retirement Benefits Authority that provides a voluntary mechanism for pooling and investing workers' savings (Kabare 2018).

The third relevant area of technological progress is part of the broader phenomenon of the massive expansion of data collection in every sphere of life, including government. As governments around the world have moved from paper to digital records and have increased the amount of information they regularly collect on individuals and households, they are increasingly able to assess socioeconomic status without necessarily observing incomes. However, this explosion of data collection and concentration also brings risks of a surveillance society that must be addressed through technological and legal safeguards.

## Know Your People: The Role of Unique Digital Identifiers

In wealthier countries, legal identity has for decades been determined through the process of civil registration. By the middle of the twentieth century, birth registration rates were close to 100 percent in advanced countries. Today, the entire populations of these countries can often be found in a digitized civil registry of some kind. Close-to-universal birth registration has also been achieved in several middle-income countries, including China.[10] However, in most low-income countries, and even in some middle-income countries, birth registration rates are far from universal and can range from as low as 15 percent to 80 percent. As a result, most people in Asian and in African countries, for example, do not have birth certificates. Numerous studies have shown the unsurprising result that people living in poverty are disproportionately represented among those not registered.[11] What serves as the initial "breeder" document for identity in rich countries is not available for much of the population in developing countries. In addition, dozens of countries continue to register births and deaths in paper-based systems of dubious quality. As a result, even in countries with good registration rates, the registration system may be an unreliable proof of identity, and there can be many individuals with multiple identities.[12]

Even if birth registration rates were to increase to 100 percent overnight, it would be many years before civil registries covered the entire population.[13] This stock-versus-flow challenge has led some countries to register older children and adults and issue them with unique identifiers in a separate process, usually as part of a national ID system. These systems typically register individuals between the ages of 15 and 18 and increasingly have ensured uniqueness using biometric deduplication. In this process, fingerprints, iris images, or both are captured and compared to all others in the database to ensure that one person is not assigned multiple identities. The most well-known case of such a system is the Aadhaar number that has been issued to more than one billion residents of India in a relatively short period. The motivation behind the project was specifically to improve the delivery of social programs. The project has also contributed to a massive increase in financial inclusion (see ID Insight 2018).

Most Sub-Saharan African countries have started to use this technology to register their populations, and a handful are close to achieving universal coverage. Mauritania and Rwanda, and, more recently, Benin and Malawi, appear to have achieved close to universal coverage of their national ID systems. In Asia, Bangladesh, Indonesia, and Pakistan have all gone this route during the past decade and have achieved high coverage rates, albeit with important gaps remaining among poor people. Thailand, which began reforming its identification system in the 1980s, has managed to seamlessly integrate its birth and death registration with its digital ID system and has achieved practically universal coverage. An integrated identification system, which assigns a unique identifier at birth that is kept throughout life and has almost universal coverage, is considered international good practice and can be found in a number of Latin American countries, such as Chile, Peru, and Uruguay.

Although ensuring that everybody has a unique digital identifier is itself a major achievement, the most significant benefits come when an authentication "ecosystem" is built around it. The ability to verify or authenticate an individual's identity is valuable to both the public and the private sectors. In the case of banks and telecom operators, the regulatory requirements to know your customer (KYC) can add significant costs unless this service is offered efficiently. A unique identifier also allows creditors, including microfinance institutions, to track borrowers more effectively. Conversely, many people cannot open bank accounts or access formal financial markets, generally due to lack of documentation.

In addition to facilitating interactions between people and the state, a robust identification system generates economic value and facilitates secure transactions. Peru's ID agency offers authentication services to private sector entities and performs millions of online authentications each year. The agency also offers this service to hospitals that biometrically authenticate patients to check that they are covered by health insurance. Government agencies administering social assistance programs can use this system to ensure that beneficiaries receive the right cash or in-kind transfers. India's Aadhaar authentication system has helped reduce fraud in several major social programs. The fiscal savings that can accrue from the elimination of fraud have been shown to be substantial (Clark 2018).

There are synergies between expanding coverage of identification systems and improving poverty-prevention programs. In Nepal, UNICEF has supported the link between a universal child grant and birth registration.

In the first district where this system was implemented, birth registration rose by 50 percentage points. A similar effect of child grants on birth registration has been observed in South Africa. Conversely, identification agencies can assist social protection programs by ensuring uniqueness and authenticating transactions. A clear case of this symbiosis can be found in Pakistan, where the identification agency, NADRA, cooperated with the Benazir Income Support Program (BISP) to enroll poor women who were the program's beneficiaries. Because of the incentive of receiving the cash transfer, coverage among rural women doubled in a few years. At the same time, BISP has benefited from having a robust mechanism to verify that the correct people are receiving benefits.

## Ditching Cash: The Transformative Power of Digital Payments

The second type of interaction that is being redefined through new technology involves digital payments and other transactions between government and individuals. In the case of employment-based contributory social insurance, for example, contributions are collected, and pensions are eventually paid. Social assistance may involve cash transfers, but it could also take the form of a good, such as food, being delivered to the eligible individual. Until recently, these transactions took place in what can be described as an analog process. In the case of transfers, it entailed the payment of cash after manual verification of the identity of the recipient. Neither cash nor this kind of authentication leaves an electronic trail, making it more difficult to detect corruption. This mode of payment is still prevalent for social assistance payments in a surprising number of countries, including the largest programs in Sub-Saharan Africa. In a few countries, including Ethiopia and Myanmar, this mode even applies to employment-based social insurance contributions and payouts.

In the past decade or so, there has been a notable shift toward digital G2P payments. Figure 5.5 shows for a selection of countries the percentage of adults aged 15 and above receiving G2P payments. It also shows the percentage of those receiving any G2P payments that receive them directly into bank accounts (the larger bar, in all cases). These figures are taken from the FINDEX tri-annual survey of 2017 and include payments of the wages of civil servants, cash transfer social assistance programs, and social insurance benefits such as pensions. The first indicator reflects the fact that larger proportions of the population receive government transfers in higher-income countries. The relatively high proportion of people in Latvia, the Russian Federation, Sweden, and the United States who receive G2P payments is largely due to maturing pension systems and

**Figure 5.5 The Potential to Ramp Up G2P Payments Varies Significantly across Countries**

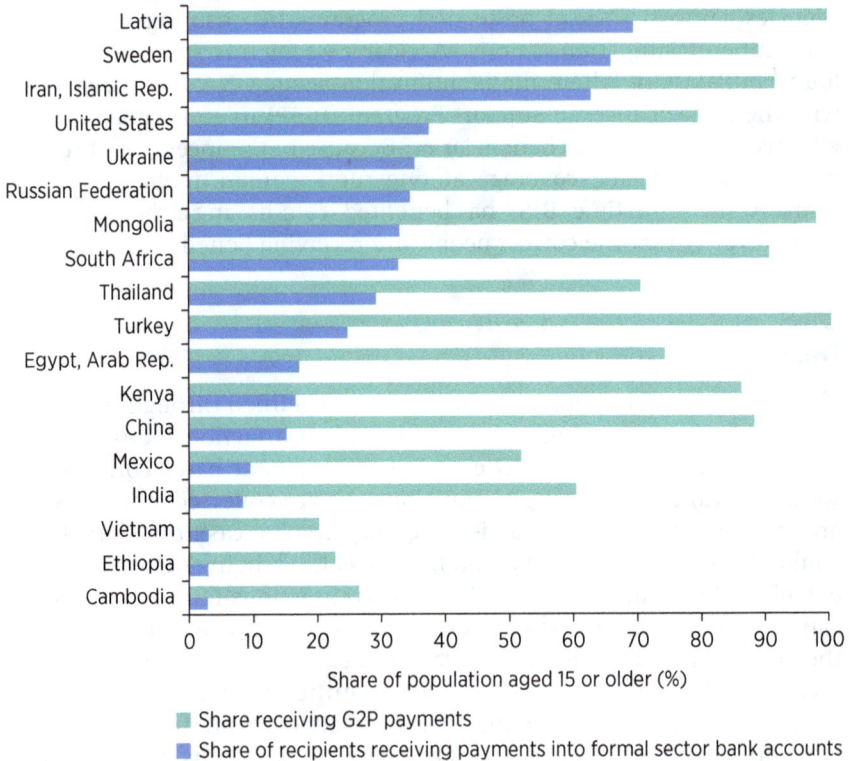

Share of population aged 15 or older (%)

■ Share receiving G2P payments
■ Share of recipients receiving payments into formal sector bank accounts

*Source:* Computations based on FINDEX data.

*Note:* This figure shows the percentage of adults receiving government-to-person (G2P) payments and the percentage of recipients who receive their payments into formal bank accounts for selected countries.

aging populations, and, not surprisingly, most payments go directly into bank accounts. In contrast, relatively few people receive such transfers in Ethiopia or Vietnam, where pension coverage is low and pension plans are still immature.

The gap between countries at different income levels is less pronounced for the second indicator, the share of G2P recipients who receive their transfers into a bank account. Between 2010 and 2017, the monetary amount of social transfers in developing countries paid digitally increased by 300 percent, reaching close to US$200 billion. One quarter of poor countries make some social transfers digitally (Bull 2018). Although the gap between low- and high-income countries is still large, many developing countries are catching up. The high percentage in the Islamic Republic of Iran, for example, is due to the quasi-universal cash transfer program introduced in 2009 to compensate for the withdrawal of energy price subsidies and the consequent increase in energy prices. To distribute these transfers, bank accounts had to be opened for millions of previously unbanked individuals, raising the Islamic Republic of Iran's financial inclusion rate to among the highest in the world. The proportion of adults who receive G2P payments in most countries is much lower than in the Islamic Republic of Iran, and in many cases, the payments are not made into transaction accounts, so the payments have a limited impact on financial inclusion. Nevertheless, the figure shows that some countries have the capacity to pay G2P recipients directly. The share paid directly is now over 60 percent in India and close to 90 percent in China and Kenya. In the latter, close to one-quarter of the payments are made through M-pesa, a mobile money transfer service.

As mobile money penetration continues to grow, so does the potential for low-cost transactions between governments and people. According to FINDEX surveys, mobile payments already make up more than one-third of G2P payments in Ghana, Haiti, and Zambia. According to the latest *Global State of Mobile Payment* report published by the GSM Association, by 2018 there were 690 million registered mobile money accounts worldwide, an increase of 25 percent since 2016. Importantly, the fastest growth in mobile money and digital commerce is taking place in Africa and Asia. Two-thirds of adults in Kenya, Rwanda, Tanzania, and Uganda actively used mobile money accounts in 2017.

This development has major implications not only for G2P payments but also for the nature of the informal economy and the potential for transfers in the opposite direction. The advances that are expanding G2P transfers also allow P2G transfers. Today in Kenya, for example, the value of annual mobile transactions is four times the size of the formal sector wage bill. In Asia, China leads the way in moving away from cash, but the shift appears imminent in South Asia's larger economies. Digital transactions formalize what were previously unobservable, anonymous cash purchases and open the possibility to tap into a different type of economic formality—digital consumption. Kenya's Mbao pension program for informal sector workers may presage a new way of saving for retirement and buying insurance, especially when these transactions can be linked to a robust digital identifier.[14] What began as a convenient way for Kenyans to send money to family in rural areas has rapidly evolved into a better way to do everything from paying merchants and bills to taking out loans.

Although East Africa led the way with mobile money, other parts of Asia are catching up rapidly. Digital payments in systems based on Quick Response (QR) codes have become widely used in China, while mobile money has expanded very rapidly in Bangladesh. With the recent introduction of PromptPay—an open-source, interoperable digital payment platform through which all G2P payments will be made—Thailand is aggressively moving away from cash. As with India's Direct Benefit Transfers, which is now used to make payments to hundreds of millions of people, the key to digital G2P payments in Thailand is the link to people's unique digital identities. All that is required is connectivity, a basic cell phone, and a bank account linked to a unique digital ID number. In India, the transfers can take place even without a phone, if the point-of-service operator has a device to read the person's fingerprint. With these technologies in place, G2P and P2G transfers are becoming cheap, secure, and transparent.

Greater coherence, coordination, and interoperability of governments' delivery systems will become even more important. Better approaches are emerging. The new solutions focus on the interoperability of information and on whole-of-government solutions to handle G2P payments efficiently from both the government's and individuals' viewpoints. Moreover, the most advanced of these approaches envision the disruption of the entire payment ecosystem, including transfers between two people and between people and businesses. The key to these approaches is interoperability, which reduces the cost of infrastructure while promoting competition. This, in turn, reduces prices for the individual and increases convenience. Importantly, the ubiquity of payment points and the ease of transferring funds digitally is particularly beneficial to those making small transactions on a frequent basis, such as people whose work has been in the previously unobservable informal economy (see photo 5.1). However, many digital payment arrangements are still managed by individual programs that enter contracts with payment providers, mostly banks. In some countries, there are half a dozen or more such arrangements within the social protection system. Social insurance and social assistance payments, not to mention government wage payments, are commonly handled under separate arrangements.

## Blurring the Line between the Formal and Informal Economies with Administrative Data

The approach to risk sharing proposed in this volume demands integrated, interoperable administrative information systems. For example, a pure universal basic income (UBI), according to the definition presented in chapter 3, would require only that individuals could be identified and authenticated, but the tapered UBI (TUBI) approach would require

**Photo 5.1    Cash Not Accepted! PromptPay in Action in Thailand**

World Bank staff photo.

more information. The prevailing approach to providing social assistance transfers involves a gradually evolving set of parallel registries corresponding to different government programs. In employment-based, contributory social insurance plans, the government mandates that employers and employees be registered and report their wages periodically so that deductions can be made. Households are mandated to report income for tax purposes (although employer withholding often plays a role). For social assistance, special processes are set up to collect the information required for targeting. In poorer countries, the data are typically gathered by going door to door, a so-called census sweep, while in middle- and high-income countries, the data are typically submitted through an application process. When combined, these registries cover almost everyone in rich countries, where most workers are in the formal sector. In contrast, a large proportion of the population in most developing countries does not show up in any of their governments' registries. Figure 5.6 presents a stylized picture of data availability in richer versus poorer countries. It suggests that about half of the global population, especially the nonpoor population working in the informal economy, are systematically excluded from any analysis of redistribution in low- and middle-income countries.

**Figure 5.6 Availability of Data on the Population Has Been Very Limited in Poor Countries**

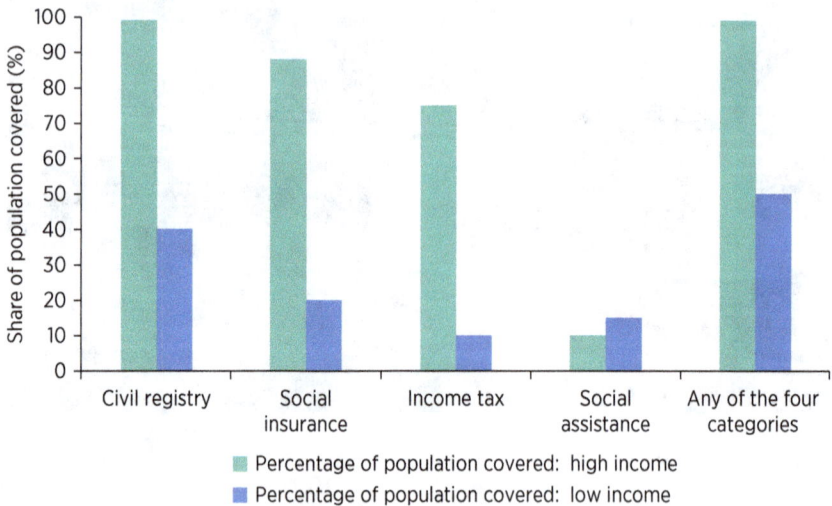

Legend:
- Percentage of population covered: high income
- Percentage of population covered: low income

*Source:* Calculations based on UNICEF data, the World Bank pension database, and World Bank 2018.

Although clearly challenged by this data gap, low- and middle-income countries are starting to fill it (see figure 5.7). Pakistan, for example, collects data on most of its population to rank the socioeconomic status of households in order to prioritize recipients of its cash transfer program. Rwanda collects information on more than 80 percent of its population. Because both countries have robust identification systems, they are better positioned than most of their peers to implement the kind of differentiated subsidies and transfers laid out in chapter 3. Recently, Rwanda introduced a differentiated subsidized pension contribution that uses these data to

**Figure 5.7   Social Registries in Low- and Middle-Income Countries Are Expanding to Cover Most Households**

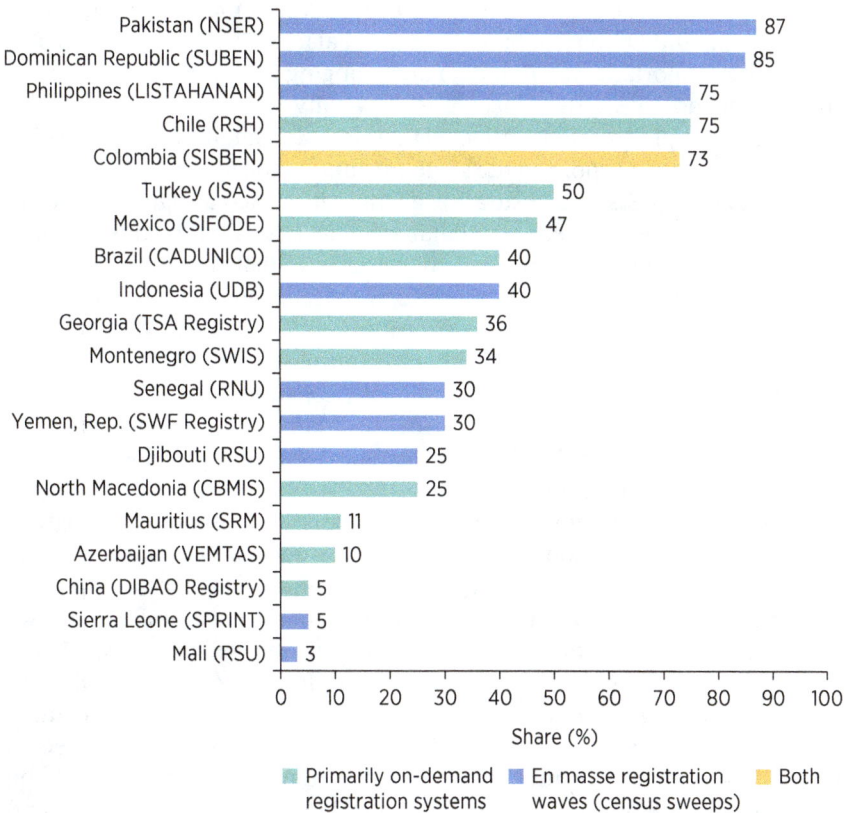

*Source:* Leite et al. 2017.

*Note:* This figure shows the population coverage of social registries (in parentheses after the country names) in selected countries circa 2015–17.

provide an old-age and survivor pension plan for informal sector workers. Internationally, there is a trend toward more complete population coverage of social registries, or the equivalent in interlinked administrative databases, as discussed below.

The cost of collecting data is surprisingly low and is falling further, partly because of better technology that allows for mobile electronic data collection. In Pakistan, the cost of data collection per household was approximately US$1.4, and the cost was around US$2.5 in Bangladesh, Indonesia, and the Philippines. These costs are a relatively small share of total program expenditures, no more than 5–10 percent of annual spending, and typically much less in poorer countries. This observation suggests that there is a strongly positive benefit-cost ratio in terms of the poverty impact of better targeting and broader coverage, which allows developing countries to phase out benefits rather than impose a 100 percent marginal rate of benefit withdrawal at some arbitrary level of income or consumption (Hanna and Olken 2018; Majoka and Palacios 2019).

Another important way that data are changing how governments assess the socioeconomic status of people is the ability to use unique identifiers to link multiple administrative databases. In addition to checking whether people are reporting the same earnings to the income tax authority as they are to the social insurance agency, it is increasingly possible to perform cross-checks between databases on assets and consumption. As land, automobile, and property registries are digitized, for example, it becomes possible to calculate the value of these assets to assess the ability to pay taxes and social insurance contributions.[15] Electricity consumption can also be used as a proxy for otherwise unobserved income. As digital transactions become pervasive, a digital "consumption footprint" will emerge. This footprint effectively formalizes many transactions and makes it possible for government to better assess needs as well as people's capacity to pay insurance premiums or to save.

These new data-intensive mechanisms make it possible to distinguish between poor and nonpoor people among households that transact mainly in the informal economy. In Egypt, using around 34 databases, the Anti-Corruption Authority has grouped 115 million people in 22 million households into five socioeconomic strata. These strata are used by many government programs to determine eligibility for different benefits or subsidies and significantly reduce leakages to ineligible groups. Turkey's Integrated Social Assistance System uses 28 databases to determine the degree to which individuals have the capacity to pay different proportions of the health insurance premium as well as eligibility for social assistance and other programs. This ability to link multiple administrative databases through a unique identifier can help countries mimic progressive income tax systems in richer countries.

These advances are welcome but raise concerns for people's sovereignty over their identity and their data. There is growing concern for safeguarding people's right to privacy and their right to know the data that governments and nongovernment entities have about them and how the data are used, as well as the right and the means to correct erroneous data. The writ of *habeas data* that protects these rights as part of the constitutions of several countries has become the legal foundation of more intentional and proactive protections as the value of data has grown with the digital economy. In countries with weak institutions or malevolent governments, advances in the state's ability to collect and use data efficiently raise the risks of misuse and selective abuse of surveillance ability. Indeed, concerns about linking multiple databases, among other things, have led some European countries to impose tight legal restrictions on data collection as well as technological barriers.[16]

Concerns over personal data protection and potential surveillance were prominent in 2018. For most of the year, India's Supreme Court grappled with the constitutionality of the Aadhaar project and its database of more than 1.2 billion individualized, unique pieces of biometric data. Although the court ultimately upheld the constitutionality of the project, it also limited the use of the data in a mandatory sense to taxation and social transfer payments. In May 2018, the European Union passed the General Data Protection Regulations, which will profoundly affect both the government and the private sector in the EU and well beyond. These checks on the potential misuse of personal data will need to be considered carefully and weighed against the benefits of proper use. The good news is that awareness about this issue has increased, and several viable mitigation measures, both technological and legal, are being proposed.[17]

## Putting it All Together

The new digital paradigms for identity, payments, and the proliferation of administrative data that can help assess needs and capacity to contribute are making the policy choices discussed in earlier chapters feasible. Harnessed properly, these technologies can make it possible to implement universal social programs that ultimately erase many of the distinctions that have separated social assistance and social insurance as well as the formal economy from the informal economy. An efficient way for governments to accurately and securely connect with their population and respond effectively to their needs in the wake of shocks is already visible on the horizon. Whether digital money is moving from government to people or in the opposite direction, the ubiquity of mobile phones, combined with unique digital IDs linked to mobile bank accounts, makes it possible to imagine an accurate, low-cost way of transacting with the entire population on the same payment platform. Using the increasingly digitized government databases to effectively mimic a progressive or negative income tax, the entire tax and transfer operation could be conducted digitally through the formal financial system.

Very few countries can claim to have all the key elements of an implementation infrastructure already in place. However, most developing countries are moving on all three fronts. The complete implementation infrastructure described in this chapter is clearly within reach with the right investments. From a practical viewpoint, there are at least seven steps that countries will have to take to get there:

1. Create a database of uniquely identified individuals covering the entire resident population,[18] and link this database to the civil registration system, which, in turn, should capture all births and deaths.
2. Ensure that all the major government registries—social assistance and insurance, tax, property, vehicle, and others—use this unique identifier[19] and that there are formal protocols in place to link the databases.
3. Develop an interoperable digital payment platform that minimizes costs for all G2P/P2G transactions, thus making these transactions accessible even to those at the bottom of the income distribution.
4. Facilitate financial inclusion by allowing the digital ID to be used for e-KYC for opening a basic transactional bank account and registering with telecom providers.
5. Develop an authentication infrastructure and ecosystem with levels of assurance appropriate to the risks involved in the transaction.
6. Use linked databases, including social registries, to rank individuals and households according to relative welfare for the purpose of determining the amount of transfers or premium subsidies they are eligible for.
7. Introduce legislation and regulations for personal data protection based on international good practice, and establish the capacity to enforce these rules.[20]

Building on this foundation, almost any conceivable risk-sharing policy can be implemented. Whether shifting out of broad energy price subsidies to more progressive and effective individual transfers, promoting long-term savings through government matching contributions and default enrollment, or paying out a UBI or TUBI, the investment in digital systems opens many possibilities. People who work in the informal economy would no longer be residuals, but an identified population of individuals with attributes that lead to a transfer in one direction or the other—G2P or P2G, ideally within the same ecosystem that is used for all private transactions. In effect, there would no longer be a clear distinction between the informal and formal sectors of the economy insofar as financing and coverage of risk-sharing policies was concerned.

## How Ready Are Countries to Shift to a New Risk-Sharing Model?

Low- and middle-income countries vary widely in their readiness to offer new guaranteed protections from poverty and catastrophic losses. The shift requires sources of financing along with an implementation infrastructure that includes digitized identification, administrative data, and payments. In some cases, where existing social insurance liabilities threaten to absorb scarce resources as the population ages, parametric pension reforms will be needed. Part of the social insurance program involving redistribution may also be replaced by expanding the guaranteed minimum core of the policy package, as we proposed in chapter 3.

The state of readiness will have to be assessed in each country before a path can be charted. Some countries may have enough financing, but their ability to effectively make transfers to individuals and households may be questionable. In other countries, projected pension deficits may crowd out any other transfers unless there are reforms. And some countries have neither the fiscal space nor the implementation capacity to move forward and will, therefore, have the most difficult road ahead.

Figure 5.8 is an attempt to describe the relative position of a range of countries in terms of fiscal space, as described earlier in this chapter, and implementation readiness, as described in the previous section. This calculation is not straightforward, and, ultimately, each country's state of readiness should be assessed on the basis of a thorough analysis that would look at several additional indicators. The indicators used here are meant to demonstrate the thinking behind such an assessment and were available for as many countries as possible. In this case, the relative rankings of 83 countries along these two dimensions has been plotted. Countries in the top right-hand corner are the most prepared to move in the direction proposed in this volume. Notably, the Islamic Republic of Iran ranks at the top of both indicators, a finding consistent with its introduction of a quasi-UBI financed by energy price subsidy reforms.

The fiscal space ranking is based on how much each country spends on energy subsidies plus social assistance. These resources are already being used to redistribute income and, therefore, are technically (if not politically) feasible to divert to risk-sharing programs without new taxes, borrowing, or cuts to unrelated programs. The range of spending levels is wide—from less than half a percent of GDP to more than 10 percent. As we argued earlier in this chapter, limiting exemptions on value added taxes and using the proceeds to increase poverty-prevention transfers would increase this resource envelope. The earmarking of these revenues would be justified by the need to offset the impact on lower-income households.

**Figure 5.8 Countries' Readiness (in Terms of Fiscal and Delivery Capacity) to Shift to Broader-Based Guaranteed Minimum Transfer Approaches Varies Widely**

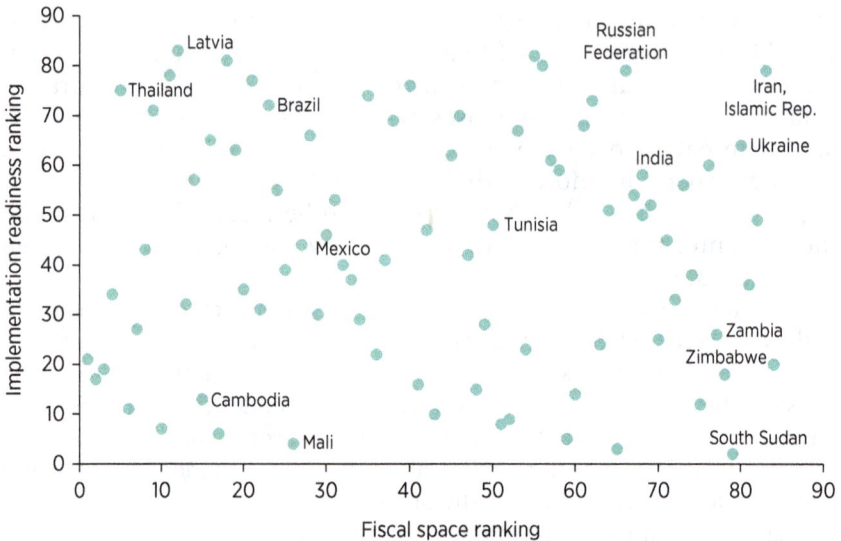

*Sources:* Calculations based on FINDEX data, UNICEF birth registration data (downloaded from https://data.unicef.org), and World Bank 2018.

Based on unpublished data from the IMF, foregone consumption tax revenues in developing countries range from roughly one-third to two-thirds of potential revenues, although it is not possible to distinguish between the effect of exemptions and that of evasion. Because consumption tax revenues are two to three times higher than revenues from income taxes in poor countries, even a fraction of these foregone revenues would significantly expand the budget envelope available for insurance-assistance and active labor measures.

The implementation readiness index considers the three areas in which new technologies are redefining the way government can interact with people, as discussed in the previous section—identification, payments, and using available data to assess socioeconomic status. It is a composite ranking based on the share of adults who have proof of identity, the share who have bank accounts,[21] and the country's e-governance ranking. The latter is a proxy for the degree of digitization of administrative databases as well as the government's potential to harness these data to mimic a progressive tax system. After a simple average of these three indicators was calculated, the 83 countries were ranked from 1 to 83, and the same was done for the fiscal space indicator.

In addition to the Islamic Republic of Iran, the more prepared countries on both fronts include India, Russia, and Ukraine. Ukraine spends more than 10 percent of its GDP on energy price subsidies and social assistance combined. It spends about the same share on pensions, and it has recently passed parametric reforms to reduce the huge deficits in its contributory plan. As a growing percentage of workers retire without these pensions due to the informalization of the economy, pressure is growing to provide noncontributory pensions. Ukraine would seem, then, to be a good candidate to implement the proposals we have described and to replace the purely poverty-prevention and redistribution components of its contributory social insurance plan with risk-pooling instruments financed from general revenues.

In the opposite corner of the figure are countries that have neither the infrastructure for implementation nor the financial resources to move quickly in the proposed direction. Cambodia and Mali fall into this category. Both countries would benefit greatly from investment in their ID and payment systems as well as from a major effort to increase financial inclusion. Both countries have grown rapidly for the past decade and could do much more to expand their revenue base. These are medium-term challenges, but they are surmountable, especially with the help of investments in proven technologies, starting with connectivity.

Countries with significant resources that are not being used effectively fall into the bottom right-hand corner. Although policy choices and conflict explain much of these countries' failures to make use of their resources, there are also shortcomings in their delivery systems that make it difficult to convert these resources into well-targeted and transparent transfers. Zimbabwe ranks very highly on the spending capacity indicator due to its high spending on energy price subsidies, but it has low banking penetration and scores poorly on the e-government index.

Finally, there are countries such as Brazil and Latvia where implementation capacity is among the highest in the world (including among many high-income countries) but fiscal space is severely limited, because their social protection systems are dominated by employment-based, contributory social insurance, especially old-age pension plans.

Readiness can be assessed, and a plausible transition path can be planned, using these and other indicators. Zambia, for example, was ranked 8th in this group for spending capacity, because it had huge energy subsidies, but 58th for implementation capacity. The government announced in 2017 that it would eliminate the subsidies, and it was supported by a loan from the IMF. In the same year, it embarked upon a plan to introduce a new digital identification system, which it hopes to roll out by 2020. It is also pursuing reforms to increase financial inclusion, having already raised the share of adults with bank accounts from 21 percent to 36 percent between 2011 and 2017. Thus, Zambia is gradually moving into the top right-hand quadrant of figure 5.8, and it may eventually be in a position to implement a completely new risk-sharing policy approach. Mexico provides an interesting case of a middle-income country that appears to have some room for financing but scores poorly on implementation, especially for its income level. Indeed, according to the FINDEX survey, Zambia has slightly higher banking coverage than Mexico. As mentioned earlier, the Mexican identification system has problems that go beyond coverage and are not completely captured in this ranking. The path forward for Mexico is to focus on improving implementation capacity and coordination across the many government agencies that lack interoperability of their systems.

The transition path from the prevailing risk-sharing model—narrowly targeted social assistance and oversized but low-coverage employment-based, contributory social insurance—to more effective risk sharing will differ in each country. Some countries will need to reform their contributory pension plans to make them more sustainable. Others will have to put in place a digital infrastructure that facilitates the delivery of benefits and the participation of people who mainly work and transact in the informal sector. And still others will have to tap new sources of revenues to fund their new risk-sharing systems. All but a select few countries will have to act on all three fronts in tandem.

## Notes

1. As Lustig (2018) argues, "analyzing the tax and spending sides simultaneously is not only desirable but necessary. Taxes can be un-equalizing but spending so equalizing that the un-equalizing effect of taxes is more than compensated. Taxes can be regressive, but when combined with transfers make the system more equalizing than without the regressive taxes."
2. Coady and Prady (2018) show how a universal basic income would reduce poverty relative to the same levels of spending on existing social programs in India.
3. Recently, emerging technologies such as biometric identification have made this idea more feasible, even in poor countries (Gelb and Majerowicz 2011). Mongolia is one of the minority of developing countries that has a biometric identification system and a population registry with which it was able to channel copper revenues into a kind of UBI.
4. The estimates by the Institute for Fiscal Studies (IFS) ranged from 22 percent to 55 percent for the four African countries analyzed.
5. As discussed in chapter 3, Antón, Hernandez, and Levy (2013) combine these two strands of the literature. The authors simulate the elimination of VAT

exemptions for Mexico combined with a reduction in payroll taxes. The cost of exemptions in Mexico was around 1 percent of GDP. The authors then simulate the effects of using the new VAT revenues and redirecting existing social spending to finance a basic package of pensions and health insurance for all workers. In a general equilibrium model, they showed positive feedback effects through increased formal employment and productivity while offsetting the regressive impact of the VAT through compensation. A recent review of tax policies in the European Union found that shifting reliance away from direct taxes and energy subsidies was also likely to contribute to economic growth. See European Union (2015).

6. Bhutan is planning to expand its plan covering public sector workers to include private sector workers.

7. These projections can be found at https://ec.europa.eu/eurostat/web/pensions.

8. See Wiener and Stokoe (2018) for a discussion of the alternative metrics.

9. On the supply side, the banking system can use robust identification to meet its know-your-customer requirements to open accounts for low-income individuals, while for the recipient, being able to receive payments into a digital account reduces the need to travel long distances to collect cash transfers.

10. Although UNICEF reports birth registration rates for almost all countries based on national data and surveys, China has a different system and is not included in those statistics. However, the coverage of the *hukou* system that registers all births is very high.

11. For birth registration by income, see UNICEF birth registration data at https://data.unicef.org; for national ID by income group, see https://id4d.worldbank.org/sites/id4d.worldbank.org/files/2018-08/ID4D%20Data%20Notes%20revised%20082918.pdf.

12. This is the case in Mexico, for example, where the number of unique ID numbers is much greater than the population and many people have been found to have more than one birth certificate.

13. The goal under Sustainable Development Goal 16.9 is universal registration by 2030, and the only indicator specified is the birth registration rate of 0- to 5-year-olds. Many countries are likely not to even meet this target.

14. The identifier ultimately becomes its owner's financial address and could facilitate automatic deductions for savings to be made, for example, when a monthly utility bill is paid. These commitment mechanisms have been shown to have a powerful impact on voluntary savings rates.

15. For example, in 2013, Jordan applied land and vehicle asset filters to determine eligibility for bread subsidies.

16. For example, Austria does not allow the unique ID number to be stored in government databases. Instead, a sector-specific number, which can only be traced to the original number under specific circumstances, is generated for each sectoral database.

17. See, for example, the proposed Data Empowerment and Protection Architecture in India at http://indiastack.org/depa and various publications at https://ID4D.worldbank.org.

18. Although the most practical approach to ensuring uniqueness is biometric deduplication, a few countries and economies (such as Taiwan) have chosen not to go this route for the moment.

19. This universal use does not mean that the same number is captured in all databases. The originating identifier, deduplicated to ensure uniqueness, can be the basis for derived identifiers that place limits on the potential for privacy infringements.
20. It could be argued that this step should be the first step implemented, although it rarely is.
21. Another indicator that could be used here is the percentage of people receiving G2P payments directly into bank accounts rather than in cash.

## References

Ali, I., F. Cawkwell, E. Dwyer, B. Barrett, and S. Green. 2016. "Satellite Remote Sensing of Grasslands: From Observation to Management—A Review." *Journal of Plant Ecology* 9 (6): 649–71.

Antón, A. 2014. "The Effect of Payroll Taxes on Employment and Wages under High Informality." *IZA Journal of Labor and Development* 3: 20.

Antón, A., F. Hernandez, and S. Levy. 2013. "The End of Informality." Inter-American Development Bank, Washington, DC.

Arze del Granado, J., D. Coady, and R. Gillingham. 2012. "The Unequal Benefits of Fuel Subsidies: A Review of Evidence for Developing Countries." *World Development* 40: 2234–48.

Baeza, C., and T. Packard. 2006. *Beyond Survival: Protecting Households from Health Shocks in Latin America*. Latin American Development Forum. Stanford, CA: Stanford University Press

Bertranou, F., O. Centrangolo, C. Grushka, and L. Casanova. 2012. "Encrucijadas en la Seguridad Social Argentina: Reforma, Cobertura y Desafios para el Sistema de Pensiones." Economic Commission for Latin America and the Caribbean and International Labour Organization, Buenos Aires.

Bird, R., and M. Smart. 2011. "Financing Social Expenditures in Developing Countries: Payroll or Value Added Taxes?" In *Social Insurance, Informality and Labor Markets: How to Protect Workers while Creating Good Jobs*, edited by M. Frolich, D. Kaplan, C. Pagés, J. Rigolini, and D. Robalino. Oxford, UK: Oxford University Press.

Bull, G. 2018. "Financial Inclusion in 2018: Big Tech Hits Its Stride." CGAP (Consultative Group to Assist the Poorest) blog, January 9. https://www.cgap .org/blog/financial-inclusion-2018-bigtech-hits-its-stride.

Centrangolo, O., and C. Grushka. 2004. "Sistema Previsional Argentino: Crisis, Reforma y Crisis de la Reforma." Serie Financiamiento del Desarrollo no. 51, Economic Commission for Latin America and the Caribbean.

Chomik, R., and J. Piggott. 2013. "Means-Testing Pensions: The Case of Australia." Policy Brief, Michigan Retirement Research Center, University of Michigan, Ann Arbor.

Clark, J. 2018. "Public Sector Savings from Identification Systems: Opportunities and Limitations." Identification for Development Working Paper series, World Bank, Washington, DC.

Coady, D., and D. Prady. 2018. "Universal Basic Income for Developing Countries: Issues, Options and Illustration for India." IMF Working Paper WP/18/174, International Monetary Fund, Washington, DC.

European Commission. 2015. *The 2015 Ageing Report: Economic and Budgetary Projections for the 28 EU Member States (2013–2060).* Brussels: European Commission.

———. 2018. *The 2018 Ageing Report: Economic and Budgetary Projections for the EU Member States (2016–2070).* Brussels: European Commission.

European Union. 2015. "Tax Reforms in EU Member States 2015: Tax Policy Challenges for Economic Growth and Fiscal Stability." European Economy Institutional Paper 008, European Commission, Brussels.

Gaspar, V., J. Harris, and A. Tieman. 2018. "The Wealth of Nations: Governments Can Better Manage What They Owe and Own." IMFBlog, October 8.

Gelb, A., and S. Majerowicz. 2011. "Oil for Uganda or Ugandans? Can Cash Transfers Prevent the Resource Curse?" Working Paper 261, Center for Global Development, Washington, DC.

Goodfellow, T. 2016. "Property Taxation and Economic Development: Lessons from Rwanda and Ethiopia." Global Political Economy Brief No. 4, Sheffield Political Economy Research Institute, University of Sheffield, Sheffield, UK.

Hanna, R., and B. Olken. 2018. "Universal Basic Incomes versus Targeted Transfers: Anti-Poverty Programs in Developing Countries." *Journal of Economic Perspectives* 32 (4): 201–26.

Harris, T., D. Philips, R. Warwick, M. Goldman, J. Jellema, K. Goraus, and G. Inchauste. 2018. "Redistribution via VAT and Cash Transfers: An Assessment in Four Low and Middle Income Countries." IFS Working Paper W18/11, Institute for Fiscal Studies, London.

HelpAge International. 2019. Pension Watch: Social Pensions Database.

ID Insight. 2018. "State of Aadhaar Report 2018." ID Insight, New Delhi, India.

International Monetary Fund (IMF). 2018. *Fiscal Monitor: Managing Public Wealth.* World Economic and Financial Surveys, October. Washington, DC: International Monetary Fund.

———. 2019. "Corporate Taxation in the Global Economy." Policy Paper No. 19/007, Fiscal Affairs Department and Legal Department, International Monetary Fund, Washington, DC.

International Monetary Fund (IMF), Organisation for Economic Co-operation and Development (OECD), World Bank, and United Nations (UN). 2015. *Options for Low-Income Countries' Effective and Efficient Use of Tax Incentives for Investment: A Report to the G-20 Development Working Group.* Platform for Collaboration on Tax. Washington, DC: World Bank.

Kabare, K. 2018. "The Mbao Pension Plan: Savings for the Informal Sector." Working Paper, Development Pathways, Kenya and UK.

Leite, P., T. George, C. Sun, T. Jones, and K. Lindert. 2017. "Social Registries for Social Assistance and Beyond: A Guidance Note & Assessment Tool." Social Protection Delivery Systems Global Solutions Group, World Bank, Washington, DC.

Lindeman, D., M. Rutkowski, and O. Sluchynskyy. 2000. "The Evolution of Pension Systems in Eastern Europe and Central Asia: Opportunities, Constraints, Dilemmas and Emerging Practices." In *Insurance and Private Pensions Compendium for Emerging Economies, Book 2*. Paris: Organisation for Economic Co-operation and Development.

Lustig, N. 2018. *Commitment to Equity Handbook: Estimating the Impact of Fiscal Policy on Inequality and Poverty*. Washington, DC: Brookings Institution Press.

Majoka, Z., and R. Palacios. 2019. "Targeting versus Universality: Is There a Middle Ground?" Social Protection and Jobs Policy Note, World Bank, Washington, DC.

Mossialos, E., A. Dixon, J. Figueras, and J. Kutzin. 2002. *Funding Health Care: Options for Europe*. European Observatory on Health Care Systems Series, World Health Organization. Buckingham, UK: Open University Press

Norregaard, J. 2013. "Taxing Immovable Property: Revenue Potential and Implementation Challenges." IMF Working Paper, International Monetary Fund, Washington, DC.

Organisation for Economic Co-operation and Development (OECD). 2018. *Tax Challenges Arising from Digitalization—Interim Report*. Paris: Organisation for Economic Co-operation and Development.

Packard, T. and T. Van Nguyen, 2014. East Asia Pacific at Work : Employment, Enterprise, and Wellbeing. World Bank East Asia and Pacific Regional Report; Washington, DC: World Bank.

Pestel, N., and E. Sommer. 2017. "Shifting Taxes from Labor to Consumption: More Employment and More Inequality?" *Review of Income and Wealth* 63 (3): 542–63.

Rofman, R., I. Apella, and E. Vezza. 2015. *Beyond Contributory Pensions: Fourteen Experiences with Coverage Expansion in Latin America*. Directions in Development—Human Development. Washington, DC: World Bank.

Santoro, M. 2017. "Pension Reform Options in Chile: Some Tradeoffs." IMF Working Paper, International Monetary Fund, Washington, DC.

Savedoff, W. 2004. "Tax-Based Financing for Health Systems: Options and Experiences." Discussion Paper No. 4; Health System Financing, Expenditure, and Resource Allocation Department; Evidence and Information for Policy Cluster; World Health Organization, Geneva.

Schwarz, A., and O. Arias. 2014. "The Inverting Pyramid: Pension Systems Facing Demographic Challenges in Europe and Central Asia." World Bank, Washington, DC.

Wiener, M., and P. Stokoe. 2018. "Discussing Accrued to Date Liabilities." *International Social Security Review* 71 (3): 27–48.

World Bank. 2016. *Live Long and Prosper: Aging in East Asia and Pacific*. East Asia and Pacific Regional Report. Washington, DC: World Bank.

———. 2018. *The State of Social Safety Nets 2018*. Washington, DC: World Bank.

———. 2019. *World Development Report 2019: The Changing Nature of Work*. Washington, DC: World Bank.

# 6

# Conclusions and Final Considerations

## Risk-Sharing Policy for a Diverse and Diversifying World of Work

Greater access to publicly organized risk pools—the unalienable essence of social insurance—financed from taxes with the broadest possible base, should underpin the foundation of any new risk-sharing model. That proposition is much less revolutionary than it seems, because the liabilities of prevailing employment-based, contributory social insurance in many low- and middle-income countries are increasingly paid with general revenue–financed budget expenditures rather than statutory earmarked levies on firms' payrolls. The key departing principle proposed in this volume is that poverty prevention and any other income redistribution objectives (that is, *vertical redistribution of income*), should be explicitly and transparently pursued with instruments financed from broad-based taxes. Statutory employer and employee contributions are a revenue channel that should be reserved to finance consumption-smoothing instruments with actuarially fair parameters (that is, *horizontal redistribution of risk*).

Furthermore, we have argued that with more effective national-level *insurance assistance* in place to help people manage risk and uncertainty, governments would no longer need to rely as heavily on mandated firm-based, employer-provided protections as they have to date. There would be more room to loosen restrictions on firms' contracting and dismissal decisions and shift government attention and resources to labor market intermediation, reemployment support services, and support for other market transitions. This *flexicurity* approach to helping people manage market shocks and transitions would be a more robust and resilient policy response to an increasingly diverse and fluid world of work and a better policy stance for governments to take given how the nature of work continues to change.

Financing the proposed protections can be achieved in many countries by reallocating existing expenditures and redeploying resources spent on energy price subsidies or other broad price subsidies. In others, government revenues will need to be increased by broadening the tax base, using existing revenue-gathering instruments better, and even deploying new tax instruments. And in some countries, governments may still, in the short run, provide insufficient resources to fully realize the vision of risk sharing proposed in this volume. In fact, many countries today provide less risk sharing than what we have proposed. But we believe that the new vision we have presented provides a helpful framework to move progressively toward more accessible, efficient, and ultimately more equitable risk-sharing institutions.

Technological change, one of the global drivers of disruption that have motivated our thinking, also offers opportunities for governments to transition away from—or leapfrog over—prevailing industrial-era policies and to offer more effective risk sharing to citizens and residents. India's Direct Benefit Transfer, an innovative use of digital technologies to directly provide subsidy transfers to the bank accounts of the poorest people, is a powerful example of what is already possible. Faced with an imperative to adopt new policy models, the lowest-income countries might actually hold an advantage: low effective coverage of industrial-era risk-sharing policies means that acquired rights and other legacy costs that will undoubtedly make transition politically and fiscally challenging are lower and opportunities to leapfrog to new risk-sharing models are easier to grasp. The investments made by many countries to develop the capacity and the systems to identify households, assess vulnerability and poverty, and deliver cash transfers more efficiently are critical assets that make the policy ideas we are proposing a realistic aspiration.

The ultimate administrative asset governments can build for effective risk sharing is a progressive tax system. Along with the proposed new packages of protection, the building of such a system should be the guiding institutional aspiration of risk-sharing policy. Although the challenges to doing so are formidable, the countries with the most effective tax systems today faced and overcame similarly formidable challenges. In the United Kingdom, the first progressive income tax was pushed through the country's parliament by Robert Peel in 1842, when about 63 percent of the U.K. labor force was still working in farming. In the United States, the first progressive income tax was established by the Revenue Act of 1862, signed into law by President Abraham Lincoln. At the time, about 58 percent of the United States' labor force worked in agriculture. In Spain, the first progressive income tax was introduced in 1900, when 70 percent of the labor force was in farming.

We have suggested more intensive use of value added tax (VAT), among other traditional and novel revenue instruments. VAT and other levies on consumption can have regressive—even impoverishing—effects on households, particularly in places where there are no compensating transfers or where those transfers fall short. However, the true impact of these instruments can only be considered as part of a comprehensive assessment of the net effect on households of the entire public transfer and tax system (Lustig 2018).

## Progressive Universality: Further Lessons from Health Policy

Over the past two decades, health discourse has been evolving decisively toward universality.[1] The principle that everyone should have "access to the health care they need without suffering financial hardship" (WHO 2019) is now mainstream. Although no country has yet achieved literally universal health coverage, such an objective is, as *The Economist* (2018) recently put it, "within reach." With a few exceptions, country trajectories point to the pursuit of universality as a legitimate and foundational goal in its own right (in addition to being good economics).

With the objective of risk sharing in mind, the similarities between health and social protection are striking, particularly when it comes to risk-sharing policies. Both sectors strive to protect people against a variety of risks. In doing so, they face an array of analogous strategic and practical trade-offs around the coverage, adequacy, and sustainability of interventions within financial, political, and administrative constraints. Quandaries around the role of the state in expanding coverage (in the formal and informal sectors of the economy), to the people who should be subsidized (whether only the poorest or the middle class as well), the composition of overall systems (contributory or noncontributory to determine eligibility for levels of coverage), and the arrangements to fund these systems (such as general revenues or payroll taxes) are central themes in both health and social protection.

Yet, there are also notable differences between the areas that must be taken into account. In the health sector, a person's entitlement is universal, but that person receives protection only when she needs it. An example is treatment of cardiac arrest: everyone is covered, but not everyone will need the actual benefit triggered by a heart attack. In other words, everyone has *contingent* coverage. The tools at the disposal of the health community—blood pressure machines, X-rays, MRIs, and so on—make a needs-based approach credible and verifiable, and they establish a relationship between causes and effects. Also, health is a distinct sector with a clear identity and a structured professional cadre of providers. Social protection, in contrast, is often cross-sectoral and multidisciplinary. For example, some countries don't have a separate social protection ministry, but instead have social protection interventions scattered across labor, agriculture, disaster management, public works, and other agencies and institutions.

Bearing these commonalities and differences in mind, one can learn important lessons for social protection from countries' universal health coverage (UHC) experiences. The following discussion identifies these lessons based on health literature and several case studies (Benach et al. 2013; Cotlear et al. 2015; Gwatkin and Ergo 2011; Jamison et al. 2013; and Marmot et al. 2010).

## Pathways to Universal Health Care

Since the 2000s, many countries seeking a more progressive path to UHC have followed two sequential steps. In the first step, countries have extended health coverage to poor people. In the second step, expanding UHC programs to the rest of their inhabitants, they have tended to take one of two pathways, either *bottom-up* or *top-down* (Cotlear et al. 2015). (See figure 6.1.)

*Step 1: Countries start by designing programs for poor people only.* Most UHC programs were initially developed for poor and vulnerable populations, with targeted public subsidies to them only. Programs providing fully subsidized coverage for poor people were introduced in two ways: (i) through embedment into existing social health insurance (SHI) agencies, such as in Ghana, the Kyrgyz Republic, the Philippines, and Vietnam, and (ii) through the creation of an ad hoc autonomous agency linked to the ministry of health, as in Georgia, India (RSBY, the national health

**Figure 6.1   The Path to Full Coverage of Effective Risk-Sharing Policies Can Follow the Steps by Which Universal Health Coverage Was Extended**

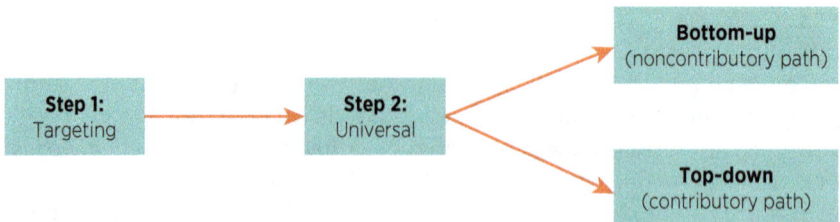

*Source:* Gentilini 2018.

insurance program), Indonesia, Peru, and Turkey (before 2012). There were concerns that the creation of ad hoc programs targeting the poor would create fragmentation and lock countries into path dependence. Yet the evidence of such effects has been limited: not only have programs targeting poor people been created within health systems that were already fragmented, but countries that began with targeted programs were later able to transition and expand their coverage to other subpopulations.

*Step 2: Countries expand coverage to nonpoor people who work in the informal sector.* After a period of targeting the poor, countries entered a second phase in which they aimed to massively cover nonpoor people working in the informal sector. In other words, the evolutionary paths followed by programs that today cover the entire informal sector have shown that starting with poor people is transitional, often a stepping-stone toward more equitable, integrated systems that cover various population groups.

Most countries have taken one of two different paths to expand coverage to the nonpoor who work in the informal economy. Some countries (such as Argentina, China, Colombia, Mexico, and Thailand) followed a noncontributory, bottom-up path, extending the tax subsidies provided to the poor to the rest of the informally employed. These programs depend mainly on general tax revenues. Others (such as Chile and Costa Rica) followed a second path of coverage from the top down: this path required nonpoor families working in the informal economy to contribute toward their health coverage.

*Bottom-up or noncontributory path.* Once the decision to expand subsidies to nonpoor informal-economy workers was made, some countries expanded coverage rapidly. For example, in Thailand, the expansion was undertaken through autonomous agencies linked to the ministry of health instead of through SHI institutions. These autonomous programs face a difficult trade-off between equity (in other words, disparities between the *non-contributory* or intentionally subsidized benefit package and the *contributory* benefits provided by the SHI) and financial sustainability. The pressures to equalize the benefits of the autonomous program with those of the SHI are substantial: the SHI requires that the nonpoor contribute to health care, regardless of whether they work in the formal or the informal sector. Instead, the autonomous informal sector program operates separately from the SHI and rarely requires contributions from nonpoor informal sector groups. The problem of sustainability arises from the incentives these programs create for job-seekers, such as to remain at small scale or even delay formalization in favor of informal employment that avoids mandated payroll deductions (Levy 2008, 2018). There is every reason to do so, if the benefits in both sectors are similar. Addressing these trade-offs may require ambitious health system reforms.

Countries with parallel systems require some of the nonpoor to pay for health coverage but allow others with similar incomes to be exempted. It is sometimes suggested that in the long run, solving this equity–sustainability trade-off may involve reforms that reduce or eliminate reliance on payroll taxes to finance health care for people in formal employment. The similarities of this debate to social protection policy debates with regard to the traditional Bismarckian systems of social insurance, which nominally rely on earmarked statutory contributions levied as payroll taxes, are evident. In the past, some member countries of the Organisation for Economic Co-operation and Development (OECD) replaced SHI with general tax financing, such as Denmark (in 1973), Italy (in 1978), and Spain (in 1986). This type of reform has been under consideration in recent years in Colombia, Mexico, and Thailand.

*Top-down or contributory path.* Governments seeking to extend program coverage often do not have the capacity to enforce mandatory contributions from informal sector workers, whose activities incomes they cannot observe; hence, countries tend to offer partial subsidies for voluntary health insurance for nonpoor informal sector participants, but this type of plan attracts only a small fraction of the sector. As capacity to enforce contributions from the informally employed grows, these programs tend to incorporate larger segments of people working in the informal economy. In the more mature programs (such as those of Chile, Costa Rica, and Turkey after 2012), participation of the poor and of people working informally is effectively mandatory: coverage for the poor is fully subsidized by general taxes, and the nonpoor who work informally are subject to a careful review of income using various mechanisms. Voluntary health insurance may indeed be helpful during the initial phase, but it doesn't appear to be a preferable path to UHC (Jamison et al. 2013).[2]

## Lessons for Relevant and Resilient Risk-Sharing Systems

For governments ready to undertake reforms of their risk-sharing policies as we have outlined in this volume, seven lessons emerge from countries' experiences in offering universal health coverage. First, simply striving for universality does not necessarily make the poorest better off. As countries expand social protection, those at the bottom of the distribution should benefit before, or at least at the same time as, others in society. This concept is encapsulated in the notion of *progressive universalism.*

Second, targeting and universalism can coexist. Progressive universalism requires information systems that can identify and prioritize those most in need during the process of expansion. In this vein, targeting and progressive universalism are compatible, mutually reinforcing concepts.

Third, in pursuing universality, countries initially develop programs for the poor only. These programs are introduced in two ways, namely, through embedment into existing social health insurance agencies (such as in Ghana, the Philippines, and Vietnam) and through the creation of an ad hoc autonomous agency linked to the ministry of health (such as in Georgia, Indonesia, and Peru).

Fourth, focusing on the poor is a stepping-stone to expanding coverage to the nonpoor who work informally. As described in the previous section, countries have taken two different paths in expanding coverage to the nonpoor: a noncontributory path (as in Argentina, China, Colombia, Mexico, and Thailand) and a path on which nonpoor informally working families contribute toward their health coverage (as in Chile and Costa Rica).

Fifth, the policy imperative of universality can provide an evolving framework and a sense of direction. Having an intended goal—reaching everyone—can help frame current operations as a means for achieving a broader end, rally different actors around a shared vision, and mobilize resources. Universal social protection is a global goal, but this goal has not yet translated into country-level priorities and plans.

Sixth, the road to universality of health and other risk-sharing policies and programs is long and comes with tough trade-offs. Social protection policy makers and practitioners have much to learn from the expansion of health coverage. Both sectors face an array of analogous quandaries around the coverage, adequacy, and sustainability of interventions under financial, political, and administrative constraints.

Finally, it is important to clarify what is meant by "universality" and to be clear about policy objectives. The definition of universality *based on needs* requires careful attention. Compared with the concept of universality more commonly used among social protection (and specifically, social assistance) policy practitioners—which is that every person gets the same benefits, no matter their circumstances—the contingent, needs-based universality that we use in this volume is more salient to social insurance specialists. However, needs-based universality could seem more conceptually coherent for social assistance specialists if framed as assistance provided to everyone, possibly with amounts that vary based on needs. Need-based universality could apply to social assistance if the entire set of such interventions is considered as a form of social insurance against poverty and its accompanying constraints on well-being, as we have conceptualized public risk pooling in chapter 2. This perspective presumes, however, that poverty can be fully explained in terms of risk management, which, as discussed earlier, is plainly not the case. Nonetheless, for societies that aspire to provide sustainable, responsive, and robust risk-sharing instruments to *all* people—no matter where or how they work today and in the future—our contingent, needs-based conception of universality opens many possible and arguably more viable options.

## Labor Market Policies for the Human Capitalist

Finally, we turn from insurance assistance to the other risk-sharing policy instruments deployed in the labor market. Throughout this volume, we have tried to make a fundamental point about the changing nature of work. Societies and markets are organic and dynamic. The disruptions discussed in chapter 1 and the changes to the demand and supply of labor they bring about are not the problem. The problems arise when these dynamic forces hit up against rigid norms and institutions, particularly policies. In chapter 4, we discussed how this clash is happening in the case of prevailing labor market policies.

Can governments take a more adaptable and resilient policy stance toward the labor market? As industrial-era risk-sharing and employment protections are scrutinized, so too should be the use of rigid legal specifications of market engagements. As we argued in chapter 4, the assumptions about the duration of employment relationships, the homogeneity of work, and the stability and exclusivity of how people engage in the market—for example, as employer, employee, sole trader, entrepreneur, equity partner, and so on—that underlie prevailing labor market institutions and regulations in many countries are being challenged. These assumptions have never accurately reflected the nature of work in low- and middle-income countries, and they are now being stretched and challenged even in high-income countries. Some new forms of work blur the distinction between being an employee and being a "dependent" self-employed worker. We argued that as a matter of urgency, labor codes should define more clearly what it means to be an employee to ensure that all receive the basic set of protections. Courts and legislators are doing their best to keep up with new work arrangements and ways in which people are engaging in markets.

But beyond this effort to keep up, an entirely new approach may be needed. The industrial-era approach to labor market regulation assumes and assigns rights and responsibilities to clearly defined categories of market engagement that are assumed to be single and stable. A new approach is needed to match the diverse and diversifying world of work in which engagements are more fluid. In the medium term, rather than incremental extensions to the labor code to reflect this diversity in detail and ensure that each category of work is protected, it is arguably more efficient and resilient to ensure that the most vital protections—of core labor standards, from catastrophic losses, and mandated worker protections—are accessible to all people no matter how they engage in the market. Following this approach also means that workers and firms in one area of the economy should have the same set of responsibilities—including in terms of taxation—as workers and firms in other areas.

A blurring of the industrial-era lines in market statutes could be particularly important to how people are remunerated and well as how they are protected from risks and uncertainty. Labor regulation should be modernized for the digital era: the *era of the human capitalist*. Intellectual property, brands, company culture, and other intangible assets are rapidly becoming the largest components of firms' value (Avent 2016). The vital input in building and sustaining these intangible assets is human capital—working people. Yet labor market policies generally, and labor regulations specifically, are still written using industrial-era distinctions between capital and labor that do not reflect the diverse, fluid, and simultaneous ways in which people engage in markets or the most important asset that most people bring to work: their human capital. The same can be said of the product market regulation and tax code of most countries.

What is the appropriate risk-sharing policy stance in the age of the human capitalist? Profit-sharing and employee-ownership structures—what the International Labour Organization (ILO) calls the *social and solidarity economy* (Borzaga, Salvarori, and Bodini 2017)—are attracting new interest as a means of blurring or eliminating the old, industrial-era distinctions, achieving an optimal distribution of risk, broadening access to wealth, and countering its seemingly mechanical concentration (Piketty 2014). Indeed, in the face of labor's declining share of gross domestic product (GDP) in a number of countries, and at a time of growing anxiety about automation, Freeman (2015) argues for calm: working people could benefit even from robots, artificial intelligence, or any labor-substituting machines *if* they own a residual claim on the profits from their production. The key to realizing a more broadly shared prosperity is to revive and reinvigorate norms and formal institutions that encourage enterprises to offer working people a stake in their growth (Blasi, Freeman, and Kruse 2013).

Risk-sharing policies extended by the state to benefit firms could be used more intentionally to broaden workers' access to shared ownership. Bringing shared ownership structures more boldly into the mainstream and broadening profit-sharing practices beyond niches of high-income economies would also help address concerns about income distribution and inequality. However, the new enthusiasm for shared ownership models has recently veered to the extremes of coercion and expropriation, which raises the risk that these models will become yet another state mandate that firms will seek to avoid and, in low- and middle-income countries, an additional implicit tax on firms that would otherwise grow to more productive scale.[3] Some proposals for "true industrial democracy" challenge bedrock principles of liberal democratic market capitalism and protections of property rights.[4] As argued in the discussion of the *plateau* in chapter 4, such extremes should be avoided. Policy makers in low- and middle-income countries could explore ways to more actively incentivize shared ownership and profit-sharing arrangements.[5]

For example, firms that shared profits or ownership with workers according to transparent rules that met minimum quality standards could be offered tax breaks.[6] Conversely, and in the face of sustained declines in labor's share of GDP, the favorable tax treatment of corporate debt and other legally conferred corporate privileges might be withdrawn from firms that failed to offer reasonable profit- and ownership-sharing plans to their employees.

Might well-regulated shared-profit and shared-ownership structures one day become as ubiquitous as (or even supplant) legislated wage floors? For the foreseeable future, policies to encourage profit-sharing and shared-ownership structures are more viable as complements for statutory minimum wages than as substitutes. In low- and middle-income countries, most working people are already in some sort of de facto shareholder or residual-earner market engagement, either as sole proprietors, self-employed workers, or informal dependent workers in a family business (Levy 2018; Packard, Koettl, and Montenegro 2012; Packard and Van Nguyen 2014). In firms offering wages where a statutory minimum wage is more likely to bind, the minimum wage imposes a large social cost. This cost is visible in the diminished job prospects of groups for whom the social benefits of work are highest. Governments could ease a considerable amount of the economic and political upward pressures on the minimum wage that increase these costs. By making it easier and attractive for firms to offer a profit-sharing structure of certain minimum-quality characteristics, governments would be better positioned to keep statutory minimum wages from rising too far too quickly. The quality of firms' profit-sharing arrangements and their compliance with these arrangements could even be monitored by social partners as part of firm-level collective bargaining arrangements. A more proactive policy approach to encourage profit sharing and employee ownership could be tested on a pilot basis, and the pilots' experiences could be analyzed to yield valuable lessons. Given the origins of many market and corporate risk-sharing institutions and how vital these arrangements are to firms' risk management and performance, a more active and purposeful use of these institutions to expand working people's stake in the changing economy has strong historical precedent.[7]

## Notes

1. This section is based on a background note, Gentilini (2018). A summary appeared as a blog post available at http://blogs.worldbank.org/development talk/what-lessons-social-protection-universal-health-coverage.
2. Although, in theory the programs in China and Rwanda are voluntary, they present procedures and political forms of organization not easily replicable elsewhere.
3. Indeed, profit sharing is mandated by several governments (e.g., the Dominican Republic, Ecuador) and is perceived as a tax and constraint on growth.

4. In his speech to the U.K. Labor Party's 2018 conference, the Shadow Chancellor, John McDonnell, MP, stood behind the slogan "Building Britain for the Many, Not the Few" and advocated an employment-ownership policy that would *mandate* that firms transfer 10 percent of their shares to "inclusive ownership funds" that would be managed collectively and would make dividend payments to workers and to the government. See https://www.youtube.com /watch?v=T4j629Dnt30.

5. Invoking many of the same trends in wealth inequality and manifestations of discontent that motivate these proposals to share profits and ownership, such as the Occupy movement, Oldham (2018) argues that the economy has become *overintermediated*—that is, that institutional investors dominate markets and that not enough individuals and households perceive themselves as having a direct stake in growth. Oldham advocates a drive for individual share ownership to be vigorously encouraged.

6. Extreme care would be required to regulate the quality and safety of profit-sharing or shared-ownership plans. After all, these mechanisms can be used to share losses with workers as well. During China's period of state-sector restructuring in the late 1990s, for example, one partial privatization approach involved providing equity to workers of failing state-owned enterprises. The equity stake was frequently used in lieu of salary (or salary increases) but often had little value when the firms failed. Encouragingly, however, the profit-sharing and shared-ownership plans of many market-leading firms provide excellent and replicable examples of quality, safety, and independent governance.

7. On the August 15, 2018, a group of prominent lawyers, economists, and financial sector participants wrote to United States Senator Elizabeth Warren to express their support for her Accountable Capitalism Act. The letter traced the history of the limited liability corporation and other specific corporate privileges in the United States, which were originally intended to encourage the owners of scarce capital to organize and finance projects for the public good, such as infrastructure, at a time when capital was scarce and public revenue systems were still being built. Listing several abuses of corporate privileges, the signatories noted how in a world of abundant capital and more reliable taxation capacity, the original intent of these policy-conferred privileges had been forgotten or outright ignored. The signatories thus espoused their support for the act and stated that they would have liked the measure to go *even further* toward "realigning our regime of incorporation with its original [public interest] purposes." See https://www.warren.senate.gov/download/federal-corporate-charter -letter-of-support.

## References

Avent, R. 2016. *The Wealth of Humans: Work and its Absence in the Twenty-First Century.* New York: St Martin's Press.

Benach, J., D. Malmusi, Y. Yasui, and J. M. Martinez. 2013. "A New Typology of Policies to Tackle Health Inequalities and Scenarios of Impact Based on Rose's Population Approach." *Journal of Epidemiology and Community Health* 67 (3): 286–91.

Blasi, J., R. Freeman, and D. Kruse. 2013. *The Citizen's Share: Reducing Inequality in the 21st Century*. Yale University Press: London.

Borzaga, C., C. Salvatori, and R. Bodini. 2017. "Social and Solidarity Economy and the Future of Work." Euricse Working Paper, International Labour Organization, Geneva.

Cotlear, D., S. Nagpal, O. Smith, A. Tandon, and R. Cortez. 2015. *Going Universal: How 24 Developing Countries Are Implementing Universal Health Coverage Reforms from the Bottom Up*. Washington, DC: World Bank.

*The Economist*. 2018. "Universal Health Coverage, Worldwide, Is within Reach." Print edition, April 26, London.

Freeman, R. 2015. "Who Owns the Robots Rules the World." IZA World of Labor, Institute of Labor Economics (IZA), Bonn, Germany.

Gentilini, U. 2018. "What Lessons for Social Protection from Universal Health Coverage?" *Let's Talk Development* (blog), August 22. http://blogs.worldbank.org /developmenttalk/what-lessons-social-protection-universal-health-coverage.

Gwatkin, D., and A. Ergo. 2011. "Universal Health Coverage: Friend or Foe of Health Equity?" *The Lancet* 377: 2160–61.

Jamison, D., et al. 2013. "Global Health 2035: A World Converging within a Generation." *The Lancet* 382: 1898–1995.

Levy, S. 2008. *Good Intentions, Bad Outcomes: Social Policy, Informality, and Economic Growth in Mexico*. Washington, DC: Brookings Institution Press.

———. 2018. *Under-Rewarded Efforts: The Elusive Quest for Prosperity in Mexico*. Washington, DC: Inter-American Development Bank.

Lustig, N. 2018. *Commitment to Equity Handbook: Estimating the Impact of Fiscal Policy on Inequality and Poverty*. Washington, DC: Brookings Institution Press.

Marmot, M., J. Allen, P. Goldblatt, T. Boyce, D. McNeish, M. Grady, and I. Geddes. 2010. "Fair Society, Healthy Lives (The Marmot Review): Strategic Review of Health Inequalities in England Post-2010." Local Government Association, London.

Oldham, G. 2018. "Egalitarian Capitalism." Unpublished.

Packard, T., J. Koettl, and C. E. Montenegro. 2012. *In from the Shadow: Integrating Europe's Informal Labor*. Washington, DC: World Bank.

Packard, T., and T. Van Nguyen. 2014. *East Asia Pacific at Work: Employment, Enterprise, and Well-Being*. World Bank East Asia and Pacific Regional Report. Washington, DC: World Bank.

Piketty, T. 2014. *Capital in the Twenty-First Century*. Cambridge, MA: Harvard University Press.

WHO (World Health Organization). 2019. "Universal Health Coverage (UHC)." Fact sheet. World Health Organization, Geneva. https://www.who.int/news-room /fact-sheets/detail/universal-health-coverage-(uhc).

# Appendix A

# Conceptual Framework: Individual Choice in the Face of Risk and Uncertainty

Individuals, households, and societies can respond in a variety of ways when faced with the prospect of losses from shocks, whether arising from job loss, extended unemployment, sickness, death or disability of an income earner, financial crises, natural disasters, structural changes, or shifts in terms of trade. Classical economic and actuarial models of risk indicate which instruments—including preventive measures—will be most effective and efficient given the nature (size and frequency) of possible losses as well as the extent to which markets fail to respond to these losses. The same models can be used to identify when coping is the most efficient course of action and to distinguish effective from ineffective forms of coping.

Risk-sharing policies come in a variety of instruments made available by the state to help households manage the shocks to their livelihood and consumption posed by a wide array of contingencies. Because they are designed to cover the losses that private insurance cannot cover—and to augment private coverage where it fails or falls short—risk-sharing policy instruments are not expected to strictly conform to the actuarial rules that are supposed to determine market provision. That said, these rules should not be ignored. Policy-relevant insights about the nature of a loss, how it is best covered, and the degree to which markets should be expected to help cover it can be drawn from the classical models on which these rules are based.

In these classical models, the challenge for individuals, households, or governments (whichever is the agent of interest) is to determine the optimal mix of market insurance, self-insurance, and self-protection.[1] As insurance, both *market insurance* and *self-insurance* transfer income from good states to bad states of the world. Market insurance *pools* risks across individuals, compensating for differences in likely exposure to bad states (adverse shocks) between them. Where it is available, market insurance can be purchased at a price—the insurance *premium*, which in the classical models is set according to the size of the prospective loss and the probability of the bad state coming about.[2] Self-insurance—essentially individual savings—does not involve risk pooling or compensation for differences in exposure to risk across individuals. While it has no explicit price, the cost of self-insurance can be implicitly determined from the expense people incur to save, for example, in forgone consumption. Individuals without access to market insurance or self-insurance must cope with losses. They can, however, lower the likelihood of the loss by *self-protecting*. Self-protection reduces the probability that losses will occur (but does not reduce the size of a loss should one occur).[3] Individuals and households that are unable (or choose not) to take preventive measures or to insure by saving or through risk-sharing structures are forced to cope with the full losses in the wake of shocks. Simpler terms are used in more recent applications of these models: market insurance is *risk pooling* or just *pooling*;[4] self-insurance is *saving*; and "self-protection" is *prevention*.

Individuals seek to smooth consumption over good and bad states of the world. Where risk pooling is missing, the individual is forced to smooth consumption using only saving and prevention. Where the options of pooling and saving both exist, the individual sees these instruments as substitutes. Pooling—available at or near actuarially fair prices—reduces the need for saving. However, greater coverage of pooling does not inevitably result in individuals spending less on prevention. If prevention leads to a lower likelihood that the bad state will occur, and if prevention is rewarded in the form of lower premiums, risk pooling and prevention can be complements—individuals can be encouraged to take up more prevention in return for cheaper risk-pooling instruments.

Figure A.1 illustrates stylized prescriptions of the classical framework drawn on two axes, each representing a different dimension of possible losses: *size* (the amount of the loss) on the vertical axis and *frequency* (the probability of occurrence of the loss) on the horizontal axis. As the simple illustration shows, full insurance is not efficient. From a financial protection perspective, it is more efficient for individuals to cope with rather than try to insure against small, rarely occurring losses (the lowermost, left-hand corner of figure A.1). However, as losses become more frequent, it is relatively more efficient to engage in prevention to lower the probability of losses and savings to cover their costs. As a probable loss becomes less frequent but increases in size, it becomes more efficient to engage in risk pooling. For many of these large, rare losses, households will have incentives to engage in prevention measures to further lower the probability that the loss will occur. However, for losses that are frequently occurring and catastrophic in size (the right-hand, uppermost corner of figure A.1) there is little that individuals, households, or markets can do on their own, and measures to create a larger risk pool are required. This is the first, clear motivation for policy intervention, particularly to help manage covariate or systemic shocks such as an economic crisis or natural disaster.

**Figure A.1 When Risk Markets Are Available and Function Well, It Is Most Efficient to Pool the Risk of Large, Infrequent Losses**

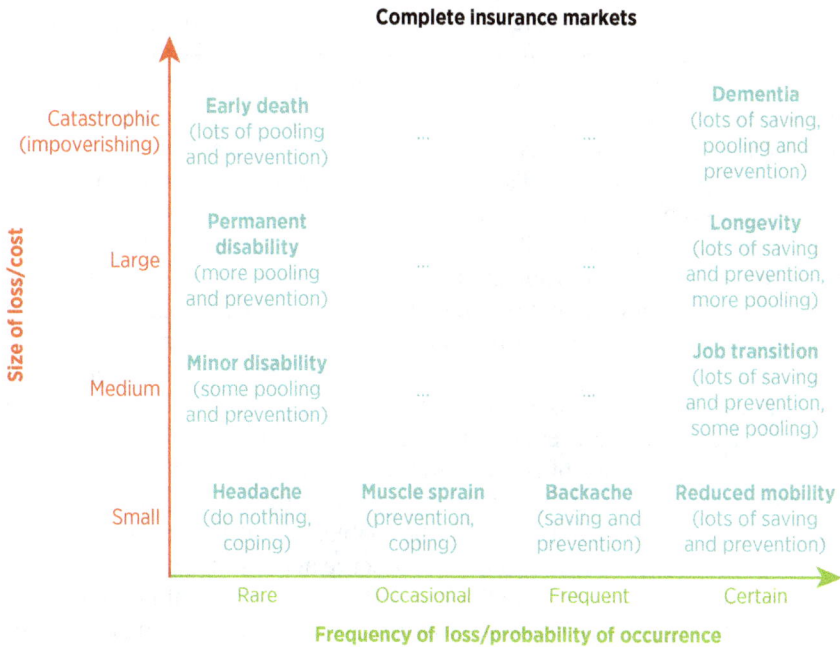

**Complete insurance markets**

| | | Rare | Occasional | Frequent | Certain |
|---|---|---|---|---|---|
| Catastrophic (impoverishing) | | **Early death** (lots of pooling and prevention) | ... | ... | **Dementia** (lots of saving, pooling and prevention) |
| Large | | **Permanent disability** (more pooling and prevention) | ... | ... | **Longevity** (lots of saving and prevention, more pooling) |
| Medium | | **Minor disability** (some pooling and prevention) | ... | ... | **Job transition** (lots of saving and prevention, some pooling) |
| Small | | **Headache** (do nothing, coping) | **Muscle sprain** (prevention, coping) | **Backache** (saving and prevention) | **Reduced mobility** (lots of saving and prevention) |

*Size of loss/cost* (vertical axis)

**Frequency of loss/probability of occurrence** (horizontal axis)

*Sources:* Baeza and Packard 2006, based on Barr 2012, Ehrlich and Becker 1972, and Gill and Ilahi 2000.

*Note:* This figure shows the optimal risk instruments with which to address a given loss by the size and frequency of the loss.

The prescriptions of the classical models are, of course, vulnerable to many of the market failures discussed extensively in the economics literature. Of particular concern are the problems posed by imperfect information. These problems can range from information problems that hinder individual consumer choice (demand-side problems) to those that hinder market provision of saving and risk-pooling instruments (supply-side problems).

For many of the assumptions of the classical models to hold, consumers and suppliers need to have information about the quality of services available; the price of these services; and the likely demand for these services in the future. Although households are fairly well informed about many of the goods and services they consume, they may be less well informed about the quality of certain sophisticated goods and services. Needs in the event of disability, old age, and illness are prime examples. Even where markets respond by providing information, either directly to consumers or through hired specialists, the information may be too complex for consumers to grasp sufficiently to make the right choices. And even with information about quality, and with new technology (mass advertising and the Internet) that allows customers to be better informed, customers may still not know whether they are getting the best quality available or buying at the right price. Further, there will always be less-than-complete knowledge about future needs—an information problem that in many ways motivates the market for risk-pooling instruments in the first place, but which nonetheless often frustrates the functioning of this market as well.[5]

This last point shifts the discussion to information problems that hinder market provision of saving and risk-pooling instruments specifically. An uneven or *asymmetrical* distribution of information between consumers and providers leads to two problems that consistently plague private markets for this form of risk mitigation: *adverse selection* and *moral hazard*. Adverse selection occurs because consumers who have the greatest interest in seeking risk-pooling services are often those who are likely to need them most. If relatively more risky consumers enter the risk pool, this will hinder the quality of the pool and eventually force the insurance provider to raise prices. The higher price of risk pooling can put off more low-risk individuals, threatening the viability of the risk pool further. When there are too many bad risks, the pool ceases to be viable. Moral hazard arises when providers of risk pooling are unable to observe actions consumers take that affect (raise or lower) the likelihood of the bad state coming about. The coverage provided by risk-pooling instruments can create strong incentives for individuals to take actions—or, more often, fail to take actions—that allow them to consume more benefits from the pool. Both these manifestations of information failures are notorious for causing private markets for risk pooling to fail or never form in the first place.

As suggested earlier, risk-pooling mechanisms cope badly with losses that occur frequently, that is, events whose likelihood approaches certainty, or events that have already occurred. This becomes a pernicious problem when considering health insurance, as many illnesses can become chronic conditions requiring sustained—and costly—medical attention. In the case of losses from involuntary-separation unemployment, an analogous "chronic condition" can be said to exist among the long-term unemployed. Similarly, although common in the past, in recent years fewer private firms in industrial and post-industrial countries have been willing to offer defined-benefit retirement plans to their employees, as increases in longevity make reaching retirement age almost a certainty.

Similarly, risk pooling fares poorly where the probability of one member of the pool suffering losses causes (or increases the probability of) another member suffering the loss (in other words, when the probabilities of suffering the loss are not independent). In the wake of these systemic losses, too many unlucky members of the pool (those who suffer the bad state) rely on the premiums of too few lucky members (those who go unscathed). Mass unemployment in a severe economic contraction (De Feranti et al. 2000), structural changes in an economy (Holzmann and Vodopivec 2012), and droughts leading to famine and other natural disasters (Siegel and Jørgensen 2013) are all examples of systemic losses to which risk-pooling markets respond badly.

But perhaps the most fundamental challenge to market supply of pooling instruments is that of distinguishing risk from uncertainty. The difference between the two concepts is more than semantic and has profound consequences for the availability of market insurance (Barr 2001). *Risk* is measurable; that is, a probability can be assessed for the risk of a given adverse event. *Uncertainty*, on the other hand, cannot be measured—the probability of an uncertain event cannot be determined. For this reason, uncertain events lie beyond the reach of the actuarial tools the market uses to price and pool risks (Barr 2001, 2012). When the uncertainty of shocks grows, the challenges to market provision of effective risk-pooling and other instruments also rise.

The market failures on the demand and supply sides are important caveats to the prescriptions of the classical models, particularly with regard to the availability of instruments that help people pool risk. These problems raise the price of risk-pooling instruments out of the reach of lower-income groups and even above what is economically viable, conspiring to create gaps in protection. These gaps typically occur among portions of the population that need protection the most, such as workers with lower levels of human capital, the elderly, children and expecting parents, people living with disabilities, and the chronically ill.

## Rationale for Policy Intervention

The problems that confound the classical economic and actuarial models usually result in one or more of the three instruments—risk pooling, individual saving, and prevention—being unavailable to households, or in constraining household uptake of these instruments from what would otherwise be optimal. Indeed, the role of the state in risk-sharing policy is to augment household options in cases where any of these instruments are unavailable or out of reach (Gill and Ilahi 2000). However, the existence of information problems and other market failures do not invalidate the classical models. On the contrary, these models are still critical to deriving how policy makers should try to correct market failures and to ensuring that policy solutions are correctly aligned with the nature of shocks and individuals' incentives.

But before turning to insights for policy makers in social protection, it is important to capture a peculiarity of the risk market immediately relevant to the discussion of health as well as education and other dimensions of well-being: the public-good nature of human capital. Although most relevant when considering adverse health events, similar threats to public goods can be identified for other prospective economic losses faced by households.

The degree of externality created by the public-good nature of many interventions introduces a third dimension to the considerations of the nature of prospective losses presented in figure A.1: the extent of market failure, and in the case discussed here, the degree of externality or extent-of-social-benefit arising from intervening to help cover the likely loss. This last market failure presents a justification for policy intervention that is even more powerful than the arguments about missing or malfunctioning markets presented earlier. Whether best covered through risk pooling, saving, or prevention measures, to the extent that prospective losses exhibit negative externalities and interventions yield public-good characteristics, the justification for intervention to ensure optimal uptake by households will grow.

Figure A.2 illustrates the three dimensions of the conceptual framework discussed so far. The first (size of loss/cost on the vertical axis) and the second (frequency of loss/probability of occurrence on the horizontal x-axis) have already been discussed. To these we add a third dimension (on the z-axis), extent of market failure, and, more specifically, the *size of the external costs imposed on others* by an individual or household's failure to take action. As we move along the z-axis away from the origin, the justification for state intervention rises.

The stylized prescriptions of this framework are simple and powerful. The size and frequency of the prospective loss should determine whether a shock is best mitigated with risk pooling, individual saving, or prevention and the relative role of each instrument. But regardless of the instrument, as we move away from the origin along the third dimension and the extent of market failure or externality posed by the prospective loss grows, the justification increases for intervention by the state to ensure that the appropriate measures are undertaken and policies are enacted to correct market failures. The rationale for risk-sharing policy actions arises when individuals or households fail to attain optimal levels of risk pooling, saving, and prevention—whether by choice or under constraint—and as the external costs of these failures grow. Such failures could occur either because one or more of the instruments are not available to the individual, or, if all three instruments are available, because market inefficiencies (information problems and other market failures we have discussed) prevent individuals from using each instrument optimally.

In short, the existence of market failures—in particular, information problems, uncertainty, and externalities—indicates when risk-sharing policy interventions are required. The framework presented here provides critical guidance on what form those interventions should take.

**Figure A.2 Market Failures—Particularly Good and Bad Externalities— Require Policy Actions to Share Risks Efficiently**

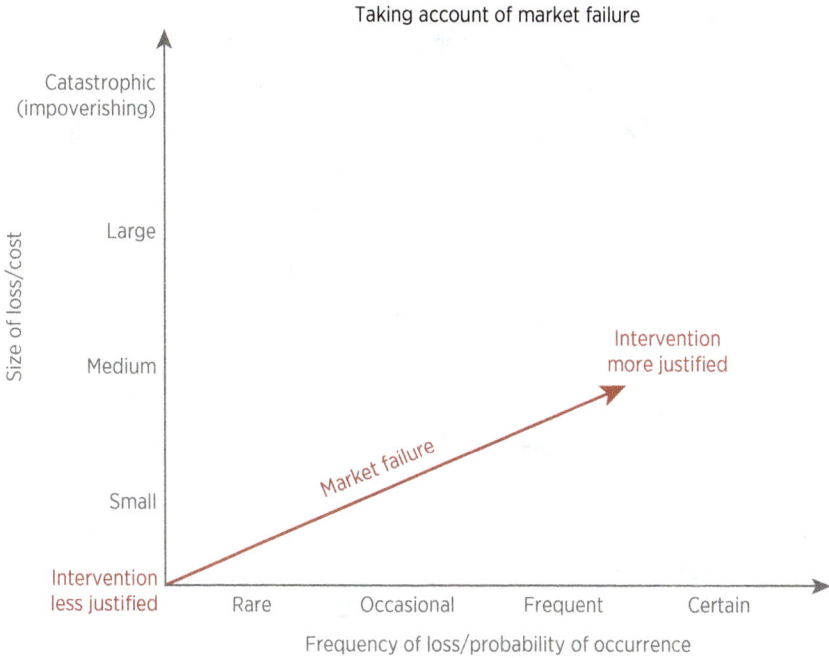

Sources: Baeza and Packard 2005, based on Barr 2012, Ehrlich and Becker 1972, and Gill and Ilahi 2000.

Note: This figure shows the optimal risk instruments to address a probable loss by the size, frequency, and extent of market failure to cover the loss.

Figure A.3 illustrates this guidance, specifying interventions, according to the three characteristics of prospective losses (size, probability of occurrence, and extent of market failure [degree of externality]) discussed above.

The types of risk-sharing policies that a government can offer on a sustainable basis to augment household options are determined by its broader policy context. Just as individuals and households facing a loss can pool risks, save, or take preventive measures (or cope with losses, should they fail to insure), governments face similar decisions. Governments can "pool" the risks of a limited (but growing) range of possible losses through private market insurance or through international, multilateral risk-pooling structures; they can "save" by accumulating surpluses in good times to spend on services during bad times (using stabilization funds and countercyclical spending policies); and they can "prevent" by practicing prudent monetary and fiscal policy, engaging in reforms that increase the efficiency and safety

**Figure A.3  Policy Options Vary According to the Size and Frequency of Losses and the Extent to Which the Risk Market Fails to Cover Them**

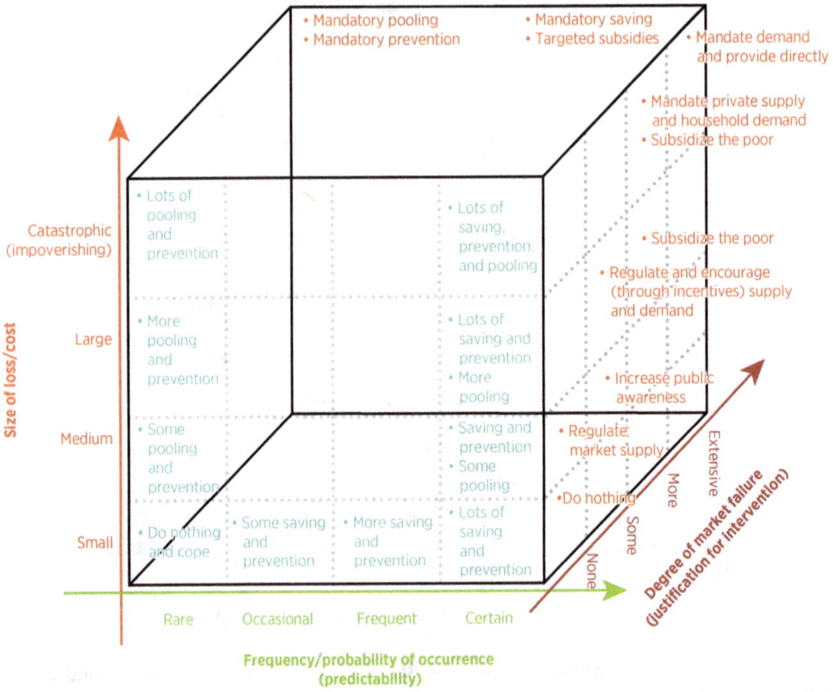

*Sources:* Baeza and Packard 2005, based on Barr 2012, Ehrlich and Becker 1972, and Gill and Ilahi 2000.

of factor, services, and product markets—thus lowering the probability of crises—and by investing in increasing their administrative capacity to collect revenue, sustain public goods, and deliver services to households. As with households, governments that fail to insure against aggregate losses from systemic shocks, or that fail to practice sound economic management to lower the likelihood of those shocks occurring, are forced to engage in coping. Governments that take preventative measures through reforms that encourage fiscal and monetary prudence and eliminate distortions in product and factor markets lower the likelihood of future shocks. In such countries, the cost of pooling the risk of unemployment, for example, will be low because the probability of the bad state will have been lowered by reforms (De Ferranti et al. 2000). Alternatively, profligate public spending, failure to reform, and lingering market inefficiencies can both raise the likelihood of macroeconomic shocks and keep prices of saving and risk pooling from adjusting to accurately reflect risks. Where prices cannot adjust and administrative capacity to correctly price risk is low, the complementary link between prevention and risk pooling is broken, increasing the likelihood that social insurance will succumb to moral hazard and adverse selection.

## Notes

1. Based on Barr (2012), Ehrlich and Becker (1972), and Gill and Ilahi (2000).
2. Conventionally, the price of market insurance $\pi$ is said to be "actuarially fair" if $\pi = (1 + \alpha)p_iL$, in which $p_iL$ is the expected loss (that is, the size of the loss $L$ weighted by the probability $p$ of the loss coming about) in the bad state and $\alpha$ is a "loading" charged by the market-insurance provider to cover administrative costs and profit (Barr 2012; Ehrlich and Becker 1972).
3. Ehrlich and Becker admit that "it is somewhat artificial to distinguish behavior that reduces the probability of the loss from behavior that reduces the size of a loss, since many actions do both" (Ehrlich and Becker 1972, 634). However, they find it helpful to separate *self-protection* from *self-insurance* because the latter clearly performs the insurance function of redistributing income from good to bad states.
4. This terminology partly reflects evolution in the literature since the Ehrlich and Becker paper and is preferred because, as discussed, not all risk-pooling arrangements are market based.
5. Barr (2012) points out how the information problems that confound the simple predictions of the classical insurance model and market provision of risk pooling are particularly treacherous when considering health risks and household demand for medical care. Information about health care is highly technical and individual-specific and is therefore costly to acquire. The costs of choosing the wrong treatment or of purchasing poor quality treatment are frequently high. And the uncertainty about future need for health care is great.

## References

Baeza, C., and T. Packard. 2006. *Beyond Survival: Protecting Households from Health Shocks in Latin America.* Palo Alto, CA: Stanford University Press.

Barr, N. 2001. *The Welfare State as Piggy Bank.* New York: Oxford University Press.

———. 2012. *The Economics of the Welfare State.* 5th ed. New York: Oxford University Press.

De Ferranti, D., G. Perry, I. Gill, and L. Serven. 2000. *Securing Our Future in a Global Economy.* World Bank Latin American and Caribbean Studies, World Bank, Washington, DC.

Ehrlich, I., and G. Becker. 1972. "Market Insurance, Self-Insurance and Self-Protection." *Journal of Political Economy* 80: 623–648.

Gill, I., and N. Ilahi. 2000. "Economic Insecurity, Individual Behavior, and Social Policy." Office of the Chief Economist, Latin America and Caribbean Region, World Bank, Washington, DC.

Holzmann, R., and M. Vodopivec, eds. 2012. *Reforming Severance Pay: An International Perspective*. Washington, DC: World Bank.

Siegel, P., and S. Jørgensen. 2013. "Global Climate Change Justice: Toward a Risk-Adjusted Social Floor." IDS Working Paper Volume 2013 No. 426, London, Institute of Development Studies.

# Appendix B

# Key Parameters of a Negative Income Tax and a Universal Basic Income

**Table B.1  Key Parameters of a Negative Income Tax and a Universal Basic Income**

| | NIT | UBI |
|---|---|---|
| Concepts | • Provision of transfers to some and phasing them out directly through means testing (taxes); an extension of progressive taxation into negative territory<br>• Just as higher-income individuals pay a higher tax rate, those below the poverty line would pay an increasingly negative tax rate—that is, they would receive a payment | • Provision of transfers to all and phasing them out indirectly through higher tax rates on higher-income individuals |
| Unit | • Household | • Individual |
| Funding | • Requires a well-functioning personal income tax system (key for determining transfer amounts and funding the transfers)<br>• Works only for formal sector workers<br>• System administrators would need to know the entire distribution of tax profiles<br>• Likely challenging to reach the poorest of the poor (who work informally and thus whose work is unobserved) | • UBI may be more flexible/may not require a full-fledged personal income tax system<br>• Can work for both formal and informal sector workers<br>• Can be funded through sources besides personal income taxes (such as carbon taxes or proceedings from natural resource revenues) |
| Transparency | • More transparent, because it makes explicit the cost borne by society<br>• Makes it more visible "who pays for whom"<br>• Politically risky, because such relationships are often unclear or lost in the plethora of different programs | • Less direct association between program and costs<br>• Possible desirable behavioral implications from more taxation (for example, if more taxation is linked to a decrease in carbon use) |
| Administration (provision by institutions) | • Administered by the tax authority<br>• Serves as a coherent transfer-tax package<br>• Single transaction<br>• Links to other SP interventions are more tenuous<br>• Provision of transfers through taxes is possibly less stigmatizing than other means-testing methods (the tax form is used as means verification) but could be more intrusive (instigating audits and such) | • Administered by a social welfare or social protection agency<br>• A two-step process of transfer and taxation (taxes more than necessary only to claw it back)<br>• Better links to other social protection services and programs<br>• No stigma, because, in principle, everyone participates (with some net payers) |

*continued next page*

**Table B.1** (*continued*)

| | NIT | UBI |
|---|---|---|
| | | • Risks downplaying implementation requirements—that is, many think "universal is easy," but IDs, MIS, recertification, robust payment mechanisms, and such are still essential |
| Administration (access by beneficiaries) | • User-friendliness depends on the tax system, but it is likely to be demanding or cumbersome<br>• By focusing on taxpayers, requires people to file their taxes even if nothing is earned, which might leave people out (same limitations as EITC concerning the poorest workers in informal settings) | • Administratively leaner for net recipients (requires no income or tax reporting, no checks, and so on)<br>• Independent of tax filing in delivery (but does require tax filing for financing); more likely to address specific bottlenecks behind low pick-up rates (such as complexity in application and awareness) |
| Payments | • Generally, operates on an annual basis<br>• Limits the ability for consumption smoothing ("poor households are middle-class in March and poor the rest of the year") | • Monthly payments<br>• Could be better suited intertemporally, that is, better at protecting against unexpected shocks, especially in contexts with imperfect credit markets |
| Incentives | • Initial income effect, with substitution attenuated by tapering (and thus less disincentive to work compared to other means-tested programs) | • Initial income effect, but no substitution effect (although, in practice, substitution occurs via taxes) |
| Design discretion | • Shape of tapering is subjective | • Less room for discretionary tapering (but tapering may occur via taxes) |
| Perception and expectations | • Perceived as *trojan horse* to dismantle state bureaucracy<br>• History of discussion and debate on the strengths and weaknesses of the approach, but never adopted in the United States (but for reasons unrelated to the instrument itself) | • Perceived as a step toward a more socialist, larger government<br>• Hype: too many objectives and too high expectations (poverty, social dividends, accountability, automation, administrative efficiency, "cheap equity," and more) |

*continued next page*

**Table B.1** (*continued*)

| | NIT | UBI |
|---|---|---|
| Cross-cutting issues | • Both are theoretical propositions that have not been fully implemented yet<br>• In principle, they can be supported by the political "left" and "right" (but for different reasons)<br>• Analytically, they can have identical net outcomes, with an NIT focused on taxing and transferring less and a UBI focused on taxing and transferring more<br>• There is no universality, per se—there are always domestic net payers and net receivers (with the exception of a UBI funded via IDA grants)<br>• Both raise issues concerning citizens versus residents<br>• Both are designed for adult individuals<br>• Can only be introduced and work if they replace other programs, raising questions as to how far substitution should go (For all social services? Part of them? Which?) and the mechanics of transition (Will it cut into social insurance? Social services? Other critical in-kind services?)<br>• Hard, but not impossible, to have a "plan B" if an NIT or UBI goes awry (as in Mongolia; see box 3.2). What would a contingency plan look like? Going back to prereform programs? How?<br>• Purchasing power is relative: would an NIT or UBI just "lift all boats" and kick the poverty problem down the road by causing inflation? | |

*Note:* EITC = earned income tax credit; IDA = International Development Agency; MIS = management information system; NIT = negative income tax; SP = social protection; UBI = universal basic income.

# Appendix C

# Policy Reform Simulations

## Integrating an Actuarially Fair Pension Plan with Alternative Risk-Sharing Instruments to Prevent Poverty and Subsidize Coverage for Catastrophic Losses

The model presented in this appendix is used to assess the distributional and fiscal implications of moving from the prevailing social insurance model to the comprehensive insurance assistance proposals in chapter 3.[1] The policy reform simulations assess the impact of interventions aiming to integrate risk pooling for poverty prevention and subsidies for the coverage of catastrophic losses (through transfers, implicit or explicit) within mandatory old-age pension systems.

The simulations show the impact a reform would have on (i) the distribution of benefits by income level and source (that is, the distribution of benefits related to individual contributions, transfers within the pension system, and transfers outside the pension system), (ii) equilibrium statutory contribution rates within the mandatory pension system, and (iii) fiscal costs, expressed as a share of total gross domestic product (GDP) and aggregate consumption.

First, the pension system, which can be defined contribution (DC) or defined benefit (DB), is modeled. In the case of DB plans, the portion of the old-age pension that results from individual contributions is separated from the portion that is financed through implicit or explicit subsidies. In this sense, the DB pension plan is "actuarially fair": individual statutory contributions are linked to expected pension benefits. Benefits not covered by individual statutory contributions are financed by taxes on labor or by broader-levies/general revenues.

The identity ensuring the financial sustainability of the pension system, whether DB or DC, is given by

$$\beta \sum\nolimits_{a=e}^{R} \omega(a)(1+r)^{R-a} = \sum\nolimits_{a=R}^{L} \frac{P(R)S(R,a)}{(1+r)^{a-R}}, \qquad (C.1)$$

in which $\omega(a)$ is the covered wage at age $a$; $e$ is the age of enrollment in the pension system; $R$ is the retirement age; $\beta$ is the contribution rate; $r$ is the sustainable rate of return of the pension system;[2] $L$ is the maximum life expectancy of *Homo sapiens*; $P(a)$ is the pension received at age $a$; and $S(R, a)$ is the probability, at age $R$, of surviving to age $a$. Essentially, the *expected present value of pension benefits* (the right-hand side of the equation) has to equal, at the age of retirement, the value of accumulated contributions plus interest (the left-hand side). If, for a given individual, including in the case of DB systems, the identity does not hold, the pension system is accumulating either assets or liabilities.

The model assumes that the level of the pension is defined by policy to replace a share, $\psi$, of average lifetime earnings for full-career individuals: those who have contributed continuously between enrollment ($e$) and retirement ($R$). Individuals who contribute less receive proportionally less. For instance, the mandate of the pension system can be to replace 40 percent of average lifetime earnings at age 65 for individuals who have contributed for 40 years to the system (the targeted replacement rate for somebody who has contributed for half of that time period would then be only 20 percent). Given this targeted replacement rate, a benefit accrual rate, $\alpha$, is defined that gives the share of average lifetime earnings that is replaced for each year of contribution:

$$\alpha = \frac{\psi}{(R-e)}. \tag{C.2}$$

The level of the pension then is given by

$$P(R) = \alpha(R-e)\sum_{a=e}^{R} \frac{\omega(a)(1+r)^{R-a}}{(R-e)} = \alpha\sum_{a=e}^{R} \omega(a)(1+r)^{R-a}, \tag{C.3}$$

in which all the salaries included in the summation are valorized at a rate $r$ (the sustainable rate of return of the plan). By inserting identity (C.3) into (C.1), we can derive the equilibrium contribution rate of the pension plan:

$$\beta = \alpha G, \tag{C.4}$$

in which $G$ is the annuity factor or so-called G factor, essentially the "discounted" life expectancy at retirement:

$$G = \sum_{a=R}^{L} \frac{S(R,a)}{(1+r)^{a-R}}. \tag{C.5}$$

Identity (C.4) shows that the level of the equilibrium contribution rate increases when the accrual rate (the level of benefits) increases or when life expectancy at retirement increases.

Assuming, for simplification, that the system is in steady state and that the growth rate, $g$, of earnings $\omega(a)$ is also equal to the rate of return $(r)$, equation (C.3) can be rewritten as

$$P(R) = \alpha \sum_{a=e}^{R} \omega(e)(1+g)^{a-e}(1+r)^{R-a} = \alpha(R-e)\omega(R). \qquad (C.6)$$

Thus, the pension can be defined as a function of the annuity factor, the vesting period $(R - e)$, and earnings at retirement. (Palacios and Robalino [2019] also account for different contribution densities.)

So far, this appendix has described the "contributory" portion of a pension plan that is actuarially fair. Often, however, pension plans offer benefits above those financed solely by individual contributions. This can be done, for instance, through a minimum pension guarantee $P_{min}$. The effective pension that individuals ultimately receive therefore will depend on their earnings. For individuals in income quantile $i$, this pension is given by

$$P(i) = \max[P_{min}, \alpha(R - e)\omega(i)]. \qquad (C.7)$$

All individuals who benefit from the minimum pension will receive replacement rates above $\psi$ because, by definition, the minimum pension would be higher than the pension that guarantees a replacement rate $\psi$. For these individuals, the equilibrium contribution rate will equal[3]

$$\beta(i) = \alpha(i)G, \qquad (C.8)$$

in which $\alpha(i) = \dfrac{P_{min}}{\omega(i)(R-e)} > \alpha$. Essentially, individuals who benefit from the minimum pension would need to pay a higher contribution rate given that they are receiving, implicitly, a higher accrual rate $\alpha(i)$.

The yearly cost of the minimum pension guarantee, that is, the value of the taxes (or general expenditure) that would need to be mobilized to finance the minimum pension, is then given by

$$C(P) = \frac{\sum_{i=1}^{i*}(\beta(i)-\beta)\omega(i)q(i)l(i)N}{Ny} = \frac{\sum_{i=1}^{i*}(\beta(i)-\beta)\omega(i)q(i)l(i)}{y}, \qquad (C.9)$$

in which $i*$ is the highest quantile for which the minimum pension becomes binding, $N$ is the country's total population, $q(i)$ is the share of the country's population in income quantile $i$, $l(i)$ is the share of this population that is enrolled in the pension system, and $y$ is GDP per capita.

In the simulations, for simplicity, the enrollment age and retirement age are fixed at 25 and R=65, respectively, and the G factor is fixed at 15. Alternative pension systems can then be characterized according to the replacement rate ($\psi$) and the level of the minimum pension guarantee $P_{min}$.

## Integrating Alternative Risk Pooling for Poverty Prevention and Subsidies for Catastrophic Coverage

To capture the impact of poverty prevention and other redistribution objectives, public risk-pooling alternatives that take the form of a universal basic income (UBI)/tapered universal basic income (TUBI) scheme are modeled. In its general form, the transfer for an individual in income quantile $i$ is given by

$$T(i) = uc - \varepsilon\omega(i). \tag{C.10}$$

When the parameter $\varepsilon$ is equal to zero, the transfer takes the form of a UBI that is expressed as a share, $u$, of consumption per capita. When $\varepsilon > 0$, the transfer is "tapered," and the UBI becomes a TUBI; it is reduced as a function of the level of income of the individual.

The aim of the reform discussion and simulations presented in chapter 3 is to integrate poverty prevention with other redistributive arrangements. This integration has two important benefits. First, it allows the expansion of the coverage of social insurance. All individuals, particularly those at the bottom of the income distribution, can thus receive a basic income during retirement even if they do not make the explicit statutory contributions to the pension plan. Second, the integration allows a reduction in the size of the mandate of the actuarially fair portion of the pension plan and therefore a reduction in the contribution rate and the "pure tax" wedge. This reduction can improve incentives for job creation and reduce incentives for firms and individuals to informalize work.

To simulate the integration, the model assumes that the level of benefits received by individuals, regardless of their position in the income distribution, does not change. Since there is a new transfer, however, the level of the pension within each quantile can be reduced proportionally. The pension for an individual in quantile $i$ is therefore given by

$$P(i)^T = \max\left[P_{min}, \alpha(R-e)\,\omega(R)\right] - T(i). \tag{C.11}$$

This change implies that both the accrual rate and the equilibrium contribution rates can be reduced within each quantile:

$$\alpha(i)^T = \frac{P(i)^T}{\omega(i)(R-e)} \leq \alpha(i), \tag{C.12}$$

$$\beta(i)^{T} = \alpha(i)^{T} G. \tag{C.13}$$

The costs of the transfer and the new minimum pension guarantee can then be computed as

$$C(T) = \frac{\sum_{i=1}^{I} T(i) q(i) l(i)}{y}, \tag{C.14}$$

$$C(P) = \frac{\sum_{i=1}^{i^*} \left( \beta(i)^{T} - \beta'(i) \right) \omega(i) q(i) l(i)}{y}, \tag{C.15}$$

in which $\beta'(i)$ is the contribution rate of individuals in quantile $i$, assumed to be set by policy; it is likely small in the lowest quantiles and equal to the equilibrium contribution rate in the other quantiles.

In the simulations, the income distribution is replaced with the consumption distributions (reflecting the data available from household surveys) of the Philippines (see table C.1). Earnings $\omega(i)$ are expressed as a share of average consumption:

$$\omega(i) = s(i)c. \tag{C.16}$$

The cost equations can therefore be written as

$$C(T) = \Sigma_{i=1}^{I} \left( u - \varepsilon s(i) \right) q(i) l(i) \theta, \tag{C.17}$$

$$C(P) = \Sigma_{i=1}^{I} \left( \beta(i)^{T} - \beta'(i) \right) s(i) q(i) l(i) \theta, \tag{C.18}$$

in which $\theta$ is the ratio of per capita consumption to per capita income, or the consumption propensity of the country's households.

The equilibrium contribution rate of the prereform system with *implicit* redistribution ($\beta^*$), the equilibrium contribution rate of the postintegration system with *implicit* redistribution ($\beta^R$), and the equilibrium contribution rate of the postintegration system without redistribution ($\beta^N$) are also tracked and reported:

$$\beta^* = \Sigma_{i=1}^{I} \beta(i) q(i) l(i), \tag{C.19}$$

$$\beta^R = \Sigma_{i=1}^{I} \beta(i)^{T} q(i) l(i), \tag{C.20}$$

$$\beta^N = \Sigma_{i=1}^{I} \beta'(i) q(i) l(i). \tag{C.21}$$

## Table C.1 Comprehensive Insurance Assistance Policy Reform Simulation: Data and Parameters for the Philippines

| Country | Deciles | Per capita consumption | Median per capita consumption | Average per capita consumption | $S(i)$ | Theta | Labor force participation |
|---|---|---|---|---|---|---|---|
| Philippines | 1 | 3,751.077 | 13,800.56 | 23,482.41 | 0.15974 | 0.74 | 0.34602052 |
| | 2 | 5,886.314 | | | 0.25067 | | 0.408889681 |
| | 3 | 7,735.046 | | | 0.3294 | | 0.446890652 |
| | 4 | 9,824.904 | | | 0.41839 | | 0.473705769 |
| | 5 | 12,337.090 | | | 0.52538 | | 0.51361692 |
| | 6 | 15,562.700 | | | 0.66274 | | 0.540712714 |
| | 7 | 19,822.000 | | | 0.84412 | | 0.567602277 |
| | 8 | 26,533.960 | | | 1.12995 | | 0.590990007 |
| | 9 | 38,984.380 | | | 1.66015 | | 0.616964042 |
| | 10 | 94,390.810 | | | 4.01964 | | 0.669670641 |

| PARAMETERS | | | | | |
|---|---|---|---|---|---|
| UBI (% of per capita consumption) | 10.81 | 6.760 | 3.38 | | |
| Slope | 0 | 0.100 | | | |
| Min. pension (% of per capita consumption) | 15 | 25.000 | | | |
| Target replacement rate | 0.4 | 0.700 | | | |
| $(R-e)$ | 40 | | | | |
| G factor | 15 | | | | |
| Decile | 1st | 2nd | 3rd | 4th | 5th |
| Max. contribution rate | 0 | 0.050 | 0.1 | 015 | 99 |

*Note:* $S(i)$ = consumption in decile $i$ relative to average consumption; Theta = consumption/GDP ratio; UBI = universal basic income.

The first two are the contribution rates that would be required if the minimum pension had to be funded only through the contributions of plan members (essentially a tax on labor). The last is the average contribution rate that would be required if the subsidized pension were financed through general revenues.

Because of the UBI/TUBI, equilibrium contribution rates in the post-integration systems, both with implicit redistribution and without redistribution, are lower than they were before the reform measure. In addition, the equilibrium contribution rate in the system without redistribution is the smallest:

$$\beta^N < \beta^R < \beta^*. \tag{C.22}$$

The parameters used in the simulations are summarized in table C.1.

## Notes

1. This appendix is based on Palacios and Robalino (2019), a technical background paper for this volume.
2. In a fully funded DC scheme, $r$ is equal to the rate of return of the portfolio of investments in the financial assets of the pension fund. In a pay-as-you-go system, $r$ is the sustainable rate of return on contributions (or the rate used to revalorize wages). It is the weighted average of the rate of return on financial assets and the pay-as-you-go asset. The latter is the present value of future contributions net of the benefits they accrue. It can be calculated through actuarial valuations (Robalino and Bodor 2009).
3. Here, for tractability, the implicit assumption is that all workers have the same mortality rates regardless of income level. Although it would be difficult in practice, given data constraints, one could calculate effective accrual rates by income groups, taking into consideration that mortality rates could be higher (and therefore equilibrium contribution rates lower) for low-income workers.

## References

Palacios, R., and D. Robalino. 2019. "Integrating Social Insurance and Social Assistance Programs for the Future World of Labor." Social Protection and Jobs Global Practice Technical Background Paper for *Protecting All: Risk Sharing for a Diverse and Diversifying World of Work*. Washington, DC: Word Bank.

Robalino, D., and A. Bodor, 2009. "On the Financial Sustainability of Earnings-Related Pension Schemes with 'Pay-as-You-Go' Financing and the Role of Government-Indexed Bonds." *Journal of Pension Economics and Finance* 8 (2): 153–87.